Beginning Sensor Networks with XBee, Raspberry Pi, and Arduino

Sensing the World with Python and MicroPython

Second Edition

Charles Bell

Apress®

Beginning Sensor Networks with XBee, Raspberry Pi, and Arduino:
Sensing the World with Python and MicroPython

Charles Bell
Warsaw, VA, USA

ISBN-13 (pbk): 978-1-4842-5795-1   ISBN-13 (electronic): 978-1-4842-5796-8
https://doi.org/10.1007/978-1-4842-5796-8

Managing Director, Apress Media LLC: Welmoed Spahr
Acquisitions Editor: Natalie Pao
Development Editor: James Markham
Coordinating Editor: Jessica Vakili

Distributed to the book trade worldwide by Springer Science+Business Media New York, 233 Spring Street, 6th Floor, New York, NY 10013. Phone 1-800-SPRINGER, fax (201) 348-4505, e-mail orders-ny@springer-sbm.com, or visit www.springeronline.com. Apress Media, LLC is a California LLC and the sole member (owner) is Springer Science + Business Media Finance Inc (SSBM Finance Inc). SSBM Finance Inc is a **Delaware** corporation.

For information on translations, please e-mail rights@apress.com, or visit http://www.apress.com/rights-permissions.

Apress titles may be purchased in bulk for academic, corporate, or promotional use. eBook versions and licenses are also available for most titles. For more information, reference our Print and eBook Bulk Sales web page at http://www.apress.com/bulk-sales.

Any source code or other supplementary material referenced by the author in this book is available to readers on GitHub via the book's product page, located at www.apress.com/978-1-4842-5795-1. For more detailed information, please visit http://www.apress.com/source-code.

Printed on acid-free paper

I dedicate this book to the countless healthcare professionals, first responders, and many unsung heroes of this difficult time we face in the world during the COVID-19 crisis. It is my hope this book and others like it help the millions of people pass the time during the crisis learning more about science and technology.

Table of Contents

About the Author

Charles Bell conducts research in emerging technologies. He is a principal software developer of the Oracle MySQL Development team. He lives in a small town in rural Virginia with his loving wife. He received his Doctor of Philosophy in Engineering from Virginia Commonwealth University in 2005.

Dr. Bell is an expert in the database field and has extensive knowledge and experience in software development and systems engineering. His research interests include microcontrollers, three-dimensional printing, database systems, software engineering, and sensor networks. He spends his limited free time as a practicing maker focusing on microcontroller projects and refinement of three-dimensional printers.

About the Technical Reviewer

Sai Yamanoor is an embedded systems engineer working for an industrial gases company in Buffalo, NY. His interests, deeply rooted in DIY and open source hardware, include developing gadgets that aid behavior modification. He has published two books with his brother, and in his spare time, he likes to contribute to build things that improve quality of life. You can find his project portfolio at http://saiyamanoor.com.

Acknowledgments

I would like to thank all of the many talented and energetic professionals at Apress. I appreciate the understanding and patience of my managing editor, Natalie Pao; coordinating editor, Jessica Vakili; and development editor, James Markham. Each was instrumental in the success of this project. I appreciate their encouragement and guidance as well as patience in dealing with my many questions. I would also like to thank the small army of publishing professionals at Apress for making me look so good in print. Thank you all very much!

I'd like to especially thank the technical reviewer, Sai Yamanoor, for his patience, insight, and impressive attention to detail. Most importantly, I want to thank my wife, Annette, for her unending patience and understanding during the many hours I spent hunched over my laptop or conducting science experiments on the dining table.

Introduction

The world of microcontrollers and increasingly capable and popular small computing platforms is enabling many more people to learn, experience, and complete projects that would previously have required dedicated (and expensive) hardware. Rather than purchase a commercial or made-for-consumers kit, enterprising developers can now build their own solutions to meet their needs. Sensor networks are just one example of how these small, powerful, and inexpensive components have made it possible for anyone with a moderate skill set to build their own sensor network.

This book presents a beginner's guide to sensor networks. I cover topics including what types of sensors exist, how they communicate their values (observations or events), how they can be used in Arduino and Raspberry Pi projects, and how to build your own home temperature sensor network.

I also include an introduction to the MySQL database server and how you can connect to, store, and retrieve data. Why, I even show you how to do it directly from an Arduino!

Better still, this edition has been updated to include updated tools and software, project examples, as well as the latest use and programming of the XBee 3 modules. Yes, we're writing code to control them in MicroPython. There's an entire chapter dedicated to MicroPython as well as extended coverage of the XBee platform.

Who This Book Is For

I have written this book with a wide variety of readers in mind. It is intended for anyone who wants to get started building their own sensor networks or those who want to learn how to use components, devices, and sensors with an Arduino or Raspberry Pi.

Whether you have already been working with sensor networks, or maybe have taken an introductory electronics course, or even have read a good Apress book on the Arduino or Raspberry Pi, you will get a lot out of this book. Best of all, if you ever wanted to know how to combine sensors, Arduinos, XBee, MySQL, and Raspberry Pi to form a cohesive solution, this book is just what you need!

Most importantly, I wrote this book to meet my own needs. Although there are some excellent books on Arduino, Raspberry Pi, sensors, and MySQL, I could not find a single reference that showed how to put all of these together. The second edition kicks it up yet another notch with more coverage of these topics with the latest versions of the tools and libraries available.

About the Projects

There are 11 chapters, 9 of which include projects that demonstrate and teach key concepts of building sensor networks. Depending on your skill level with the chapter topic, you may find some of the projects easier to complete than others. It is my hope that you find the projects challenging and enlightening (but, more importantly, informative) so that you can complete your own sensor network projects.

In this section, I present some guidance on how best to succeed and get the most out of the projects.

Strategies

I have tried to construct the projects so that the majority of readers can accomplish them with little difficulty. If you encounter topics that you are very familiar with, I recommend working through the projects anyway instead of simply reading or skipping through the instructions. This is because some of the later projects build on the earlier projects.

On the other hand, if you encounter topics that you are unfamiliar with, I recommend reading through the chapter or section completely at least once before attempting the project. Take some time to fully absorb the material, and pay particular attention to the numerous links, tips, and cautionary portions. Some of those are pure gold for beginners.

Perhaps the most significant advice I can offer when approaching the projects is to attempt them one at a time. By completing the projects one at a time, you gain knowledge that you can build on for future projects. It also helps you establish a pace to work through the book. Although some accomplished readers can probably complete all the projects in a weekend, I recommend working through the book at a pace best suited for your availability (and enjoyment).

With some exceptions, the earlier chapters are independent and can be tackled in any order. This is especially true for the Raspberry Pi (Chapter 5) and Arduino (Chapter 6) chapters. Regardless, it is a good idea to read the book and work on the projects in order.

Tips for Buying Hardware

The hardware list for this book contains a number of common components such as temperature sensors, breadboards, jumper wires, and resistors. Most of these items can be found in electronics stores that stock supplies for electronics enthusiasts. The list also includes a number of specialized components such as XBee modules, XBee adapters, XBee shields, Arduino boards, and Raspberry Pi boards.

Each chapter has a list of the components used at the end of the chapter. In some cases, you reuse the hardware from previous chapters. I include a separate list for these items. I have placed the component lists at the end of each chapter to encourage you to read the chapter before attempting the projects.

The lists include the name of each component and at least one link to an online vendor that stocks the component. In addition, I include the quantity needed for the chapter and an estimated cost. If you add up all the components needed and sum the estimated cost, the total may be a significant investment for some readers.

The following sections are for anyone looking to save a little on the cost of completing the projects in this book or wanting to build up their own inventory of sensor network hardware on a budget.

Buy Only What You Need When You Need It

One way to mitigate a significant initial investment in hardware is to pace your buying. If you follow previous advice and work on one project at a time, you can purchase only the hardware needed for that project. This will allow you to spread the cost over however long you plan to work through the book.

However, if you are buying your hardware from an online retailer, you may want to balance ordering the hardware for one project at a time against the potentially higher total shipping cost for multiple orders.

As mentioned, the more common electronics like LEDs, breadboards, and so on can be found in traditional brick-and-mortar stores, but the cost may be a little higher. Once again, the cost of shipping to your location may dictate whether it would be cheaper to buy the higher-priced items from a local electronics shop vs. an online retailer.

Online Auctions

One possible way to save money is to buy your components at a discount on online auction sites. In many cases, the components are the very same ones listed. In other cases, the components may be from vendors that specialize in making less expensive alternatives. I have had a lot of success in buying quality hardware from online auction sites (namely, eBay).

If you are not in a hurry and have time to wait for auctions to close and the subsequent shipping times, you can sometimes find major components like Arduinos, shields, power supplies, and the like at a reduced price by bidding for them. For example, open source hardware manufacturers sometimes offer their products via auctions or at special pricing for quantities. I have found a number of Arduino clones and shields at nearly half the cost of the same boards found on other sites or in electronics stores.

Hey, Buddy, Can You Spare an Arduino?

Another possible way to save some money on the hardware is to borrow it from your friends! If you have friends who are electronics, Arduino, or Raspberry Pi enthusiasts, chances are they have many of the components you need. Just be sure you return the components in working order![1]

A NOTE ABOUT NEWER ARDUINO BOARDS

The projects in this book are designed for a current, readily available version of the Arduino as well as the most recently retired boards. The projects can be completed with the Uno or Mega 2560 boards without modification. Although you can use the Leonardo (see specific notes in the chapters about the differences), you should consider the newer boards carefully before buying.

---

[1]And replace the components you implode, explode, or otherwise turn into silicon slag. Hey, it happens.

Downloading the Code

The code for the examples shown in this book is available on the Apress website, www.apress.com. A link can be found on the book's information page under the Source Code/Downloads tab. This tab is located underneath the Related Titles section of the page.

Reporting Errata

Should you find a mistake in this book, please report it through the Errata tab on the book's page at www.apress.com. You will find any previously confirmed errata in the same place.

CHAPTER 1

Introduction to Sensor Networks

Sensor networks are no longer expensive industrial constructs. You can build a simple sensor network from easily procured, low-cost hardware. All you need are some simple sensors and a microcontroller or computer with input/output capabilities. Yes, your Arduino and Raspberry Pi are ideal platforms for building sensor networks. If you've worked with either platform and have ever wanted to monitor your garden pond, track movement in your home or office, monitor the temperature in your house, monitor the environment, or even build a low-cost security system, you're halfway there!

As inviting and easy as that sounds, don't start warming up the soldering iron just yet. There are a lot of things you need to know about sensor networks. It's not quite as simple as plugging things together and turning them on. If you want to build a reliable and informative sensor network, you need to know how such networks are constructed.

In addition, you may have heard of something called the Internet of Things (IoT). This phrase refers to the use of devices that can communicate over a network (local or Internet). IoT devices are therefore network-aware devices that can send data to other resources, thereby virtualizing the effects of the devices on users and their experience. Sensor networks play a prominent role in the IoT. What you will learn in this book will provide a firm foundation for building IoT solutions using sensor networks.

© Charles Bell 2020
C. Bell, *Beginning Sensor Networks with XBee, Raspberry Pi, and Arduino*,
https://doi.org/10.1007/978-1-4842-5796-8_1

If you want to know more about IoT in general, several books have been written on the topic, including the following. If you're interested in learning more about the IoT and how sensor networks are used, check out some of these titles:

- *Building Internet of Things with the Arduino* by Charalampos Doukas (CreateSpace Independent Publishing Platform, 2012)

- *Architecting the Internet of Things* by Dieter Uckelmann, Mark Harrison, and Florian Michahelles (Springer, 2011)

- *Getting Started with the Internet of Things: Connecting Sensors and Microcontrollers to the Cloud* by Cuno Pfister (O'Reilly, 2011)

In this chapter, we will explore sensor networks through a brief description of what they are and how they are constructed. We will also examine the components that make up a sensor network including an overview of sensors, the types of sensors available, and the things that they can sense.

Anatomy of a Sensor Network

Sensor networks are everywhere. They're normally thought of as complicated monitoring systems for manufacturing and medical applications. However, they aren't always complicated, and they're all around you.

In this section, we will examine the building blocks of a sensor network and how they're connected (logically). First, let's look at some examples of sensor networks to visualize the components.

Examples of Sensor Networks

Although some of these examples may not be as familiar to you as others, it's a good idea as you read through these examples to try and imagine the components of the application. Visualize the sensors themselves—where they're placed and what data they may be reading and sending to another part of the network for processing and recording.

Automotive

Almost every modern automobile has a network of sophisticated sensors that monitor the performance of the engine and its subsystems. Some cars have additional sensors for monitoring external air temperature, tire pressure, and even proximity to objects and other vehicles. Newer vehicles have a host of safety mechanisms including lane departure, obstacle avoidance, auto braking, and more.[1]

If you take a late-model car in for service and get a chance to look in the garage area, you may notice several machines that resemble computer terminals, tablet computers, or in some cases an iPad. These systems are diagnostic machines designed to connect to your car and read all the data the sensors and computer have stored. Some manufacturers use the industry standard interface called onboard diagnostics (OBD).[2] There are several versions of this interface and its protocols; most dealerships have equipment that supports all the latest protocols.

---

[1]Interestingly, I have heard a few motorists who despise some of these features because their driving habits place the vehicle more to one side of the road or another, which triggers the lane departure warning. Similarly, those that habitually cross the center line when driving on curving roads tend to turn off the departure warning. Clearly one of these is an understandable annoyance, whereas the other is exactly why the feature is needed.

[2]http://en.wikipedia.org/wiki/On-board_diagnostics

However, some manufacturers use their own proprietary diagnostic systems, but many use the same connector as OBD-II. You may want to ask about this before purchasing a vehicle. If your new vehicle requires proprietary electronic tools for maintenance, you may be required to take it to a qualified mechanic or another dealer to get it serviced. For those that live in rural areas, finding a dealership or even a trained mechanic to work on your car may require some travel and therefore advanced planning.

For example, Porsche uses what it calls Porsche Integrated Workshop Information System (PIWIS). While PIWIS uses the same connector as OBD-II, Porsche implemented a proprietary system to read and alter the data. Only those mechanics who are trained (and who purchase) the proprietary tools can service the vehicle.

Interestingly, while manufacturers that use proprietary diagnostic systems require you to service your car at an authorized dealer, some enterprising technologists have created compatible systems. In the case of Porsche, Durametric (`www.durametric.com/default.aspx`) manufactures a host of products that enable basic maintenance features like fault and servicereminder reset and even advanced troubleshooting features for many Porsche models. Figure 1-1 shows one of the screens of the Durametric software reading the sensor data from a Porsche Cayman.

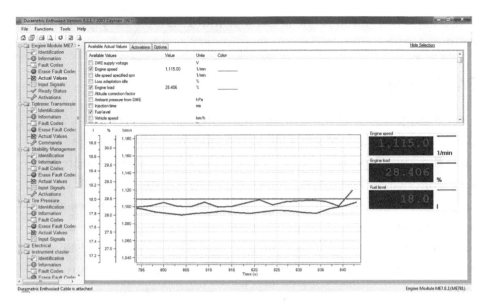

Figure 1-1. *Porsche diagnostic data from Durametric*

Notice the level of detail displayed. The image shows three metrics in the trace, but if you look at the top of the screen, you will see many more metrics that can be monitored. The data shown in the graph was gathered in real time and displayed using the sophisticated sensor networks Porsche employs.

The use of sensors in automobiles has begun to spill over into related machinery such as motorcycles, boats, and even the venerable farm tractor. Many modern farm machines such as combines have sophisticated sensors that enable amazing capabilities such as auto header height, auto pilot, and more.

For example, modern combines can be purchased with a suite of GPS-based tools that permit the operator to plot the boundaries of the harvest field and calculate the best paths for minimal time and maximum harvest. In the case where the harvest field is very large, the operator can practically take a nap while the combine does the work.[3] This is a far cry from older combines that required manual adjustment of the header.

Environment

The environment is on many peoples' minds, and many scientists are actively monitoring it. Motives for monitoring the environment range from checking a specific area or room for gases and tracking the area's temperature and humidity to monitoring and reporting anomalies for sensitive equipment, such as running chemical analyses for clean rooms. Examples of environment sensor networks include those used to monitor air pollution, detect and track forest fires, detect landslides, provide earthquake early warnings, and provide industrial and structural monitoring.

Sensor networks are ideal for all forms of environmental monitoring. Due to the sensors' small size, low energy requirements, and low cost, they can be easily installed at specific locations or on specific machines for precise reporting. For example, a clean-room environment often requires very precise temperature and humidity control as well as extremely low levels of contaminants (loose particles floating in the air). Sensors can be used to measure these observations at key locations (windows, doors, air vents, and so on); the data is sent to a computer that records it and generates threshold alerts. Most sophisticated clean rooms tie the filtration, heat, and cooling systems into the same computer system (using their own sensors) to control the environment based on the data collected from the sensor network.

---

[3]It may be hard to imagine a 46,000-pound plus machine that resembles a medieval torture device or a serial killer's weapon being driven by a computer, but it's true. Some of the most expensive combines have more sophisticated technology than your favorite sports sedan including air conditioning, cruise control, and fully adjustable seats.

Environmental sensors aren't limited to temperature, humidity, dew point, and air quality. Sensors for monitoring electromagnetic interference and radio frequencies may be used in hospitals to protect patients who rely on sensitive electronic medical equipment such as heart pacemakers and similar lifesaving electronics.[4] Sensors for monitoring water purity, oxygen level, and contaminants may be used in fish farms to maximize crop yield.

Scientists and industrial engineers aren't the only ones who build environmental sensor networks. You can build your own using relatively low-cost sensors. In their book, *Environmental Monitoring with Arduino: Building Simple Devices to Collect Data About the World Around Us* (Make, 2012), Emily Gertz and Patrick Di Justo show how to build simple sensor networks to monitor noise, water purity, and, of course, weather.

If this sounds too good to be true, consider for the moment your average home heating, ventilation, and cooling system (HVAC). It has a very simple sensor network, often in the form one or more sensors for ambient temperature (the thermostats on the wall) that feed data to a control board that turns on the mechanisms to pump gases through the system and the fan to move air. Some modern HVACs use additional sensors to monitor air quality and engage additional active electronic filters[5] or to divert heat and cooling to areas where it's needed most. If you have purchased a modern Wi-Fi thermostat, you may be surprised that it is an IoT device because most allow you to control your HVAC system from any room or even when you're not at home.

---

[4]This will become very important to you should a family member need such a device.

[5]Electronic filters are an absolute necessity for those of us with allergies living in areas with a high concentration of pollutants, both natural and man-made.

7

IS A THERMOSTAT A SENSOR NODE?

If you've ever been in a home with a thermostat that used a sliding or rotating arm to set the desired temperature, it's likely you've encountered a simple sensor node. Older thermostats use a combination of a temperature-sensitive coil and a tilt switch mounted to it. This coil is in turn mounted to a plate that can be tilted one way or the other to adjust the desired temperature. As the room temperature changes, the coil expands or contracts, reorienting the tilt switch. Once the coil expands or contracts so that the tilt switch disengages, the flow of voltage to the HVAC unit ceases, thereby turning off the unit.

Some manufacturers are creating increasingly sophisticated thermostats. Some are even capable of recording data and predicting trends. For example, the Nest Learning Thermostat (www.nest.com/living-with-nest/) can detect when someone is at home and can be accessed remotely via the Internet.

Atmospheric

Closely related to environmental monitoring is atmospheric monitoring: a sensor network designed to monitor air quality. Atmospheric monitoring is a form of environment monitoring, but there is a great deal more emphasis on studying the atmosphere. The obvious reason is that mammals simply can't survive without air (at least, not for long).

As in environment sensor networks, there are specialized sensors to measure all forms of air quality including free gases, particle contamination, smoke, humidity, and so on. Other motivations for building atmospheric sensor networks include measuring pollution from factories and automobiles (most cars have several atmospheric sensors incorporated into engine and cabin systems), ensuring clean drinking water from water treatment plants, and measuring the effects of aerosols.

Fortunately for the hobbyist and aspiring atmospheric scientist, gas sensors are plentiful, and many are inexpensive. Better still, many example projects available on the Internet demonstrate how to construct atmospheric sensor networks.

ENVIRONMENT VS. ATMOSPHERE: WHAT'S THE DIFFERENCE?

If you're wondering what the difference is between environment and atmosphere, you aren't alone. Simply stated, environment is an aggregate of things around a subject (a person, an object, or an event) that influences the subject. Thus, it can be all the things around you including the ambient temperature, moisture content, and so on.

Atmosphere (literally, air) refers to the collection of gases that fills the spaces around objects. Atmosphere is one of the elements in an environment. Scientists have defined many layers of atmosphere surrounding planet Earth. Most atmospheric sensors are designed to measure the unique gases for a specific level. The lower atmosphere where we live is called the troposphere.

Like the environmental monitoring sensor networks discussed earlier, you can build your own atmospheric sensor network. In their book, *Atmospheric Monitoring With Arduino: Building Simple Devices to Collect Data About the Environment* (Make, 2012), Emily Gertz and Patrick Di Justo also show how to build simple sensor networks that measure gases such as butane and methane, light wavelengths, ozone, and more.

Security

Some of the most popular and prolific sensor networks are those used for security and surveillance. You may not think of security systems as sensor networks, but let's consider what is involved in a typical home or office security system.

A basic security system is designed to record and alert whenever a door or window is opened. The sensors in such a network are switches (the simplest of all sensors) that detect when a door or window is opened or closed. A central processor or microcontroller can be used to monitor the sensors and act: for example, generating a signal with a buzzer or bell.

A surveillance system includes more than just a set of switches. Typically, such a system includes video sensors (cameras—with or without infrared capabilities to enhance photos at night), boundary sensors (motion, line-of-sight breaks, etc.), and even audio sensors (microphones). The system may also include some form of monitor that records the data and enables users to view that data (see when doors were opened, listen to audio, and view video).

Most home surveillance systems include a digital video recorder (DVR) or similar dedicated system and one or more cameras. One popular home system includes four cameras with audio. The system allows you to record data from the sensors programmatically as well as view the video in real time. Figure 1-2 shows a typical and affordable home surveillance system from Harbor Freight (`www.harborfreight.com`).

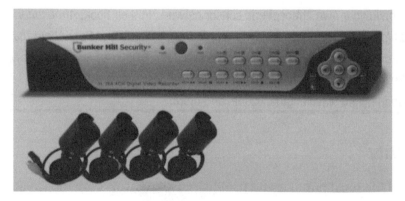

Figure 1-2. Security sensor network: home surveillance system from Harbor Freight

Surveillance systems used in businesses are like home surveillance systems but typically include additional sensors and data tracking such as employee badging, equipment monitoring, and integration, along with offsite support services such as night watchmen and data archiving.

Another example includes the addition of cameras to doorbells, security lights, and similar outside facing devices. For example, some of the newest camera doorbells have motion and similar sensors to detect movement or even enhance video at night. Some, like the ring doorbell, permit two or more doorbells to link together to form a "neighborhood watch" system (https://shop.ring.com/pages/neighbors). Best of all, they provide real-time alerts, which can help you detect crime and alert authorities sooner. And, yes, this is an IoT device too!

Although they aren't as inexpensive as temperature, humidity, light, or gas sensors, microphones and cameras are becoming cheaper. You can find these sensors at electronics stores such as Adafruit Industries. For example, Adafruit has a camera (http://adafruit.com/products/397) that you can connect to your Arduino or Raspberry Pi to record images and low-frame-rate video (see Figure 1-3).

Figure 1-3. *Camera sensor from Adafruit Industries (courtesy of Adafruit)*

Many security sensor networks are available for the consumer. They range from simple audio/visual monitoring to remote monitored systems that integrate into your home, tracking everything from movement to portal breaches, and even temperature and lighting.

The Topology of a Sensor Network

Now that you've seen a few examples, let's discuss the components of a sensor network: in this case, a garden pond–monitoring system. Specifically, the system monitors the health of a fishpond. Thus, the system is an environmental sensor network.

The motivation is to ensure a safe environment for the fish. This means the water temperature should be within tolerance for the species of fish, the water depth should be maintained to avoid over- or under-filling, and the oxygen level of the water should be monitored to ensure that there is sufficient oxygen for the fish to survive. Similarly, sensors may be employed to ensure a healthy level of symbiotic life such as other aquatic animals or algae.

Most pond owners have learned to build their ponds with the cycle of life in mind, to be sure the pond can sustain its environment. However, things can go wrong. The introduction of another species (like amphibians[6] or the dreaded algae infestation) can cause an imbalance that could threaten your prized Koi. Having the ability to detect when an imbalance begins can make the solutions much easier to implement.

Figure 1-4 shows a simple drawing depicting the sensors and their placement. In this system, there are three sensors, a monitoring control or recording system, and a communication medium—a way for the sensors to send their data to the monitor. Let's begin by discussing the sensors.

---

[6]Each pond I've built has eventually given seeming spontaneous birth to frogs. Where do they all come from?

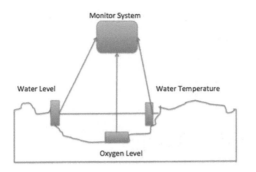

Figure 1-4. *Typical fishpond-monitoring system*

If I were to build this system, I would use sensors that operate on low voltage so that I could use battery or solar to power them. Most sensors are discrete components that take voltage in and produce either digital or analog data. They require another component to read the data and send it to the pond-monitoring control system. If you're thinking this would be a good use for an Arduino, you're right! The Arduino is an excellent platform for reading data from one or more sensors and sending it to another system for processing. Some enterprising Arduino enthusiasts have built monitoring systems using only a single Arduino and multiple sensors.

Let's assume for this example that the pond-monitoring system is a computer with an Arduino attached to it so that you can record, view, or access the data remotely. You now have the sensors connected to an Arduino (called a sensor node) and the pond-monitoring system connected to another Arduino (called the aggregator node). What is missing is how to get the data from the sensor node to the aggregate node.

There are many ways to get two Arduinos to communicate or share data, but this book limits the discussion to media that permit long-distance communication—wired or wireless. Wired communication in this case can be via an Ethernet shield (a special daughter board designed to sit on top of the Arduino) or a wireless fidelity (Wi-Fi) shield fitted to each Arduino.

As you can see, many levels of hardware and protocols are involved in building sensor networks. Now that you have a general idea of what the major components are, let's examine the communication media and then discuss the types of sensor nodes.

Communication Media

Now that you understand the topology of a sensor network, let's consider how sensors communicate their data to the other nodes in the network. They do so through two basic forms of network communication: wired and wireless.

Wired Networks

Wired networks can take several forms involving some form of hardware designed to permit electrical signals to be sent from one device to another via a wire or cable. Thus, sensor networks that employ wired communication must also add network hardware to the nodes in the network.

As I mentioned earlier, you can use an Arduino with an Ethernet shield to connect the sensor node(s) to the aggregate or data-collection nodes. If your sensors were hosted with Raspberry Pi computers, you would already have the necessary hardware to connect two Raspberry Pi computers— they all have RJ-45 LAN ports.

Of course, using wired Ethernet isn't as simple as plugging a cable in to two devices. Unless you use a crossover cable, you need some form of Ethernet switch to connect the devices. A detailed discussion of Ethernet networks and hardware is beyond the scope of this book, but it's a viable communication medium for sensor networks.

While the use of wired networks isn't as popular today due mostly to the availability of manyWi-Fi-enabled solutions, the use of wired networks can help improve transmission speed, reliability, and, in some cases, improve security.

Wireless Networks

A more popular and more versatile medium is wireless communication. In this case, you use a wireless device such as a Wi-Fi shield for each Arduino or Wi-Fi adapters for Raspberry Pi computers. Like wired Ethernet, wireless Ethernet (Wi-Fi) requires the addition of a wireless router. However, Wi-Fi has a much shorter maximum distance, so it may not be suitable for some networks.

But you have another form of wireless at your disposal. You can use XBee wireless modules instead of Ethernet (Wi-Fi). XBee provides a specialized, lightweight protocol that is ideal for use in sensor nodes and small microcontrollers and embedded systems. There is even modules that support Bluetooth Mesh, but we will focus on the Wi-Fi modules. The rest of this book uses XBee modules for the communication mechanism of the example sensor network projects.

One of the features of XBee modules is that they are low power and can be placed into a periodic sleep mode to conserve power. However, the best feature is that XBee modules can be connected directly to sensors, allowing you to build even lighter weight (and cheaper) sensor nodes. XBee modules are discussed in more detail in Chapter 2.

Hybrid Networks

Some sophisticated sensor networks require the mixing of both communication media. For example, an industrial sensor network may collect data using sensor nodes installed in many different buildings or rooms. You may want to isolate the sensor networks into subsystems because each area may require a different form of sensor network. In this case, it may be better to use wireless for certain segments in which the use of wired networks is difficult (e.g., a sensor on a moving industrial robot) and wired Ethernet to link the subsystems to a central data-recording or data-monitoring system.

Types of Sensor Nodes

Sensor nodes are composed of one or more sensors (although this book uses only one sensor per node) and a communication device to transmit the data. As mentioned, the communication device can be a microcontroller like an Arduino, an embedded system, or even a small-footprint computer like a Raspberry Pi. Typically, sensor nodes are designed for unattended operation; they're sometimes installed on mobile objects or in locations where wired communication is impractical. In these situations, sensor nodes can be designed to operate without being tethered to a power or communication source.

Logically, sensor nodes can be classified into different types based on how they're used. The following sections detail type of sensor node used in this book. It helps to think of the sensor nodes by role so that you can design and plan the sensor network using logical building blocks.

Basic Sensor Nodes

At the lowest (or leaf) level of the sensor network is a basic sensor node. This is the type of node described thus far—it has a single sensor and a communication mechanism. These nodes don't store or manipulate the captured data in any way—they simply pass the data to another node in the network.

Data Nodes

The next type of node is a data node. Data nodes are sensor nodes that store data. These nodes may send the data to another node, but typically they're devices that send the data to a storage mechanism such as a data card, to a database via a computer, or directly to a visual output device like an LCD screen, panel meter, or LED indicators.

Data nodes require a device that can do a bit more than simply pass the data to another node. They need to be able to record or present the data. This is an excellent use for a microcontroller, as you'll see in later chapters. Digi, the makers of the XBee, has dedicated sensor nodes that measure temperature, humidity, and light information and transmit the data on the network. Where is the fun in that? In this book, you build your own sensor nodes.

Data nodes can be used to form autonomous or unattended sensor networks that record data for later archiving. Returning to the fishpond example, many commercial pond-monitoring systems employ self-contained sensor devices with multiple sensors that send data to a data node; the user can visit the data node and read the data for use in analysis on a computer.

Aggregator Nodes

Another type of node is an aggregate node. These nodes typically employ a communication device and a recording device (or gateway) and no sensors. They're used to collect data from one or more data or sensor nodes. In the examples discussed thus far, the monitoring system would have one or more aggregator nodes to read the data from the sensors. Figure 1-5 shows how each type of nodes would be used in a fictional sensor network.

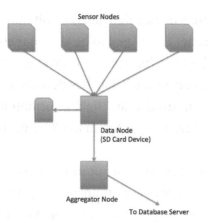

Figure 1-5. Types of nodes in a sensor network

For the more general case, the diagram should probably show multiple data nodes (so that the aggregator node is aggregating stuff).

In this example, several sensor nodes at the top send data wirelessly to a data node in the middle. The data node collects the data and saves it to a secure digital card, which then sends the data to an aggregator node that communicates with a database server via a wired computer network to store the data. Mixing data nodes with aggregator nodes ensures that you won't lose any data if your aggregator node fails or the recording and monitoring system fails or goes offline.

Now that you understand the types of nodes in a sensor network, let's examine sensors: how they can measure data and examples of sensors available for building low-cost sensor networks.

Sensors

With all this talk of sensors and what sensor networks are and how they communicate data, you may be wondering what exactly sensors are and what makes them sense. This section and its subsections answer those questions and more. Let's begin with the definition of a sensor.

A sensor is a device that measures phenomena of the physical world. These phenomena can be things you see, like light, gases, water vapor, and so on. They can also be things you feel, like temperature, electricity, water, wind, and so on. Humans have senses that act like sensors, allowing us to experience the world around us. However, there are some things your sensors can't see or feel, such as radiation, radio waves, voltage, and amperage. Upon measuring these phenomena, it's the sensors' job to convey a measurement in the form of either a voltage representation or a number.

There are many forms of sensors. They're typically low-cost devices designed for a single purpose and with a limited capability for processing. Most simple sensors are discrete components; even those that have more sophisticated parts can be treated as separate components. Sensors are either analog or digital and are typically designed to measure only one thing. But an increasing number of sensor modules are designed to measure a set of related phenomena, such as the USB Weather Board from SparkFunElectronics (`www.sparkfun.com/products/10586`) (see Figure 1-6).

Figure 1-6. *USB Weather Board (courtesy of SparkFun and Juan Pena)*

Notice the blue module with XBee written on it. This is a wireless module that permits the sensor board to send its data to another node or multiple nodes. The XBee is discussed in more detail in Chapter 2.

The following sections examine how sensors measure data, how to store that data, and examples of some common sensors.

How Sensors Measure

Sensors are electronic devices that generate a voltage based on the unique properties of their chemical and mechanical construction. They don't manipulate the phenomena they're designed to measure. Rather, sensors sample some physical variable and turn it into a proportional electric signal (voltage, current, digital, and so on).

For example, a humidity sensor measures the concentration of water (moisture) in the air. Humidity sensors react to these phenomena and generate a voltage that the microcontroller or similar device can then read and use to calculate a value on a scale. A basic, low-cost humidity sensor is the DHT-22 available from most electronics stores (see Figure 1-7).

Figure 1-7. *DHT-22 humidity sensor (courtesy of Adafruit)*

The DHT-22 is designed to measure temperature as well as humidity. It generates a digital signal on the output (data pin). Although simple to use, it's a bit slow and should be used to track data at a reasonably slow rate (no more frequently than about once every 3 or 4 seconds).

When this sensor generates data, that data is transmitted as a series of high (interpreted as a 1) and low (interpreted as a 0) voltages that the microcontroller can read and use to form a value. In this case, the microcontroller reads a value 40 bits in length (40 pulses of high or low voltage)—that is, 5 bytes—from the sensor and places it in a program variable. The first two bytes are the value for humidity, the second two are for temperature, and the fifth byte is the checksum value to ensure an accurate read. Fortunately, all this hard work is done for you in the form of a special library designed for the DHT-22 and similar sensors. Let's see how this works in practice.

Listing 1-1 shows an excerpt from the DHT library provided by Adafruit for the Arduino platform. You can find this library at https://github.com/adafruit/DHT-sensor-library. The listing shows the method used to read the humidity from the DHT-22 sensor library on the Arduino.

Listing 1-1. Reading Temperature and Humidity with a DHT-22

```
/*
  Beginning Sensor Networks, 2nd Edition

  This sketch demonstrates a basic sensor node using a DHT22
  sensor to read temperature and humidity printing the results
  in the serial monitor.

  Dr. Charles Bell
*/
#include <DHT.h>
#include <DHT_U.h>
```

```
#define DHTPIN 2          // Digital pin connected to the DHT sensor
#define DHTTYPE DHT22    // DHT 22  (AM2302), AM2321

DHT dht(DHTPIN, DHTTYPE);

void setup() {
}

void loop() {
  float humidity = dht.readHumidity();
  float temperature = dht.readTemperature();

  // Make sure they are numbers or fail.
  if (isnan(temperature) || isnan(humidity)) {
    Serial.println("ERROR: DHT values are not numbers!");
  } else {
    Serial.print("Temperature (C): ");
    Serial.print(temperature);
    Serial.print("Humidity: ");
    Serial.print(humidity);
  }
}
```

Notice that the DHT library provides methods to make it very easy to read the temperature (in Celsius) and humidity and display those values.[7] Yes, it's that easy! If you'd like to experiment with the DHT-22, there is an excellent tutorial on Adafruit's site (http://learn.adafruit.com/dht).

Recall that the DHT-22 produces a digital value. Not all sensors do this; some generate a voltage range instead. These are called analog sensors. Let's take a moment to understand the differences. This will become essential information as you plan and build your sensor nodes.

---

[7]Using the serial monitor feature of the Arduino IDE. See Chapter 3 for details on how to use the serial monitor.

Analog Sensors

Analog sensors are devices that generate a voltage range, typically between 0 and 5 volts.[8] An analog-to-digital circuit is needed to convert the voltage to a number. Most microcontrollers have this feature built in, and the Arduino is a fine example. The Arduino has a limited set of pins that operate on analog data and incorporate analog-to-digital (A/D) conversion circuits.

But it isn't that simple (is it ever?). Analog sensors work like resistors and, when connected to microcontrollers, often require another resistor to "pull up" or "pull down" the voltage to avoid spurious changes in voltage known as floating. This is because voltage flowing through resistors is continuous in both time and amplitude. Thus, even when the sensor isn't generating a value or measurement, there is still a flow of voltage through the sensor that can cause spurious readings. Your projects require a clear distinction between OFF (zero voltage) or ON (positive voltage). Pull-up and pull-down resistors ensure that you have one of these two states. It's the responsibility of the A/D converter to take the voltage read from the sensor and convert it to a value that can be interpreted as data.

WHAT IS A RESISTOR?

A resistor is one of the standard building blocks of electronics. Its job is to impede current and impose a reduction in voltage (which is converted to heat). Its effect, known as resistance, is measured in ohms. A resistor can be used to reduce voltage to other components, limiting frequency response, or protect sensitive components from over voltage.

---

[8]There are also sensors with a 4–20mA output, but for this book, we will focus on those with output (signals) in the 0–5V range.

When a resistor is used to pull up voltage (by attaching one end to positive voltage) or pull down voltage (by attaching one end to ground) (resistors are bidirectional), it eliminates the possibility of the voltage floating in an indeterminate state. Thus, a pull-up resistor ensures that the stable state is positive voltage, and a pull-down resistor ensures that the stable state is zero voltage (ground).

An excellent getting-to-know-electronics book is the *Encyclopedia of Electronic Components* by Charles Platt (O'Reilly, 2012).

When sampled (when a value is read from a sensor), the voltage read must be interpreted as a value in the range specified for the given sensor. Remember that a value of, say, 2 volts from one analog sensor may not mean the same thing as 2 volts from another analog sensor. Each sensor's datasheet shows you how to interpret these values.

When you use a microcontroller like the Arduino, the A/D converters conveniently change the voltage into a value that uses 10 bits, resulting in an integer value between 0 and 1023. For example, a sensor may measure phenomena in a range consisting of 200 points on a scale. The lowest value typically represents 0 and the highest 1023. The Arduino in this case can be programmed to convert the value read from the A/D converter into a value on the sensor's scale.

As you can see, working with analog sensors is a lot more complicated than using the DHT-22 digital sensor from the previous section. With a little practice, you will find that most analog sensors aren't difficult to use once you understand how to attach them to a microcontroller and how to interpret their voltage on the scale in which the sensor is calibrated to work.

Digital Sensors

Digital sensors like the DHT-22 are designed to produce a string of bits using serial transmission (one bit at a time). However, some digital sensors produce data via parallel transmission (one or more bytes[9] at a time). As described previously, the bits are represented as voltage, where high voltage (say, 5 volts) or ON is 1 and low voltage (0 or even –5 volts) or OFF is 0. These sequences of ON and OFF values are called discrete values because the sensor is producing one or the other in pulses—it's either ON or OFF.

Digital sensors can be sampled more frequently than analog signals because they generate the data more quickly and because no additional circuitry is needed to read the values (such as A/D converters and logic or software to convert the values to a scale). Thus, digital sensors are generally more accurate and reliable than analog sensors. But the accuracy of a digital sensor is directly proportional to the number of bits it uses for sampling data.

The most common form of digital sensor is the pushbutton or switch. What, a button is a sensor? Why, yes, it is a sensor. Consider for a moment the sensor attached to a window in a home security system. It's a simple switch that is closed when the window is closed and open when the window is open. When the switch is wired into a circuit, the flow of current is constant and unbroken (measuring positive volts using a pull-up resistor) when the window is closed and the switch is closed, but the current is broken (measuring zero volts) when the window and switch is open. This is the most basic of ON and OFF sensors.

Most digital sensors are small circuits of several components designed to generate digital data. Unlike analog sensors, reading their data is easy because the values can be used directly without conversion (except to

---

[9]This depends on the width of the parallel buffer. An 8-bit buffer can communicate 1 byte at a time, a 16-bit buffer can communicate 2 bytes at a time, and so on.

other scales or units of measure). Some may suggest this is more difficult than using analog sensors, but that depends on your point of view. An electronics enthusiast would see working with analog sensors as easier, whereas a programmer would think digital sensors are simpler to use.

So, what do you do with the data once it's measured? The following section briefly describes some aspects of sensor data and considerations for storing that data.

Storing Sensor Data

Storing sensor data depends on how the data is interpreted and ultimately how it will be used. If you plan to use a computer—or, better, a database— to store the data, you should store it in a way that makes sense.

For example, storing a sequence of voltages from an analog signal may be considered preserving the data in its purest form, but without context or an A/D converter, the data may be meaningless. Storing the digital conversion of the voltage may not be wise either, because you must remember the scale and range to derive the values intended to be represented. Thus, it makes much more sense to store the resulting conversion to scale. Fortunately, when you're using digital sensors, the only thing you need to remember is what unit of measure is being used (Celsius, Fahrenheit, feet, meters, and so on). Therefore, it's best to save the final form of the measurement.

But where do you store this information? Commercial sensor networks store the data in an embedded database or file-storage device, transmit it to another system for storage, or store it on removable digital media. Older sensor networks (like a polygraph or EKG machine) store the data as hard copy using graphs (making them very obsolete).

There are several simple storage devices and technologies you can use to build your own sensor networks, ranging from local devices for the Arduino to modern hard drives on the Raspberry Pi. These storage mechanisms are listed here and discussed in more detail when this book examines the types of hardware used and application of technologies in building sensor networks:

- Hard-copy printer

- Secure digital card

- USB hard drive

- Web server

- Database server (MySQL)

Now let's look at some of the sensors available and the types of phenomena they measure.

Examples of Sensors

All sensor networks begin with one sensor and a means to read and interpret the data. This chapter has presented a lot of information about sensors. You may be thinking of all manner of useful things you can measure in your home or office or even in your yard or surroundings. You may want to measure the temperature changes in your new sun room, detect when the mail carrier has tossed the latest circular in your mailbox, or perhaps keep a log of how many times your dog uses his doggy door. I hope that by now you can see these are just the tip of the iceberg when it comes to imagining what you can measure. You should be thinking about what kind of sensor network you want to build; you can use this book to learn how to build it.

What types of sensors are available? The following list describes some of the more popular sensors and what they measure. This is just a sampling of what is available. Perusing the catalogs of online electronics vendors like Mouser Electronics (www.mouser.com), SparkFun Electronics (`www.sparkfun.com`), and Adafruit Industries (`http://adafruit.com/`) will reveal many more examples:

- *Accelerometers*: These sensors measure motion or movement of the sensor or whatever it's attached to. They're designed to sense motion on several axes (velocity, inclination, vibration, etc.). Some include gyroscopic features. Most are digital sensors. A Wii Nunchuck (or WiiChuck) contains a sophisticated accelerometer for tracking movement. Aha: now you know the secret of those funny little thingamabobs that came with your Wii.

- *Audio sensors*: Perhaps this is obvious, but microphones are used to measure sound. Most are analog, but some of the better security and surveillance sensors have digital variants for higher compression of transmitted data.

- *Barcode readers*: These sensors are designed to read barcodes. Most often, barcode readers generate digital data representing the numeric equivalent of a barcode. Such sensors are often used in inventory-tracking systems to track equipment through a plant or during transport. They're plentiful, and many are economically priced, enabling you to incorporate them into your own projects.

- *RFID sensors*: Radio frequency identification uses a passive device (sometimes called an RFID tag) to communicate data using radio frequencies through electromagnetic induction. For example, an RFID tag can be a creditcard–sized plastic card, a label, or something similar that contains a special antenna, typically in the form of a coil, thin wire, or foil layer that is tuned to a specific frequency. When the tag is placed near the reader, the reader emits a radio signal; the tag can use the electromagnet energy to transmit a nonvolatile message embedded in the antenna, in the form of radio signals which is then converted to an alphanumeric string.[10]

- *Biometric sensors*: A sensor that reads fingerprints, irises, or palm prints contains a special sensor designed to recognize patterns. Given the uniqueness inherit in patterns such as fingerprints and palm prints, they make excellent components for a secure access system. Most biometric sensors produce a block of digital data that represents the fingerprint or palm print.

- *Capacitive sensors*: A special application of capacitive sensors, pulse sensors are designed to measure your pulse rate and typically use a fingertip for the sensing site. Special devices known as pulse oximeters (called pulseox by some medical professionals) measure pulse rate with a capacitive sensor and determine the oxygen content of blood with a light sensor. If you own modern electronic devices, you may have *encountered touch-sensitive* buttons that use special capacitive sensors to detect touch and pressure. Some newer versions can be used to measure liquid levels.

- *Coin sensors*: This is one of the most unusual types of sensors.[11] These devices are like the coin slots on a typical vending machine. Like their commercial

---

[10]http://en.wikipedia.org/wiki/Radio-frequency_identification
[11]www.sparkfun.com/products/11719

equivalent, they can be calibrated to sense when a certain size of coin is inserted. Although not as sophisticated as commercial units that can distinguish fake coins from real ones, coin sensors can be used to add a new dimension to your projects. Imagine a coin-operated Wi-Fi station. Now, that should keep the kids from spending too much time on the Internet!

- *Current sensors*: These are designed to measure voltage and amperage. Some are designed to measure change, whereas others measure load.

- *Flex/force sensors*: Resistance sensors measure flexes in a piece of material or the force or impact of pressure on the sensor. Flex sensors may be useful for measuring torsional effects or to measure finger movements (like in a Nintendo Power Glove). Flex-sensor resistance increases when the sensor is flexed.

- *Gas sensors*: There are a great many types of gas sensors. Some measure potentially harmful gases such as LPG and methane and other gases such as hydrogen, oxygen, and so on. Other gas sensors are combined with light sensors to sense smoke or pollutants in the air. The next time you hear that telltale and often annoying low-battery warning beep[12] from your smoke detector, think about what that device contains. Why, it's a sensor node!

---

[12]Here's a good home owner tip. Instead of running around trying to figure out which detector is intermittently signaling a dead battery (or a false positive), consider replacing them with the newer versions that have 10-year batteries (www.lowes.com/pd/First-Alert-Micro-Photoelectric-Smoke-Alarm-with-10-Year-Battery/1000456457).

- *Light sensors*: Sensors that measure the intensity or lack of light are special types of resistors: light-dependent resistors (LDRs), sometimes called photo resistors or photocells. Thus, they're analog by nature. If you own a Mac laptop, chances are you've seen a photo resistor in action when your illuminated keyboard turns itself on in low light. Or, your phone can change brightness using light sensors. Special forms of light sensors can detect other light spectrums such as infrared (as in older TV remotes).

- *Liquid-flow sensors*: These sensors resemble valves and are placed inline in plumbing systems. They measure the flow of liquid as it passes through. Basic flow sensors use a spinning wheel and a magnet to generate a Hall effect (rapid ON/OFF sequences whose frequency equates to how much water has passed).

- *Liquid-level sensors*: A special resistive solid-state device can be used to measure the relative height of a body of water. One example generates low resistance when the water level is high and higher resistance when the level is low.

- *Location sensors*: Modern smartphones have GPS sensors for sensing location, and of course GPS devices use the GPS technology to help you navigate. Fortunately, GPS sensors are available in low-cost forms, enabling you to add location sensing to your sensor network. GPS sensors generate digital data in the form of longitude and latitude, but some can also sense altitude.

- *Magnetic-stripe readers*: These sensors read data from magnetic stripes (like that on a credit card) and return the digital form of the alphanumeric data (the actual strings).

- *Magnetometers*: These sensors measure orientation via the strength of magnetic fields. A compass is a sensor for finding magnetic north. Some magnetometers offer multiple axes to allow even finer detection of magnetic fields.

- *Proximity sensors*: Often thought of as distance sensors, proximity sensors use infrared or sound waves to detect distance or the range to/from an object. Made popular by low-cost robotics kits, the Parallax Ultrasonic Sensor uses sound waves to measure distance by sensing the amount of time between pulse sent and pulse received (the echo). For approximate distance measuring,[13] it's a simple math problem to convert the time to distance. How cool is that?

- *Radiation sensors*: Among the more serious sensors are those that detect radiation. This can also be electromagnetic radiation (there are sensors for that too), but a Geiger counter uses radiation sensors to detect harmful ionizing. In fact, it's possible to build your very own Geiger counter using a sensor and an Arduino (and a few electronic components).

- *Speed sensors*: Like flow sensors, simple speed sensors like those found on many bicycles use a magnet and a reed switch to generate a Hall effect. The frequency

---

[13]Accuracy may depend on environmental variables such as elevation, temperature, and so on.

combined with the circumference of the wheel can be used to calculate speed and, over time, distance traveled. Yes, a bicycle computer is yet another example of a simple sensor network: the speed sensor on the wheel and fork provides the data for the monitor on your handlebars.

- *Switches and pushbuttons*: These are the most basic of digital sensors used to detect if something is set (ON) or reset (OFF).

- *Tilt switches*: These sensors can detect when a device is tilted one way or another. Although very simple, they can be useful for low-cost motion-detection sensors. They are digital and are essentially switches.

- *Touch sensors*: The touch-sensitive membranes formed into keypads, keyboards, pointing devices, and the like are an interesting form of sensor. You can use touch-sensitive devices like these for sensor networks that need to collect data from humans.

- *Video sensors*: As mentioned previously, it's possible to obtain very small video sensors that use cameras and circuitry to capture images and transmit them as digital data.

- *Weather sensors*: Sensors for temperature, barometric pressure, rainfall, humidity, wind speed, and so on are all classified as weather sensors. Most generate digital data and can be combined to create comprehensive environmental sensor networks. Yes, it's possible to build your own weather station from about a dozen inexpensive sensors, an Arduino (or a Raspberry Pi), and a bit of programming to interpret and combine the data.

Summary

Sensors are everywhere. They're in your office, your car, your home, and our personal electronic devices (which, for most people, means we always have a sensor nearby). Most of the sensors you encounter are discrete, like a smoke detector or thermostat. Sometimes they're part of a much larger collection of sensors designed to realize some feature, such as the sensors in your car that keep your speed constant when you set the cruise control, engaging the windshield wipers when it rains, or vibrating your seat if you veer too close to lane demarcations.

Now that you've learned more about the types of sensors and the data they communicate, you've probably started to think of some cool projects to build. This book will prepare you to realize those projects. This chapter examined what sensor networks are, how they're constructed, how they communicate, and how sensors work. You even saw a bit of code!

The next chapter focuses on the communication medium used in this book, by diving into a short tutorial of the new XBee 3 wireless modules. You see how to set up and configure these devices for use in transmitting sensor data to data and aggregate nodes.

CHAPTER 2

Tiny Talking Modules: An Introduction to XBee Wireless Modules

The application of sensor networks often precludes the use of wired sensors. Although it's possible to use wired sensors installed in a controlled environment that supports a cable plant, you seldom have this luxury. Sometimes you can connect some parts of a sensor network to a wired network, but the sensors are located in areas where running wires is impractical. Thus, most sensor networks require using wireless technology to transmit data from the sensors to other nodes in the network.

There are many forms of wireless communication. This book uses one of the easiest: the XBee wireless module from Digi. In this chapter, you explore the basics of using the XBee modules, from choosing a module to configuring it for use with a microcontroller and finally to creating a simple network.

© Charles Bell 2020
C. Bell, *Beginning Sensor Networks with XBee, Raspberry Pi, and Arduino*,
https://doi.org/10.1007/978-1-4842-5796-8_2

What Is an XBee?

An XBee is a self-contained, modular, cost-effective component that uses radio frequency (RF) to exchange data between XBee modules. XBee modules transmit on 2.4 GHz or long-range 900 MHz and have their own network protocols.

The XBee module itself is very small—about the size of a large postage stamp—making it easy to incorporate in small projects like sensor nodes. The modules are also low power and can use a special sleep mode to further reduce power consumption.

Although the XBee isn't a microcontroller, it does have a limited amount of processing power that you can use to control the module. One of these features, the sleep mode, can help extend battery life for battery-powered (or solar-powered) sensor nodes. You can also instruct the XBee module to monitor its data pins and transmit the data read to another XBee module. Aha! So, you can use XBee modules to link a sensor node to a data-aggregator node.

While the XBee can be used to read sensor data, its limited processing power may mean it is not suitable for all sensor nodes. For example, sensors that require algorithms to interpret or extrapolate meaningful data may not be suited for using an XBee alone. You may need to use a microcontroller or computer to perform the additional calculations.

Even better, the newest model of XBee (version 3) can be programmed on chip using MicroPython. You can even interface with (talk to) the module and execute your MicroPython code interactively (very much like you would with Python on a PC). We will see more about this exciting new feature later in this chapter.

Note   To configure an XBee module, you must use the Digi configuration tool, XCTU, which is (now) available on Windows, macOS, and Linux. Older versions were limited to Windows.

The following sections explore how to get started using XBee modules, beginning with how to choose an XBee module. I encourage you to read through the chapter before embarking on the project. I list the materials needed to complete this chapter's projects before the chapter summary.

XBee Primer

This section describes the types of XBee modules available, how to choose modules for your project, and how to configure them. I have kept this section short and terse while providing enough information to explain what XBee modules you will be using and why.

But there is one thing that confuses most new to the world of XBee: how to configure the modules. So, let's clarify that first. The XBee modules have numerous controls and settings that allow you to configure it for your project. There are two ways to alter these settings:(1) using the Digi-supplied XCTU desktop application and(2) using a terminal application with an XBee USB explorer board to manually change settings. This is done using a set of commands (called AT commands) in a specific mode (called amazingly enough AT mode).

You will learn about the different connection methods as well as the two operating modes. You will also see demonstrations of both methods to configure XBee modules. With that out of the way, let's dive into our XBee tutorial starting with choosing XBee modules.

Choosing XBee Modules

If you visit the Digi XBee website (www.digi.com/products/embedded-systems/digi-xbee/rf-modules), you will see a list of the latest modules to choose. There are modules that support proprietary (Digi) protocols, WiFi (UART or SPI to 802.11 b/g/n), and ZigBee[1] and 802.15.4 protocols. So how do you know which to choose?

Some of the most popular XBee modules are those that support the ZigBee protocol. You will be using these modules for the projects in this book. If you click the link for the ZigBee modules (www.digi.com/products/embedded-systems/digi-xbee/rf-modules/2-4-ghz-modules/xbee3-zigbee-3), you will find there are three form factors to choose to match your hardware requirements and that the modules support a variety of protocols including the ZigBee feature set, Digi Mesh, Bluetooth low energy (BLE), and 802.15.4[2] protocols. This book uses the modules that support the ZigBee Pro feature set.

There are many XBee modules available in one of three form factors including through-hole and two surface-mount options. If you click the Part Numbers & Accessories link, you will see a long list of modules grouped by the form factor. Figure 2-1 shows two of the formats available with the through-hole format on the left. Both are available at most retailers.

---

[1]ZigBee is based on the 802.15.4 protocol that provides power management, addressing, and error control, as well as networking features.

[2]For more information, see http://en.wikipedia.org/wiki/IEEE_802.15.4.

Figure 2-1. *XBee 3 form factors*

OK, WHAT'S A ZIGBEE?

ZigBee is an open standard for network communication based on the IEEE 802.15.4 standard. The protocol supports the formation of mesh networks that can automatically configure (via the coordinator and router roles), heal broken links, and allow transmission of data over longer ranges using intermediate nodes (data is passed through the mesh from node to node). Despite the name, ZigBee is not owned by Digi, nor is it limited to the similarly named XBee module.

For this book, we will be using the through-hole format. Digi offers these options to allow even more freedom of design so that the XBee modules can be used in almost any application where a low-cost wireless option is needed.

Furthermore, you will notice there are two versions of each form factor: a standard model and a pro model. Both models have the same pinout and you can mix and match them in the same network. The pro models may be slightly larger (longer), use more power, cost a bit more, but offer greater range than the standard (also called "regular modules") modules. However, you may not be able to tell the XBee 3 pro and regular modules apart without connecting them to your computer. For example, the PCB option XBee 3 pro and regular modules appear identical, but there is a subtle difference printed in black ink on the top of the board. The regular modules (of the batch I'm using) are stamped with "109 202," whereas the pro module is stamped with "941 201." If you're using XBee 3 modules, you may want to place a small mark on your pro modules to make them easier to identify.

Although you won't find them on the Digi website, there are several iterations (called series or versions) of XBee-ZB modules. Series 1 modules use an older chipset that supports point-to-point communication.[3] Series 2 and 2.5 have a newer chipset that supports several forms of communication, including mesh networks. Series 3 have the latest chipset and feature on-chip MicroPython for faster and easier development. You will use series 2 and series 3 modules for this book.

WHICH SERIES SHOULD I USE?

With so many series of XBee modules available, you may be wondering which you should choose to use. The answer depends on how you want to use them and your own experience level. For some, using the series 2 and 2.5 will meet all of their needs. For others, the added ease of use of the series 3 may be a better fit.

Another aspect may be the cost of the modules. With the release of the series 3 modules, the older series modules may be found cheaper.

So, which should you use? If you already have some modules, it turns out it doesn't matter since the series 3 is backward compatible with the series 2 modules. Thus, you can use your existing modules and add the new series 3 modules if you need more. If you don't have any modules, using the series 3 may be the easiest route to get your sensor network operating.

---

[3]Sometimes called cable replacement because it effectively links two devices together without a cable.

But you're not done yet. You also have to choose the antenna type you want to use. There are three antenna options for either regular or pro modules.[4] Figure 2-2 depicts each type available for the XBee-ZB modules. The following list describes each in more detail:

- *U.FL*: This option has a very small connector that requires an adapter cable (called a pigtail) to permit the connection to an external antenna. These antennas have the advantage that the XBee module can be enclosed in a casing (even metal) and the antenna mounted to the exterior of the case. These modules tend to cost a few dollars more and require the purchase of the pigtail as well as the antenna.

- *RPSMA*: Like the U.FL option, this one provides for an external antenna; but it uses the much larger RPSMA connector. You can mount a swivel antenna to the connector directly, but the risk of stress on the antenna is too great. Thus, you should use an extension cable and mount the antenna externally. Like the U.FL option, these modules cost a bit more and require the purchase of an antenna.

- *PCB*: The antenna is printed or embedded as a wire trace onto the module itself. This type of module is similar to the chip antenna and may be a bit less expensive to manufacture. Currently, only the PRO modules are available with this antenna option.

---

[4]Series 2 modules had five antenna options for the PRO module and four for the standard modules.

Figure 2-2. *XBee module antenna options (courtesy of SparkFun)*

WHERE'S THE WHIP?

If you've encountered XBee modules in the past, you may be familiar with an antenna option where a small wire was mounted on the module called a "whip" or wire antenna. These were available in the series 2.5 and earlier. They were a bit cheaper and offered an omni-directional signal, making them easier to use in certain applications. If you can find these modules, you may be able to save a few dollars on your project.

However, the wire antenna is not durable and can be easily broken if flexed too often. Fortunately, you can solder a replacement antenna using a bit of stranded wire of the same gauge and length. Soldering the old antenna back in place by stripping a bit of the insulation is another option, but that does change its radiation properties slightly.

Now you know that there are many types of XBee modules and that this book's projects are limited to the XBee-ZB series 2 and 3 modules, let us discuss how to communicate with the modules.

Interacting with an XBee-ZB Module

When you examine the XBee module, the first thing you notice is that the pin layout is much smaller than that of a typical discrete component designed for breadboard use. Furthermore, you cannot connect your computer directly to the XBee. You need a USB adapter to mount the XBee to allow communication with the module. Fortunately, several variants are available. You use the USB adapter to configure the module.

You can use a USB dongle like the XBee Explorer dongle from SparkFun Electronics (`www.sparkfun.com/products/11697`). This option allows you to mount the XBee module in the headers (the two rows of ten-pin connectors) on the PCB and plug the entire unit into your USB port. Since it is only a bit larger than the XBee module itself and has no need for a cable, it may be the best choice for using your XBee in remote locations.

Figure 2-3 shows the XBee Explorer dongle without the XBee module. It accepts series 1, 2, 2.5, and 3 standard or PRO models.

Figure 2-3. *XBee Explorer dongle (courtesy of SparkFun)*

Notice the white outline of the XBee module on the right side of the PCB. This indicates the correct orientation of the module on the board. Be sure to check pin alignment before inserting it into your USB port.

A similar option is the XBee Explorer USB, also from SparkFun (`www.sparkfun.com/products/11812`). Instead of being made as a dongle, it is a separate PCB base unit with a miniUSB connector. It also supports series 1, 2, 2.5, and 3 standard or PRO modules. It requires a USB-to-mini USB cable. Figure 2-4 shows the XBee Explorer USB unit.

Figure 2-4. *XBee Explorer USB (courtesy of SparkFun)*

Both options from SparkFun include the mounting holes for headers that can be used with breadboards, giving you access to all the pins of the XBee module. Although they do not come with the pins soldered in place, the pins are easy to add if you so desire. You will see in later chapters where this would be helpful.

SparkFun also carries several other XBee Explorer boards including a regulated breakout board (`www.sparkfun.com/products/11373`) and an Arduino shield (`www.sparkfun.com/products/12847`). If you plan to use an Arduino to host the XBee, the SparkFun shield is a must-have. Figure 2-5 shows the SparkFunXBeeshield.

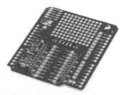

Figure 2-5. *XBee Arduino shield (courtesy of SparkFun)*

There are also several boards in their "SparkFun Thing" range of boards that support XBee modules such as the SparkFun Thing Plus (`www.sparkfun.com/products/15454`).

WHAT IS A SHIELD?

A shield is a PCB designed to mount on top of an Arduino by connecting
to the headers on the Arduino. Shields are used to extend the hardware
features of the Arduino. There are shields for controlling LCDs, Ethernet,
XBees, and much more.

Digi also produces an XBee 3 development kit that contains three XBee
standard surface-mount modules with antenna and three USB interface
boards. It also includes all the cables you need to get started including
a handy storage box. Although the cost is rather intimidating ($110.95
suggested retail), it does provide a one-stop shopping option for those
looking for maximum practicality and no assembly (other than plugging
the modules into the interface boards). Figure 2-6 shows the Digi ZigBee
Development Kit sold by SparkFun (www.sparkfun.com/products/15216).

Figure 2-6. *Digi ZigBee Development Kit*

One nice feature of this kit is the explorer boards support the plug-
and-play Grove interface (also called the Grove system), which makes
wiring the modules to Grove-enabled sensors as simple as plugging them
together. For more information about the Grove interface, see http://
wiki.seeedstudio.com/Grove_System/.

While there are other options available from many vendors, including older serial interface modules, these are among the best and easiest-to-use options I have found for working with XBee modules. When you get to the point where we are using XBee modules with Arduino, you'll see an example of an XBee shield that enables direct connection of the XBee to the Arduino pins.

Pin Layout

If you look at the XBee module, you will see a total of 20 pins. If you view the module from the top (the side with the antenna), the pins are labeled 1–10 starting on the upper left and 11–20 starting from the lower right. Thus, pin 1 is in the upper left, and pin 20 is in the upper right. But what do all these things do?

You will be exploring these pins in more detail in later chapters, but for now (if you are curious), Table 2-1 depicts the pin layout for a typical XBee module. In this case, I am presenting the pin layout of an XBee-ZB series 2 module. Series 3 modules have one difference in the pins; pin 14 is not supported on the series 3 modules and should not be used with those modules.

Table 2-1. *XBee Pin Layout*

Pin	Name	Description	Direction	Default
1	VCC	Power supply	N/A	N/A
2	DOUT	UART data out	OUT	OUT
3	DIN/CONFIG	UART data in	IN	IN
4	DIO12	Digital I/O 12	BOTH	DISABLED
5	RESET	Module reset	BOTH	Open collector with pull-up

(continued)

Table 2-1. (*continued*)

Pin	Name	Description	Direction	Default
6	RSSI PWM/DIO10	RX signal strength, digital I/O 10	BOTH	OUT
7	DIO11	Digital I/O 11	BOTH	IN
8	Reserved	No connection	NA	DISABLED
9	DTR/SLEEP_RQ/ DIO08	Sleep control, digital I/O 8	BOTH	IN
10	GND	Ground	N/A	N/A
11	DIO4	Digital I/O 4	BOTH	DISABLED
12	CTS/DIO7	Clear to send, digital I/O 7	BOTH	OUT
13	ON/SLEEP	Status, digital I/O 9	OUT	OUT
14	VREF	No connection	IN	N/A
15	ASSOCIATE/DIO5	Associated indicator, digital I/O 5	BOTH	OUT
16	RTS/DIO6	Request to send, digital I/O 6	BOTH	IN
17	AD3/DIO3	Analog I/O 3, digital I/O 3	BOTH	DISABLED
18	AD2/DIO2	Analog I/O 2, digital I/O 2	BOTH	DISABLED
19	AD1/DIO1	Analog I/O 1, digital I/O 1	BOTH	DISABLED
20	AD0/DIO0	Analog I/O 0, digital I/O 0	BOTH	DISABLED

To find more information about the XBee 3 module hardware, see the hardware reference document from Digi at www.digi.com/resources/documentation/digidocs/pdfs/90001543.pdf.

In the next section, you will see how to get started configuring the modules for use in your projects.

Configuring Modules

Configuring XBee modules is not very difficult. Because you are using ZigBee modules, you need to set the address for each module, choose a role to perform in the network, and configure your modules to interface with whatever sensor or microcontroller you are using to process the sensor data. Let's begin by discussing ZigBee addressing.

CAN SENSORS BE CONNECTED DIRECTLY TO THE XBEE?

The XBee module can read sensor data via its I/O ports. However, not all sensors can be connected directly to an XBee module. If the sensor requires direct I/O using special communication protocols, you need a microcontroller to read the sensor data and then send it to the XBee for transmission. You will see this in action when you explore using a DHT-22 temperature sensor in the next chapter.

Addresses

The XBee modules are branded with a specific serial number or address located on the bottom of the module. This is a little inconvenient given that you normally cannot see the back of the module when it is mounted. However, you can find the address using either the Digi configuration application or a simple serial terminal application.

Figure 2-7 shows the underside of an XBee 3 module (enlarged for better viewing). Notice the numbers printed under the model number. You use these together to form a 64-bit address unique to each XBee module. This is referred to by many publications as the radio address and is split into two parts: a high and low address (or value). For example, the address shown in the figure, 0013A200, is the "high" address and 4192DA30 is the "low" address. We will need these in an upcoming example.

Figure 2-7. *XBee address printed on the back of the module*

Tip   It is common to see the XBee referred to as either a module or a radio. These terms are often interchanged. I refer to the XBee in general terms with module and with radio when referring to the transmit and receive capabilities of the radio itself.

The radio's address is used to target messages for delivery. In many ways, it is similar to an IP address, but in this case, it is a specific radio address.

Along with the specific 64-bit radio address, ZigBee networks use a 16-bit address within each network that is assigned to each radio. In addition, you can assign a short text string to identify each radio. Along with that, there is a personal area network (PAN) address that can be used to logically group the radios in a network. Finally, all radios must be transmitting and receiving on the same channel (frequency). To recap, when an XBee radio wants to send a message to another radio, it must use the same channel and set the destination PAN and a specific 16-bit radio address. You see these options in action in the following sections.

ZigBee Networks

Like Ethernet networks, ZigBee networks are based on a predefined network stack where each layer in the stack is responsible for a specific transformation of the data messages. Also like other networks, ZigBee networks support message routing, ad hoc network creation, and self-healing mesh topologies. Thus, the radio address and the PAN address are needed to support these features.

Support for mesh topologies is made possible with the addition of different roles that each node (radio) can perform in the network. The following list describes each role in more detail, starting from the most complex:

- *Coordinator*: A single coordinator is needed for each network. This node is responsible for administering addresses and forming and managing the network. All other nodes search for the coordinator and exchange handshake information at startup.

- *Router*: A node that is configured as a router is designed to pass on (route) information to other radios. Routers enable the healing of mesh networks by joining networks and exchanging messages from other nodes. Routers are typically powered with reliable sources because they must be dependable. Thus, a data-aggregation node would be a good choice for the router radio mode.

- *End device*: An end device is a node that sends or receives information to the router nodes and the coordinator. It has an advantage in that less processing is going on, so power consumption is lower. End devices support a sleep mode to reduce power requirements still further. Most of your sensor nodes will be configured as end devices.

You can configure your XBee modules in any way you want, provided you have at least one coordinator in the network. To form a mesh, simply employ several routers, where one or more end devices exchange messages and the routers exchange messages with a coordinator. Figure 2-8 shows a typical mesh network.

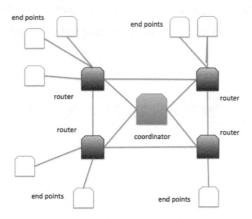

Figure 2-8. *ZigBee mesh network*

Configuring XBee modules can sometimes go wrong. When this happens, the issue can be very frustrating to diagnose and correct. I include a troubleshooting section at the end of this chapter that will help you solve many of the common things that can go wonky and drive you batty. If you get stuck, check out the troubleshooting section.

Updating Firmware

The first thing you should do when starting to configure XBee modules is to load the latest version of the firmware and set the role. Firmware in this case refers to the program for the XBee's embedded microcontroller. You should only need to change the firmware if any of your series 2 or 2.5 modules are using an older version or if you want to experiment with different configurations. Similarly, if you want to use a series 3 module with older modules, you will have to load a different firmware on the series 3 modules. For example, if you want to use a series 2 and a series 3 together using the 802.15.14 protocol, you should install the same firmware on each module.

Digi makes this easy by providing a nice configuration application named XCTU. Loading firmware can only be done with the XCTU application. Figure 2-9 shows XCTU running without any modules attached.

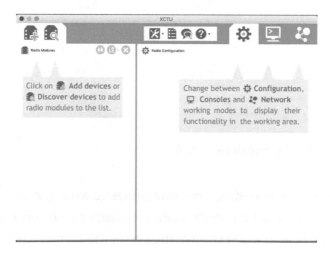

Figure 2-9. *XCTU main window*

As you can see, the XCTU software will give you friendly reminders and tips on how to do things. In the following paragraphs, we will see how to contact and configure modules. You can download the latest version of the XCTU software from the following URL:

`www.digi.com/products/embedded-systems/digi-xbee/digi-xbee-`
`tools/xctu#productsupport-utilities`

You will find installers for most platforms including macOS, Windows, and Linux as well as links to the release notes and license documents. Simply download the installer for your platform and install it using the methods common to the platform. For example, on Windows, you would run and execute the installer, and on macOS, you must first extract the installer from a compressed file and then execute the installer.

Once the software is installed and you launch the XCTU software, you need to connect to your XBee modules. To connect to the XBee, simply insert the XBee module into the adapter and connect it to your computer. For example, if you are using the SparkFun Explorer USB dongle, you need only insert the XBee module into the dongle first. Once you insert the dongle into a USB slot, you should see the power LED glow.

Once the explorer is connected to your computer, you can add the module using either of the buttons in the top left portion of the window as shown in Figure 2-10. The one on the left allows you to add a module by specifying its serial connection parameters, and the one on the right scans all serial connections for modules. Let's use the *add module* button.

Figure 2-10. *Add and scan modulebuttons*

When ready, click the *add radio* button. You should see a dialog open that permits you to choose the serial connection and set the connection parameters. The default serial connection parameters are 9600 baud, no flow control, 8 bits, no parity, and 1 stop bit (also written as 96008N1). If you find your XBee won't communicate, chances are it is operating at a different baud rate. If you change the baud rate, you should change it for all modules. Figure 2-11 shows the add module dialog. If you elected to use the discover option, you can select multiple serial configurations to search.

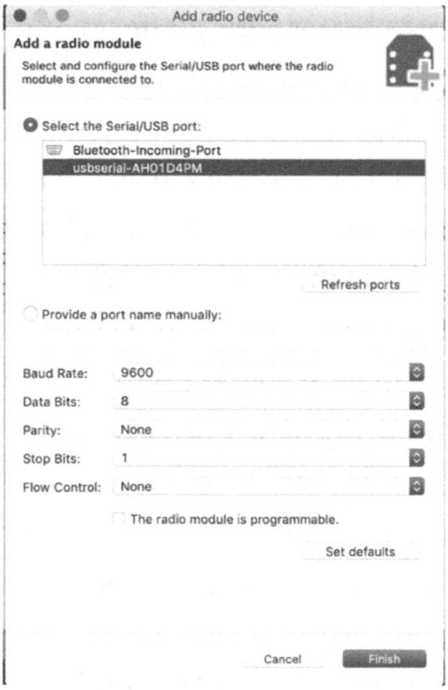

Figure 2-11. *Add module dialog*

Simply select the serial connection, verify the connection parameters, and click Finish. It takes a few seconds for XCTU to make the connection, and once it does, you will see the module appear in the left column of the main window as shown in Figure 2-12. Newer series 3 modules will appear with a black background, and older series modules will appear with a blue background. This permits you to look at the list and quickly identify your older modules.

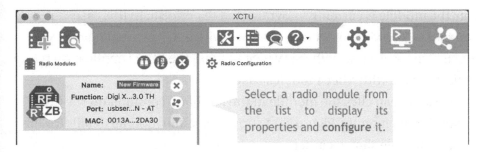

Figure 2-12. *Radio module added*

The list of radios also shows the role the module is assigned. For example, a router will appear with an "R" and the coordinator will appear with a "C" icon over the module image. You will also see the protocol icon change depending on what firmware is loaded. Icons to the right of each module allow you to close the radio connection, run a discovery operation to find other modules on the same network, and hide the module details. Figure 2-13 shows an example of a series 3 module.

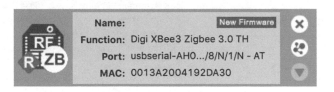

Figure 2-13. *Radio entry—overview*

Notice in the center there is additional data including the name of the module (you can change the name), function (the firmware loaded), serial connection, and media access control (MAC) address.[5] Recall, each module has a unique MAC address and is printed on the bottom of the module. Notice also there is a diamond with an "R" in it. This indicates the

---

[5]https://en.wikipedia.org/wiki/MAC_address

role the module is currently programmed to perform. In this case, it is a router. The coordinator would be shown with a "C" and end devices with an "E". This is just one of the very nice touches the XCTU application has to make working with XBee modules easy.

Next, we can click the module in the left-hand column and see the details for the module. Figure 2-14 shows the radio module details for the series 3 module shown earlier.

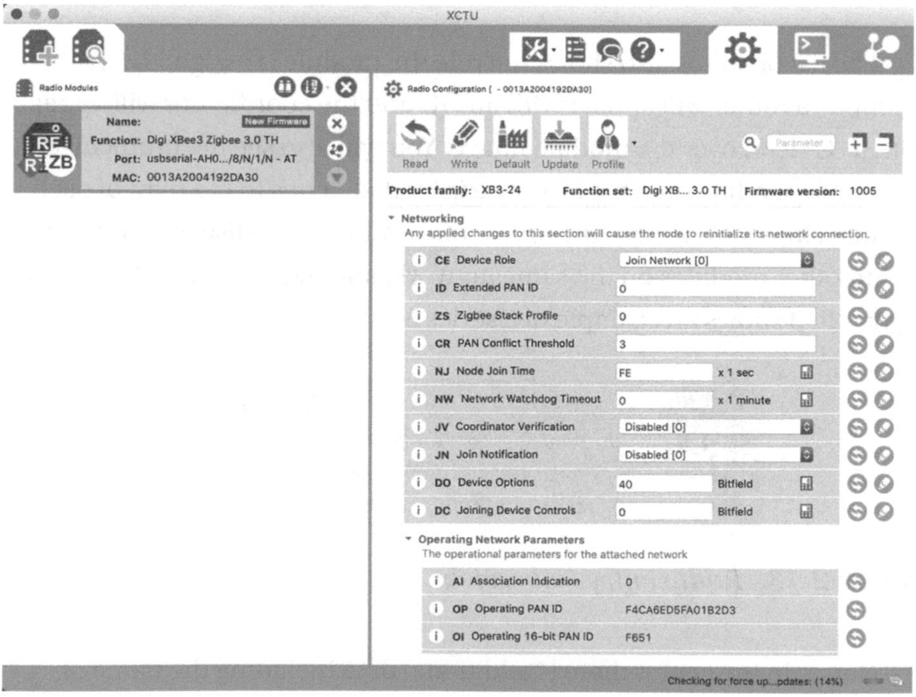

Figure 2-14. *XCTU radio module settings*

The radio module settings include a long list of things you can change. While most are things you would not normally change, some are those you will need to change when you configure your modules. For example, you may need to set the role and other parameters for using in a ZigBee mesh. Fortunately, the settings are grouped into categories that you can collapse or expand to make it easier to find the settings you want. Just click the triangle for each category to collapse or open it. There is also a search box that lets you search for a setting. That's a nice touch.

Let's see how to make a small change. Notice the series 3 module shown in the figures does not have a name. Whenever you make a change to any setting, you first find the setting, make the change, and then write the changes to the module. In this case, we want the name whose parameter is node identifier or NI. To find it in the settings, simply type NI in the search box. You can then change the name as shown in Figure 2-15.

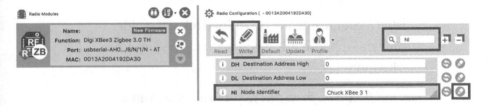

Figure 2-15. *Change the name identifier for a module*

Notice I changed the node identifier. To write the changes to the module, I click the pencil icon next to the setting. You can also make changes to other parameters applying each in turn or wait and update all changes by clicking the *Write* button to write all changes to the module. Figure 2-16 shows the radio with changes applied.

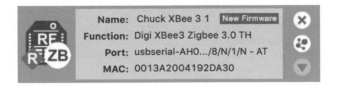

Figure 2-16. *Radio module name changed*

Naming your modules can also help identify them in the list of radio modules. In fact, XCTU allows you to sort the modules in a variety of ways including by name. Setting other parameters are just as easy. For example, you may want to set the PAN address, destination address, and node identifier.

There is one more aspect you should understand about XBee modules—managing the firmware. If you have older modules, you may be prompted if you want to download the legacy firmware. A dialog box like that shown in Figure 2-17 may be shown. You have three download options:

- *Look for and install new firmware*: Download updates for XCTU and "known" modules only.

- *Install legacy firmware*: Download all of the older firmware—choose this if you want to use any older series modules.

- *Install firmware from file*: Load firmware from a file—use this if you have downloaded a custom firmware (used rarely).

The first time you use XCTU or the first time you use an older series module, you should choose the second option and install the legacy firmware packages. Otherwise, the first option is the default and, in fact, XCTU checks for updates automatically (but you can turn that off in the preferences).

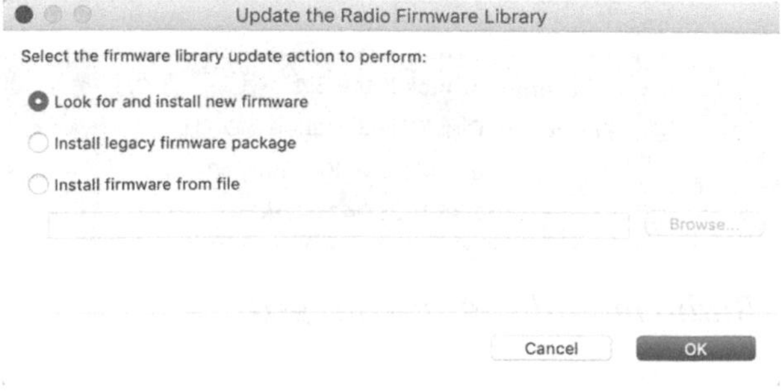

Figure 2-17. Downloading firmware

Depending on the speed of your Internet connection, it may take a while to download the older firmware, but you should do so in order to keep your modules up to date. Having the older firmware also permits you to load the correct firmware on newer series 3 modules so that they match in protocol and features.

There are two modes for XBee modules to communicate: AT or API. AT means the module accepts AT commands via its local serial connection and displays information in a human-readable format using a derivative of the Hayes modem command set. API means the module is configured to send and receive data via its protocol stack. Thus, when you want to communicate with a module to configure it using a console connection, you use the AT method. The API method is used throughout the rest of this book. All modules must use the same communication firmware (AT or API) and version for their roles.

In this chapter, we will use the AT mode. To ensure you have the correct firmware loaded, you should insert your module into an explorer, plug the explorer into your computer, and then add the radio module in XCTU. Then, click the *Update* button as shown in Figure 2-18.

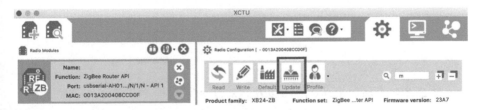

Figure 2-18. *Choosing to update firmware*

You will be presented with a dialog that allows you to choose the firmware you want to download onto (update) the module. Figure 2-19 shows an example of choosing the ZigBee protocol firmware in AT mode and the latest version for the series 2.5 and older modules. Firmware for the XBee series 3 modules are listed differently.

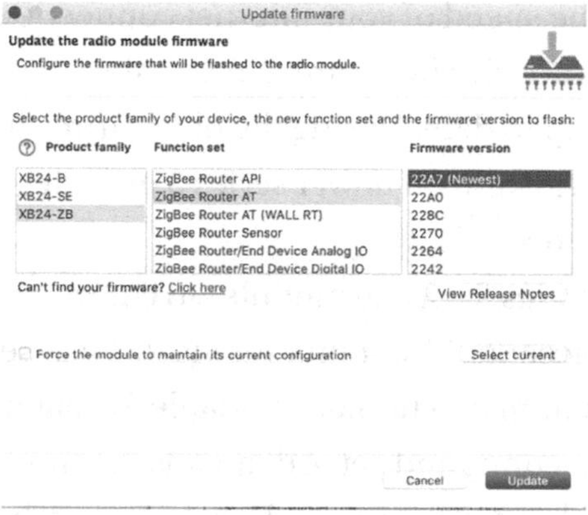

Figure 2-19. *Choose the firmware (series 2.5 and older)*

Figure 2-20 shows the firmware choices for the XBee series 3 modules.

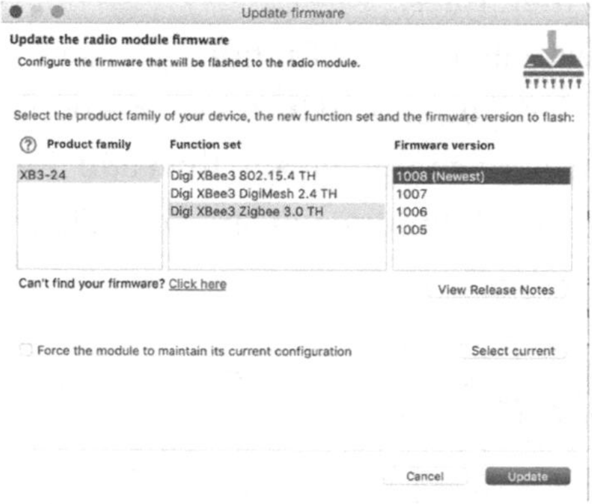

Figure 2-20. *Choose the firmware (series 3)*

When you have selected the firmware you want, click the *Update* button. You may have to respond to one or more "are you sure?" queries. This is because updating the firmware erases any settings you've made including any programming. Clearly, only say "OK" if you are sure you don't need to save anything first. Once the firmware is updated, you will get an "OK" dialog. When that is closed, XCTU will reload the radio into your list of radios.

Now that you have seen how to manage the XBee module's firmware and settings, let's look at an easier way to set the user-defined values.

Changing Settings with a Terminal Application

Most of the settings for an XBee module can be changed using a terminal application (AT mode). In the past, we had to use a console application, but XCTU now provides a console mode that works very well. The console has all of the features you need to work with the XBee modules. You can connect, disconnect, and even record your session. You can also send commands or form packets and send them to the module. For this section, we will be sending commands. The interface also allows us to see the commands in hexadecimal, which can help in diagnosing connections or deciphering data.

The XBee module has two modes: command and transparent. Command mode is initiated with a special command, +++, where the module sends a response back via the serial connection. Transparent mode is the default mode: the module sends data to the radio destination specified. In other words, use command mode when you want to talk to the module and transparent mode when you want to talk via or through the module to another. For example, sending data via the XBee to another XBee uses transparent mode.

Thus, to configure your XBee modules after loading the correct firmware, you open a terminal application and issue the appropriate command. Table 2-2 shows some of the more common AT commands you use to configure XBee modules.

Table 2-2. *Common XBee AT Commands*

Command	Description	Use	Response
+++	Enter command mode	Put the module in command mode	OK
ATCN	Exit command mode	Return to transparent mode	OK
AT	Attention	Check to see if the module is available	OK
ATWR	Save	Write settings to firmware	OK
ATID	PAN ID	Display the PAN ID	PAN ID
ATID nnnn	PAN ID	Change the PAN ID	OK
ATSH	64-bit serial high	Display the high part of the 64-bit serial number	Address
ATSL	64-bit serial low	Display the low part of the 64-bit serial number	Address
ATDH	64-bit destination high	Display the high part of the 64-bit destination address	Address
ATDH nnnn	64-bit destination high	Set the high part of the 64-bit destination address	OK
ATDL	64-bit destination low	Display the low part of the 64-bit destination address	Address
ATDL nnnn	64-bit destination low	Set the low part of the 64-bit destination address	OK
ATMY	16-bit address	Display the 16-bit address assigned by the coordinator	Address

(continued)

Table 2-2. (*continued*)

Command	Description	Use	Response
ATNI	Node ID	Display the text string node identifier	id
ATNI text	Node ID	Set the text string node identifier	OK
ATRE	Reset	Reset the XBee to factory defaults	OK

Tip   For more information about AT commands, see the XBee 3 manual at www.digi.com/resources/documentation/ digidocs/pdfs/90001539.pdf.

Some commands require a value for setting variables. Omitting the variable results in displaying the current value. All commands except +++ require you to press Enter to execute. If you press the +++ command and nothing happens, try it again, waiting a second or two between each attempt. You can also try typing a little faster (or a little slower) until the command-mode switch takes effect.

Tip   All numeric values are entered as hexadecimal values.

To demonstrate how these commands work, let's use XCTU's console dialog to connect to a module that has been loaded with the ZigBee ROUTER AT firmware. First, select your radio in the left-hand list and then click the *console* tab as shown in Figure 2-21.

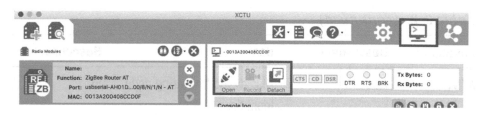

Figure 2-21. *Selecting console mode*

The console pane allows you to do three things with the three icons to the left. You can open a connection (connect to a module), record the session (only selectable once connected), and detach, which allows you to detach the console into its own window. If you are following along, go ahead and disconnect the console now and then click the *Open* button. Figure 2-22 shows a typical configuration session starting with connecting to the module and displaying its values and then exiting command mode.

Note   The first time you run the ATDH, ATDL, or ATMY command without a parameter, you may see a result of 0. This indicates the value has not been set.

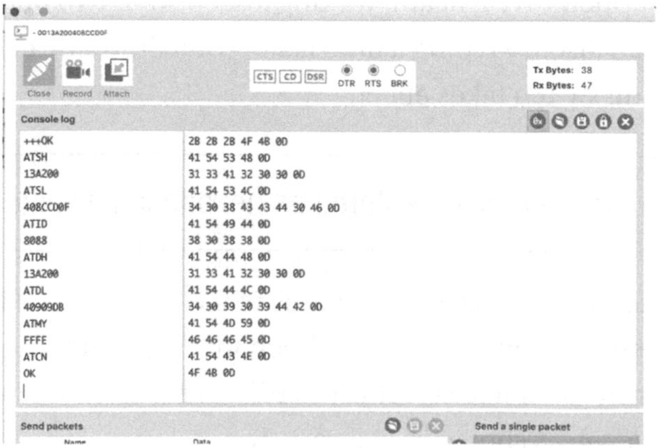

Figure 2-22. *Getting information about a module (AT mode) in a console*

Tip   When in command mode, you have only 10 seconds to enter a command before the module returns to transparent mode. If this happens, you see no response when entering commands. Simply issue the +++ command again and reissue the command.

Next, Figure 2-23 shows a session where you set the destination address (the XBee to which you want to connect) and its PAN ID using the XCTU console.

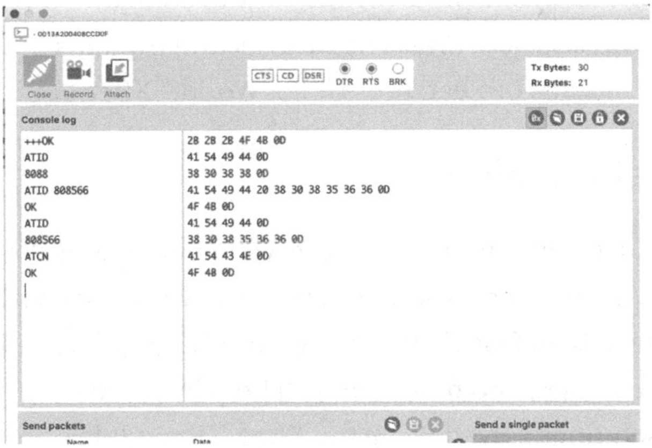

Figure 2-23.   *Configuring a module (AT mode) in a console*

While the XCTU application has a very nice serial terminal that works very well (and I prefer to use it when working with XBee modules in AT mode), you can use any terminal application you want such as CoolTerm. You need only setup the serial connection to match your XBee (baud rate, etc.) and connect to the serial port where your XBee is connected. Figure 2-24 shows an example of using CoolTerm on macOS.

Figure 2-24. *Configuring a module (AT mode) using CoolTerm*

Now that you know the types of modules you need to form wireless networks using the ZigBee protocol and how to configure them, you can start building wireless networks. The next section explains how to create the most basic of XBee project: the "Hello, World!" XBee equivalent.

For More Information

If you would like to learn more about the XBee modules and how they communicate, an excellent resource is the Digi website (`www.digi.com`). You can also search on Google for "XBee" and "ZigBee" to find a number of blogs, how-to pages, and more that will help by presenting different projects and solutions solved using the XBee-ZB modules.

If you are using older series modules, there are also a couple of excellent books that you can refer to for additional information, project ideas, and more. I list two of the better titles here:

- *Building Wireless Sensor Networks: With ZigBee, XBee, Arduino, and Processing*, by Robert Faludi (O'Reilly, 2010), ISBN 978-0596807733

- *The Hands-on XBEE Lab Manual: Experiments that Teach You XBEE Wireless Communications*, by Jonathan Titus (Newnes, 2012), ISBN 978-0123914040

However, there are some excellent resources from Digi that you should consider exploring including the XCTU documentation, XBee module hardware manuals, and ZigBee manuals. You can find all of these documents at the following site:

```
www.digi.com/support/productdetail?pid=5637&type=documentation
```

Before we embark on our first sample application using XBee modules, let's discuss one of the most powerful options for the series 3 modules: MicroPython.

Introducing MicroPython

The use of the Python language for controlling hardware has been around for some time. Users of the Raspberry Pi, pcDuino, and other low-cost computers and similar boards have had the advantage of using Python for controlling hardware. In this case, they used full versions of the Python programming language on the native Linux-based operating system.

However, this required special libraries built to communicate with the hardware. These libraries were designed to interface with the general-purpose input output (GPIO) pins. The GPIO pins normally appear on the board in one or more rows of male pins on the board. Some boards used female header pins.

While these boards made it possible for those who wanted to develop electronics projects, it required users to buy the board as well as peripherals like a keyboard, mouse, and monitor. Not only that, but users also had to learn the operating system. For those not used to Linux, this can be a challenge in and of itself.

The vision for MicroPython was to combine the simplicity of learning Python with the low cost and ease of use of microcontroller boards, which would permit a lot more people to work with electronics for art and science projects. Beginners would not have to learn a new operating system or learn one of the more complex programming languages. MicroPython was the answer.

MicroPython[6] was created and is maintained by Damien P. George, Paul Sokolovsky, and other contributors. It was designed to be a lean, efficient version of the Python 3 language and installed on a small microcontroller. Since Python is an interpreted language and thus slower (in general) than compiled languages, MicroPython was designed to be as efficient as possible so that it can run on microcontrollers that normally are slower and have much less memory than a typical personal computer.

Another aspect is microcontroller boards like the Arduino require a compilation step that you must perform on your computer and load the binary executable onto the board first. In contrast, since MicroPython has its interpreter running directly on the hardware, we do not need the intermediate step to prepare the code; we can run the interpreted language directly on the hardware!

This permits hardware manufacturers to build small, inexpensive boards that include MicroPython on the same chip as the microprocessor (typically). This gives you the ability to connect to the board, write the code, and execute it without any extra work.

You may be thinking that to reduce Python 3 to a size that fits on a small chip with limited memory that the language is stripped down and lacking features. That can't be further than the truth. In fact, MicroPython is a complete implementation of the core features of Python 3 including a compact runtime and interactive interpreter. There is support for reading

---

[6]Copyright 2014-2017, Damien P. George, Paul Sokolovsky, and contributors. Last updated on March05, 2017.

and writing files, loading modules, interacting with hardware such as GPIO pins, error handling, and much more. Best of all, the optimization of Python 3 code allows it to be compiled into a binary requiring about 256K of memory to store the binary and runs with as little as 16K of RAM.

MicroPython therefore allowed Digi to put a functional programming language and interpreter on the XBee series 3 module itself! Yes, this means we can connect to our XBee series 3 boards, write code, and execute it. This opens a whole new world for working with XBee modules and sensor networks.

Note   MicroPython only works with series 3 modules.

XCTU has a MicroPython console that you can use to connect to a series 3 module. To use MicroPython, we must make a few changes to the modules. Recall, we set the changes using the update icon (pencil) to the right after changing the setting. These include changing the baud rate (faster), enabling API + MicroPython mode. Figure 2-25 shows the settings in XCTU.

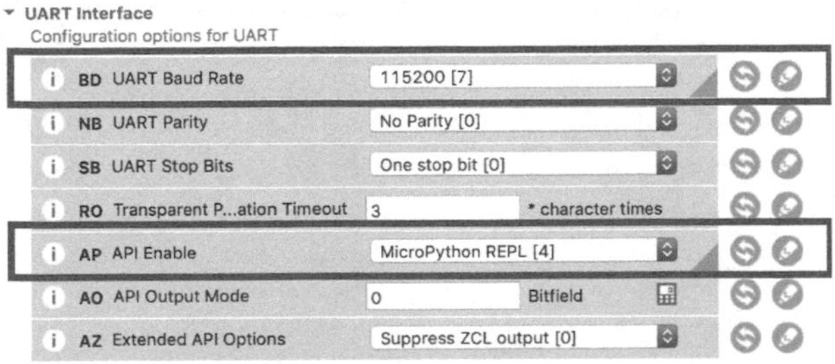

Figure 2-25. *Setup module for MicroPython*

Once these settings are written to the module, simply connect your XBee series 3 module to a USB XBee Explorer, plug it into your computer, and add the radio to XCTU. Once there, you can click thetools icon and select *MicroPython Terminal.* Figure 2-26 shows the selections.

Figure 2-26. *Opening a MicroPython console*

This opens the MicroPython console where you can issue Python commands. Figure 2-27 shows a simple example in the form of the ubiquitous "hello, world!" program.

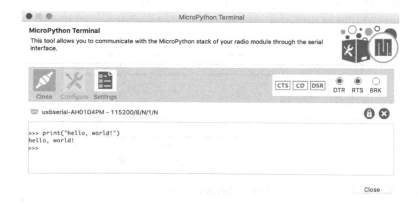

Figure 2-27. *Example MicroPythonsession*

This example was shown using a ZigBee series 3 module. MicroPython features may be slightly different depending on which module you use. Table 2-3 shows the major features and their availability on certain series 3 modules.

Table 2-3. *XBee Series 3 MicroPython Features by Model*

Feature	XBee 3 Cellular	XBee 3 ZigBee, DigiMesh, and 802.15.4
Digital I/O	Yes	Yes
I2C	Yes	Yes
Power management	Yes	Yes
Digi Remote Manager	Yes[1]	No
Secondary UART	Yes	No
Real-time clock	Yes	No
File system	Yes	Yes
File system—concurrent file writes	Yes	No
File system—rename	Yes	No
File system—Edit files after creation	Yes	No
File System—delete	Yes	No[2]
File System—secure files	Yes	No
File System preserved across updates	Yes	No

We will see more about MicroPython in the next chapter. But first, let's see the XBee modules in action with a short demonstration project where we use AT mode for setup and configuration via a terminal connection.

An XBee Wireless Chat Room

For this example, you need two XBee modules, two USB adapters and required cables, and either one or two computers. You can use one computer with each module connected to a different USB serial port.

This example uses one series 2 and one series 3 XBee module to demonstrate how to work with each series. If you have only one series, you can skip the sections that demonstrate the other series. The biggest difference is in how you load the firmware. Programming the modules in AT mode is the same.

This project is a sort of "Hello, World!" test for the XBee at the hardware level. Rather than writing a simple program to print the messages, you will use two XBee modules configured as a simple point-to-point network with one coordinator and one router. In the example, I included one series 2 and one series 3 module, but you can use two of the same series (either) if you want. Just follow the series-specific instructions in the following sections.

You'll set both modules to use AT firmware so you can demonstrate the transparent mode and see the messages you are passing in clear text. This is what will make the chat work. What is typed on or message entered on one module will appear on another. Cool, eh?

Loading the Firmware for the Modules

The first thing you need to do is to load the firmware for each module. Recall that you use the XCTU application to load the firmware. We will review the specifics for loading firmware for series 2.5 and earlier as well as series 3 modules.

Series 2.5 and Earlier

The older series 2.5 and earlier modules have firmware that is preconfigured for one of the three roles. This is indicated by the version number. For the XBee modules I used in writing this chapter, the version number for a coordinator is 20A7. The first two digits are the role, and the last two digits are the version. It is not critical if your modules have a version other than A7, as long as they both have the same. The following are some of the major roles and their values:

- 20xx, coordinator, AT/transparent operation

- 21xx, coordinator, API operation

- 22xx, router, AT/transparent operation

- 23xx, router, API operation

- 28xx, end device, AT/transparent operation

- 29xx, end device, API operation

Series 3

Series 3 modules are configured a little differently. These modules have only three choices for the ZigBee firmware as follows. To use series 3 modules together with older ZigBee modules, be sure to load the ZigBee firmware:

- *Digi XBee3 802.15.4 TH*: Use this firmware when working with other modules that use the older 802.15.4 protocol.

- *Digi XBee3 DigiMesh 2.4 TH*: Use this firmware when working with other modules that use the Digi Mesh protocol.

- *Digi XBee3 ZigBee 3.0 TH*: Use this firmware when working with other modules that use the ZigBee protocol.

Since we use the ZigBee protocol in this book, if you are using any series 3 modules, you will want to load the ZigBee firmware. Currently, the latest version is 1008. Again, it is not critical to have the latest, but it never hurts to keep up to date.

You may be wondering how the series 3 modules can be configured for one of the three roles. This is done by selecting a combination of two settings. First, we choose the *device role* (CE) and set it to either *form network* (1) or *join network* (0). Second, we choose the *sleep mode* (SM) and set it to either 0 for a router or > 0 for use as an end device. Table 2-4 shows a matrix to help you choose the correct settings.

Table 2-4. *Setting the Series 3 Role*

ZigBee Role	AT Command	
	Device Role (CE)	Sleep Mode (SM
Coordinator	1	0
Router	0	0
End Device	0	> 0

For example, to set a series 3 module as the coordinator using the AT mode, we issue the ATCE and ATSM commands. Or, better, we can use the XCTU application and set the parameters there.

But there is one other setting specific to series 3 modules. Notice there is no choice for AT or API firmware. This is controlled using the *API Enable* (AP) setting. Set it to 0 for AT mode or 1 for API mode. You can do this with the ATAP command or by using the application.

Tip Remember to click the *Write* button next to a setting when changing it or if you've changed two or more settings, click the *Write* button on the toolbar.

Loading the Firmware for the Coordinator

Use the XCTU application to configure the first XBee module as the coordinator AT function set. In this case, we will use a series 3 module.

Connect the module and click the *Add* or *Discover* button (in the upper-left hand corner of the XCTU window). Follow the dialogs, and once the module is added and its configuration is read, you're ready to update the firmware.

Click the *Update* icon and select the ZigBee firmware in the dialog. Figure 2-28 shows the correct selection to load the ZigBee 3.0 firmware. Once you have that selected, click the *Update* button in the dialog.

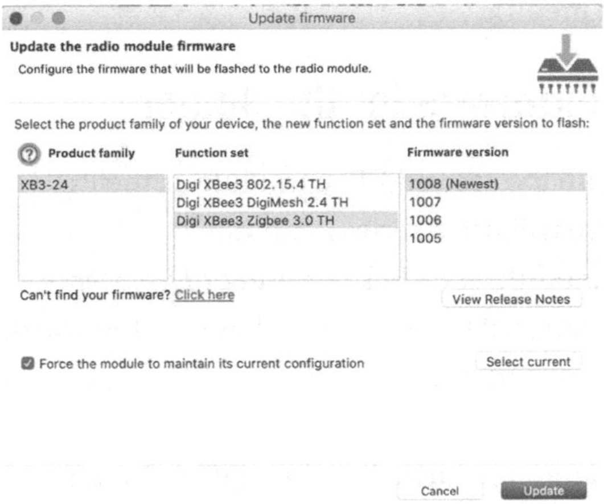

Figure 2-28. *Loading firmware for the coordinator (series 3)*

When the write process is done, you must set the *Device Role* and *Sleep Mode* as shown in Table 2-4. You also need to ensure the *API Mode* is set to 0. The following code shows how to do this using the terminal connection. Recall, we can click the *Terminal* icon in the upper-right corner of the XCTU interface and then click the *Open* button to start a session. Remember to type the +++ command (in the left-hand side of the console log) and wait a few seconds for a response before entering the commands.

```
+++
ATCE 1
ATSM 0
ATAP 0
ATWR
ATCN
```

If you want to set the parameters using the XCTU application, remember to click the *Configuration* icon to switch to the configuration mode (or use the menu).

Loading the Firmware for the Router

Now, let's configure the second XBee module as the ROUTER AT function set. In this case, we will use a series 2 module.

Connect the module and click the *Add* or *Discover* button (in the upper-left hand corner of the XCTU window). Follow the dialogs, and once the module is added and its configuration is read, you're ready to update the firmware.

Click the *Update* icon and select the ZigBee Router AT firmware in the dialog. Figure 2-29 shows the correct selection to load the ZigBee Router AT firmware. Once you have that selected, click the *Update* button in the dialog.

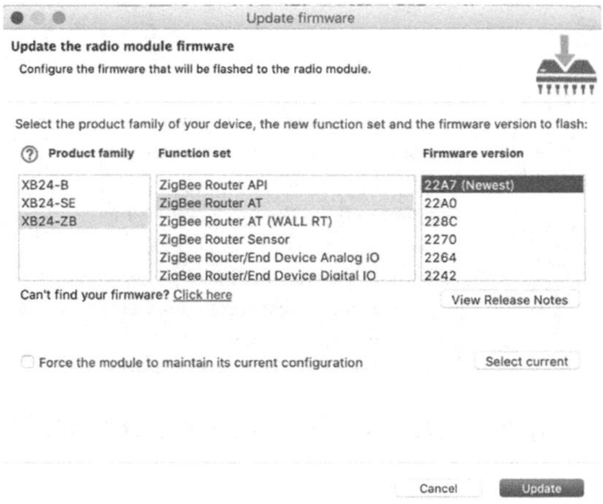

Figure 2-29. *Loading firmware for the router (series 2.5 and earlier)*

Next, we need to set the destination addresses for each module to point to each other. Hence, the point-to-point nomenclature.

Capturing Serial Numbers

Recall that XBee radios require the 64-bit address (serial number—also named the MAC address) of the destination radio to send data. You need to record these before you begin the project. Take a moment to record the 64-bit serial numbers for each of your XBee modules.

If you have inserted your XBee modules into their adapters, you can see the addresses easily using the XCTU application. Figure 2-30 shows a series 3 and series 2 module attached. Notice the addresses indicated. We will set each module's destination to the address of the other module.

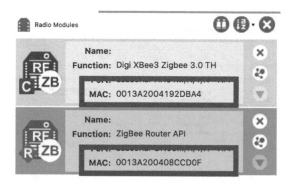

Figure 2-30. *Identifying the 64-bit address using XCTU*

You can also use a terminal application to query the modules for the address using the ATSH and ATSL commands if you prefer or require that operation mode.

Once you identify the addresses, write the information in Table 2-5.[7] There are spaces for additional information that you will be using, so refer to this table as you proceed with the project.

Table 2-5. *XBee Configuration Data*

Role	Serial High	Serial Low	PAN ID	Node ID
Coordinator AT				
Router AT				

Now, let's configure the AT mode parameters starting with the coordinator.

---

[7]If you prefer not to write in your book, take a piece of paper and make a chart like Table 2-5 to store the information. If the paper is thin, you can fold it and use it as a bookmark.

Configuring the Coordinator

To configure the coordinator, you want to set the destination address of this radio to the serial number of the other radio (the router). Thus, you set the destination address on the coordinator to the address of the router. We also need to set the PAN ID for the network.

We'll use the XCTU application to change the settings, but you can use a terminal if you prefer and issue the ATDH, ATDL, and ATID commands.

You must also choose a PAN ID to use on the network. Let's use the iconic 8088.[8] In this case, it does not matter what you use as long as all modules on the network have the same PAN ID and the value is in the range 0000–FFFF (hexadecimal). Also set the Node ID to COORDINATOR to make it easier to identify. Figure 2-31 shows the configuration session for the coordinator.

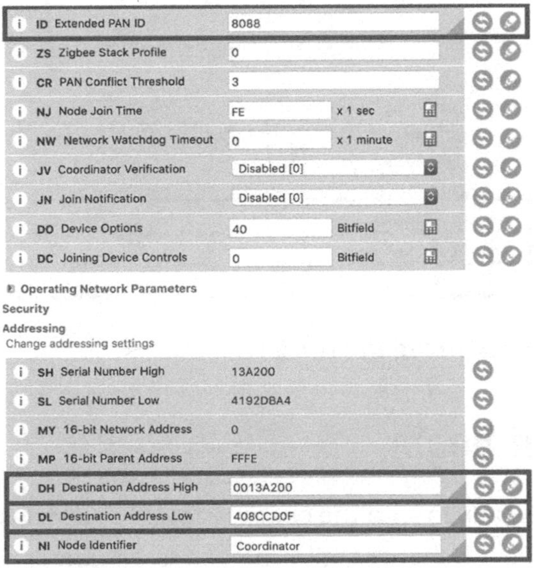

Figure 2-31. *Configuring the coordinator*

---

[8]Does that number mean anything to you? Hint: IBM PC.

Configuring the Router

To configure the router, you want to set the destination address of this radio (router) to the serial number of the other radio (coordinator). Like the coordinator, you set the PAN ID to 8088. Also set the Node ID to ROUTER to make it easier to identify. Figure 2-32 shows the configuration session for the router.

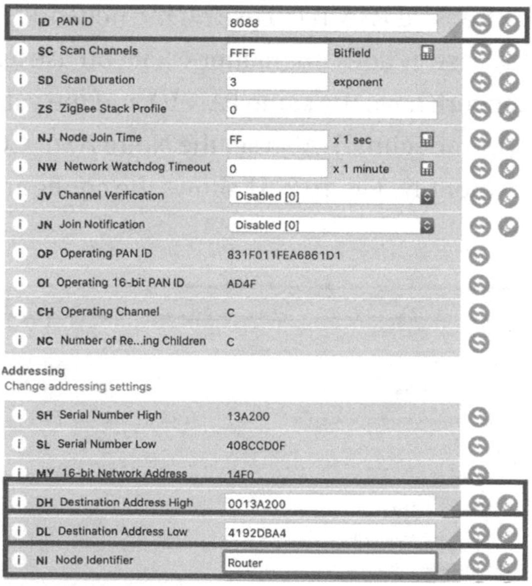

Figure 2-32. Configuring the router

Let the Chat Begin

That's it: you are ready to start the chat session. If you've been using a terminal to make the changes, all you need to do now is return the modules to transparent mode by either using the ATCN command or simply waiting 10 seconds.

Once you've setup the destination addresses for the modules, they will "find" each other and start the chat. To see the chat in action, simply click one of the modules and open a terminal connection. You should click the *Detach* button so that you can click the other module and open a terminal for that module.

Next, click the *Open* button in each terminal. You may not see anything happen at this point since the modules are waiting for data from the other. We can do that ourselves by clicking in the left side of the console output. Go ahead and type something in there.

If your configurations worked, you should see text from one terminal appear in the other and vice versa. If you do, congratulations—you have just set up your first XBee network (albeit a very simple point-to-point network). Figure 2-33 shows the results of the test I ran from my PC using XCTU. This terminal feature is nice, in that it color-codes the messages. If you run it yourself, you should see red text is text received, and the blue is text sent.

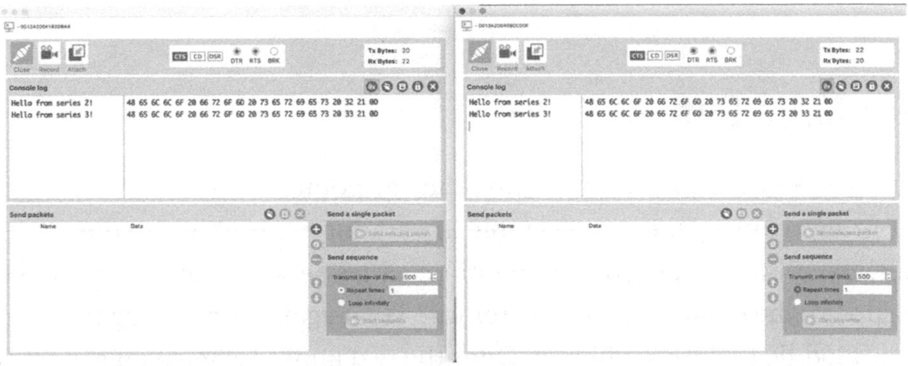

Figure 2-33. *Successful chat*

For bonus points, unplug your USB adapters and switch them from one computer to the other; then restart your terminal programs. Notice anything special? That's a trick question, because you should see the chat example working as before. It matters not which is the coordinator in this case; and because you wrote the values to the XBee nonvolatile memory, the modules "remember" their settings even if unplugged. Very nice, eh?

IS POINT-TO-POINT GOOD ENOUGH?

You may be wondering if you can use point-to-point networking in sensor networks. The short answer is that in some cases you can. For example, if you have a small number of nodes that are unlikely to be taken offline, you may be able to form a network with point-to-point networks. In this case, you would be forming a star topology network.

However, there are limitations, such as the fact that if a node in the middle goes down, it orphans all the nodes on one side of the node from the other. You also cannot form multiple-point connections, and broadcasting may require extra programming to accomplish. For these reasons and more, sophisticated sensor networks can benefit from using a mesh topology.

For More Fun

If you'd like experiment more with point-to-point networks and the AT firmware using the chat example, try adding a third XBee to the network. Connect it to your router node and type some data. Where does it appear: the coordinator or the router? Try it again, connecting the new module to the coordinator. Does the text appear where you expect it? Hint: Make the new module a router as well and set its destination address to the first router.

GOT HUB?

If you want to test your XBee networks but your PC doesn't have enough USB ports, the ports are too close together,[9] or you don't want to use a second (or third) PC, the USB XBee Explorers will work using a powered hub and even some of the better unpowered hubs as shown here.

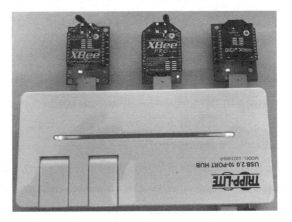

However, I've discovered some hubs don't work. I have a very nice (and very expensive) USB 3 hub that works great for everything except my XBee Explorer boards. So, your mileage may vary here. Oddly enough, my older powered USB 2.0 hub works great and has plenty of room for the XBee Explorer boards.

---

[9]Or, they're on the floor and you don't want to stand on your head to plug them in.

Building an XBee-ZB Mesh Network

Now that you know what an XBee module is, how to select models for use in your projects, and how to configure them for sending and receiving data in a point-to-point network, let's look at something a bit more complicated and more inline with sensor networks.

In this project, you configure three XBee modules: one as a coordinator, another as a router, and the last as an end device. I will use a series 3 module for the coordinator, but as before it is not required, and the project will work with earlier modules.

However, instead of the AT firmware, you use the API firmware that is required for forming mesh networks. The goal isn't to explore the API firmware in depth; rather, it is to see how the XBee modules can be used to transmit the data through the network.

Recall that the API firmware is designed to implement the full ZigBee protocol, meaning the data messages are encapsulated inside a packet layered with headers. In other words, messages are transmitted as binary data rather than text as you saw with the AT firmware.

There is a lot to the API firmware and the ZigBee protocol. Fortunately, you do not have to get too far into the specifics in order to use it. However, it does help to know how the packets are formed so that you can diagnose and debug your data messages. I shall present some of the frequently encountered packets as you progress through the book.

If you would like to know more about the ZigBee protocol and its many packet formats (called frame types), see one of the following resources:

- *Building Wireless Sensor Networks: With ZigBee, XBee, Arduino, and Processing*, by Robert Faludi (O'Reilly, 2010), ISBN 978-0596807733[10]

---

[10]Does not cover series 3 modules.

- "ZigBee RF Modules," Digi International, 2018,
  www.digi.com/resources/documentation/digidocs/
  pdfs/90000976.pdf

Loading the Firmware for the Modules

The first thing you need to do is to load the firmware for each module using the XCTU application. In this example, we will use a series 3 module for the coordinator and two series 2 modules for the router and end device.

Since we are using a series 3 module, recall we need only set the API Mode (AP) to 1 to turn on the API mode. For earlier modules, we will have to load the correct firmware. More specifically, we load the END DEVICE API function set on one module, the ROUTER API function set on another, and if we do not have the series 3 module, we will need to load the COORDINATOR API function set on a third module.

Configuring the XBee Modules

It is recommended when starting a new project to reset your XBee modules with the factory defaults. You can do this with the XCTU application on the configuration page. Click the *Default* button to set the factory defaults, and then click *Yes* to confirm. That is all you need to do! You can also use the ATRE command from a terminal in AT command mode.

But what about all those addresses and PAN IDs and stuff? Simply put, you don't need them. The modules will automatically connect to the coordinator (or router), and the coordinator will assign the 16-bit addresses to each module. Clearly, this is a lot easier to configure than the AT point-to-point mode.

Although that is true, it is also harder to experiment using the API firmware. Recall that the API firmware transmits and receives data messages in binary form. In order to see this network in action, you need to form special packets called transmission request packets.

Forming Test Messages

The test message is a simple numeric value embedded in a packet called a transmit request packet. (It's called a transmit request frame in some of the documentation.) The packet requires a very specific format.

If you have ever worked with low-level data packets like those encountered in Ethernet networks (TCP packets) or other communication protocols like the MySQL client protocol, you are already familiar with the basic concepts. However, if you haven't, the layout of the data may seem strange. Table 2-6 shows the layout of an example transmission request packet. It's described in more detail later.

Table 2-6. *Transmission Request Packet*

Field	Offset	Example	Description
Delimiter	0	7E	Start of packet delimiter
Length	1	00 10	Bytes between length and checksum
Frame Type	3	10	Request transmission
Frame ID	4	01	UART data frame
Destination Address 64-bit	5	00 00 00 00 00 00 00 00 FF FF	64-bit address of coordinator
Destination Address 16-bit	13	00 00	16-bit destination address
Broadcast Radius	15	00	Maximum number of hops
Options	16	00	Options
RF Data	17	99 99	Data payload
Checksum	19	BC	0xff minus sum of bytes in packet

The important parts of this packet are the length, addresses, and data payload. These are the parts you would most likely want to change. In this case, the 64-bit address is the default address for the coordinator. The coordinator gets this address using the default settings. The same is true for the 16-bit address. The example makes a payload of hexadecimal 99 99 (39321 in decimal). Because you use only 2 bytes for this, the length (the length in bytes of all parts of the packet following the length part, up to but not including the checksum part) is 16 (1+1+8+2+1+1+2). The checksum is calculated as 0xff minus the 8-bit sum of the bytes between the length and the checksum.

Sound complicated? It can be. Fortunately, you do not need to do this manually very often. In fact, the programming libraries you use when communicating with the XBee itself will build these packets for you when you use it to send data. The libraries you use to talk to the XBee from the Arduino and Raspberry Pi will also make life much easier for you.

So, what do you do for this project? Do you create the packets yourself? If you are concerned about counting bytes and figuring out the checksum, fear not. Digi has built the XCTU application with a nifty packet creation dialog called the frames generator tool. You can use this too to create any ZigBee packet you want easily.

You can use this when you have opened a terminal and connected to the module from which you want to send the packet. Simply click the *Add New Frame* button in the Send frames section of the interface. Figure 2-34 shows an example of a terminal session.

Figure 2-34. *Adding a new frame packet*

Once you click the *Add Frame* button, you will see a dialog that permits you to either edit an existing packet or add a new one with the frames generator tool. To add a new packet, click the *Create frame using 'Frames Generator' tool* button as shown in Figure 2-35.

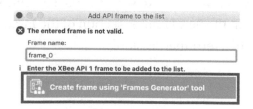

Figure 2-35. *Open the Frames Generator tool*

Next, you will get a dialog that permits you to populate the packet, but first you must select the packet type. For this project, we want to choose the transmit request packet (0x10). The dialog will automatically refresh with the correct fields for that packet type. Figure 2-36 shows the dialog for the transmit request packet. Recall, this packet is used to send data to another module.

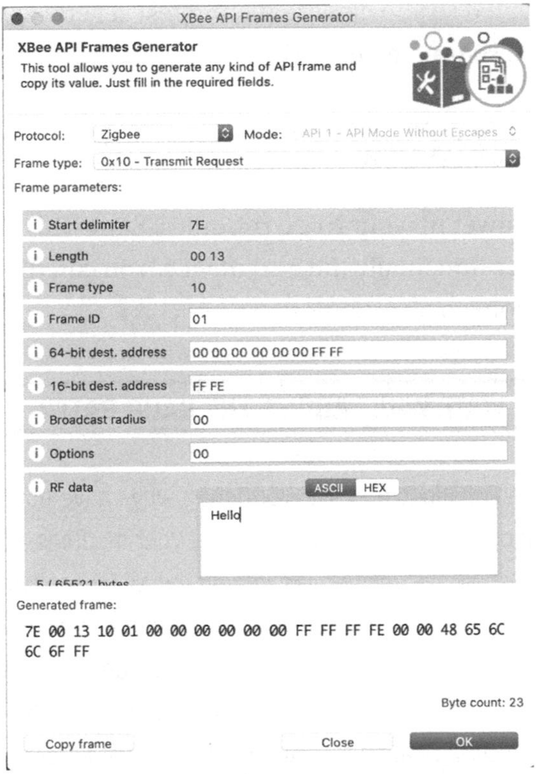

Figure 2-36. *Creating the transmit request packet*

Notice here I have set the destination address with 00 00 00 00 00 00 FF FF. This is the broadcast address, which causes the packet to be sent to all modules. If you wanted to send the packet to a specific module, you would fill in the 64-bit MAC address for that module. Since we are using the broadcast, we would see this packet received by all of the modules in the network.

Notice also I added a message in the RF Data box. I simply entered the word, Hello. Thus, this is a Hello, World! Type exercise.

Take a moment to open a terminal and create this frame yourself. One very nice thing about the new XCTU interface is it will save the packet frames you've created so you can create and test several at a time. Now, let's look at how to setup the network.

Testing the Network

Now it is time to power up your XBee modules. Start with the coordinator, then the first router, and finally the end device. You can then connect terminal applications to all modules.

WAIT, WHAT ABOUT THE BAUD RATE?

If you've been reading along and are wondering why I have not demonstrated how to the serial options (such as baud rate) of your modules and whether you need to set them at all, the answer lies in how the XCTU application works. It allows you to use modules at whatever parameters you want. On the other hand, if you want to use a different terminal application, you may need to change the parameters. Fortunately, this is easy to do in the XCTU application. Simply go into the configuration for each module and look for the serial parameters as shown here.

Serial Interfacing
Change modem interfacing options

i	BD Baud Rate	115200 [7]	
i	NB Parity	No Parity [0]	
i	SB Stop Bits	One stop bit [0]	
i	RO Packetization Timeout	3 x character times	
i	D7 DIO7 Configuration	CTS flow control [1]	
i	D6 DIO6 Configuration	Disable [0]	

Change the settings you want and then write the changes to the module. But again, you don't need to do that, and you do not need to have all the modules using the same connection parameters with the XCTU application. Cool, eh?

For this example, I used a single computer with XCTU connected to all three modules using the terminal mode. Once you have all the modules connected to a terminal application, you should give the modules five to ten minutes to self-configure before proceeding.

So, how do you know everything is working? Well, it's actually quite easy. XCTU has a network mode that you can use. This will show you the layout of the network by reading all the modules are creating a map for the network. The *network* button is in the upper-right corner of the XCTU window. Next, click the *Scan* button. Once you click that button, it may take a moment to discover the network, but it should show you a layout similar to Figure 2-37.

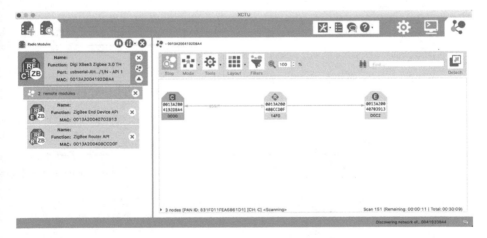

Figure 2-37. *Network mode in XCTU*

Notice the map shows the 64-bit address (MAC address) for each module as well as the communication pathways displayed as a solid line. Nice.

OK, so you've waited, and everything should be working. Let's find out. On any module connection, click the *Add Frame* button, and create a transmit request packet with a broadcast address as shown in Figure 2-36 including the payload of "Hello". Be sure to click the *Add Frame* button to save the packet.

To send the packet, select it in the left side and click the *Send selected frame* button. If you are watching the terminals in the other modules, you may see a number of packets go by. This is because the default is to show all packets, but you can use the filter to reduce the clutter. I leave that as an exercise—just click the *filter* button and select the packet types you want to see (or not see). Once the packet is received by all of the modules, you can click the packet and see the data. Figure 2-38 shows the results of entering the command.

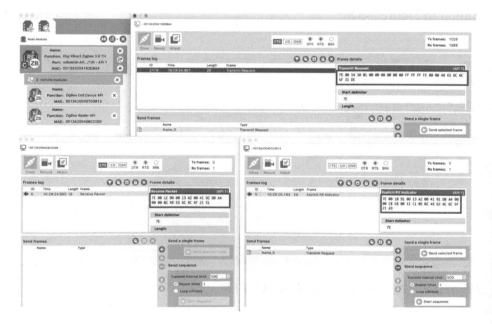

Figure 2-38. Broadcast packet received by all modules

Notice the box around the packets on each of the modules. Here, we see the packet was sent from the coordinator and received on the other modules. But, where's the data payload? It's there, just embedded in the message. In this case, it's in hexadecimal form and Hello in Hexadecimal is 48 65 6C 6C 6F. See if you can spot that in the image.

A broadcast message might be handy for sending power-down or sleep-mode commands to all of your sensor nodes or perhaps a command to send to all of your data-aggregate nodes to save their data to the media they are using.

Next, let's create a new transmit request message and specify the 64-bit address for one of the other modules. Add whatever you want for the data and send the frame. For example, I set the destination address to the router in my sample network (0013A200408CCD0F). I also typed in a random number in the RF Data field (90125[11]). Figure 2-39 shows the frame I created and then added.

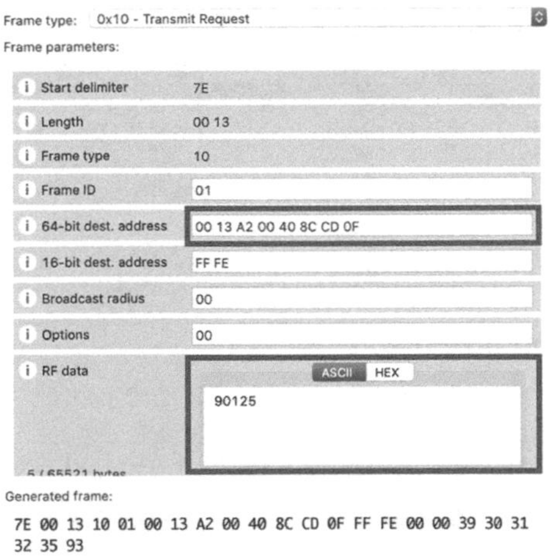

Frame type: 0x10 - Transmit Request

Frame parameters:

i	Start delimiter	7E
i	Length	00 13
i	Frame type	10
i	Frame ID	01
i	64-bit dest. address	00 13 A2 00 40 8C CD 0F
i	16-bit dest. address	FF FE
i	Broadcast radius	00
i	Options	00
i	RF data	ASCII HEX
		90125

Generated frame:
7E 00 13 10 01 00 13 A2 00 40 8C CD 0F FF FE 00 00 39 30 31 32 35 93

Figure 2-39. *Transmit request frame with destination*

---

[11]Some classic rock fans may claim that random number has a bigger story. Here's a hint: yes, it does.

When I sent the packet, it showed up on the router but not on the other modules. This is because this was a message sent to a particular module; the others ignored the message. Figure 2-40 shows the results with the "sending" module on top and "receiving" below.

Figure 2-40. *Frame sent and received*

Notice the small arrows in the left side of the frames log. An arrow pointing to the right is a sent event, and the arrow pointing to the left is a receive event. Nice, eh?

Tip You've seen only a very small portion of the capabilities of the XCTU application. You should spend some time reading the manual to learn more about its capabilities. For example, savvy users may want to check out the over-the-air capabilities of XBee modules.

At this point, you have seen how messages can be sent from one module to the coordinator directly and how broadcast messages can be sent to all modules. If you were able to duplicate or perform similar operations on your own XBee modules, congratulations! You now have a very simple wireless mesh network.

Although this project did not contain any sensor nodes, if you consider the end device as the sensor node and the keyboard as the sensor sending data, you can see how a typical sensor network will perform. In this case, the end device sends its data packet to the coordinator by default and can broadcast data if needed. Sending all data to the coordinator is also a clue as to how a data-aggregate node may be configured with an XBee module. You build on this premise in upcoming chapters.

For More Fun

If you'd like some more practice creating test packets, try sending a network node-detection command from the router and see what you get. Hint: You want an ATND command.

Component Shopping List

You need a number of components to complete the projects in this chapter. Table 2-7 lists them.

Table 2-7. *Components Needed*

Item	Vendors	Est. Cost USD	Qty Needed
XBee-ZB (ZB) Series 2, 2.5, or 3	www.sparkfun.com	$25.00–48.00	3
	www.adafruit.com		
	www.makershed.com		
XBee Explorer Dongle	www.sparkfun.com/products/11697	$24.95	1**
XBee Explorer USB	www.sparkfun.com/products/11812	$29.95	1**
USB-to-mini USB cable for use with the XBee Explorer USB	www.sparkfun.com/products/11301	$3.95	1***
USB XBeeAdapter	www.adafruit.com/product/247	$29.95	1**

** *You need only three of any of the USB adapters.*

*** *One needed for each XBee USB Adapter—not needed for the dongle.*

Be sure to get the correct cables. Also remember that you need three matching XBee-ZB modules. The adapter boards need not be the same, but you should have three of them.

CABLE TROUBLE SOLUTION

If you are like me and have many USB projects, one of the first frustrations you may encounter is the seeming randomness of choice of USB connectors. It seems like every time I buy a new component it takes a different USB cable! Rather than carry a set of cables in my kit, I've found a solution from SparkFun that has made my life much easier. The USB Cerberus cable (www.sparkfun. com/products/12016) includes a standard USB A-type male connector on one end and a set of three common connectors on the other (B, mini-B, and micro-B). I recommend buying one for each of your electronics kits.

Another frustration concern is powering devices with USB hubs and the like. Once again, I used to carry around a bunch of power cables to power all of my components. In this case, SparkFun comes to the rescue again with its Hydra power cable (sparkfun.com/products/11579). This cable has a standard USB A-type connector on one end and a set of three connectors on the other (barrel plug for Arduino, JST, and alligator clips). Very cool.

Troubleshooting Tips and Common Issues

If you encounter problems getting either of the chapter projects working, don't feel bad, and don't give up! Despite their diminutive size and powerful feature sets, these little pests can cause you a lot of grief if they are not configured correctly. This section explores some best practices for solving some of the more common problems.

Things to Check

The following is a list of tips for helping you determine what is wrong and how to fix it:

- *Cabling*: It may sound silly, but check to ensure that all of your modules are powered correctly—either by the host microcontroller or USB adapter (or USB hub!). You'd be surprised how easy it is to tell your OS to eject a USB dongle. If this happens, it is likely your adapter may have all its power LEDs lit but the terminal cannot connect. Try removing the cable and reinserting it. Also check the serial port, because some operating systems may reassign the serial port if moved from one port to another.

- *Is it plugged in?* You should also check that the module is plugged into its socket in the proper orientation and no pins are skipped (misaligned).

- *Serial settings*: If you are using a different terminal than what is available in XCTU, check your baud rate. If you've changed it on the XBee, your terminal application may not have saved the setting. If you want to change the setting, be sure to set it the same for all of your XBee modules as well as your terminal applications.

- *AT address*: If you are building point-to-point systems with the AT firmware, be sure to check your addresses! Remember that the destination address needs to point to the address of the module where you wish to send data (ATDH/ATDL). Be sure to use the ATWR command to save the values.

- *Version*: It is best to make sure the version you use for the firmware is the same on all modules. Some versions are incompatible with others. It is best to always use the same version.

- *Is the XBee dead?* If your XBee module cannot be read by your terminal application or it stops responding to XCTU, you may have encountered what some refer to as bricking, which makes the module worthless except as a doorstop or brick. If this happens, try resetting the module. If your adapter does not have a *reset* button (only a few do), you can connect the adapter and then gently (very gently) remove the module and reinsert it. When the module starts responding, reload the firmware. For extreme cases, see www.instructables. com/id/Restoring-your-broken-XBee/.

- *Old values keep coming back*: If you change your settings in the AT firmware but the old values keep coming back even after you use ATWR, use the reset command (ATRE) to return all values to their factory defaults.

Common Issues

The following are some of the more common scenarios you may encounter and what to do about them:

- *AT commands don't work*: If the +++ command won't wake up the module, make sure the module has the AT firmware loaded. I fussed for nearly 15 minutes with what I thought was a dead module, only to discover it was loaded with the API firmware. Don't fall prey to that self-induced prank!

- *Strange errors in AT mode*: Make sure your modules are configured with the same version of the AT firmware. You can use the ATVR command to check each module.

- *Settings go missing or revert*: One of the most common errors is making all of your settings and failing to write the values with ATWR. You need to use this command to save the values. The XBee modules may not work until you have done this and returned to transparent mode.

- *Inability to use Backspace*: It can be very frustrating to try to enter commands with values using the AT firmware because the Backspace key doesn't work in most terminal applications. When you make a mistake, press Enter and try the command again. Always check the setting with the command's display option (the command with no value).

- *API firmware doesn't work*: If you are sure you have all of your modules configured for the same version of the API firmware, try unplugging all the modules and plugging the coordinator in first followed by the routers and then your end devices. It may take as long as ten minutes for the coordinator to join all the nodes to the network.

You can also visit Robert Faludi's web page for common XBee mistakes (www.faludi.com/projects/common-xbee-mistakes/). He lists a lot of things that go wrong when you are unfamiliar with XBees and how to configure them. As he states, they aren't as unreliable or quirky as they seem to be. Most quirks are a result of user error. Sadly, it isn't always obvious that that is the case.

Finally, use the Digi website and its knowledgebase (www.digi.com/support/kbase/). There is a wealth of information out there. Chances are someone has had a similar problem, and a simple search of the knowledgebase and forums may reveal the solution.

Summary

Wow, we covered a lot of ground in this chapter. You were introduced to the XBee-ZB module and the ZigBee protocol, and you experimented with the AT and API firmware. You also learned a great deal about the XBee, and its many features include a little about the MicroPython features of the series 3 modules. Although it seems like I discussed a lot, the truth is that you have only just begun learning about the XBee and how to use it in your sensor networks.

I will be returning to the XBee topic throughout the rest of this book. Chapter 4 explores how to host sensors with XBee modules, Chapter 5 examines how to host sensors with a Raspberry Pi, and Chapter 6 explores how to host sensors with an Arduino microcontroller. If you enjoyed the projects in this chapter, the projects in the next chapter are likely to be even more enjoyable because you get to see a real sensor in action.

But first, let's learn more about programming MicroPython. The next chapter introduces MicroPython along with a brief tutorial. Let's get coding!

CHAPTER 3

Programming in MicroPython

Now that we have a basic understanding of the XBee modules, we can learn more about programming in MicroPython—a very robust and powerful language that you can use to write very powerful applications. Mastering MicroPython is very easy, and some may suggest it doesn't require any formal training to use. This is largely true, and thus you should be able to write MicroPython scripts with only a little bit of knowledge about the language.

Given that MicroPython is Python, we can learn the basics of the Python language first through examples on our PC. Thus, this chapter presents a crash course on the basics of Python programming including an explanation about some of the most commonly used language features. As such, this chapter will provide you with the skills you need to understand the Python IoT project examples available on the Internet. The chapter also demonstrates how to program in Python through examples that you can run on your PC. So, let's get started!

Note I use the term Python to describe programming concepts in this chapter that apply to both MicroPython and Python. Concepts unique to MicroPython use the term MicroPython.

© Charles Bell 2020
C. Bell, *Beginning Sensor Networks with XBee, Raspberry Pi, and Arduino*,
https://doi.org/10.1007/978-1-4842-5796-8_3

Now let's learn some of the basic concepts of Python programming. We will begin with the building blocks of the language such as variables, modules, and basic statements and then move into the more complex concepts of flow control and data structures. While the material may seem to come at you in a rush, this tutorial on Python covers only the most fundamental knowledge of the language and how to use it on your PC and XBee modules. It is intended to get you started writing MicroPython code for the XBee.

If you know the basics of Python programming, feel free to skim through this chapter. However, I recommend working through the example projects at the end of the chapter, especially if you've not written many Python applications.

The following sections present many of the basic features of Python programming that you will need to know to understand the example projects in this book.

Note   MicroPython on the XBee (and similar) modules and boards do not support the full library of functions available on the PC version of Python. However, all facilities that you need to use on the XBee module are available in MicroPython. Regardless, learning Python on the PC is an excellent way to gain the skills you need to program your XBee modules.

Before we jump into Python programming, let's discuss what features and libraries are available for MicroPython as well as the common limitations.

MicroPython Features and Limitations

While MicroPython will look and feel exactly like Python, there are a few things that MicroPython doesn't implement from the Python 3 language. The following sections give you an idea of what you can do with MicroPython and what you cannot do with MicroPython.

MicroPython Features

The biggest feature of MicroPython is, of course, it runs Python. This permits you to create simple, efficiently specified, and easy-to-understand programs. That alone, I think, is its best advantage over other boards like the Arduino. The following list is a few of the features that MicroPython supports. We will see these features in greater detail throughout this book:

- *Interactive interpreter*: MicroPython boards have built in a special interactive console that you can access by connecting to the board with a USB cable (or in some cases, over Wi-Fi). This console is called a read-evaluate-print loop that allows you to type in your code and execute it one line at a time. It is a great way to prototype your code or just run a project as you develop it.

- *Python standard libraries*: MicroPython also supports many of the standard Python libraries. In general, you can expect to find MicroPython supports more than 80% of the most commonly used libraries. These include parsing JavaScript Object Notation (JSON),[1] socket programming, string manipulation, file input/output, and even regular expression support.

---

[1]www.json.org/

- *Hardware-level libraries*: MicroPython has libraries built in that allow you to access hardware directly either to turn on or off analog pins, read analog data, read digital data, and even control hardware with pulse-width modulation (PWM)—a way to limit power to a device by rapidly modulating the power to the device, for example, making a fan spin slower than if it had full power.

- *Extensible*: MicroPython is also extensible. This is a great feature for advanced users who need to implement some complex library at a low level (in C or C++) and include the new library in MicroPython. Yes, this means you can build in your own unique code and make it part of the MicroPython feature set.

To answer your question "But, what can I do with MicroPython?", the answer is quite a lot! You can control hardware connected to the XBee module, send data to other nodes, and much more. The hardware you can connect to include turning LEDs on and off, controlling servos, and reading sensors. You can create just about any form of sensor node just like you can with a Raspberry Pi or Arduino (or another MicroPython board).

But if you don't yet possess any MicroPython boards, you can check out the online MicroPython interpreter at `https://micropython.org/unicorn/`.

However, there are a few limitations to running MicroPython on the chip.

MicroPython Limitations

The biggest limitation of MicroPython is its ease of use. The ease of using Python means the code is interpreted on the fly. And while MicroPython is highly optimized, there is still a penalty for the interpreter. This means that projects that require a high degree of precision such as sampling data at a high rate or communicating over a connection (USB, hardware interface, etc.)

may not run at PC speeds. For these areas, we can overcome the problem by extending the MicroPython language with optimized libraries for handling the low-level communication.

MicroPython also uses a bit more memory than other microcontroller platforms such as the Arduino. Normally, this isn't a problem but something you should consider if your program starts to get large. Larger programs that use a lot of libraries could consume more memory than you may expect. Once again, this is related to the ease of use of Python— another price to pay.

Finally, as mentioned previously, MicroPython doesn't implement all the features of all the Python 3 libraries. However, you should find it has everything you need to build IoT projects (and more).

Now, let's learn to program in Python!

Basic Concepts

Python is a high-level, interpreted, object-oriented scripting language. One of the biggest goals of Python is to have a clear, easy-to-understand syntax that reads as close to English as possible. That is, you should be able to read a Python script and understand it even if you haven't learned the language. Python also has less punctuation (special symbols) and fewer syntactical machinations than other languages. The following lists a few of the key features of Python:

- An interpreter processes Python at runtime. No external (separate) compiler is used. You just "run" your code via the Python interpreter.

- Python supports object-oriented programming constructs by way of a class.

- Python is a great language for the beginner-level programmers and supports the development of a wide range of applications.

- Python is a scripting language but can be used for a wide range of applications.

- Python is very popular and used throughout the world giving it a huge support base.

- Python has few keywords, simple structure, and a clearly defined syntax. This allows the student to pick up the language quickly.

- Python code is more clearly defined and visible to the eyes.

Python is available for download (`python.org/downloads`) for just about every platform that you may encounter or use—even Windows! Python is a very easy language to learn with very few constructs that are even mildly difficult to learn. Rather than toss out a sample application, let's approach learning the basics of Python in a Python-like way: one step at a time.

Tip   If you have not installed Python on your PC, you should do so now so that you can run the examples in this chapter.

Code Blocks

The first thing you should learn is that Python does not use a code block demarcated with symbols like other languages. More specifically, code that is local to a construct such as a function or conditional or loop is designated using indentation. Thus, the lines in Listing 3-1 are indented (by spaces or, gag, tabs) so that the starting characters align for the code body of the construct. Listing 3-1 shows this concept in action.

Caution   Python interpreters will complain and could produce strange results if the indentation is not uniform.

Listing 3-1. Using Code Blocks

```
if (expr1):
    print("inside expr1")
    print("still inside expr1")
else:
    print("inside else")
    print("still inside else")
print("in outer level")
```

Here we see a conditional or if statement. Notice the function call print() is indented. This signals the interpreter that the lines belong to the construct above it. For example, the two print statements that mention expr1 form the code block for the if condition (and executes when the expression evaluates to true). Similarly, the next two print statements form the code block for the else condition. Finally, the non-indented lines are not part of the conditional and thus are executed after either the if or else depending on the expression evaluation.

As you can see, indentation is a key concept to learn when writing Python. Even though it is very simple, making mistakes in indentation can result in code executing that you did not expect or worse errors from the interpreter.

Tip   I use "program" and "application" interchangeably with "script" when discussing Python. While technically Python code is a script, we often use it in contexts where "program" or "application" are more appropriate.

There is one special symbol that you will encounter frequently. Notice the use of the colon (:) in the preceding code. This symbol is used to terminate a construct and signals the interpreter that the declaration is complete and the body of the code block follows. We use this for conditionals, loops, classes, and functions.

Comments

One of the most fundamental concepts in any programming language is the ability to annotate your source code with non-executable text that not only allows you to make notes among the lines of code but also forms a way to document your source code.

To add comments to your source code, use the pound sign (#). Place at least one at the start of the line to create a comment for that line repeating the # symbols for each subsequent line. This creates what is known as a block comment as shown. Notice in Listing 3-2 I used a comment without any text to create whitespace. This helps with readability and is a common practice for block comments.

Listing 3-2. Adding Comments to Source Code

```
#
# Beginning Sensor Networks, 2nd Edition
#
# Example Python application.
#
# Created by Dr. Charles Bell
#
```

You can also place comments on the same line as the source code. The compiler will ignore anything from the pound sign to the end of the line. For example, the following code shows a common style of documenting variables:

```
zip = 35012# Zip or postal code
address1= "123 Main St."  # Store the street address
```

Arithmetic

You can perform many mathematical operations in Python including the usual primitives but also logical operations and operations used to compare values. Rather than discuss these in detail, I provide a quick reference in Table 3-1 that shows the operation and example of how to use the operation.

Table 3-1. *Arithmetic, Logical, and Comparison Operators in Python*

Type	Operator	Description	Example
Arithmetic	+	Addition	int_var + 1
	–	Subtraction	int_var – 1
	*	Multiplication	int_var * 2
	/	Division	int_var / 3
	%	Modulus	int_var % 4
	–	Unary subtraction	-int_var
	+	Unary addition	+int_var
Logical	&	Bitwise and	var1&var2
	|	Bitwise or	var1|var2
	^	Bitwise exclusive or	var1^var2
	~	Bitwise complement	~var1
	and	Logical and	var1 and var2
	or	Logical or	var1 or var2
Comparison	==	Equal	expr1==expr2
	!=	Not equal	expr1!=expr2
	<	Less than	expr1<expr2
	>	Greater than	expr1>expr2
	<=	Less than or equal	expr1<=expr2
	>=	Greater than or equal	expr1>=expr2

Bitwise operations produce a result on the values performed on each bit. Logical operators (and, or) produce a value that is either true or false and are often used with expressions or conditions.

Tip   True and false are represented as `True` and `False` in Python (initial cap).

Output to Screen

We've already seen a few examples of how to print messages to the screen but without any explanation about the statements shown. While it is unlikely that you would print output from your XBee module for projects that you deploy, learning Python is much easier when you display messages to the screen.

Some of the things you may want to print—as we have seen in Listing 3-1—is to communicate what is going on inside your program. This can include simple messages (strings), but can also include the values of variables, expressions, and more.

As we have seen, the built-in `print()` function is the most common way to display output text contained within single or double quotes. We have also seen some interesting examples using another function named `format()`. The `format()` function generates a string for each argument passed. These arguments can be other strings, expressions, variables, and so on. The function is used with a special string that contains replacement keys delimited by curly braces { } (called string interpolation[2]). Each replacement key contains either an index (starting at 0) or a named keyword. The special string is called a format string. Let's see a few examples to illustrate the concept. You can run these yourself on your PC. I include the output so you can see what each statement does.

---

[2]`https://en.wikipedia.org/wiki/String_interpolation`

Notice the >>> symbol in Listing 3-3. This indicates I am executing the code using the Python interpreter. You can start the Python interpreter from any command window (terminal) by typing the command python or python3 for running the 3.X version of Python.

Listing 3-3. Python Interpreter Example

```
>>> a = 42
>>> b = 1.5
>>> c = "seventy"
>>> print("{0} {1} {2} {3}".format(a,b,c,(2+3)))
42 1.5 seventy 5
>>> print("{a_var} {b_var} {c_var} {0}".format((3*3),c_var=c,
b_var=b,a_var=a))
42 1.5 seventy 9
```

Note   For those who have learned to program in another language like C or C++, Python allows you to terminate a statement with the semicolon (;); however, it is not needed and considered bad form to include it.

Notice I created three variables (we will talk about variables in the next section) assigning them different values with the equal symbol (=). I then printed a message using a format string with four replacement keys labeled using an index. Notice the output of that print statement. Notice I included an expression at the end to show how the format() function evaluates expressions.

The last line is more interesting. Here, I use three named parameters (a_var, b_var, c_var) and used a special argument option in the format() function where I assign the parameter a value. Notice I listed them in a different order. This is the greatest advantage of using named parameters;

they can appear in any order but are placed in the format string in the position indicated.

As you can see, it's just a case of replacing the { } keys with those from the format() function, which converts the arguments to strings. We use this technique anywhere we need a string that contains data gathered from more than one area. We can see this in the preceding examples.

Tip   For more information about format strings and the options available, see https://docs.python.org/3/library/string. html#formatstrings.

Now let's look at how we can use variables in our programs (scripts).

Variables and Data Types

Now that we've seen the basic construction of simple Python code, let's explore the fundamental concepts you will need to master first: variables and data types. In this section, we discover how to create variables to store data including how they are typed (what kind of data they can store) and simple statements for working with variables. We will learn more about complex data types in the next section.

Variables

Python is a dynamically typed language, which means the type of the variable (the type of data it can store) is determined by context as it is encountered or used. This contrasts with other language such as C and C++ where you must declare the type before you use the variable.

Variables in Python are simply named memory locations that you can use to store values during execution. We store values by using the equal sign to assign the value. Python variable names can be anything you want, but there are rules and conventions most Python developers follow. The rules are listed in the Python coding standard.[3]

However, the general, overriding rule requires variable names that are descriptive, have meaning in context, and can be easily read. That is, you should avoid names with random characters, forced abbreviations, acronyms, and similar obscure names. By convention, your variable names should be longer than a single character (with some acceptable exceptions for loop counting variables) and short enough to avoid overly long code lines.

WHAT IS A LONG CODE LINE?

Most will say a code line should not exceed 80 characters, but this harkens from the darker days of programming when we used punched cards that permitted a maximum of 80 characters per card (or less) and later display devices with the same limitation. With modern, widescreen displays, this is not as big a deal, but I still recommend keeping lines short to ensure better readability. No one likes to scroll down to read! Or, worse, require turning on word wrap or use a 34" widescreen monitor to read your code.

Thus, there is a lot of flexibility in what you can name your variables. There are additional rules and guidelines in the PEP8 standard, and should you wish to bring your project source code up to date with the standards, you should review the PEP8 naming standards for functions, classes, and more. See the PEP8 coding guidelines for Python coding at www.python.org/dev/peps/pep-0008 for a complete list of the rules and standards.

Listing 3-4 shows some examples of simple variables and their dynamically determined types.

---

[3]www.python.org/dev/peps/pep-0008

Listing 3-4. Simple Variable Examples

```
# floating point number
length = 10.0
# integer
width = 4
# string
box_label = "Tools"
# list
car_makers = ['Ford', 'Chevrolet', 'Dodge']
# tuple
porsche_cars = ('911', 'Cayman', 'Boxster')
# dictionary
address = {"name": "Joe Smith", "Street": "123 Main", "City":
"Anytown", "State": "New Happyville"}
```

So, how did we know the variable width is an integer? Simply because the number 4 is an integer. Likewise, Python will interpret "Tools" as a string. We'll see more about the last three types and other types supported by Python in the next section.

Tip   For more information about naming conventions governed by the Python coding standard (PEP8), see `www.python.org/dev/peps/pep-0008/#naming-conventions`.

Types

As mentioned, Python does not have a formal type specification mechanism like other languages. However, you can still define variables to store anything you want. In fact, Python permits you to create and use variables based on context and you can use initialization to "set" the data type for the variable. Listing 3-5 shows several examples.

Listing 3-5. Setting the Variable Data Type

```
# Numbers
float_value = 9.75
integer_value = 5

# Strings
my_string = "He says, he's already got one."

print("Floating number: {0}".format(float_value))
print("Integer number: {0}".format(integer_value))
print(my_string)
```

For situations where you need to convert types or want to be sure values are typed a certain way, there are many functions for converting data. Table 3-2 shows a few of the more commonly used type conversion functions. I discuss some of the data structures in a later section.

Table 3-2. *Type Conversion in Python*

Function	Description
int(x [,base])	Converts x to an integer. Base is optional (e.g., 16 for hex)
long(x [,base])	Converts x to a long integer
float(x)	Converts x to a floating point
str(x)	Converts object x to a string
tuple(t)	Converts t to a tuple
list(l)	Converts l to a list
set(s)	Converts s to a set
dict(d)	Creates a dictionary
chr(x)	Converts an integer to a character
hex(x)	Converts an integer to a hexadecimal string
oct(x)	Converts an integer to an octal string

However, you should use these conversion functions with care to avoid data loss or rounding. For example, converting a float to an integer can result in truncation. Likewise, printing floating-point numbers can result in rounding.

Now let's look at some commonly used data structures including this strange thing called a dictionary.

Basic Data Structures

What you have learned so far about Python is enough to write the most basic programs and indeed more than enough to tackle the example project later in this chapter. However, when you start needing to operate on data—either from the user or from sensors and similar sources—you will need a way to organize and store data as well as perform operations on the data in memory. The following sections introduce three data structures in order of complexity: lists, tuples, or dictionary.

While it is less likely you would use these constructs with your XBee MicroPython scripts, any tutorial on Python would be remiss to not include these. That doesn't mean you cannot use these constructs in MicroPython—you can—but the MicroPython scripts for most small projects may not use all data structures in the same script. Again, if you need to use them, then do so!

Lists

Lists are a way to organize data in Python. It is a free-form way to build a collection. That is, the items (or elements) need not be the same data type. Lists also allow you to do some interesting operations such as adding things at the end, beginning, or at a special index. Listing 3-6 demonstrates how to create a list.

Listing 3-6. Creating a List

```
# List
my_list = ["abacab", 575, "rex, the wonder dog", 24, 5, 6]
my_list.append("end")
my_list.insert(0,"begin")
for item in my_list:
  print("{0}".format(item))
```

Here, we see I created the list using square brackets ([ ]). The items in the list definition are separated by commas. Note that you can create an empty list simply by setting a variable equal to [ ]. Since lists, like other data structures, are objects, there are several operations available for lists such as these:

- append(x): Add x to the end of the list.

- extend(l): Add all items to the end of the list.

- insert(pos,item): Insert item at a position pos.

- remove(value): Remove the first item that matches (==) the value.

- pop([i]): Remove and return the item at position i or end of list.

- index(value): Return index of first item that matches.

- count(value): Count occurrences of value.

- sort(): Sort the list (ascending).

- reverse(): Reverse sort the list.

Lists are like arrays in other languages and very useful for building dynamic collections of data.

Tuples

Tuples, on the other hand, are a more restrictive type of collection. That is, they are built from a specific set of data and do not allow manipulation like a list. In fact, you cannot change the elements in the tuple. Thus, we can use tuples for data that should not change. Listing 3-7 shows an example of a tuple and how to use it.

Listing 3-7. Using Tuples

```
# Tuple
my_tuple = (0,1,2,3,4,5,6,7,8,"nine")
for item in my_tuple:
  print("{0}".format(item))
if 7 in my_tuple:
  print("7 is in the list")
```

Here, we see I created the tuple using parenthesis (). The items in the tuple definition are separated by commas. Note that you can create an empty tuple simply by setting a variable equal to (). Since tuples, like other data structures, are objects, there are several operations available such as the following including operations for sequences such as inclusion, location, and so on:

- x in t: Determine if t contains x.

- x not in t: Determine if t does not contain x.

- s + t: Concatenate tuples.

- s[i]: Get element i.

- len(t): Length of t (number of elements).

- min(t): Minimal (smallest value).

- max(t): Maximal (largest value).

If you want even more structure with storing data in memory, you can use a special construct (object) called a dictionary.

Dictionaries

A dictionary is a data structure that allows you to store key, value pairs where the data is assessed via the keys. Dictionaries are a very structured way of working with data and the most logical form we will want to use when collecting complex data. Listing 3-8 shows an example of a dictionary.

Listing 3-8. Using Dictionaries

```
# Dictionary
my_dictionary = {
   'first_name': "Chuck",
   'last_name': "Bell",
   'age': 36,
   'my_ip': (192,168,1,225),
   42: "What is the meaning of life?",
}
# Access the keys:
print(my_dictionary.keys())
# Access the items (key, value) pairs
print(my_dictionary.items())
# Access the values
print(my_dictionary.values())
# Create a list of dictionaries
my_addresses = [my_dictionary]
```

There is a lot going on here! We see a basic dictionary declaration that uses curly braces to create a dictionary. Inside that, we can create as many key, value pairs we want separated by commas. Keys are defined using strings (I use single quotes by convention but double quotes will work) or integers, and values can be any data type we want. For the my_ip attribute, we are also storing a tuple

Following the dictionary, we see several operations performed on the dictionary from printing the keys, printing all the values, and printing only the values. Listing 3-9 shows the output of executing this code snippet from the Python interpreter.

Listing 3-9. Performing Operations on Dictionaries

```
[42, 'first_name', 'last_name', 'age', 'my_ip']
[(42, 'what is the meaning of life?'), ('first_name', 'Chuck'),
('last_name', 'Bell'), ('age', 36), ('my_ip', (192, 168, 1, 225))]
['what is the meaning of life?', 'Chuck', 'Bell', 36,
(192, 168, 1, 225)]
'42': what is the meaning of life?
'first_name': Chuck
'last_name': Bell
'age': 36
'my_ip': (192, 168, 1, 225)
```

As we have seen in the example in Listing 3-9, there are several operations (functions or methods) available for dictionaries including the following. Together this list of operations makes dictionaries a very powerful programming tool:

- len(d): Number of items in d.

- d[k]: Item of d with key k.

- d[k] = x: Assign key k with value x.

- del d[k]: Delete item with key k.

- k in d: Determine if d has an item with key k.

- `d.items()`: Return a list (view) of the (key, value) pairs in `d`.

- `d.keys()`: Return a list (view) of the keys in `d`.

- `d.values()`: Return a list (view) of the values in d.

Best of all, objects can be placed inside other objects. For example, you can create a list of dictionaries like I did earlier, a dictionary that contains lists and tuples, and any combination you need. Thus, lists, tuples, and dictionaries are a powerful way to manage data for your program.

In the next section, we learn how we can control the flow of our programs.

Flow Control Statements

Now that we know more about the basics of Python, we can discover some of the more complex code concepts you will need to complete your project such as conditional statements and loops.

Conditional Statements

We have also seen some simple conditional statements: statements designed to alter the flow of execution depending on the evaluation of one or more expressions. Conditional statements allow us to direct execution of our programs to sections (blocks) of code based on the evaluation of one or more expressions. The conditional statement in Python is the `if` statement.

We have seen the `if` statement in action in our example code. Notice in the example, we can have one or more (optional) `else` phrases that we execute once the expression for the if conditions evaluates to false. We can chain `if`/`else` statements to encompass multiple conditions where the code executed depends on the evaluation of several conditions. Listing 3-10 shows the general structure of the if statement. Notice in the comments how I explain how execution reaches the body of each condition.

Listing 3-10. Conditional Statements

```
if (expr1):
    # execute only if expr1 is true
elif ((expr2) or (expr3)):
    # execute only if expr1 is false *and* either expr2 or
       expr3 is true
else:
    # execute if both sets of if conditions evaluate to false
```

While you can chain the statement as much as you want, use some care here because the more elif sections you have, the harder it will become to understand, maintain, and avoid logic errors in your expressions.

There is another form of conditional statement called a ternary operator. Ternary operators are more commonly known as conditional expressions in Python. These operators evaluate something based on a condition being true or not. They became a part of Python in version 2.4. Conditional expressions are a short-hand notation for an if-then-else construct used (typically) in an assignment statement as shown here:

```
variable = value_if_true if condition else value_if_false
```

Here, we see if the condition is evaluated to true, the value preceding the if is used, but if the condition evaluates to false, the value following the else is used. Listing 3-11 shows a short example.

Listing 3-11. Evaluation of Conditional Statements

```
>>> numbers = [1,2,3,4]
>>> for n in numbers:
...    x = 'odd' if n % 2 else 'even'
...    print("{0} is {1}.".format(n, x))
...
```

```
1 is odd.
2 is even.
3 is odd.
4 is even.
>>>
```

Conditional expressions allow you to quickly test a condition instead of using a multi-line conditional statement, which can help make your code a bit easier to read (and shorter).

Loops

Loops are used to control the repetitive execution of a block of code. There are three forms of loops that have slightly different behavior. All loops use conditional statements to determine whether to repeat execution or not. That is, they repeat if the condition is true. The two types of loops are while and for. I explain each with an example.

The while loop has its condition at the "top" or start of the block of code. Thus, while loops only execute the body if and only if the condition evaluates to true on the first pass. The following code illustrates the syntax for a while loop. This form of loop is best used when you need to execute code only if some expression(s) evaluate to true, for example, iterating through a collection of things whose number of elements is unknown (loop until we run out of things in the collection):

```
while (expression):
    # do something here
```

For loops are sometimes called counting loops because of their unique form. For loops allow you to define a counting variable and a range or list to iterate over. The following code illustrates the structure of the for loop. This form of loop is best used for performing an operation in a collection.

In this case, Python will automatically place each item in the collection in the variable for each pass of the loop until no more items are available.

```
for variable_name in list:
  # do something here
```

You can also do range loops or counting loops. This uses a special function called `range()` that takes up to three parameters, `range([start], stop[, step])`, where start is the starting number (an integer), stop is the last number in the series, and step is the increment. So, you can count by 1, 2, 3, and so on through a range of numbers. The following code shows a simple example:

```
for i in range(2,9):
  # do something here
```

There are other uses for `range()` that you may encounter. For more information, see the documentation on this function and other built-in functions at `https://docs.python.org/3/library/functions.html`.

Python also provides a mechanism for controlling the flow of the loop (e.g., duration or termination) using a few special keywords as follows:

- `break`: Exit the loop body immediately.

- `continue`: Skip to next iteration of the loop.

- `else`: Execute code when loop ends (not executed if the loop was stopped with a break statement).

There are some uses for these keywords, particularly break, but it is not the preferred method of terminating and controlling loops. That is, professionals believe the conditional expression or error handling code should behave well enough to not need these options.

Modularization: Modules, Functions, and Classes

The last group of topics are the most advanced and include modularization (code organization). As we will see, we can use functions to group code, eliminate duplication, and encapsulate functionality into objects. Once again, you may not use these constructs in your MicroPython code for XBee, but you should be aware of these techniques as you are likely to encounter them at some point.

Including Modules

Python applications can be built from reusable libraries that are provided by the Python environment. They can also be built from custom modules or libraries that you create yourself or download from a third party. These are often distributed as a set of Python code files (e.g., files that have a file extension of .py). When we want to use a library (function, class, etc.) that is included in a module, we use the import keyword and list the name of the module. The following code shows some examples:

```
import os
import sys
```

The first two lines demonstrate how to import a base or common module provided by Python. In this case, we are using or importing modules for the os and sys modules (operating system and Python system functions).

Tip It is customary (but not required) to list your imports in alphabetical order with built-in modules first, then third-party modules listed next, and finally your own modules.

Functions

Python allows you to use modularization in your code. While it supports object-oriented programming by way of classes (e.g., a more advanced feature that you are unlikely to encounter for most Python GPIO examples on the Raspberry Pi), on a more fundamental level, you can break your code into smaller chunks using functions.

Functions use a special keyword construct (rare in Python) to define a function. We simply use def, followed by a name for the function and a comma-separated list of parameters in parenthesis. The colon is used to terminate the declaration. Listing 3-12 shows an example.

Listing 3-12. Defining Functions

```python
def print_dictionary(the_dictionary):
    for key, value in the_dictionary.items():
      print("'{0}': {1}".format(key, value))

# define some data
my_dictionary = {
  'name': "Chuck",
  'age': 37,
}
```

You may be wondering what this strange code does. Notice the loop is assigning two values from the result of the items() function. This is a special function available from the dictionary object.[4] The items() function returns the key, value pairs, hence the names of the variables.

The next line prints out the values. The use of formatting strings where the curly braces define the parameter number starting at 0 is common for Python 3 applications. See the Python documentation for more

---

[4]Yes, dictionaries are objects! So are tuples and lists and many other data structure.

information about formatting strings (https://docs.python.org/3/
library/string.html#format-string-syntax).

The body of the function is indented. All statements indented under
this function declaration belong to the function and are executed when the
function is called. We can call functions by name providing any parameters
as follows. Notice how I referenced the values in the dictionary by using
the key names.

```
print_dictionary(my_dictionary)
print(my_dictionary['age'])
print(my_dictionary['name'])
```

This example together with the preceding code, when executed,
generates the output shown in Listing 3-13.

Listing 3-13. Output of Function Example

```
$ python3
Python 3.6.0 (v3.6.0:41df79263a11, Dec 22 2016, 17:23:13)
[GCC 4.2.1 (Apple Inc. build 5666) (dot 3)] on darwin
Type "help", "copyright", "credits" or "license" for more
information.
>>> def print_dictionary(the_dictionary):
...     for key, value in the_dictionary.items():
...         print("'{0}': {1}".format(key, value))
...
>>> # define some data
... my_dictionary = {
...     'name': "Chuck",
...     'age': 41,
... }
>>> print_dictionary(my_dictionary)
'name': Chuck
```

```
'age': 41
>>> print(my_dictionary['age'])
41
>>> print(my_dictionary['name'])
Chuck
```

Now let's look at the most complex concept in Python—object-oriented programming. Once again, you may not want to use these concepts in your MicroPython—but you can—you should still understand the basics to ensure your Python knowledge is complete.

Classes and Objects

You may have heard that Python is an object-oriented programming language. But what does that mean? Simply, Python is a programming language that provides facilities for describing objects (things) and what you can do with the object (operations). Objects are an advanced form of data abstraction where the data is hidden from the caller and only manipulated by the operations (methods) the object provides.

The syntax we use in Python is the class statement, which you can use to help make your projects modular. By modular, we mean the source code is arranged to make it easier to develop and maintain. Typically, we place classes in separate modules (code files), which helps organize the code better. While it is not required, I recommend using this technique of placing a class in its own source file. This makes modifying the class or fixing problems (bugs) easier.

So, what are Python classes? Let's begin by considering the construct as an organization technique. We can use the class to group data and methods together. The name of the class immediately follows the keyword class, followed by a colon. You declare other class methods like any other method, except the first argument must be self, which ties the method to the class instance when executed.

FUNCTION OR METHOD: WHICH IS CORRECT?

I prefer to use terms that have been adopted by the language designers or community of developers. For example, some use "function," but others may use "method." Still others may use subroutine, routine, procedure, and so on. It doesn't matter which term you use, but you should strive to use terms consistently. One example, which can be confusing to some, is I use the term method when discussing object-oriented examples. That is, a class has methods, not function. However, you can use function in place of method and you'd still be correct (mostly).

Accessing the data is done using one or more methods by using the class (creating an instance) and using dot notation to reference the data member or function. Let's look at an example. Listing 3-14 shows a complete class that describes (models) the most basic characteristics of a vehicle used for transportation. I created a file named vehicle.py to contain this code.

Listing 3-14. Vehicle Class

```
#
# Beginning Sensor Networks 2nd Edition
#
# Class Example: A generic vehicle
#
# Dr. Charles Bell
#
```

```
class Vehicle:
    """Base class for defining vehicles"""
    axles = 0
    doors = 0
    occupants = 0

    def __init__(self, num_axles, num_doors):
        self.axles = num_axles
        self.doors = num_doors

    def get_axles(self):
        return self.axles

    def get_doors(self):
        return self.doors

    def add_occupant(self):
        self.occupants += 1

    def num_occupants(self):
        return self.occupants
```

Notice a couple of things here. First, there is a method with the name
__init__(). This is the constructor and is called when the class instance is
created. You place all your initialization code like setting variables in this
method. We also have methods for returning the number of axles, doors,
and occupants. We have one method in this class: to add occupants.

Also, notice we address each of the class attributes (data) using
self.<name>. This is how we can ensure we always access the data that is
associated with the instance created.

Let's see how this class can be used to define a family sedan. Listing 3-15
shows code that uses this class. We can place this code in a file named
sedan.py.

Listing 3-15. Using the Vehicle Class

```
#
# Beginning Sensor Networks 2nd Edition
#
# Class Example: Using the generic Vehicle class
#
# Dr. Charles Bell
#
from vehicle import Vehicle

sedan = Vehicle(2, 4)
sedan.add_occupant()
sedan.add_occupant()
sedan.add_occupant()
print("The car has {0} occupants.".format(sedan.num_
occupants()))
```

Notice the first line imports the Vehicle class from the vehicle module. Notice I capitalized the class name but not the file name. This is a very common naming scheme. Next in the code, we create an instance of the class. Notice I passed in 2, 4 to the class name. This will cause the __init__() method to be called when the class is instantiated. The variable, sedan, becomes the class instance variable (object) that we can manipulate, and I do so by adding three occupants and then printing out the number of occupants using the method in the Vehicle class.

We can run the code on our PC using the following command. As we can see, it tells us there are three occupants in the vehicle when the code is run. Nice.

```
$ python ./sedan.py
The car has 3 occupants.
```

Object-Oriented Programming (OOP) Terminology

Like any technology or concept, there comes a certain number of terms that you must learn to be able to understand and communicate with others about the technology. The following list briefly describes some of the terms you will need to know to learn more about object-oriented programming:

- *Attribute*: A data element in a class.

- *Class*: A code construct used to define an object in the form of attributes (data) and methods (functions) that operate on the data. Methods and attributes in Python can be accessed using dot notation.

- *Class instance variable*: A variable that is used to store an instance of an object. They are used like any other variable and, combined with dot notation, allow us to manipulate objects.

- *Instance*: An executable form of a class created by assigning a class to a variable initializing the code as an object.

- *Inheritance*: The inclusion of attributes and methods from one class in another.

- *Instantiation*: The creation of an instance of a class.

- *Method overloading*: The creation of two or more methods with the same name but with a different set of parameters. This allows us to create methods that have the same name but may operate differently depending on the parameters passed.

- *Polymorphism*: Inheriting attributes and methods from a base class adding additional methods or overriding (changing) methods.

There are many more OOP terms, but these are the ones you will encounter most often.

Now, let's see how we can use the vehicle class to demonstrate inheritance. In this case, we will create a new class named PickupTruck that uses the vehicle class but adds specialization to the resulting class. Listing 3-16 shows the new class. I placed this code in a file named pickup_truck.py. As you will see, a pickup truck is a type of vehicle.

Listing 3-16. Pickup Truck Class

```
#
# Beginning Sensor Networks 2nd Edition
#
# Class Example: Inheriting the Vehicle class to form a
# model of a pickup truck with maximum occupants and maximum
# payload.
#
# Dr. Charles Bell
#
from vehicle import Vehicle

class PickupTruck(Vehicle):
    """This is a pickup truck that has:
    axles = 2,
    doors = 2,
    __max occupants = 3
    The maximum payload is set on instantiation.
    """
    occupants = 0
    payload = 0
    max_payload = 0

    def __init__(self, max_weight):
```

```
        super().__init__(2,2)
        self.max_payload = max_weight
        self.__max_occupants = 3

    def add_occupant(self):
        if (self.occupants < self.__max_occupants):
            super().add_occupant()
        else:
            print("Sorry, only 3 occupants are permitted in the
            truck.")

    def add_payload(self, num_pounds):
        if ((self.payload + num_pounds) < self.max_payload):
            self.payload += num_pounds
        else:
            print("Overloaded!")

    def remove_payload(self, num_pounds):
        if ((self.payload - num_pounds) >= 0):
            self.payload -= num_pounds
        else:
            print("Nothing in the truck.")

    def get_payload(self):
        return self.payload
```

Notice a few things here. First, notice the class statement: class
PickupTruck(Vehicle). When we want to inherit from another class, we
add the parenthesis with the name of the base class. This ensures Python
will use the base class allowing the derived class to use all its accessible
data and memory. If you want to inherit from more than one class, you
can (called multiple inheritance); just list the base (parent) classes with a
comma-separated list.

Next, notice the __max_occupants variable. Using two underscores in a class for an attribute or a method makes that, through convention, the item private to the class.[5] That is, it should only be accessed from within the class. No caller of the class (via a class variable/instance) can access the private items nor can any class derived from the class. It is always a good practice to hide the attributes (data).

You may be wondering what happened to the occupant methods. Why aren't they in the new class? They aren't there because our new class inherited all that behavior from the base class. Not only that, but the code has been modified to limit occupants to exactly three occupants.

I also want to point out the documentation I added to the class. We use documentation strings (use a set of three double quotes before and after) to document the class. You can put documentation here to explain the class and its methods. We'll see a good use of this a bit later.

Finally, notice the code in the constructor. This demonstrates how to call the base class method, which I do to set the number of axles and doors. We can do the same in other methods if we wanted to call the base class method's version.

Now, let's write some code to use this class. Listing 3-17 shows the code we used to test this class. Here, we create a file named pickup.py that creates an instance of the pickup truck, adds occupants and payload, and then prints out the contents of the truck.

---

[5]Technically, it is called name mangling, which simulates making something private, but can still be accessed if you provide the correct number of underscores. For more information, see https://en.wikipedia.org/wiki/ Name_mangling.

Listing 3-17. Using the PickupTruck Class

```
#
# Beginning Sensor Networks 2nd Edition
#
# Class Example: Exercising the PickupTruck class.
#
# Dr. Charles Bell
#
from pickup_truck import PickupTruck

pickup = PickupTruck(500)
pickup.add_occupant()
pickup.add_occupant()
pickup.add_occupant()
pickup.add_occupant()
pickup.add_payload(100)
pickup.add_payload(300)
print("Number of occupants in truck = {0}.".format(pickup.num_
occupants()))
print("Weight in truck = {0}.".format(pickup.get_payload()))
pickup.add_payload(200)
pickup.remove_payload(400)
pickup.remove_payload(10)
```

Notice I add a couple of calls to the add_occupant() method, which the new class inherits and overrides. I also add calls so that we can test the code in the methods that check for excessive occupants and maximum payload capacity. When we run this code, we will see the results as shown here:

```
$ python ./pickup.py
Sorry, only 3 occupants are permitted in the truck.
```

```
Number of occupants in truck = 3.
Weight in truck = 400.
Overloaded!
Nothing in the truck.
```

There is one more thing we should learn about classes: built-in attributes. Recall the __init__() method. Python automatically provides several built-in attributes each starting with __ that you can use to learn more about objects. The following lists a few of the operators available for classes:

- __dict__: Dictionary containing the class namespace

- __doc__: Class documentation string

- __name__: Class name

- __module__: Module name where the class is defined

- __bases__: The base class(es) in order of inheritance

The following code shows what each of these attributes returns for the preceding PickupTruck class. I added this code to the pickup.py file.

```
print("PickupTruck.__doc__:", PickupTruck.__doc__)
print("PickupTruck.__name__:", PickupTruck.__name__)
print("PickupTruck.__module__:", PickupTruck.__module__)
print("PickupTruck.__bases__:", PickupTruck.__bases__)
print("PickupTruck.__dict__:", PickupTruck.__dict__)
```

When this code is run, we see the following output:

```
PickupTruck.__doc__: This is a pickup truck that has:
    axles = 2,
    doors = 2,
    max occupants = 3
```

The maximum payload is set on instantiation.

```
PickupTruck.__name__: PickupTruck
PickupTruck.__module__: pickup_truck
PickupTruck.__bases__: (<class 'vehicle.Vehicle'>,)
PickupTruck.__dict__: {'__module__': 'pickup_truck', '__doc__':
'This is a pickup truck that has:\n    axles = 2,\n    doors
= 2,\n    max occupants = 3\n    The maximum payload is set
on instantiation.\n    ', 'occupants': 0, 'payload': 0, 'max_
payload': 0, '_PickupTruck__max_occupants': 3, '__init__':
<function PickupTruck.__init__ at 0x1018a1488>, 'add_occupant':
<function PickupTruck.add_occupant at 0x1018a17b8>, 'add_
payload': <function PickupTruck.add_payload at 0x1018a1840>,
'remove_payload': <function PickupTruck.remove_payload at
0x1018a18c8>, 'get_payload': <function PickupTruck.get_payload
at 0x1018a1950>}
```

You can use the built-in attributes whenever you need more information about a class. Notice the _PickupTruck__max_occupants entry in the dictionary. Recall that we made a pseudo-private variable, __max_ occupants. Here, we see how Python refers to the variable by prepending the class name to the variable. Remember, variables that start with two underscores (not one) indicate they should be considered private to the class and only usable from within the class.

Tip   For more information about classes in Python, see https://docs.python.org/3/tutorial/classes.html.

FOR MORE INFORMATION

Should you require more in-depth knowledge of Python, there are several excellent books on the topic. I list a few of my favorites here:

- *Pro Python*, Second Edition (Apress 2014), J. Burton Browning, Marty Alchin

- *Learning Python*, Fifth Edition (O'Reilly Media 2013), Mark Lutz

- *Automate the Boring Stuff with Python: Practical Programming for Total Beginners* (No Starch Press 2015), Al Sweigart

A great resource is the documentation on the Python site: python.org/doc/.

Summary

Wow! That was a wild ride, wasn't it? I hope that this short crash course in Python has explained enough about the sample programs shown so far that you now know how they work. This crash course also forms the basis for understanding the other Python and MicroPython examples in this book.

If you are learning how to work with sensor network projects and don't know how to program with Python, learning Python can be fun given its easy-to-understand syntax. While there are many examples on the Internet you can use, very few are documented in such a way as to provide enough information for someone new to Python to understand or much less get started and deploy the sample! But at least the code is easy to read.

This chapter has provided a crash course in Python that covers the basics of the things you will encounter when examining most of the smaller example projects. We discovered the basic syntax and constructs of a Python application including all the fundamental statements and data structures you will likely encounter writing Python and MicroPython scripts.

In the next chapter, we'll dive deeper into MicroPython programming and start writing MicroPython for our XBee modules.

CHAPTER 4

XBee-Based Sensor Nodes

Thus far into our journey of sensor networks, we have discovered how sensor networks can be formed, the type of nodes, and their roles that comprise a sensor network, and we've spent some time learning about XBee modules and how to program them with MicroPython.

Now it is time to see how we can use XBee modules to read sensor data. As you will see, this can be accomplished in one of two ways: using the extensive native capabilities of the XBee to read sensors and broadcast the data to several or even a single node and using MicroPython written to read and manage sensor data passing it on to other nodes. We will concentrate on the first method, but we will see a short example of both methods.

Let's begin with a brief overview of what we can do with the XBee modules.

© Charles Bell 2020

C. Bell, *Beginning Sensor Networks with XBee, Raspberry Pi, and Arduino*,

https://doi.org/10.1007/978-1-4842-5796-8_4

How to Host Sensors with XBee

There are two basic methods[1] of hosting sensors with an XBee module. You can configure the XBee module to sample a sensor and send its data on a time schedule (XBee hardware option), or you can write a MicroPython script (MicroPython option) to do the same. There is one major difference. Using the MicroPython option means you can do some additional processing on the sensor data prior to transmitting it. This can include basic error handling, data transformation, and more. If you need to do any work on the sensor data prior to transmitting it or if you want to control other devices connected to the XBee module, MicroPython is a clear advantage.

For example, you could connect an LED to the XBee that you turn on whenever data is read from a sensor. This might be helpful in solutions such as a radio frequency identification (RFID) reader where swiping a card over the sensor unlocks a door. In this case, you can use MicroPython to trigger a light-emitting diode (LED) to let the user know when the lock is disengaged (or engaged).

Conversely, the hardware option permits you to configure the XBee to capture the sensor data in its raw form and there is no provision to modify it (easily). Thus, the data sent is the raw data the sensor generated. While this is one of the best practices—storing the data in its raw form— sometimes you may want to manipulate the data prior to transmission. We will see how to do that with the MicroPython option.

---

[1]These are the basic methods. Other methods including using XBee modules to control other devices are possible but are more advanced and beyond the scope of this work.

In both cases, sensors are connected directly to the XBee via the input/output pins. More specifically, you connect your sensor(s) to the XBee, read the data, and send it to one or more XBee modules on your network. You can send the data to a specific module by address or you can broadcast the data sending it to all modules on the network.

In the next section, we will see examples of both methods using the same hardware setup for a simple environmental sensor.

Building an XBee Environment Sensor

The XBee environmental sensor node in this example is a single XBee module with a simple analog temperature sensor (TMP36) connected to one of the analog input pins, which uses an analog-to-digital converter (ADC) to convert voltage to a number in range 0–1024. For this project, you tell the XBee to send data using short time periods; but for a real project, you would want to consider using a slower sampling rate or perhaps using sleep mode, in which the XBee sleeps for some time, then sends data, and repeats. We set the sampling rate when we configure the XBee module later in this chapter. For now, let's let the XBee send samples more frequently so you can see something happening.

The XBee also has a really nifty feature for monitoring battery power. You can tell the XBee to send the current supply power as part of the data packet. In this case, it sends whatever voltage is being supplied to the XBee. This is helpful because it allows you to build into your solution a trigger to remind you to change the batteries in your sensor node(s).

If you have a home or apartment with smoke detectors, you may have already experienced a similar circuit in the form of a tone or alarm that sounds when the battery voltage drops. For those of us with homes that have multiple smoke detectors, it can be somewhat of a "Where's Waldo?" game to find the detector that is chirping! This is why whenever the first detector starts chirping, I change the batteries in all of them.

145

Hardware Setup

To keep the project easy to build, you will use a breadboard for the sensor node. Using a breadboard makes it easier to experiment with the components, and once you perfect the circuit, you can move them to printed circuit board (PCB) breadboards for semi-permanent installation or perhaps design and build your own custom PCB for your sensor nodes.

The hardware for the XBee sensor node consists of a breadboard, a breadboard power supply, a TMP36 temperature sensor, and a 0.10mF capacitor. You also need an XBee Explorer board and a set of male headers (0.1" spacing for breadboards) like those available from Adafruit or SparkFun. Figure 4-1 shows the SparkFun regulated explorer board. The regulated board is a bit more expensive, but it has power regulation built in, so if you accidentally connect 5V, it won't fry your XBee. As an owner of a now completely useless XBee (it's not even big enough to use as a coaster), I can tell you that it is worth the extra cost.

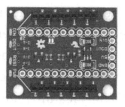

Figure 4-1. *SparkFun regulated XBee Explorer (courtesy of SparkFun)*

Note   Most breakout boards do not come with the breadboard headers installed. You have to solder them yourself, get someone to do it for you.

Once you have the components assembled, plug them in to your breadboard as shown in Figure 4-2. Notice the figure is shown without the XBee module installed so you can see the connections clearly. Be sure to set the breadboard power supply to 3.3V.

Caution   Be sure to double-check your wiring before powering on the sensor node.

There is no need to install the XBee module just yet since you need to configure its settings before you can use it with the circuit. You do that in the next section.

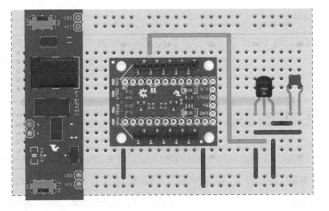

Figure 4-2. *XBee temperature sensor node*

It is important to note that the drawing shows positive power going to pin 1 of the XBee. Be sure to check the pins on your breakout board to be certain you are connecting to the right pin. For example, the SparkFun regulated explorer input voltage is not on pin 1.

Note   The breadboard power supply can be any 6V to 12V power supply. The 9V wall wart that most use to power their Arduino will do nicely.

Notice that you also connect your data line from the TMP36 to pin 17 (analog 3 on the XBee or DIO3 on the explorer board), and you connect ground to the ground pin on the breakout board (or explorer). Be sure to orient the TMP36 with the flat side as shown in the drawing. That is, with the flat side facing you, pin 1 is on the left and is to be connected to input power, the middle pin is data, and pin 3 is to be connected to ground. You can place the capacitor in either orientation, but be sure it is connected to pins 1 and 3 of the TMP36.

Caution   Ensure your breakout board power supply is set to 3.3V.

ALTERNATIVE TO A BREADBOARD POWER SUPPLY

If you plan to make a few XBee sensor nodes for semi-permanent installation, you may not want to use a breadboard. Rather, you may want to use a PCB breadboard and solder your XBee breakout board, sensor, and supporting electronics in place. In this case, a breadboard power supply might not be convenient. Similarly, if you want to keep costs down, you can build a basic power supply from a few parts that can accept up to 12V and still regulate the power to your XBee at 3.3V.

All you need are a 7833-voltage regulator, a 1mF capacitor, a 10mF, and a two-terminal terminal block (or similar power connector). In total, you should be able to buy these components for a few dollars even at an electronics retail store—and less from an electronics online store. Arranging the circuit is easy. The following picture shows the components wired to a breadboard.

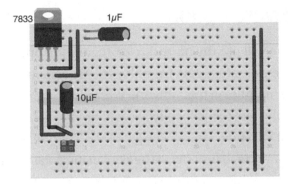

You need only a little imagination and some wire to transfer the circuit to a PCB breadboard. Notice the orientation of the capacitors—keep the white strip on the negative side!

Now that we have the hardware portion set up, let's see how to enable the sensor on the XBee with each method described earlier.

For each option, we will test the sensor node using the XCTU application to observe the data. This will allow us to test reading the sensor without setting up a complete sensor network. In fact, it is recommended that you test each sensor node in a similar manner. Once all of the nodes are working with a single connection, you can start connecting them together in a larger network. This will save you untold time and frustration later.[2]

We will start with the XBee hardware option.

---

[2]This is a common novice mistake: building the entire sensor network including data collection without testing the individual components. The best method is to build your network in stages after testing each node separately (or in as small a configuration as possible). Debugging a network with many nodes is much harder than building the network with networks that have been assembled in stages.

XBee Hardware Option

In this section, we will use the hardware configuration options of the XBee module to read temperature data from the TMP36 sensor and pass it on to another XBee module on the network. We will use a ZigBee network to keep things simple. More specifically, we will not be using the destination address (DH and DL codes) to set a target node. This will permit the XBee acting as a sensor node to broadcast the data using a data sample packet.

We will need one XBee module to read the sensor and another to receive the data. To keep the example simple and easy to set up, we will use XBee series 2 modules for this example. You can use one of the modules you used in Chapter 2 for the sensor node, provided you don't use the coordinator and you clear the destination address (DH and DL). You will use the XBee module configured as the coordinator to test the XBee sensor node. The following section details all of the settings you will need to make.

Configuring the XBee Sensor Node

The XBee module you use as the XBee sensor node is either an end device or a router with API firmware. You use the XCTU application to connect to the XBee with a USB adapter. Recall, we must connect the XBee using the USB dongle, then open XCTU, and add the module (or search for all modules). Once the module is found, open the *configuration mode* tab. From there, we will set several settings to enable the XBee to read the sensor. If you have not uploaded the router or end device firmware, you should do that first.

In this case, you want the XBee module to send data every 15 seconds (15,000 milliseconds), read data on analog line 3 (digital I/O 3 or DIO3), and include the reference voltage. Thus, in the XCTU application, you want to change the corresponding settings. Table 4-1 shows the settings you need to change. Use the code shown in the search box to find each setting quickly. Recall that all values are entered in hexadecimal and that you can change the value in XCTU by searching for the code and then either choosing a value or typing it into the text box for that setting. Change the settings as shown, and then click *Write* to save the settings to the XBee module.

Table 4-1. *XBee Sensor Node Options and Values*

Code	Setting Name	Description	Value
D3	AD3/DIO3	Trigger analog or digital data recording	2—ADC
ID	PAN ID	Id for the network	8088
IR	I/O Sampling Rate	Time to wait to send data	3A98—15,000ms
NI	Node Identifier	Name for the node	Sensor Node
V+	Supply Voltage Threshold	Supply voltage	FFFF (always send)

Setting Up the Coordinator

Next, remove the XBee sensor node and plug it into the explorer on the breadboard. Make sure you have loaded the coordinator firmware and use the settings in Table 4-2.

Table 4-2. *XBee Coordinator Options and Values*

Code	Setting Name	Description	Value
ID	PAN ID	Id for the network	8088
NI	Node Identifier	Name for the node	Coordinator

Now we are ready to test our sensor node.

Testing the XBee Sensor Node

To test the XBee sensor node, you use your XBee coordinator with API firmware installed on the USB adapter connected to your PC. Do this first so the coordinator can be up and running when you start the XBee sensor node. Plug it into your computer, and open the XCTU application. Use XCTU to discover the XBee module and then open a terminal. See Chapter 2 for instructions on how to do this.

Next, connect your power supply to your XBee sensor node. It will take a few moments for the XBee to connect to the coordinator and join the network. Once it does, you start to see the coordinator receiving data, as shown in Figure 4-3.

Tip   It can take some time for the network to form. If you do not see data samples on the coordinator, power off the sensor node and power it on again. If you still do not see any data, double-check your settings to ensure both nodes are on the same network PAN ID.

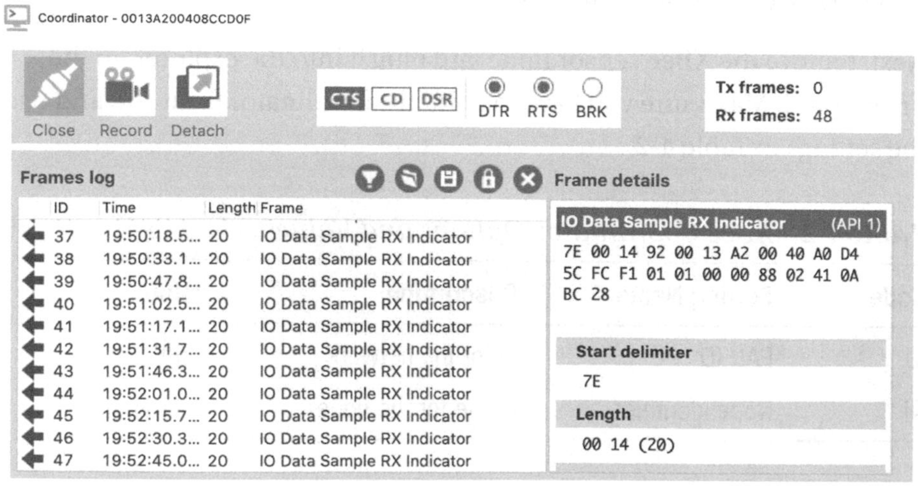

Figure 4-3. Serial monitor output

You should see one or more *IO Data Sample receive RX Indicator* packets. Notice in the image that the first row begins with 7E (hex). This is the start-of-packet delimiter. You should see to the right data that looks like the following. This is a series of hexadecimal values.

7E 00 14 92 00 13 A2 00 40 A0 D4 5C FC F1 01 01 00 00 88 02 41 0A BC 28

All ZigBee packets have a specific format or layout. Table 4-3 shows the layout for the *IO Data Sample RX Indicator* packet.

Table 4-3. *IO Data Sample Rx Indicator Packet*

Value	Field Name	Notes
7E	Start delimiter	
00 14	Packet length	20 bytes to checksum
92	Frame type	I/O Data Sample Rx Indicator
00 13 A2 00 40 A0 D4 5C	64-bit address	Address of XBee sensor node
FC F1	16-bit address	
01	Options	
01	Number of samples	1 data sample
00 00	Digital mask	Digital pins that have data
88	Analog mask	Analog pins that have data
02 41	Sample	Temperature from sensor
0A BC	Supply voltage	
28	Checksum	

This data packet represents the data sent from the XBee sensor node. In this case, you set the XBee to send any value from the analog pin 3 (digital IO 3) every 15 seconds. You also set the option to send the value of the supply voltage. Notice the value for the analog mask: the value 88 in hexadecimal is converted to 1000 1000 in binary. The first part of the byte is an indicator that the supply voltage is also included in the data packet. The second part of the byte indicates that AD3/DIO3 (pin 3) was the source of the sample. If you were sampling multiple sensors, the mask would have the bits for the data pin set or 0001 for pin 0, 0010 for pin 1, and 0100 for pin 2.

From the table, you see there is indeed one data sample with a value of 02 41 (hex, 577 decimal). The value is 577 because this is the voltage in millivolts read from the sensor. To calculate the temperature, you must use the following formula:

```
temp =  ((sample * 1200/1024) - 500)/10
```

Thus, you have ((577 * 1200/1024)-500)/10 = 17.61 degrees Celsius. The supply voltage is a similar formula:

```
voltage = (sample * 1200/1024)/1000
```

Here, you convert the data read to volts rather than millivolts. Thus, the data packet contained 0A BC (hex, 2748), and the voltage read is 3.22 volts. If you are powering an XBee sensor from a battery, you can use this value to determine when you need to change or charge the battery.

Take a few moments to study the other samples in the example and check the data samples for the temperature read. If you are really careful, you can place your finger on the TMP36 and observe the temperature change (it should start increasing after one or two more samples). Once you are convinced your XBee sensor node is sending similar data, you can conclude that the sensor node is working correctly.

Next, let's look at the MicroPython option.

MicroPython Option

In this section, we will use a MicroPython script on the XBee module to read temperature data from the TMP36 sensor and pass it on to another XBee module on the network. We will use a ZigBee network to keep things simple. More specifically, we will supply the destination address (DH and DL codes) to send the data to a specific node.

We will need one XBee module to read the sensor and another to receive the data. We must use an XBee series 3 module for the sensor node in this example, but we can use the same coordinator from the previous example. You can use one of the modules you used in Chapter 2 for the sensor node, provided you don't use the coordinator and you clear the destination address (DH and DL). You will use the XBee module configured as the coordinator to test the XBee sensor node. The following section details all of the settings you will need to make.

Configuring the XBee Sensor Node

The XBee module you use as the XBee sensor node is either an end device or a router with API firmware configured to run MicroPython. Once again, you use the XCTU application to connect to the XBee with a USB adapter.

Recall, we will be placing the XBee module into MicroPython mode. While will we still be using the ZigBee network, we will set up the module to connect to (join) the network. Thus, we will require one coordinator. Fortunately, we can use the same coordinator as the last section.

Table 4-4 shows the settings you need to change. Recall that all values are entered in hexadecimal and that you can change the value in XCTU by searching for the code and then either choosing a value or typing it into the text box for that setting. Change the settings as shown, and then click *Write* to save the settings to the XBee module.

155

Table 4-4. *XBee Sensor Node Options and Values*

Code	Setting Name	Description	Value
AP	API Enabled	Set API mode	4—MicroPython
BD	UART Baud Rate	Speed of serial connection	115200
CE	Device Role	Role in ZigBee Network	0—Join Network
D3	AD3/DIO3	Trigger analog or digital data recording	2—ADC
ID	PAN ID	Id for the network	8088
NI	Node Identifier	Name for the node	Python TMP36
PS	MicroPython Auto start	Auto start REPL	1—Enabled

Programming the Sensor Node

Go ahead and make the configuration changes for the sensor node and then write (save) them to the module. Recall from Chapter 2, we can either write our MicroPython script interactively and then save it to a file or write it to a file and upload it to the module. In this example, we will see the interactive mode.

Next, we will open the MicroPython Terminal by selecting it from the menu as shown in Figure 4-4.

Figure 4-4. *Open MicroPython Terminal*

Once the *MicroPython Terminal* is opened, press *Enter* a few times to get a response. You should see the prompt >>>. If you are reusing an XBee module from a previous project that was loaded with a MicroPython script where the main.py script was overwritten either by copying a file or using the interactive mode of the REPL console, you may need to press *Ctrl+C* to stop the main.py script.

Next, we are going to type in the code shown in Listing 4-1. You can download the source code for this book and open the example file named listing4-1.py and copy and paste the code once in interactive file mode. You can omit the comment lines if you'd like. Also recall you must press *Ctrl+C* to interrupt a MicroPython script that you've loaded previously. You can then place the terminal in file mode with *Ctrl+F*.

Listing 4-1. Reading a TMP36 Sensor

```
#
# Beginning Sensor Networks 2nd Edition
#
# XBee Sensor Node Example: Reading a TMP36 temperature sensor.
#
# Dr. Charles Bell
#
from machine import ADC
from time import sleep
import xbee

# Target address to send data
TARGET_64BIT_ADDR = b'\x00\x13\xA2\x00\x40\x8C\xCD\x0F'
wait_time = 15 # seconds between measurements
cycles = 10 # number of repeats

for x in range(cycles):
    # Read temperature value & print to debug
    temp_pin = ADC("D3")
    temp_raw = temp_pin.read()
    print("Raw pin reading: %d" % temp_raw)

    # Convert temperature to proper units
    temp_c = ((float(temp_raw) * (1200.0/4096.0)) - 500.0) / 10.0
    print("Temperature: %.2f Celsius" % temp_c)
    temp_f = (temp_c * 9.0 / 5.0) + 32.0
    print("Temperature: %.2f Fahrenheit" % temp_f)

    # Send data to coordinator
    message = "raw: %d, C: %.2f, F: %.2f" % (temp_raw, temp_c,
    temp_f)
    print("Sending: %s" % message)
```

```
try:
    xbee.transmit(TARGET_64BIT_ADDR, message)
    print("Data sent successfully")
except Exception as e:
    print("Transmit failure: %s" % str(e))

# Wait between cycles
sleep(wait_time)
```

Listing 4-2 shows the interactive session to copy and paste the preceding code (without comments). Notice at the end, we used *Ctrl+D* to save the file to main.py, pressing *Y* to confirm.

Tip   If you encounter problems when you copy and paste the entire file, try copy and paste one line at a time. This can happen if you omit the blank lines, which trigger the REPL console to close code blocks and execute code.

Listing 4-2. Interactive File Mode for TMP36 Sensor Example

```
flash compile mode; Ctrl-C to cancel, Ctrl-D to finish
  1^^^ from machine import ADC
  2^^^ from time import sleep
  3^^^ import xbee
  4^^^
  5^^^ # Target address to send data
  6^^^ TARGET_64BIT_ADDR = b'\x00\x13\xA2\x00\x40\x8C\xCD\x0F'
  7^^^ wait_time = 15 # seconds between measurements
  8^^^ cycles = 10 # number of repeats
  9^^^
 10^^^ for x in range(cycles):
 11^^^     # Read temperature value & print to debug
 12^^^     temp_pin = ADC("D3")
```

```
13^^^        temp_raw = temp_pin.read()
14^^^        print("Raw pin reading: %d" % temp_raw)
15^^^
16^^^        # Convert temperature to proper units
17^^^        temp_c = ((float(temp_raw) * (1200.0/4096.0)) -
             500.0) / 10.0
18^^^        print("Temperature: %.2f Celsius" % temp_c)
19^^^        temp_f = (temp_c * 9.0 / 5.0) + 32.0
20^^^        print("Temperature: %.2f Fahrenheit" % temp_f)
21^^^
22^^^        # Send data to coordinator
23^^^        message = "raw: %d, C: %.2f, F: %.2f" % (temp_raw,
             temp_c, temp_f)
24^^^        print("Sending: %s" % message)
25^^^        try:
26^^^            xbee.transmit(TARGET_64BIT_ADDR, message)
27^^^            print("Data sent successfully")
28^^^        except Exception as e:
29^^^            print("Transmit failure: %s" % str(e))
30^^^
31^^^        # Wait between cycles
32^^^        sleep(wait_time)
33^^^
Erasing /flash/main.mpy...
Compiling 1008 bytes of code...
Saved compiled code to /flash/main.mpy (619 bytes).
Automatically run this code at startup [Y/n]? Y
Stored code will run at startup.
```

Once you save the file, we can run the file by pressing *Ctrl+R* as shown in Listing 4-3. However, remember that we are using the REPL console, which will execute the code interactively. Since we have not connected the TMP36 sensor yet, you may see spurious values when the code executes. Let it run for a few iterations and then press *Ctrl+C* to stop execution.

Listing 4-3. Interactive Execution of TMP36 Example

```
MicroPython v1.11-1290-g9da1b0c on 2019-11-14; XBee3 Zigbee
with EFR32MG
Type "help()" for more information.
Press CTRL-R in the REPL to run the code at any time.

Try running it with CTRL+R. Interrupt with CTRL+C.

Loading /flash/main.mpy...
Running bytecode...
Raw pin reading: 4095
Temperature: 69.97 Celsius
Temperature: 157.95 Fahrenheit
Sending: raw: 4095, C: 69.97, F: 157.95
Data sent successfully
Raw pin reading: 4095
Temperature: 69.97 Celsius
Temperature: 157.95 Fahrenheit
Sending: raw: 4095, C: 69.97, F: 157.95
Data sent successfully
Raw pin reading: 4095
Temperature: 69.97 Celsius
Temperature: 157.95 Fahrenheit
Sending: raw: 4095, C: 69.97, F: 157.95
Data sent successfully
Traceback (most recent call last):
  File "<stdin>", line 32, in <module>
KeyboardInterrupt:

>>>
```

Now, let's return to the code paying attention to the formulas for calculating the Celsius value from the raw input shown as follows for clarity. You may notice that the formula uses a different value for the maximum value read (4096 instead of 1024). This is because MicroPython returns a range of 0–4095 from the ADC so we must take that into consideration in the formula.

```
temp_raw = temp_pin.read()
print("Raw pin reading: %d" % temp_raw)

# Convert temperature to proper units
temp_c = ((float(temp_raw) * (1200.0/4096.0)) - 500.0) / 10.0
```

Once you are convinced this formula is correct, you can shut down the *MicroPython Terminal*, disconnect your XBee from XCTU, and remove the USB explorer. Next, move the XBee module to the breadboard set up from before.

You do not need to power on the circuit, but if you have already configured the coordinator or are using from the previous example, you can power on the circuit skipping the following section.

Setting Up the Coordinator

Next, remove the XBee sensor node and plug it into the explorer on the breadboard. If you are reusing the coordinator from the last section, you do not need to make the changes. If you are using a new XBee module or one from another project, make sure you have loaded the coordinator firmware and use the settings in Table 4-5.

Table 4-5. *XBee Coordinator Options and Values*

Code	Setting Name	Description	Value
ID	PAN ID	Id for the network	8088
NI	Node Identifier	Name for the node	Coordinator

Once the settings are written and the sensor node is powered on, take a look at the network to ensure your module is connecting. Figure 4-5 shows an example of what you should see. Recall, you can select the coordinator, open the network view from the main window, and then click *Scan*.

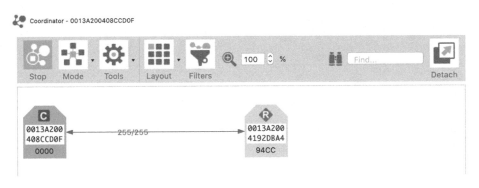

Figure 4-5. *Checking the network*

Tip   It is always a good idea to check your ZigBee network to ensure the modules have connected correctly. If you do not see the modules you expect, double-check all settings and rescan the network.

Now we are ready to test our sensor node.

Testing the XBee Sensor Node

To test the XBee sensor node, you use your XBee coordinator with API firmware installed on the USB adapter connected to your PC. Do this first so the coordinator can be up and running when you start the XBee sensor node. Plug it into your computer, and open the XCTU application. Use XCTU to discover the XBee module and then open a terminal. See Chapter 2 for instructions on how to do this.

Next, connect your power supply to your XBee sensor node. It will take a few moments for the XBee to connect to the coordinator and join the network. Once it does, you start to see the coordinator receiving data, as shown in Figure 4-6.

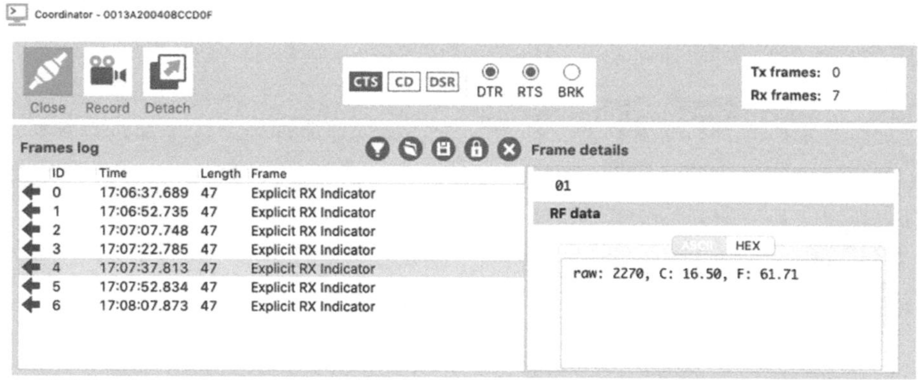

Figure 4-6. *Serial monitor output*

You should see one or more *Explicit RX Indicator* packets. We get this packet instead of the broadcast because we're transmitting the packet directly to the coordinator by address. Notice in the image that the first row begins with 7E (hex). This is the start-of-packet delimiter. You should see to the right data that looks like the following. This is a series of hexadecimal values.

```
7E 00 2F 91 00 13 A2 00 41 92 DB A4 94 CC E8 E8 00 11 C1 05 01
72 61 77 3A 20 32 32 37 30 2C 20 43 3A 20 31 36 2E 35 30 2C 20
46 3A 20 36 31 2E 37 31 24
```

You may be wondering where the message is we transmitted. It is there, but hard to see in the hexadecimal output. It appears at the end of the message. The following shows the message from the example.

```
72 61 77 3A 20 32 32 37 30 2C 20 43 3A 20 31 36 2E 35 30 2C 20
46 3A 20 36 31 2E 37 31
```

If you convert the hex values to American Standard Code for Information Interchange (ASCII),[3] you will see the message. A somewhat tedious lookup using an ASCII chart will reveal the following 29 hexadecimal values are represented in ASCII as follows. Nifty, yes?

```
raw: 2270, C: 16.50, F: 61.71
```

Now, let's take a closer look at the packet. All ZigBee packets have a specific format or layout. Table 4-6 shows the layout for the *Explicit RX Indicator* packet.

Table 4-6. *Explicit Rx Indicator Packet*

Value	Field Name	Notes
7E	Start delimiter	
00 2F	Packet length	47 bytes to checksum
91	Frame type	Explicit Rx Indicator
00 13 A2 00 41 92 DB A4	64-bit address	Address of XBee sensor node
94 CC	16-bit address	
E8	Source endpoint	
E8	Destination endpoint	
00 11	Cluster Id	
C1 05	Profile Id	
01	Receive options	0x01—Packet Acknowledged
0A BC	Supply voltage	
N bytes	Received data	Example: 29
N+1 byte	Checksum	Example: 0x24

---

[3]https://en.wikipedia.org/wiki/ASCII

This data packet represents the data sent from the XBee sensor node. In this case, you set the XBee to send any value from the analog pin 3 (digital IO 3) every 15 seconds for ten cycles.[4]

Take a few moments to study the other samples in the example and check the data samples for the temperature read. If you are really careful, you can place your finger on the TMP36 and observe the temperature change (it should start increasing after one or two more samples). Once you are convinced your XBee sensor node is sending similar data, you can conclude that the sensor node is working correctly.

Next, we will look at an example of this project done a bit easier using a different form of sensor.

Example: Using XBee Modules to Gather Data

In this example, we will kick up the configuration a bit by switching to an easier (but slightly more expensive) option to connect sensors to XBee modules. We will also see a different form of sensor that communicates with a different interface.

We will use the XBee Grove Development Board to host our XBee module as shown in Figure 4-7. The XBee Grove Development Board has several connectors along with six grove connectors, user *controllable* button and LED, and much more. For complete details about the board, see the guide at www.digi.com/resources/documentation/ Digidocs/90001457-13/.

---

[4]We leave it as an exercise to module the script to send readings without stopping (e.g., continuously).

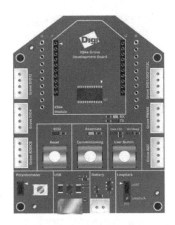

Figure 4-7. *XBee Grove Development Board*

Grove is a hardware prototyping standard made by Seeed Studio (seeedstudio.com) designed to simplify connecting devices together using a simple, four-wire connection. You can find all manner of sensors and output components for creating your projects quickly. See the Seeed Studio wiki about the Grove system to learn more (http://wiki. seeedstudio.com/Grove_System/).

The sensor we will use is the BMP280 temperature/humidity sensor. You can find this sensor at Adafruit (adafruit.com) or SparkFun (sparkfun.com). Figure 4-8 shows the BMP280 module from Adafruit. You can get one here at www.adafruit.com/product/2651. There is a Grove module for the BMP280 (http://wiki.seeedstudio.com/Grove-Barometer_Sensor-BMP280/), but it is harder to find because it is an older module.

Figure 4-8. *BMP280 breakout board*

This sensor uses the Inter-Integrated Circuit (I2C) interface[5] with 7-bit addressing. This requires four connections: power, ground, clock (SCL), and data (SDA). Since you can connect multiple sensors to the same I2C bus, each sensor has its own address so that you can "talk" to the sensor you want. Unfortunately, each I2C sensor (device) has its own communication protocol, so communicating with the module to get data requires a special library (called a driver) to use the sensor. Fortunately, there is a MicroPython I2C driver for the BMP280. We will download it and copy it to our XBee module. However, since it is written to a MicroPython version that is a bit different than the XBee MicroPython, we need to make some minor alterations.

While this example is terse and shows the bare minimal needed to get it working, we will learn more about I2C interfaces in the next two chapters.

Let's begin by configuring the hardware for the XBee sensor node.

Hardware Setup

Setting up the hardware for this project is easier than the previous examples. All you need is a Grove to Female Jumper cable or (4) female-to-female jumper wires, the XBee Grove Development Board, and the BMP280 module. If your BMP280 module doesn't have the header soldered, you may need to solder it yourself or find someone to solder it for you.

---

[5]https://en.wikipedia.org/wiki/I%C2%B2C

To connect the sensor to the board, we will be using only four of the connections on the BMP280. The module from Adafruit supports I2C and x (SPI) interfaces, so we only need those for I2C. These are marked on the board as follows: 3V0 (3V power), GND (ground), SDK (SCL on the development board), and SDI (SDA on the development board). We can use the Grove PWM connector for power and ground, but must use the Grove D10 connector for the I2C interface. Several options for making the connections are shown as follows. Go ahead and make the connections now. Do not insert the XBee module or connect the board to your PC at this time.

BMP280 with Jumper Wires

If you want to use individual jumper wires, you should use two of the Grove connectors: the first for the SCL and SDA connections and another for power. This is because the jumper wires are slightly larger than the pins in the Grove connectors.

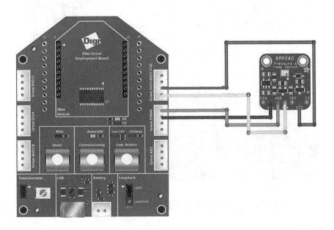

Figure 4-9. Connecting the BMP280 breakout board using jumper wires

BMP280 with Grove Breakout Cable

The Grove breakout cable from Seeed Studio is an excellent alternative to jumper wires. These have a Grove connector on one end and female connectors for each wire on the other end, making them ideal for connecting to breakout boards like the BMP280 in this example. See `www.seeedstudio.com/Grove-4-pin-Female-Jumper-to-Grove-4-pin-Conversion-Cable-5-PCs-per-Pack.html` for more details. Like the Grove BMP280 module, these cables are harder to find. They also make a Grove to male cable. See `www.seeedstudio.com/Grove-4-pin-Male-Jumper-to-Grove-4-pin-Conversion-Cable-5-PCs-per-Pack.html`.

Figure 4-10 shows how to make the connections using the Grove to jumper wire cable.

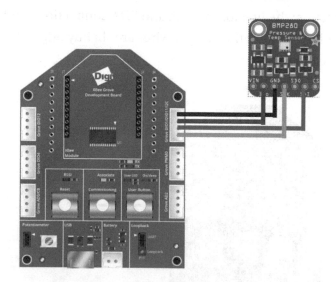

Figure 4-10. *Connecting the BMP280 breakout board using Grove to jumper wire cable*

Grove BMP280 Module Connections

If you purchased the BMP280 Grove module, all you need to do is connect the module to the board using a Grove cable as shown in Figure 4-11.

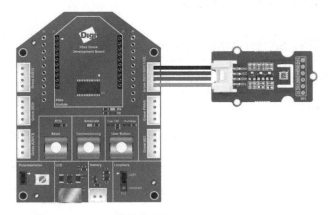

Figure 4-11. *Connecting the BMP280 Grove module*

Next, let's configure the XBee sensor node.

Configuring the XBee Sensor Node

The XBee module you use as the XBee sensor node is either an end device or a router with API firmware configured to run MicroPython. Once again, you use the XCTU application to connect to the XBee. In this case, we will use the XBee Grove Development Board.

Simply connect your XBee module to the board and then connect the board to your PC using the provided micro-USB cable. This will act like the USB explorer that we've been using in the other projects. If you are reusing the XBee module we used as the sensor node from the previous, many of the settings will remain the same except for the digital IO pin setting (D1).

Table 4-7 shows the settings you need to change. Recall that all values are entered in hexadecimal and that you can change the value in XCTU by searching for the code and then either choosing a value or typing it into the text box for that setting. Change the settings as shown, and then click *Write* to save the settings to the XBee module.

Table 4-7. *XBee Sensor Node Options and Values*

Code	Setting Name	Description	Value
AP	API Enabled	Set API mode	4—MicroPython
BD	UART Baud Rate	Speed of serial connection	115200
CE	Device Role	Role in ZigBee Network	0—Join Network
D1	DIO1	Digital data read/write	6—I2C SCL
ID	PAN ID	Id for the network	8088
NI	Node Identifier	Name for the node	Python BMP280
PS	MicroPython Auto start	Auto start REPL	1—Enabled

Programming the Sensor Node

Go ahead and make the configuration changes for the sensor node and then write (save) them to the module. Recall from Chapter 2, we can either write our MicroPython script interactively and then save it to a file or write it to a file and upload it to the module. In this example, we will see the file copy mode.

In this case, we will need to copy the BMP280 I2C library to the lib folder on the XBee module and copy our MicroPython script to the XBee module renaming it as main.py. Rather than jumping into the project by blindly copying the files, let's learn how to use custom MicroPython libraries using the BMP280 library.

When you want to use an I2C sensor or device, you will need to have a MicroPython driver library for it. Recall, this is because each device has its own protocol requiring writing certain values to a specific byte or bytes to trigger or set some option and then read the data using yet another address. Sound complicated? It can be. Fortunately, someone has done all the work for us.

Use your browser and navigate to `https://github.com/dafvid/micropython-bmp280/`. This library was written by David Wahlund and is an excellent example of how to write an I2C driver in MicroPython. If you want to write your own driver for another I2C device, this code is a very good template to follow.

To download the driver, click the *Clone or download* button and save the Zip file to your PC. Once it has downloaded, open the Zip library and extract the files. You will need to find the `bmp280.py` file. We will be copying this file to our XBee module after we modify it.

Tip   A modified version of the module is available on the source code download for the book from the Apress website.

In short, we must add a new import and comment out a few lines in the constructor. These modifications will permit the code to work on the XBee modules. We also need to remove some of the methods in the module because the code size is a bit too large for the XBee.

Caution   If you find other modules you want to use with your XBee and encounter memory errors, you may need to reduce the size of the module. You can do so by removing unneeded methods, constants, and similar features. Be careful to only remove things you don't need (and are not needed by the remaining methods).

Open the downloaded file and add this line at the top of the file:

```
from micropython import const
```

Next, locate the following lines and either comment them (placing a # at the start of the line). You will find both in the constructor. You may encounter errors such as an invalid I2C operation or memory error if you forget to remove these lines:

```
self._bmp_i2c.start()
self.use_case(BMP280_CASE_HANDHELD_DYN)
```

Finally, to reduce the size of the module, remove all methods after the pressure() method and then save the file. Listing 4-4 shows the resulting code. Your edits should be very similar (allowing for minor improvements by the author of the module).

Tip   Also included in the source code for the book is a difference file (bmp280.diff) that you can use to apply to the code if you are familiar with *diff* and *patch*.

Listing 4-4. Modified bmp280.py Module

```
from micropython import const
from ustruct import unpack as unp

# Author David Stenwall Wahlund (david at dafnet.se)

# Power Modes
BMP280_POWER_FORCED = const(1)
BMP280_POWER_NORMAL = const(3)
```

```
BMP280_SPI3W_ON = const(1)
BMP280_SPI3W_OFF = const(0)

BMP280_TEMP_OS_SKIP = const(0)
BMP280_TEMP_OS_1 = const(1)
BMP280_TEMP_OS_2 = const(2)
BMP280_TEMP_OS_4 = const(3)
BMP280_TEMP_OS_8 = const(4)
BMP280_TEMP_OS_16 = const(5)

BMP280_PRES_OS_SKIP = const(0)
BMP280_PRES_OS_1 = const(1)
BMP280_PRES_OS_2 = const(2)
BMP280_PRES_OS_4 = const(3)
BMP280_PRES_OS_8 = const(4)
BMP280_PRES_OS_16 = const(5)

# Standby settings in ms
BMP280_STANDBY_0_5 = const(0)
BMP280_STANDBY_62_5 = const(1)
BMP280_STANDBY_125 = const(2)
BMP280_STANDBY_250 = const(3)
BMP280_STANDBY_500 = const(4)
BMP280_STANDBY_1000 = const(5)
BMP280_STANDBY_2000 = const(6)
BMP280_STANDBY_4000 = const(7)

# IIR Filter setting
BMP280_IIR_FILTER_OFF = const(0)
BMP280_IIR_FILTER_2 = const(1)
BMP280_IIR_FILTER_4 = const(2)
BMP280_IIR_FILTER_8 = const(3)
BMP280_IIR_FILTER_16 = const(4)
```

```
# Oversampling setting
BMP280_OS_ULTRALOW = const(0)
BMP280_OS_LOW = const(1)
BMP280_OS_STANDARD = const(2)
BMP280_OS_HIGH = const(3)
BMP280_OS_ULTRAHIGH = const(4)

# Oversampling matrix
# (PRESS_OS, TEMP_OS, sample time in ms)
_BMP280_OS_MATRIX = [
    [BMP280_PRES_OS_1, BMP280_TEMP_OS_1, 7],
    [BMP280_PRES_OS_2, BMP280_TEMP_OS_1, 9],
    [BMP280_PRES_OS_4, BMP280_TEMP_OS_1, 14],
    [BMP280_PRES_OS_8, BMP280_TEMP_OS_1, 23],
    [BMP280_PRES_OS_16, BMP280_TEMP_OS_2, 44]
]

# Use cases
BMP280_CASE_HANDHELD_LOW = const(0)
BMP280_CASE_HANDHELD_DYN = const(1)
BMP280_CASE_WEATHER = const(2)
BMP280_CASE_FLOOR = const(3)
BMP280_CASE_DROP = const(4)
BMP280_CASE_INDOOR = const(5)

_BMP280_CASE_MATRIX = [
    [BMP280_POWER_NORMAL, BMP280_OS_ULTRAHIGH, BMP280_IIR_
    FILTER_4, BMP280_STANDBY_62_5],
    [BMP280_POWER_NORMAL, BMP280_OS_STANDARD, BMP280_IIR_
    FILTER_16, BMP280_STANDBY_0_5],
    [BMP280_POWER_FORCED, BMP280_OS_ULTRALOW, BMP280_IIR_
    FILTER_OFF, BMP280_STANDBY_0_5],
```

```
    [BMP280_POWER_NORMAL, BMP280_OS_STANDARD, BMP280_IIR_
    FILTER_4, BMP280_STANDBY_125],
    [BMP280_POWER_NORMAL, BMP280_OS_LOW, BMP280_IIR_FILTER_OFF,
    BMP280_STANDBY_0_5],
    [BMP280_POWER_NORMAL, BMP280_OS_ULTRAHIGH, BMP280_IIR_
    FILTER_16, BMP280_STANDBY_0_5]
]

_BMP280_REGISTER_ID = const(0xD0)
_BMP280_REGISTER_RESET = const(0xE0)
_BMP280_REGISTER_STATUS = const(0xF3)
_BMP280_REGISTER_CONTROL = const(0xF4)
_BMP280_REGISTER_CONFIG = const(0xF5)  # IIR filter config

_BMP280_REGISTER_DATA = const(0xF7)

class BMP280:
    def __init__(self, i2c_bus, addr=0x76):
        self._bmp_i2c = i2c_bus
        self._i2c_addr = addr

        self.chip_id = self._read(_BMP280_REGISTER_ID, 2)

        # read calibration data
        # < little-endian
        # H unsigned short
        # h signed short
        self._T1 = unp('<H', self._read(0x88, 2))[0]
        self._T2 = unp('<h', self._read(0x8A, 2))[0]
        self._T3 = unp('<h', self._read(0x8C, 2))[0]
        self._P1 = unp('<H', self._read(0x8E, 2))[0]
        self._P2 = unp('<h', self._read(0x90, 2))[0]
        self._P3 = unp('<h', self._read(0x92, 2))[0]
        self._P4 = unp('<h', self._read(0x94, 2))[0]
```

177

```
        self._P5 = unp('<h', self._read(0x96, 2))[0]
        self._P6 = unp('<h', self._read(0x98, 2))[0]
        self._P7 = unp('<h', self._read(0x9A, 2))[0]
        self._P8 = unp('<h', self._read(0x9C, 2))[0]
        self._P9 = unp('<h', self._read(0x9E, 2))[0]

        # output raw
        self._t_raw = 0
        self._t_fine = 0
        self._t = 0

        self._p_raw = 0
        self._p = 0

        self.read_wait_ms = 0  # interval between forced
        measure and readout
        self._new_read_ms = 200  # interval between
        self._last_read_ts = 0

    def _read(self, addr, size=1):
        return self._bmp_i2c.readfrom_mem(self._i2c_addr,
        addr, size)

    def _write(self, addr, b_arr):
        if not type(b_arr) is bytearray:
            b_arr = bytearray([b_arr])
        return self._bmp_i2c.writeto_mem(self._i2c_addr,
        addr, b_arr)

    def _gauge(self):
        # TODO limit new reads
        # read all data at once (as by spec)
        d = self._read(_BMP280_REGISTER_DATA, 6)
```

```
    self._p_raw = (d[0] << 12) + (d[1] << 4) + (d[2] >> 4)
    self._t_raw = (d[3] << 12) + (d[4] << 4) + (d[5] >> 4)

    self._t_fine = 0
    self._t = 0
    self._p = 0

def reset(self):
    self._write(_BMP280_REGISTER_RESET, 0xB6)

def load_test_calibration(self):
    self._T1 = 27504
    self._T2 = 26435
    self._T3 = -1000
    self._P1 = 36477
    self._P2 = -10685
    self._P3 = 3024
    self._P4 = 2855
    self._P5 = 140
    self._P6 = -7
    self._P7 = 15500
    self._P8 = -14600
    self._P9 = 6000

def load_test_data(self):
    self._t_raw = 519888
    self._p_raw = 415148

def print_calibration(self):
    print("T1: {} {}".format(self._T1, type(self._T1)))
    print("T2: {} {}".format(self._T2, type(self._T2)))
    print("T3: {} {}".format(self._T3, type(self._T3)))
    print("P1: {} {}".format(self._P1, type(self._P1)))
    print("P2: {} {}".format(self._P2, type(self._P2)))
```

```
        print("P3: {} {}".format(self._P3, type(self._P3)))
        print("P4: {} {}".format(self._P4, type(self._P4)))
        print("P5: {} {}".format(self._P5, type(self._P5)))
        print("P6: {} {}".format(self._P6, type(self._P6)))
        print("P7: {} {}".format(self._P7, type(self._P7)))
        print("P8: {} {}".format(self._P8, type(self._P8)))
        print("P9: {} {}".format(self._P9, type(self._P9)))

    def _calc_t_fine(self):
        # From datasheet page 22
        self._gauge()
        if self._t_fine == 0:
            var1 = (((self._t_raw >> 3) - (self._T1 << 1)) *
            self._T2) >> 11
            var2 = (((((self._t_raw >> 4) - self._T1)
                        * ((self._t_raw >> 4)
                            - self._T1)) >> 12)
                    * self._T3) >> 14
            self._t_fine = var1 + var2

    @property
    def temperature(self):
        self._calc_t_fine()
        if self._t == 0:
            self._t = ((self._t_fine * 5 + 128) >> 8) / 100.
        return self._t

    @property
    def pressure(self):
        # From datasheet page 22
        self._calc_t_fine()
        if self._p == 0:
            var1 = self._t_fine - 128000
```

```
        var2 = var1 * var1 * self._P6
        var2 = var2 + ((var1 * self._P5) << 17)
        var2 = var2 + (self._P4 << 35)
        var1 = ((var1 * var1 * self._P3) >> 8) +
        ((var1 * self._P2) << 12)
        var1 = (((1 << 47) + var1) * self._P1) >> 33

        if var1 == 0:
            return 0

        p = 1048576 - self._p_raw
        p = int(((((p << 31) - var2) * 3125) / var1)
        var1 = (self._P9 * (p >> 13) * (p >> 13)) >> 25
        var2 = (self._P8 * p) >> 19

        p = ((p + var1 + var2) >> 8) + (self._P7 << 4)
        self._p = p / 256.0
    return self._p
```

To copy the modified file to our XBee module, connect your XBee
to your PC using the Grove Development Board and then open the *File
System Manager* using the *Tools* menu as shown in Figure 4-12.

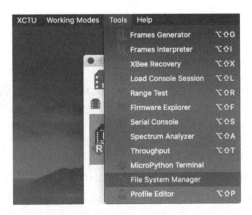

Figure 4-12. *Open the File System Manager*

Once the *File System Manager* is open, you will need to connect to the XBee. If you select the XBee module in XCTU before opening the *File System Manager*, you can click the *Open* button and the manager will connect to your module. Otherwise, you can use the *Settings* button to choose the UART (serial) parameters for the XBee and then connect to it.

Use the manager to locate the bmp280.py file using the left side of the interface and navigate to the lib folder on the XBee using the right side of the interface. Then, click bmp280.py and drag it to the right and drop it. This will copy the file to your XBee module. The result should resemble Figure 4-13.

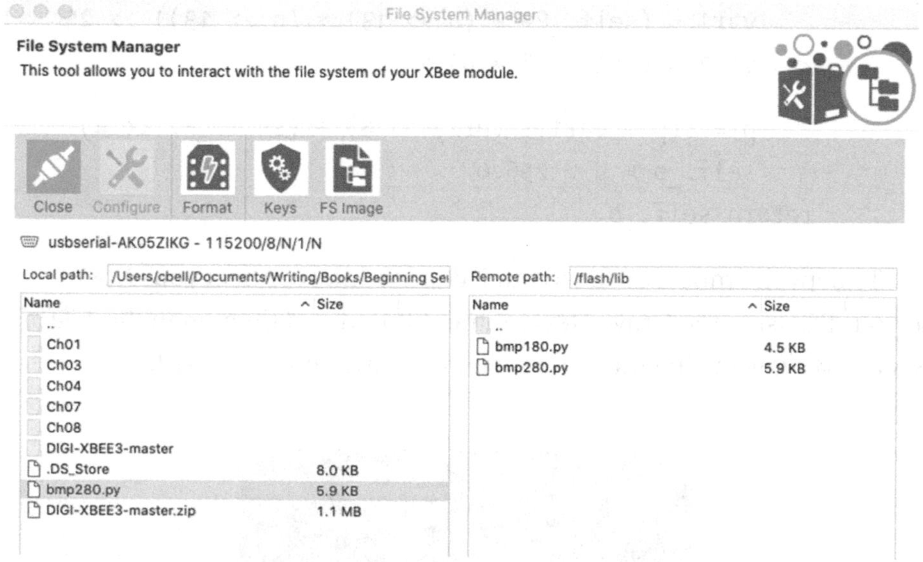

Figure 4-13. *Copying the BMP driver using the File System Manager*

Now, let's test the library using a bare minimal script. We'll use the MicroPython Terminal in interactive mode to do that. But first, click the *Close* button in the upper left and then the *Close* button in the lower right to close the manager.

Next, open the *MicroPython Terminal* from the *Tools* menu and then connect to your XBee module. Recall, you may need to press *ENTER* or *Ctrl+C* to get the >>> prompt. Once there, enter the following lines of code:

```
from machine import I2C
from bmp280 import BMP280
bmp280 = BMP280(I2C(1, freq=100000), 0x77)
print(bmp280.temperature)
print(bmp280.pressure)
```

This code shows how to use the I2C BMP280 driver by telling the driver the sensor is on DIO 1 and use a sample frequency of 100,000 and the I2C address of 0x77 (hexadecimal). We then read the temperature, print it, and repeat for the barometric pressure. The following code shows the results you should see (values may differ):

```
>>> from machine import I2C
>>> from bmp280 import BMP280
>>> bmp280 = BMP280(I2C(1, freq=100000), 0x77)
>>> print(bmp280.temperature)
21.71
>>> print(bmp280.pressure)
102357.4
>>>
```

If you get errors such as address or NOENV errors, double-check your wiring connections. Sometimes the jumper wires can be a little loose. Crimp them on the development board side and the connection should improve.

Now that we have the BMP driver copied and tested, we can write the script for reading the sensor. Listing 4-5 shows the complete code. It should look very familiar as it follows the same template as the previous examples. Take a moment to examine the code to see how it works.

Listing 4-5. Reading a BMP280 Sensor

```
#
# Beginning Sensor Networks 2nd Edition
#
# XBee Sensor Node Example: Reading a BMP280 sensor.
# This demonstrates how to use an I2C driver.
#
# Dr. Charles Bell
#
from machine import I2C
from bmp280 import BMP280

import xbee

# BMP280 address
BMP_ADDR = 0x77
# Target address to send data
TARGET_64BIT_ADDR = b'\x00\x13\xA2\x00\x40\x8C\xCD\x0F'
wait_time = 15 # seconds between measurements
cycles = 10 # number of repeats
bmp280 = BMP280(I2C(1, freq=100000), BMP_ADDR)

for x in range(cycles):
    # Read temperature & barometric pressure
    temp_c = bmp280.temperature
    pressure = bmp280.pressure

    # Convert temperature to proper units
    print("Temperature: %.2f Celsius" % temp_c)
    temp_f = (temp_c * 9.0 / 5.0) + 32.0
    print("Temperature: %.2f Fahrenheit" % temp_f)
    print("Barometric Pressure: %.4f" % pressure)
```

```
# Send data to coordinator
message = "C: %.2f, F: %.2f, B: %.4f" % (temp_c, temp_f,
pressure)
print("Sending: %s" % message)
try:
    xbee.transmit(TARGET_64BIT_ADDR, message)
    print("Data sent successfully")
except Exception as e:
    print("Transmit failure: %s" % str(e))

# Wait between cycles
sleep(wait_time)
```

If you have downloaded the sample code from the Apress book website, you can extract this file and copy it to your PC. Rename it as main. py and then copy it to your XBee using the *File System Manager* like we did earlier. Be sure to copy it to the root folder on the XBee as shown in Figure 4-14.

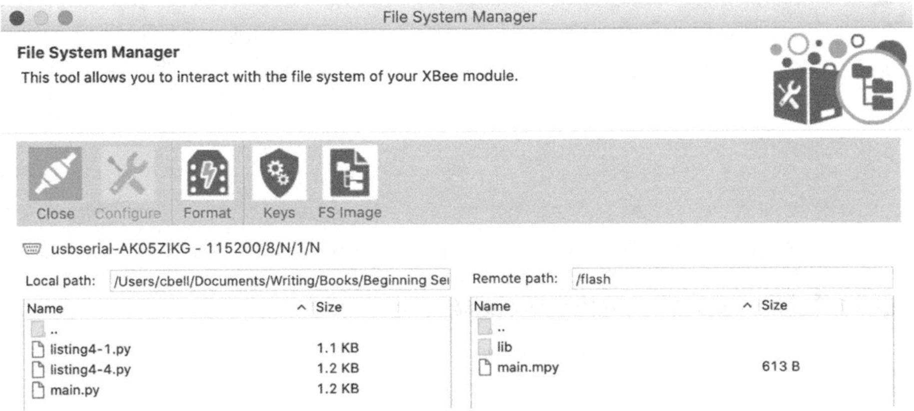

Figure 4-14. *Copying the main.py using the File System Manager*

Now we are ready to test our sensor node.

Testing the XBee Sensor Node

To test the XBee sensor node, you use your XBee coordinator with API firmware installed on the USB adapter connected to your PC. Do this first so the coordinator can be up and running when you start the XBee sensor node. Plug it into your computer, and open the XCTU application. Use XCTU to discover the XBee module and then open a terminal. See Chapter 2 for instructions on how to do this.

Next, connect your power supply to your XBee sensor node. It will take a few moments for the XBee to connect to the coordinator and join the network. Once it does, you start to see the coordinator receiving data, as shown in Figure 4-15.

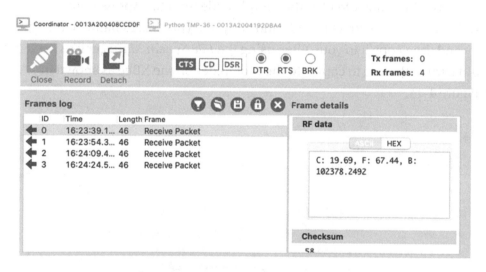

Figure 4-15. *Serial monitor output*

You should see one or more *Receive Packet* packets. We get this packet instead of the broadcast because we're transmitting the packet directly to the coordinator by address. Notice in the image that the first row begins with 7E (hex). This is the start-of-packet delimiter. You should see to the right data that looks like the following. This is a series of hexadecimal values.

```
7E 00 2E 90 00 13 A2 00 41 92 DB A4 94 CC 01 43 3A 20 31 39 2E
36 39 2C 20 46 3A 20 36 37 2E 34 34 2C 20 42 3A 20 31 30 32 33
37 38 2E 32 34 39 32 58
```

You may be wondering where the message is we transmitted. It is there, but hard to see in the hexadecimal output. It appears at the end of the message. The following shows the message from the example:

```
43 3A 20 31 39 2E 36 39 2C 20 46 3A 20 36 37 2E 34 34 2C 20 42
3A 20 31 30 32 33 37 38 2E 32 34 39 32
```

If you convert the hex values to ASCII, you will see the message revealed as follows:

```
C: 19.69, F: 61.44, B: 102378.2492
```

Now, let's take a closer look at the packet. All ZigBee packets have a specific format or layout. Table 4-8 shows the layout for the *Receive Packet* packet.

Table 4-8. *Receive Packet Packet*

Value	Field Name	Notes
7E	Start delimiter	
00 2E	Packet length	47 bytes to checksum
90	Frame type	Receive Packet Indicator
00 13 A2 00 41 92 DB A4	64-bit address	Address of XBee sensor node
94 CC	Reserved	
01	Options	0x01 = Packet was a broadcast packet
N bytes	Received data	Example: 34
N+1 byte	Checksum	Example: 0x58

Take a few moments to study the other samples in the example and check the data samples for the temperature read. If you are really careful, you can place your finger on the BMP280 and observe the temperature change (it should start increasing after one or two more samples). Once you are convinced your XBee sensor node is sending similar data, you can conclude that the sensor node is working correctly.

Component Shopping List

You need a number of components to complete the projects in this chapter. Table 4-9 lists them. Note that the Grove components can be considered option if you do not intend to implement the last example.

Table 4-9. Components Needed

Item	Vendors	Est. Cost USD	Qty Needed
XBee-ZB (ZB) Series 2, 2.5, or 3	www.sparkfun.com	$25.00–48.00	2
	www.adafruit.com		
BMP280 breakout board	www.adafruit.com/product/2651	$9.95–14.95	1
	www.sparkfun.com/products/15440		
BMP280 Grove Sensor (optional)	www.seeedstudio.com/catalogsearch/result/?q=bmp280	$8.95	1
Grove to Female Jumper (optional)	www.seeedstudio.com/Grove-4-pin-Female-Jumper-to-Grove-4-pin-Conversion-Cable-5-PCs-per-PAck.html	$3.90	1
XBee Grove Development Board (optional)	www.digikey.com/products/en?mpart=76000956&v=602	$25.00	1
Breadboard (not mini)	www.sparkfun.com/products/9567	$4.95	1
Breadboard jumper wires	www.sparkfun.com/products/8431	$3.95	1

(continued)

189

Table 4-9. (*continued*)

Item	Vendors	Est. Cost USD	Qty Needed
XBee Explorer Regulated with headers	www.sparkfun.com/products/11373	$10.95	1
TMP36 sensor	www.sparkfun.com/products/10988	$1.50	1
	www.adafruit.com/products/165		
0.10uF capacitor	www.sparkfun.com/products/8375	$0.25	1

Summary

The XBee modules are a fantastic inexpensive way to transmit data wirelessly from one device to another. They can also be used to collect data in the form of hosting (connecting) one or more sensors.

We can either configure the XBee to collect the raw data from the sensor and transmit (broadcast) it to other nodes in the network—without programming. Or, we can use the robust MicroPython programming language to write a script to read the data and format it or perform calculations before sending it to another node.

In this chapter, we saw examples of both forms of hosting sensors. We learned how to connect sensors to the XBee module using an analog temperature sensor (TMP36) as well as an I2C digital sensor (BMP280).

We also saw a short glimpse at the Grove prototyping platform offered by Seeed Studio. Grove makes connecting sensors easier by removing the need to build circuits on a breadboard. We will see more about Grove sensors in later chapters.

In the next chapter, we will explore the Raspberry Pi including a short tutorial on how to use the Raspberry Pi as well as example projects on how to host sensors.

CHAPTER 5

Raspberry Pi–Based Sensor Nodes

Using XBee modules and microcontrollers to host sensors is an economical way to build a sensor network. But what do you do when you need more computational power than a microcontroller can provide? What if you need to convert the data to a different format, incorporate the data in an application, or print a hard copy of the sensor data? In these situations, you likely need a computer that has more processing power, can allow the use of common applications, permits the use of scripting languages, and affords access to peripherals.

Although personal computers are relatively inexpensive, there are a few distinct disadvantages to using personal computers in your sensor networks—especially as sensor nodes. If the sensors are located in areas where mains power is unreliable or unavailable, or where there is a risk of overheating, or where there is simply no room to install a personal computer, you must either transmit the data to another node for processing or store it locally and process it later.

However, there is another limitation to using a personal computer as a sensor node: a personal computer has no general input/output (I/O) ports. You can purchase expansion cards for collecting data, but these are often built for use in server or desktop computers. If you consider the cost of the computer and the data-collection card, the cost of the sensor node becomes uneconomical.

© Charles Bell 2020
C. Bell, *Beginning Sensor Networks with XBee, Raspberry Pi, and Arduino*,
https://doi.org/10.1007/978-1-4842-5796-8_5

So, what do you do in these cases? If only there were a low-cost computer with sufficient processing power and memory that used standard peripherals, supported programmable I/O ports,[1] and had a small form factor. That's exactly what the Raspberry Pi can do.

This chapter explores getting started with the Raspberry Pi, including how to use the system and how to read sensors using the I/O ports. You also explore a few types of sensors and examine the differences in how you read data from them.

Note   We will cover both the Raspberry Pi 3B and the newest Raspberry Pi 4B. You can use either for the projects in this book, but most figures depict the Raspberry Pi 3B and 3B+. Fortunately, all GPIO connections are the same on 3B, 3B+, and 4B boards.

What Is a Raspberry Pi?

The Raspberry Pi is a small, inexpensive personal computer. Although it lacks the capacity for RAM (random access memory) expansion and it doesn't have onboard devices such as CD, DVD, and hard drives,[2] it has everything a simple personal computer requires. That is, it has four USB ports (the Raspberry Pi 3 has 2.0 ports, the Raspberry Pi 4B has two USB 2.0 and two USB 3 ports), an Ethernet port, HDMI video, and even an audio connector for sound.

---

[1]In this case, you require I/O ports that can be used as components in an electronic circuit and can be accessed (read from and written to) by programming libraries.

[2]Most USB hard drives and DVD drives work.

194

The Raspberry Pi has an SD drive[3] that you can use to boot the computer into any of several Linux operating systems. All you need is an HDMI cable and monitor (or DVI cable and monitor with an HDMI to DVI adapter), a USB keyboard and mouse, and a 5V power supply, and you're off and running.

Note   As of this writing, it is not possible to boot from a USB drive on the Raspberry Pi 4B. Blogs suggest this feature will be available soon. When it becomes available, you can easily create a faster boot system by moving the operating system to a USB drive.

You can also power your Raspberry Pi using a USB port on your computer. In this case, you need a USB type A male to micro-USB type B male cable (Raspberry Pi 3B) or a USB type A male to USB-C male cable. Plug the type A side into a USB port on your computer and the micro-USB type B/USB-C side into the Raspberry Pi power port.

The board is available in several versions and comes as a bare board costing as little as $35.00. The newer Raspberry Pi 4B comes in 1GB, 2GB, 4GB, or 8GB variants (only the memory differs) ranging in price from $35.00 to $65.00. It can be purchased online from electronics vendors such as SparkFun and Adafruit. Some Best Buy retailers have started carrying the Raspberry Pi 4B 2GB boards as well as the basic accessories (e.g., case, power supply). Most online vendors have a host of accessories that have been tested and verified to work with the Raspberry Pi. These include small monitors, miniature keyboards, and even cases for mounting the board.

---

[3]Secure Digital (SD): a small removable memory drive the size of a postage stamp. See http://en.wikipedia.org/wiki/Secure_Digital.

In this section, you explore the origins of the Raspberry Pi, take a tour of the hardware connections, and discover what accessories are needed to get started using the Raspberry Pi.

Noble Origins

The Raspberry Pi was designed to be a platform to explore topics in computer science. The designers saw the need to provide inexpensive, accessible computers that could be programmed to interact with hardware such as servo motors, display devices, and sensors. They also wanted to break the mold of having to spend hundreds of dollars on a personal computer and thus make computers available to a much wider audience.

The designers observed a decline in the experience of students entering computer science curriculums. Instead of having some experience in programming or hardware, students are entering their academic years having little or no experience with working with computer systems, hardware, or programming. Rather, students are well versed in Internet technologies and applications. One of the contributing factors cited is the higher cost and greater sophistication of the personal computer, which means parents are reluctant to let their children experiment on the family PC.

This poses a challenge to academic institutions, which have to adjust their curriculums to make computer science palatable to students. They have had to abandon lower-level hardware and software topics due to students' lack of interest or ability. Students no longer wish to study the fundamentals of computer science such as assembly language, operating systems, theory of computation, and concurrent programming. Rather, they want to learn higher-level languages to develop applications and web services. Thus, some academic institutions are no longer offering courses in fundamental computer science.[4] This could lead to a loss of knowledge and skill sets in future generations of computer professionals.

To combat this trend, the designers of the Raspberry Pi felt that, equipped with the right platform, youth could return to experimenting with personal computers as in the days when PCs required a much greater commitment to learning the system and programming it in order to meet your needs. For example, the venerable Commodore 64, Amiga, and early Apple and IBM PC computers had very limited software offerings. Having owned a number of these machines, I was exposed to the wonder and discovery of programming at an early age.[5]

WHY IS IT CALLED RASPBERRY PI?

The name was partly derived from design committee contributions and partly chosen to continue a tradition of naming new computing platforms after fruit (think about it). The Pi portion comes from Python, because the designers intended Python to be the language of choice for programming the computer. However, other programming language choices are available.

The Raspberry Pi is an attempt to provide an inexpensive platform that encourages experimentation. The following sections explore more about the Raspberry Pi, including the models available, required accessories, and where to buy the boards.

---

[4]My alma mater has made this very sad transition. I mourn for the loss of knowledge.

[5]My first real computer was an IBM PCjr. I followed it by building my own IBM PC AT computer, complete with a 10MB hard drive. Ah, those were the glory days of personal computers!

Models

There are currently two model classifications of Raspberry Pi boards: Model A and Model B. The early Model A boards were the first mass-produced boards with 256MB of RAM, one USB port, and no Ethernet port. This was followed closely by the first Model B board, which had 512MB of RAM, two USB ports, and an Ethernet port. Figure 5-1 shows the version 3 variant of the Model A board designated as Raspberry Pi 3A+.

Figure 5-1. *Raspberry Pi 3A+ (courtesy of the Raspberry Pi Foundation)*

WHAT DOES THE "+" MEAN?

The "+" symbol in the model designation indicates it is a newer release of the same version only with some improvements. For example, the 3B+ included a slightly faster processor and a host of minor refinements. Typically, the boards are effectively the same and you may not notice a difference, but if you want the "latest" or "better" board, you'll want the one with the "+" designation.

Figure 5-2 shows the version 3 Model B board designated as Raspberry Pi 3B+. Notice the board is a bit larger and has more connections.

Figure 5-2. *Raspberry Pi 3B+ (courtesy of the Raspberry Pi Foundation)*

Figure 5-3 shows the latest Model B board designated as the Raspberry Pi 4B. The figure depicts some of the improvements from the 3B+ model including more RAM, USB-C power, two HDMI ports, and USB 3 support. Plus, it is the fastest Raspberry Pi computer to date!

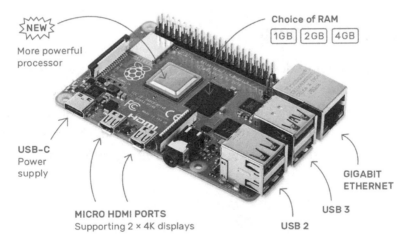

Figure 5-3. *Raspberry Pi 4B (courtesy of the Raspberry Pi Foundation)*

You can often find the Raspberry Pi 3A+ at online retailers and auction sites for a bit less than the Raspberry Pi 3B+ board. The newest Raspberry Pi 4B are still in high demand so you may pay more for those boards but shop around to find retailers that offer the board at suggested retail prices of $35 (1GB), $45 (2GB), $55 (4GB), or $91 (8GB). If you plan to use the Raspberry Pi for experimentation and do not need the extra memory to run memory-intensive applications, you can use the Raspberry Pi 3A+.

Tip   It is recommended to use the Raspberry Pi 3B+ or the newest, the Raspberry 4B, for the projects in this book. The examples in this chapter and the remaining chapters use the Model B variant—either the Raspberry Pi 3B+ or 4B.

A Tour of the Board

Not much larger than a deck of playing cards, the Raspberry Pi board contains a number of ports for connecting devices. This section presents a tour of the board. If you want to follow along with your board, hold it with the Raspberry Pi logo faceup. I will work around the board clockwise. Figure 5-4 depicts a drawing of the board with all the major connectors labeled.

Figure 5-4. *Raspberry Pi 3B+ (courtesy of the Raspberry Pi Foundation)*

In the center of the near side, you see an HDMI connector. To the left of the HDMI connector is the micro-USB power connector and to the right is the camera connector and audio connector. The power connector is known to be a bit fragile on some boards, so take care plugging and unplugging it. Be sure to avoid putting extra strain on this cable while using your Raspberry Pi.

On the left side of the board, we see the location of the WiFi chip. On the underside of the board is where the microSD card connector is located. Interestingly, most cases are not designed to protect the microSD card. When installed, the microSD card protrudes a few centimeters out of the board.

On the far side of the board is the general-purpose input/output (GPIO) header (a double row of 20 pins), which can be used to attach to sensors and other devices. You will work with this connector later in this chapter.

On the right side of the board are four USB connectors and the Ethernet connector. An external powered USB hub connected to the USB ports on the Raspberry Pi can power some boards, but it is recommended that you use a dedicated power supply connected to the micro-USB connector.

Caution   Because the board is small, it is tempting to use it in precarious places like in a moving vehicle or on a messy desk. Ensure that your Raspberry Pi is in a secure location. The micro-USB power and microSD card slots seem to the most vulnerable to damage.[6]

Take a moment to examine the top and bottom faces of the board. As you can see, components are mounted on both sides. This is a departure from most boards that have components on only one side. The primary reason the Raspberry Pi has components on both sides is that it uses multiple layers for trace runs. This permits the board to be much smaller and enables the use of both surfaces for mounting its components. This is probably the most compelling reason to consider using a case—to protect the components on the bottom of the board and thus avoid shorts and board failure.

Required Accessories

The Raspberry Pi is sold as a bare system board with no case, power supply, or peripherals. Depending on how you plan to use the Raspberry Pi, you need a few commonly available accessories. If you have been accumulating spares like me, a quick rummage through your stores may locate most of what you need.

---

[6]Guess how I know this. Yep, I've had to repair both connectors on various boards at least once.

If you want to use the Raspberry Pi in console mode (no graphical user interface), you need a USB power supply (USB-C for the Raspberry Pi 4B), a keyboard, and an HDMI cable and monitor. The power supply should have a minimal rating of 2500mA or greater for the Raspberry Pi 3B, 3B+ boards, and 3000mA USB-C (15 Watt) or greater for the Raspberry Pi 4B. If you want to use the Raspberry Pi with a graphical user interface, you also need a mouse.

If you have to purchase these items, stick to the commonly available brands and models without extra features. For example, avoid the latest multifunction keyboard and mouse. Chances are they require drivers that are not available for the various operating system choices for the Raspberry Pi.

You also must have a microSD card. I recommend a 16GB or higher version. Recall that the microSD is the only onboard storage medium available. You will need to put the operating system on the card, and any files you create will be stored on the card.

If you want to use sound in your applications, you also need a set of powered speakers that accept a standard 3.5mm audio jack. Finally, if you want to connect your Raspberry Pi to the Internet, you need access to a WiFi access port or an Ethernet hub.

Recommended Accessories

I highly recommend at least adding small rubber or silicone self-adhesive bumpers to keep the board off your desk. On the bottom of the board are many sharp prongs that can come into contact with conductive materials, which can lead to shorts or, worse, a blown Raspberry Pi. These bumpers are available at most home-improvement and hardware stores.

If you plan to move the board from room to room or you want to ensure that your Raspberry Pi is well protected against accidental damage, you should consider purchasing a case to house the board. Many cases are available, ranging from simple snap-together models to models made from laser-cut acrylic or even milled aluminum. The following list includes several excellent choices, complete with vendor links.

Pi Tin

The Pi Tin from SparkFun is a basic, clear, two-piece case that snaps together. It uses light pipes to make reading the status LEDs easier and has cutouts for the GPIO header. It is inexpensive and an excellent choice for the budget minded. It is made for the Raspberry Pi 3B+. Figure 5-5 shows the Pi Tin from SparkFun (www.sparkfun.com/products/13103).

Figure 5-5. *Pi Tin (courtesy of SparkFun)*

Aluminum Heatsink Case for Raspberry Pi 4B

The Aluminum Heatsink Case for Raspberry Pi 4B from SparkFun is an example of a good metal case with heat sink made for the Raspberry Pi 4B. It is made with two pieces of metal that have built-in heat sink pads that bolt together. It is a minimalist design that doesn't make the board much larger (but is heavier). It is a bit more expensive than the basic plastic cases and provides better cooling and protection, and, to me, it also looks better than others. Figure 5-6 shows the Aluminum Heatsink Case from SparkFun (www.sparkfun.com/products/15773). I have also seen versions of this design that have one or two fans on top if you need extra cooling.

Figure 5-6. *Aluminum Heatsink Case for Raspberry Pi 4B (courtesy of SparkFun)*

Pibow Coupé

The Pibow Coupé (www.adafruit.com/products/2083) is available from Adafruit and other vendors and comes in various colors for both the Raspberry Pi 3B+ and 4B (there are also available for other Raspberry Pi boards). It is made from pieces of acrylic, but they're arranged in a novel slice pattern. To assemble the Pibow, you place the Raspberry Pi on the bottom plate and stack the layers, finishing with the top plate. Key layers provide cutouts for all ports including the GPIO header. Four nylon fasteners secure the case as a unit. Once assembled, the case looks great and is very solid. Figure 5-7 shows the Pibow Coupé for Raspberry Pi 3B+ from Adafruit.

Figure 5-7. *Pibow Coupé (courtesy of Adafruit)*

Tip   If none of these cases meet your needs or aesthetic choices, you can find a host of options from Adafruit at `www.adafruit.com/category/395`. You're sure to find what you want there!

Aside from a case, you should also consider purchasing (or pulling from your spares) a powered USB hub. The USB hub power module should be 2500mA or more (some suggest you need only a 1500mA, but more is better especially if you want to connect USB devices to your board). A powered hub is required if you plan to use USB devices that draw a lot of power, such as a USB hard drive or a USB soft missile launcher.

Where to Buy

The Raspberry Pi has been available in Europe for some time. It is getting easier to find, but very few brick-and-mortar stores stock the Raspberry Pi. Fortunately, a number of online retailers stock it, as well as a host of accessories that are known to work with the Raspberry Pi. The following are some of the more popular online retailers with links to their Raspberry Pi catalog entry:

- SparkFun (`www.sparkfun.com/categories/233`)
- Adafruit (`www.adafruit.com/category/105`)
- PiShop.us (`www.pishop.us`)
- The PiHut (ships internationally) (`www.thepihut.com`)

The next section presents a short tutorial on getting started using the Raspberry Pi. If you have already learned how to use the Raspberry Pi, you can skip to the following section to begin learning how to connect sensors to your board.

Raspberry Pi Tutorial

The Raspberry Pi is a personal computer with a surprising amount of power and versatility. You may be tempted to consider it a toy or a severely limited platform, but that is far from the truth. With the addition of onboard peripherals like USB, WiFi, Ethernet, and HDMI video, the Raspberry Pi has everything you need for a lightweight desktop computer. This is especially true for the Raspberry Pi 4B with 2GB or 4GB or 8GB of RAM—those make nice desktop computers!

Furthermore, if you consider the addition of the GPIO header, the Raspberry Pi becomes more than a simple desktop computer and fulfills its role as a computing system designed to promote hardware experimentation.

The following sections present a short tutorial on getting started with your new Raspberry Pi, from a bare board to a fully operational platform. A number of excellent works cover this topic in much greater detail. If you find yourself stuck or wanting to know more about beginning to use the Raspberry Pi and more about the Raspbian operating system, see *Computing with the Raspberry Pi* by B. Schell (Apress, 2019). If you want to know more about using the Raspberry Pi in hardware projects, an excellent in-depth resource is *Advanced Raspberry Pi* by W. Gay (Apress, 2018).

Getting Started

As mentioned in the "Required Accessories" section, you need a microSD card (16GB is recommended), a USB power supply rated at 2500mA or better with a male micro-USB connector (or USB-C for Raspberry Pi 4B), a keyboard, a mouse (optional), and an HDMI cable and monitor or a DVI monitor with an HDMI adapter. However, before you can plug these things in to your Raspberry Pi and bask in its brilliance, you need to create a boot image for your microSD card.

Installing a Boot Image

The process of installing a boot image involves choosing an image, downloading it, and then copying it to your microSD (hence simply SD) card. The following sections detail the steps involved.

Choosing the Image

The first thing you need to do is decide which operating system variant you want to use. There are several excellent choices, including the standard Raspbian "buster" variant. Each is available as a compressed file called an image or card image. You can find a list of recommended images along with links to download each on the Raspberry Pi foundation download page: `www.raspberrypi.org/downloads`. The following images are a few of the images available at the site:

- *Raspbian Buster*: The basic or default image. It is based on Debian and contains a graphical user interface, development tools, and rudimentary multimedia features.

- *Ubuntu MATE*: Provides a complete, familiar (if you know Ubuntu), desktop environment for basic desktop computing.

- *Ubuntu Core*: A hardened Ubuntu core operating system for uses where security is of great importance.

- *Ubuntu Server*: A scaled down version of the Ubuntu server for running server applications.

If you are just starting with the Raspberry Pi, you should use the Raspbian image. This image is also recommended for the examples in this book.

There are two ways to go about making an image for your Raspberry Pi. The easiest way is to use a special boot loaded called New Out Of the Box Software (NOOBS), which is used to help streamline the setup of your board. The other is to download a specific image and format the SD card with the image. I will show you both methods in the following sections.

Installing Using NOOBS

This is by far the easiest method to build your SD card. All you need to do is download and unzip NOOBS from www.raspberrypi.org/downloads/noobs/, format an SD card, and then copy the files. Once you boot from NOOBS, you will be guided to install the default operating system (Raspbian) or another of your choice (requires additional downloads).

There are some excellent resources for learning how to install Raspbian with NOOBS. There is a nice video at www.raspberrypi.org/help/videos/#noobs-setup.

There is also a complete setup guide that steps you through the process. See projects.raspberrypi.org/en/projects/raspberry-pi-setting-up. For those completely new to working with the Raspberry Pi or have never done any formatting or SD card setup, those links are the way to go. However, I will summarize the steps here to those who feel comfortable working with their PC:

1. Download the NOOBS binary from www.raspberrypi.org/downloads/noobs/. There are two options: a smaller one that will use the Internet to download during the install and a larger one that has the Raspbian image. If you have a slow Internet connection or cannot connect your Raspberry Pi to the Internet during install, you should choose the version with Raspbian (not the Lite one). This is a Zip file that you can download and unzip.

2. You must format the SD card. For best results, use a 16GB or 32GB card. You can use any application you want, but the best I've found is to download SD Formatter from `www.sdcard.org/downloads/formatter/index.html`, which is available for most platforms.

3. Next, locate the files from the NOOBS archive that you unzipped earlier and copy all of them to the SD card.

4. Insert the SD card into your Raspberry Pi; connect your mouse, keyboard, and monitor; and power it on.

5. Follow the onscreen instructions to install Raspbian.

That's it! Once again, the online tutorial and videos are much more detailed, but now that you have a sense of the process, following the online tutorial will be very easy.

Installing Raspbian

If you want to install Raspbian to the SD card or don't want to use NOOBS, you can download Raspbian from `www.raspberrypi.org/downloads/raspbian/`. For this book, you should choose the one named "Raspbian Buster with desktop and recommended software". Unlike the NOOBS option, this file is a bootable image file that requires a special process to build a new bootable image on your SD card.

Tip   See `www.raspberrypi.org/documentation/installation/installing-images/README.md` for a tutorial on installing images for the Raspberry Pi.

Once you have downloaded the image, you first unzip the file and then transfer (sometimes called "write") the image to your SD card. There are a variety of ways to do this. The following sections describe some simplified methods for a variety of platforms. You must have an SD card reader/writer connected to your computer. Some systems have SD card drives built in (Lenovo laptops, Apple laptops and desktops, and so on).

Windows

To create the SD card image on Windows, you can use the Win32 Disk Imager software from Launchpad (`https://launchpad.net/win32-image-writer`). Download this file, and install it on your system. Unzip the image if you haven't already, and then insert your SD card into your SD card reader/writer. Launch the Win32 Disk Imager application, select the image in the top box, and then click *WRITE* to copy the image to the SD.

Caution   The copy process overwrites anything already on the SD card, so be sure to copy those photos to your hard drive first!

Mac OS X

To create the SD card image on the Mac, download the image and unzip it. Insert your SD card into your SD card reader/writer. Be sure the card is formatted with FAT32. Next, open the System report. (Hint: Use the *Apple* menu ➤ *About This Mac.*)

Click the card reader if you have a built-in card reader, or navigate through the *USB* menu and find the SD card. Take note of the disk number. For example, it could be disk4.

Next, open the *Disk Utility* and unmount the SD card. You need to do this to allow the *Disk Utility* to mount and connect to the card. Now things get a bit messy. Open a terminal, and run the following command, substituting the disk number for n and the path and name of the image file for <image_file>:

```
sudo dd if=<image_file> of=/dev/diskn bs=1m
```

At this point, you should see the disk-drive indicator flash (if there is one), and you need to be patient. This step can run for some time with no user feedback. You will know it is complete when the command prompt is displayed again.

Linux

To create the SD card image using Linux, you need to know the device name for the SD card reader. Execute the following command to see the devices currently mounted:

```
df -h
```

Next, insert the SD card or connect a card reader, and wait for the system to recognize it. Run the command again:

```
df -h
```

Take a moment to examine the list and compare it to the first execution. The "extra" device is your SD card reader. Take note of the device name, for example, /dev/sdc1. The number is the partition number. So, /dev/sdc1 is partition 1, and the device is /dev/sdc. Next, unmount the device (I will use the previous example):

```
umount /dev/sdc1
```

Use the following command to write the image, substituting the device name for <device> and path and name of the image file for <image_file> (e.g., /dev/sdc and my_image.img):

```
sudo dd bs=4M if=<image_file> of=<device>
```

At this point, you should see the disk-drive indicator flash (if there is one), and you may need to be patient. This step can run for some time with no user feedback. You will know it is complete when the command prompt is displayed again.

Booting Up

To boot your Raspberry Pi, insert the SD card with the new image and plug in your peripherals. Wait to plug in the USB power last. Because the Raspberry Pi has no On/Off switch, it will start as soon as power is supplied. The following describes the process you will see and follow to boot Raspbian for the first time. The setup steps are executed only once (but you can change the settings later if you want).

When you power on the Raspberry Pi, the system bootstraps and then starts loading the OS. You see a long list of statements that communicate the status of each subsystem as it is loaded, followed by a welcome banner. You don't have to try to read or even understand all the rows presented,[7] but you should pay attention to any errors or warnings.

You may also see a message about resizing the boot device and your Raspberry Pi may reboot. This is automatic and nothing to be concerned about. In fact, it is ensuring the boot volume is expanded to the maximum size your microSD supports. When the boot sequence is complete, you will see the Raspbian desktop as shown in Figure 5-8.

---

[7]They go by so fast; it is unlikely you can read them anyway. Basically, they're noise unless there is an error, and those usually appear in the last few lines displayed.

Figure 5-8. *Raspbian desktop*

Notice there is a dialog open in the center of the desktop. Once again, these steps will execute only once on first boot. The steps include the following:

- *Welcome to Raspberry Pi*: Click *Next* to start the setup. You can cancel and run the setup later.

- *Set Country*: Choose your country, language, and timezone. Click *Next* to continue.

- *Set Password*: Choose the password for the default user. Click *Next* to continue.

- *Set Up Screen*: If your screen shows a black rectangle around the edge, you can tick the checkbox to have the video adapter synchronize properly on the next boot. Click *Next* to continue.

- *Select WiFi Network*: Choose your WiFi access point to connect to the Internet. You can click *Skip* to skip the step or click *Next* to continue.

- *Update Software*: If you have connected to the Internet, you can optionally download and install updates for Raspbian. This is highly recommended, and when you choose this option, you will go through several more informational dialogs that show you the progress of the updates. You can click *Skip* to skip the step. Click *Next* to continue when done.

- *Setup Complete*: The setup is done. Click *Next* to continue, and if you selected any options that require a reboot, the system will reboot now.

Figure 5-9 shows each step starting from the upper left working left to right.

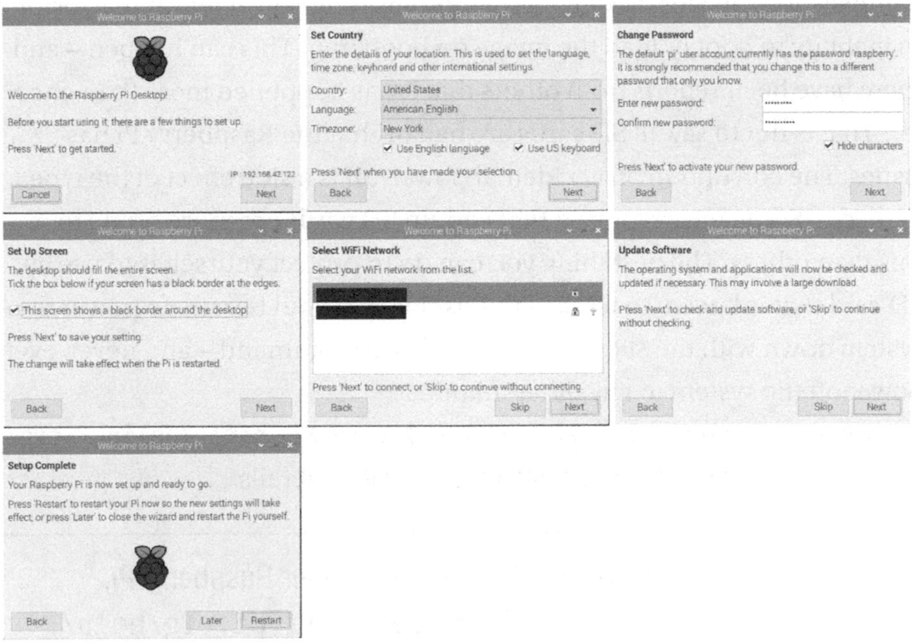

Figure 5-9. *First boot setup sequence*

When the system next boots, you will see the Raspbian desktop with your settings configured. If you set up a WiFi connection, it will automatically reconnect. Nice.

Care and Feeding of the SD Card

Imagine this scenario. You're working away on creating files, downloading documents, and so on. Your productivity is high, and you're enjoying your new low-cost, super-cool Raspberry Pi. Now imagine the power cable accidentally gets kicked out of the wall, and your Raspberry Pi loses power. No big deal, yes? Well, most of the time.

The SD card is not as robust as your hard drive. You may already know that it is unwise to power off a Linux system abruptly, because doing so can cause file corruption. Well, on the Raspberry Pi, it can cause a complete loss of your disk image. Symptoms range from minor read errors to inability to boot or load the image on bootstrap. This can happen—and there have been reports from others that it has happened more than once.

That is not to say all SD cards are bad or that the Raspberry Pi has issues. The corruption on accidental power-off is a side effect of the type of media. Some have reported that certain SD cards are more prone to this than others. The best thing you can do to protect yourself is to use an SD card that is known to work with Raspberry Pi and be sure to power the system down with the sudo shutdown -h now command—and never, ever power off the system in any other manner.

You can also make a backup of your SD card. See http://elinux.org/RPi_Beginners#Backup_your_SD_card for more details.

Tip   If you need any help at all when using your Raspberry Pi, there are very helpful articles at www.raspberrypi.org/help/, and the official documentation is at www.raspberrypi.org/documentation/.

GPIO Pin Mapping

The Raspberry Pi has a special hardware feature called the general-purpose I/O (GPIO) header. It is located in the upper-left portion of the board and resembles a floppy drive header.[8] The header consists of two rows of 20 male pins.

All GPIO pins can be configured as either input (reading) or output (writing). The voltage read can be used for digital I/O. Specifically, when the voltage is less than 1.7V, the value is 0; greater than 1.7V is a value of 1. For output pins, you can set the voltage from 0 to 3.3V.

Figure 5-10 shows the layout of the GPIO header of the Raspberry Pi 3B+ (and 4B).

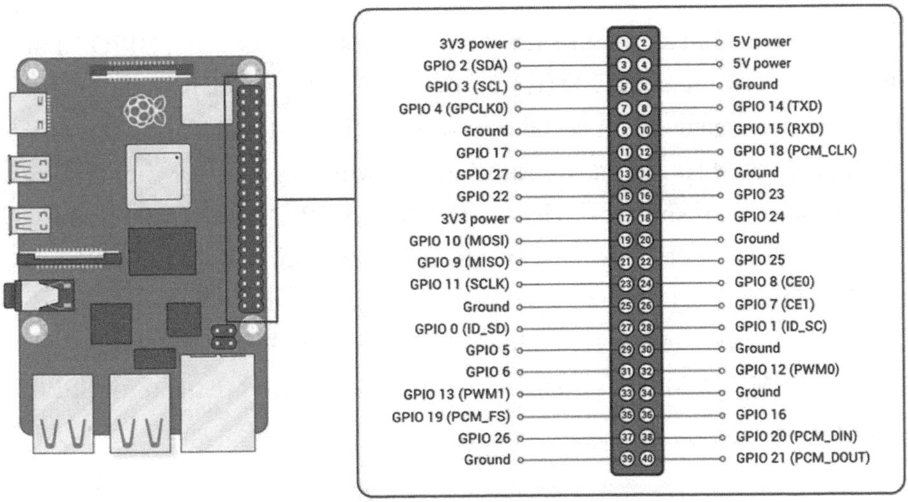

Figure 5-10. GPIO pin assignments (courtesy of raspberrypi.org)

---

[8]What? Never heard of floppy drives? The original ones were indeed floppy. For bonus points, what was the storage capacity of the 8″ dual-sided, double-density floppy medium?

Notice that the pins are not named in order. For example, there are GPIO 1 and GPIO 2, but they aren't next to each other on the header (GPIO 1 is on the right at position or pin 28 and GPIO 2 is on the left at header position or pin 3). This naming may be a source of confusion because it doesn't follow what you would expect, nor does it mirror the neat layout of microcontrollers like the Arduino. Thus, when working with the GPIO header, you should check your pin choices carefully.

Caution   Do not mistake pin number for GPIO number. Always double-check the name of the connection you want to use with the position or pin number it uses on the header. For example, GPIO 16 is not at pin 16, it is at pin 36.

Also notice that some pins have two names. For example, GPIO 14 and GPIO 15 are also named TXD (transmit) and RXD (receive), respectively. These pins can be used for serial communication. GPIO 18 and GPIO 21 are labeled PWM (pulse wave modulation), which is used for powering LEDs, motors, and similar devices. GPIO 0 and GPIO 1 are also named SDA and SCL, respectively, and are used for I2C communication. I2C is a fast digital protocol that uses two wires (plus power and ground) to read data from circuits (or devices). Finally, GPIO 9, GPIO 10, and GPIO 11 are also named MISO, MOSI, and SCKL, respectively, and are used for SPI communication.

Caution   All pins are limited to 3.3V. Attempting to send more than 3.3V will likely damage your Raspberry Pi. Always test your circuit for maximum voltage before connecting to your Raspberry Pi. You should also limit current to no more than 5mA.

Adafruit has a nifty accessory that makes working with the GPIO a lot easier. It is a small PCB with the layout of the GPIO imprinted on it. It's called the GPIO reference card and can be found at https://www.adafruit.com/product/2263. Figure 5-11 shows what the card looks like (rotated for brevity and enlarged for detail). I recommend buying one the next time you order from Adafruit.

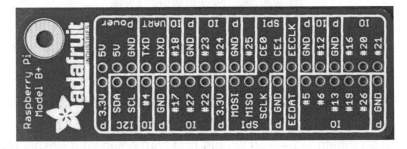

Figure 5-11. *GPIO reference card (courtesy of Adafruit)*

If you want to ensure that you are protecting your Raspberry Pi from higher voltage and current, most expansion boards have additional circuitry for power protection. A number of expansion boards are available, including the Gertboard (www.element14.com/community/docs/DOC-51726?ICID=raspberrypi-gert-banner). This book does not cover the use of expansion boards, but you may want to consider using expansion boards if your sensors involve complex circuitry that requires more ports or additional features like motor controllers or relays.

Rather than expansion boards, here you use a simple prototyping board instead. The one I've chosen is called the Pi T-Cobbler Plus breakout board and is available from Adafruit (www.adafruit.com/products/2028). It features a ribbon cable and a breadboard-compatible connector with the pins arranged in the same order as those on the Raspberry Pi. Figure 5-12 shows the Pi T-Cobbler Plus. The board does not provide any additional functionality other than making it easier to work with GPIO by connecting the Raspberry Pi to a breadboard.

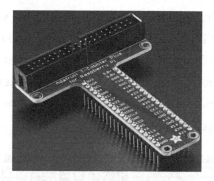

Figure 5-12. *Pi T-Cobbler Plus breakout board (courtesy of Adafruit)*

Caution   Whenever you want to connect sensors or circuits to the GPIO header—either directly (not recommended) or via a breakout board (recommended)—you should first shut down your Raspberry Pi. This may sound inconvenient and even like a pain when you're working through a project, but it is the best method for ensuring that you do not accidentally short some pins or make the wrong connections.

I've found it best to make the connections with the Raspberry Pi powered off and to take a couple of passes verifying the connections are connected to the right pins. It is very easy to connect to the wrong pin—there are so many, and they are in close proximity. The odd arrangement of the pin numbers doesn't help either. Properly admonished, let's jump into working with your Raspberry Pi GPIO and hook up some sensors!

A smaller alternative of the Pi T-Cobbler places the ribbon connector in the center and takes up less room on a breadboard. This version is called the Pi Cobbler Plus and is available at www.adafruit.com/products/2029. Figure 5-13 shows the Pi Cobbler Plus.

Figure 5-13. *Pi Cobbler Plus breakout board (courtesy of Adafruit)*

Note   The Pi T-Cobbler Plus and Cobbler Plus may come partially assembled. You may need to solder (or have someone solder) the breadboard headers to the breakout board.

You can also find several variants on the Pi T-Cobbler Plus and Cobbler Plus on popular online auction and electronics discount sites. One fine example is the SparkFun Pi Wedge from SparkFun (`www.sparkfun.com/products/13717`). This board has a similar layout to the Pi T-Cobbler Plus but arranges the GPIO pins in a slightly different order (but is printed on the PCB for easy reference).

Whichever breakout board you choose, it will permit you to connect your Raspberry Pi to a breadboard, making experimentation with electronics (and sensors) much easier. It won't protect you against accidental power overload, so be mindful of that. The following projects use a breadboard; so, if you have a Pi Cobbler, connect your Raspberry Pi to your breadboard.

Now that you know how to connect hardware to the GPIO pins, you need to know what software is required to allow you to write programs to read from and write to those pins.

Required Software

You need to install a number of software packages to work with the GPIO header. This section examines the required software for using the Python programming language. You can use C and Scratch language extensions, but Python is the best to learn because it is syntactically easy to read and easy to master. Also, the designers of the Raspberry Pi chose Python initially as its only language, so you are likely to find more examples on the Internet to which to refer for ideas and help. We have already seen a tutorial on MicroPython, and the Python we will be using on the Raspberry Pi is nearly identical at least in terms of how we write the code.

By default, the Raspbian includes Python and a host of supporting libraries. But it does not include everything you need. To fully access all the GPIO features, you also need the Raspberry Pi Python GPIO module (RPi. GPIO) for communicating with the GPIO pins, pySerial for connecting to serial devices, and python-smbus for accessing the I2C bus. If you use an expansion board, the manufacturer may also have special modules you need to install. No special modules are needed for the Pi T-Cobbler breakout board. If you are interested in writing games, you may also want to install the python-game package.

But first, you need some prerequisites. You must install additional Python modules using the following commands. Your Raspberry Pi needs to be connected to the Internet to execute these commands, because they download the modules from the Internet:

```
sudo apt-get update
sudo apt-get install python-dev
```

To install the RPi.GPIO module, pySerial, and python-smbus modules, issue the following commands:

```
sudo apt-get install python-rpi.gpio
sudo apt-get install python-serial
sudo apt-get install python-smbus
```

Now that you have the software loaded, it's time to experiment! If you haven't plugged in your breakout board, shut down your Raspberry Pi (using `sudo shutdown -h now` from a terminal or the shutdown from the *Raspbian* menu) and connect the breakout board, and then restart your Raspberry Pi.

Project: Hardware "Hello, World!"

In this project, you will build a "Hello, World!" project for the Raspberry Pi. This project uses an LED that the Raspberry Pi turns on and off through calls to a Python library function. That's a fine project for getting started, but it does not relate to how sensors could be used.

Thus, in this section, you will use a modified LED project where we simply trigger an LED by adding a sensor. In this case, you still keep things simple by using what is arguably the most basic of sensors: a pushbutton. The goal is to illuminate the LED whenever the button is pushed.

Hardware Connections

Let's begin by assembling a Raspberry Pi, Pi T-Cobbler from Adafruit (optional), breadboard, one LED, and one pushbutton. You start with the Raspberry Pi powered down.

Plug the breakout board into the breadboard. Wire the 3.3V pin, not the 5V pin, to the breadboard power rail, the ground pin to the ground rail, and a loop around to the other side of the board. This connection provides power to the breakout board. Thus, you do not need a breadboard power supply.

Place the LED and pushbutton to one side of the breadboard, as shown in Figure 5-14. Remember, the longest leg on the LED is the positive side. Notice that I show the Raspberry Pi and the Pi Cobbler breakout board but not the cable to the Raspberry Pi, for brevity. The Raspberry Pi is connected via a ribbon cable to the Pi Cobbler Plus (you can use the

T-Cobbler Plus in the same manner). Be sure to align the cable so the colored stripe (indicating pin 1) is aligned with pin 1 on the connector. Do this for both the Raspberry Pi and the breakout board.

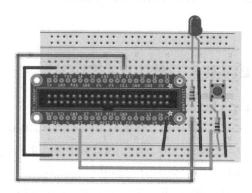

Figure 5-14. *Diagram of an LED with a pushbutton*

Caution   Connecting the 5V pin to any other pin on the GPIO header can damage your Raspberry Pi. If you use a sensor that requires 5V input, be sure to double-check that its maximum output is 3.3V or less.

You're almost there. Now wire a jumper from the power rail to one side of the pushbutton, and wire the other side of the pushbutton to pin GPIO 17 on the breakout board (pin 6 on the left side). Wire the LED to ground on the breadboard and a 150 Ohm resistor (colors: brown, green, brown, gold). The other side of the LED should be wired to pin GPIO 7 on the breakout board (see Figure 5-13).

You also need a resistor to pull the button low when the button is not pressed. Place a 10K Ohm resistor (colors: brown, black, orange, gold) on the side of the button with the wire to pin GPIO 17 and ground. The shortest side of the LED is the ground side. This side should be the one connected to the resistor. It does not matter which direction you connect the resistor. It is used to limit the current to the LED. Check the drawing again to ensure that you have a similar setup.

A COOL GADGET

One of the coolest gadgets for working with the Raspberry Pi is the Raspberry Pi Dish mounting plate from Adafruit (www.adafruit.com/products/942). This small acrylic plate has space for a full-sized breadboard and a Raspberry Pi. It even has mounting holes for bolting the Raspberry Pi to the plate and small rubber feet to keep the plate off the work surface. The following figure shows the mounting plate in action. Note that this image shows an older Raspberry Pi board, but all of the latest Raspberry Pi boards fit.

Although you can make your own Raspberry Pi mounting plate from Lexan or Plexiglas, the Adafruit product is a notch better than what you can make yourself. For about $23.00, you can keep your Raspberry Pi and breadboard together and avoid scratches to your table and shorts caused by components on the bottom of the Raspberry Pi coming into contact with conductive material.

Writing the Script

The script you need for this project requires two pins: one output and one input. The output pin will illuminate the LED, and the input pin will detect the pushbutton engagement. You connect positive voltage to one side of the pushbutton and the other side to the input pin. When you detect voltage on the input pin, you tell the Raspberry Pi processor to send positive voltage to the output pin. In this case, the positive side of the LED is connected to the output pin.

Now, open a text editor with the following command to create a new Python module (or use the editor of your choice such as the Thonny Python IDE from the *Programming* menu):

```
nano hello_raspi.py
```

When the editor opens, type the following code to set up the GPIO module and establish the pin assignments:

```
import RPi.GPIO as GPIO    # GPIO library
LED_PIN = 7
BUTTON_PIN = 17
GPIO.setmode(GPIO.BCM)
GPIO.setup(LED_PIN, GPIO.OUT)
GPIO.setup(BUTTON_PIN, GPIO.IN)
```

As you can see in the drawing in Figure 5-13, the input pin is pin GPIO 17 and the output pin is pin GPIO 7. Let's use a variable to store these numbers so you do not have to worry about repeating the hard-coded numbers (and risk getting them wrong). Use the GPIO.setup() method to set the mode of each pin (GPIO.IN, GPIO.OUT).

You also need to place the code to turn on the LED when the input pin state is *HIGH* (==1). In this case, you use the GPIO.output() method to set the output pin to *HIGH* when the input pin state is *HIGH* (1) and similarly set the output pin to *LOW* when the input pin state is *LOW* (0).

We encapsulate the code in a try...except...finally block to capture the keyboard interrupt and clean up the GPIO assignments at the end (turns off output pins). The following code shows the statements needed:

```
GPIO.output(LED_PIN, GPIO.LOW)
while 1:
    if GPIO.input(BUTTON_PIN) == 1:
        GPIO.output(LED_PIN, GPIO.HIGH)
    else:
        GPIO.output(LED_PIN, GPIO.LOW)
```

Tip   Recall, indentation is important in Python. Indented statements form a code block. For example, to execute multiple statements for an if statement, indent all the lines that you want to execute when the conditions are evaluated as true.

Now let's see the entire script in Listing 5-1, complete with proper documentation.

Listing 5-1. Simple Sensor Script

```
#
# RasPi Simple Sensor - Beginning Sensor Networks 2nd Edition
#
# For this script, we explore a simple sensor (a pushbutton)
  and a simple response to sensor input (a LED). When the
  sensor is activated (the button is pushed), the LED
  is illuminated.

import RPi.GPIO as GPIO
```

```python
# Pin assignments
LED_PIN = 7
BUTTON_PIN = 17

# Setup GPIO module and pins
GPIO.setmode(GPIO.BCM)
GPIO.setup(LED_PIN, GPIO.OUT)
GPIO.setup(BUTTON_PIN, GPIO.IN)

# Set LED pin to OFF (no voltage)
GPIO.output(LED_PIN, GPIO.LOW)
try:
    # Loop forever
    while 1:
        # Detect voltage on button pin
        if GPIO.input(BUTTON_PIN) == 1:
            # Turn on the LED
            GPIO.output(LED_PIN, GPIO.HIGH)
        else:
            # Turn off the LED
            GPIO.output(LED_PIN, GPIO.LOW)
except KeyboardInterrupt:
    print("Done!")
finally:
    GPIO.cleanup()
```

Tip   To save yourself a lot of typing, you can download the code for this chapter or any of the examples in the book from the Apress website.

Once you've entered the script as written or downloaded it onto your Raspberry Pi, you are ready to run it. To run the Python script, launch it as follows:

```
python3 hello_raspi.py
```

Note   I use `python3` and later `pip3`, which execute for Python version 3. Use this on the latest version of Raspbian. Older releases or other distributions may not support Python3, in which case you can omit the "3" from the command.

Testing the Sensor

Once the script is started, what do you see on your Raspberry Pi? If you've done everything right, the answer is "Nothing." It's just staring back at you with that one dark LED—almost mockingly. Now, press the pushbutton. Did the LED illuminate? If so, congratulations: you're a Raspberry Pi Python GPIO programmer!

If the LED did not illuminate, hold the button down for a second or two. If that does not work, check all of your connections to make sure you are plugged in to the correct runs on the breadboard and that your LED is properly seated with the longer leg connected to the resistor and to pin GPIO 7.

On the other hand, if the LED stays illuminated, try reorienting your pushbutton 90 degrees. You may have set the pushbutton in the wrong orientation.

Try the project a few times until the elation passes. If you're an old hand at Raspberry Pi, that may be a very short period. If this is all new to you, go ahead and push that button and bask in the glory of having built your first sensor node!

Now, how do you stop it? Because you coded an endless loop (intentionally), you need to use `Ctrl+C` to cancel the script. This will not harm your Raspberry Pi or the GPIO or the circuitry.

The next section examines a more complicated sensor node using a temperature and humidity sensor.

For More Fun

To make the script a bit more user-friendly, you can change the code to exit more gracefully. The following are some interesting suggestions:

- Loop for no more than 10,000 iterations. Hint: Use a variable and increment it.

- Use a second LED, and set up the code to toggle both LEDs so that when the button is pressed, one illuminates and the other turns off.

- Use a *second* button so that when the *second* button is pressed, the loop terminates. Hint: Use `sys.exit()` or `break`.

Hosting Sensors with Raspberry Pi

The GPIO pins of the Raspberry Pi make it an ideal platform for hosting sensors. Because most sensors need very little in the way of supporting components, you can often host multiple sensors on one Raspberry Pi. For example, it is possible to host a temperature sensor or even multiple temperature, barometric, humidity, and other sensors for sampling weather conditions from a given site.

ANALOG ONLY?

The Raspberry Pi GPIO pins do not support digital signals—they are all analog pins. This is one of the many small cost considerations that help keep the price down. To access digital signals, you need an analog-to-digital controller. If you encounter a situation in which you want to use a digital sensor, you can look at the 12-bit ADC—4 Channel with Programmable Gain Amplifier from Adafruit (`www.adafruit.com/products/1083`).

As I discussed in Chapter 1, a host of sensors are available. SparkFun and Adafruit each have excellent websites that provide a great deal of information about the products they sell. You can also google for examples of using analog sensors with the Raspberry Pi.

Although this chapter demonstrates how to host sensors with the Raspberry Pi using a breakout board connected to a breadboard, the restriction of using analog only and 3.3V maximum voltage makes the Raspberry Pi less versatile than the Arduino. Add to that the fact that you must run Python scripts using root, and hosting sensors on a Raspberry Pi becomes a bit harder to do (but not overly so) and more cumbersome than doing so with an Arduino.

You can still connect sensors directly to the Raspberry Pi, as you see in the next section. However, you may want to consider using the Raspberry Pi as an aggregate node using an XBee connected to XBee-hosted sensors or even Arduino-hosted sensors. But first, let's see how to connect a sensor to the Raspberry Pi and read some data.

To make things easier, you use a project similar to the one you used in Chapter 3. More specifically, you build a sensor node with a Raspberry Pi and a single temperature sensor. Before you begin, let's discuss some safety factors related to working with the Raspberry Pi GPIO header.

Project: Building a Raspberry Temperature Sensor Node

The next project you explore is another temperature sensor example. This time, you use a temperature sensor that utilizes a special digital protocol to send. As mentioned previously, the Raspberry Pi does not have an analog-to-digital converter.

Although this may be yet another temperature sensor node, the project also gives you experience in reading digital sensors that use the one-wire protocol—which is built into the Raspberry Pi GPIO. Specifically, you use the DS18B20 digital temperature sensor available from SparkFun and Adafruit.

In some respects, the hardware portion of this project is easier than the previous project because there are fewer parts; but the code is more complex. Let's begin with the hardware setup.

Hardware Setup

The hardware needed for this project is a breadboard, a breakout board for the Raspberry Pi (such as Pi Cobbler+), a DS18B20 digital temperature sensor, a 0.10mF capacitor, and some jumper wires. Insert your breakout board into the breadboard, aligning pin 1 (3.3V) to position 1 on the breadboard. This will help you orient the pins more easily by using the numbers on the breadboard to quickly find the pins without counting (and miscounting) them. Figure 5-15 shows the correct orientation of the breakout board. I omit the ribbon cable for brevity.

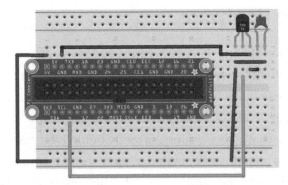

Figure 5-15. *Connecting a temperature sensor to a Raspberry Pi*

Next, install the temperature sensor to the right of the breakout board with pin 1 to the left. If you hold the sensor such that the flat side is facing you, pin 1 is on the left of the flat side of the sensor. Connect the 0.10mF capacitor between pin 3 (right) and pin 2 (center) or use jumpers as shown in Figure 5-15.

Connect power from the breakout board to the power rail of the breadboard and ground from the breakout board to the ground rail of the breadboard, as shown in Figure 5-14. Next, connect power to pin 3 of the sensor and ground to pin 1. Finally, connect pin 2 of the sensor to GPIO 4. Why GPIO 4? Because the sensor is a digital sensor, and you can use the one-wire facility (because it uses only a single data wire) to read the data. Cool, eh?

WHAT ABOUT THE WATERPROOF VERSION?

If you have the waterproof version of the DS18B20 digital temperature sensor, the sensor has four wires. Typically, the wires are colored red, black, white or yellow or orange, and copper or silver. The copper or silver wire is not used; it is part of the shielding. The red wire is connected to power, the black wire is connected to ground, and white or yellow or orange is the data wire.

Testing the Hardware

Once you have double-checked your connections, go ahead and boot up your Raspberry Pi. Because the sensor uses the one-wire protocol to read data, you can use features built into the Raspberry Pi to read data from the sensor. This isn't nearly as elegant as writing a Python script, but it will permit you to see that all is working correctly before you start programming.

You will use a special utility called modprobe. This utility loads (or unloads) modules into the Linux kernel. In the vernacular of other operating systems, it loads device drivers. The modprobe utility can do far more than just load modules (drivers); to learn more about it, see http://linux.die.net/man/8/modprobe.

The modules you want to load are named w1-gpio and w1-therm. The w1-gpio module registers and loads the new sensor connected to pin GPIO 4. The w1-therm module registers and loads a module that has support for temperature sensors.

To use the modules, we must enable them by editing the need to add the following line to /boot/config.txt, before rebooting your Pi. Use the command sudo nano /boot/config.txt and add the following line anywhere in the file (near the end is best with the other examples). Note that this enables PIN4 as the default. You can specify the pin you want to use by adding the option gpiopin=N to the line. Edit the file and then shut down your Raspberry Pi prior to wiring the sensor. For more information about editing the file including adding multiple sensors, see https://pinout.xyz/pinout/1_wire#.

dtoverlay=w1-gpio

When you use modprobe to load each of these modules (w1-gpio first), the Raspberry Pi enables data collection on pin GPIO 4 and reads data from the sensor and stores it in a file. The file is named starting with 28 and followed by a unique file name. If you had other sensors, there would be a file for each one.

Note   The file is created whether there is a sensor created or not, but to see meaningful data, you should shut down, wire the sensor, and then reboot before checking the file.

The file contains the raw data read from the sensor. You can open this file and inspect its contents to see the raw data. You will likely see data that makes little sense, but we will decipher the data in the code. Listing 5-2 shows the commands you use to load the modules and then inspect the file along with the output that shows the name of the file created.

Listing 5-2. Testing the Temperature Sensor Hardware

```
pi@raspberrypi:~ $ sudo modprobe w1-gpio
pi@raspberrypi:~ $ sudo modprobe w1-therm
pi@raspberrypi:~ $ cd /sys/bus/w1/devices/28-1a1970a65dff
pi@raspberrypi:/sys/bus/w1/devices/28-1a1970a65dff $ ls
driver  hwmon  id  name  power  subsystem  uevent  w1_slave
pi@raspberrypi:/sys/bus/w1/devices/28-1a1970a65dff $ cat w1_slave
3e 01 55 00 7f ff 0c 10 8d : crc=8d YES
3e 01 55 00 7f ff 0c 10 8d t=19875
pi@raspberrypi:/sys/bus/w1/devices/28-1a1970a65dff $ cat w1_slave
3f 01 55 00 7f ff 0c 10 ce : crc=ce YES
3f 01 55 00 7f ff 0c 10 ce t=19937
pi@raspberrypi:/sys/bus/w1/devices/28-1a1970a65dff $ cat w1_slave
3f 01 55 00 7f ff 0c 10 ce : crc=ce YES
3f 01 55 00 7f ff 0c 10 ce t=19937
pi@raspberrypi:/sys/bus/w1/devices/28-1a1970a65dff $ cat w1_slave
3e 01 55 00 7f ff 0c 10 8d : crc=8d YES
3e 01 55 00 7f ff 0c 10 8d t=19875
```

```
pi@raspberrypi:/sys/bus/w1/devices/28-1a1970a65dff $ cat w1_slave
5e 01 55 00 7f ff 0c 10 6c : crc=6c YES
5e 01 55 00 7f ff 0c 10 6c t=21875
```

Notice that in the example I ran the cat[9] (concatenate and print) utility to print out the data in the file several times. I placed my hand over the sensor while running the utility in order to simulate an increase in temperature. Can you see how the values changed?

Software Setup

The software required for this project is already installed. You will write a short Python script to read the data from the sensor and display it to standard out (the terminal window). Begin by importing the required modules as shown here:

```
import glob
import os
import time
```

Next, you use the Python module named os to make a system call to run the two modprobe commands from previous example. In this case, you use the os.system() method:

```
os.system('modprobe w1-gpio')
os.system('modprobe w1-therm')
```

---

[9]In case you were curious, there is no dog command.

Before you jump into the code to read the file, let's make it easier by declaring a few variables to contain the directory and the file name. In this case, you don't know the file name, but you do know the directory. You can use the glob module to search for files matching a wildcard in a specific directory. You do so with the following code:

```
base_dir = '/sys/bus/w1/devices/'
datadir = glob.glob(base_dir + '28*')[0]
datafile = datadir + '/w1_slave'
```

Notice that you know the parent directory and the starting portion of the directory. The glob module does all the work for you. If there were multiple directories matching the wildcard, the call would return a list. In this case, you have only one sensor, so you can expect only one directory.

Now you are ready to read the data from the file. You can design your own code however you like, but I've elected to write two methods (defined with the def directive). I will use one method to open the file and read all the lines (data) in the file and another method to use the data read to calculate the temperature in Celsius and Fahrenheit. Let's look at the first method. I've named it read_data():

```
def read_data():
    f = open(datafile, 'r')
    lines = f.readlines()
    f.close()
    return lines
```

As you can see, it is very straightforward and reads like the steps you would imagine. Specifically, you open the file, read all the lines in the file, close the file, and return what you read.

Now let's look at the second method. I've named it get_temp():

```
def get_temp():
    temp_c = None
    temp_f = None
    lines = read_data()

    while not lines[0].strip().endswith('YES'):
        time.sleep(0.25)
        lines = read_data()
    pos = lines[1].find('t=')
    if pos != -1:
        temp_string = lines[1][pos+2:]
        temp_c = float(temp_string) / 1000.00
        temp_f = temp_c * 9.00 / 5.00 + 32.00
    return temp_c, temp_f
```

This method has two parts. The first part reads the data from the file using the previous method and checks the first line (arrays and lists start with index 0 in Python) to see if the status is YES. If it isn't, you read the line from the file again and repeat until you find a file that has the correct, valid status.

The next part looks in the file for the data read. In this case, you look for a substring that starts with t= and then read the data after that and convert it to Celsius and Fahrenheit. You return those values for use in printing the data.

Let's put it all together. Listing 5-3 shows the completed script, including documentation. Open an editor, create a file named pi_temp.py, and enter the source code shown. Feel free to modify it to suit your mood or particular brand of humor.

Take some time to explore this completed code until you understand how it all works. There are several Pythonisms[10] in this file, so do not be intimidated if some of the code isn't clear right away. For example, look at the print statement in the next-to-last line. This statement could be written differently, but what is shown is the accepted standard most Python programmers adopt.

Listing 5-3. The pi_temp.py Script

```
# RasPi Temperature Sensor - Beginning Sensor Networks Second
  Edition
#
# For this script, we explore connecting a digital temperature
  sensor to the Raspberry Pi and reading the data. We display
  the temperature in Celsius and Fahrenheit.

# Import Python modules (always list in alphabetical order)
import glob
import os
import time

# Issue the modprobe statements to initialize the GPIO and
# temperature sensor modules
os.system('modprobe w1-gpio')
os.system('modprobe w1-therm')
```

---

[10]Meaning it is the preferred way. Sometimes code can be described as "pythonic," which also means it was written in the preferred Python style or with specific syntax. Learning to program Python with Pythonisms comes second to everyone who learns Python, but it is the mark of a true Pythonista to be able to know the difference.

```
# Use glob to search the file system for files that match the
  prefix.
base_dir = '/sys/bus/w1/devices/'
# Save the directory to the file.
datadir = glob.glob(base_dir + '28*')[0]
# Create the full path to the file
datafile = datadir + '/w1_slave'

# Procedure for reading the raw data from the file.
# Open the file and read all of the lines then close it.
def read_data():
    f = open(datafile, 'r')
    lines = f.readlines()
    f.close()
    return lines

# Read the temperature and return the values found.
def get_temp():
    # Initialize the variables.
    temp_c = None
    temp_f = None
    lines = read_data()

    # If the end of the first line ends with something other
      than 'YES'
    # Try reading the file again until 'YES' is found.
    while not lines[0].strip().endswith('YES'):
        time.sleep(0.25)
        lines = read_data()

    # Search the second line for the data prefixed with 't='
    pos = lines[1].find('t=')
```

```
# A return code of -1 means it wasn't found.
if pos != -1:

    # Get the raw data located after the 't=' until the end
        of the line.
    temp_string = lines[1][pos+2:]

    # Convert the scale for printing
    temp_c = float(temp_string) / 1000.00

    # Convert to Fahrenheit
    temp_f = temp_c * 9.00 / 5.00 + 32.00

# Return the values read
return temp_c, temp_f

# Main loop. Read data then sleep 1 second until cancelled with
    CTRL+C.
while True:
    temp_c, temp_f = get_temp()
    print("Temperature is {0} degrees Celsius, "
            "{1} degrees Fahrenheit.".format(temp_c, temp_f))
    time.sleep(1)
```

Take a few minutes to double-check your file to make sure you have typed all the statements correctly. If you have an editor on your desktop or laptop, you might want to use it to create and edit the file using the syntax-checking feature to catch any errors. The script won't run correctly on your desktop or laptop, but checking the syntax can be a big help.

Now that the software is written, let's see what it does.

Testing the Sensor

As in the previous project, you need to run the script as root using sudo python ./pi_temp.py. When you do so, you may not see any output right away, but within a second or two, you should start seeing output like that shown here:

```
$ python ./pi_temp.py
Temperature is 20.062 degrees Celsius, 68.11160000000001
degrees Fahrenheit.
Temperature is 20.187 degrees Celsius, 68.3366 degrees
Fahrenheit.
Temperature is 21.25 degrees Celsius, 70.25 degrees Fahrenheit.
Temperature is 21.437 degrees Celsius, 70.5866 degrees
Fahrenheit.
Temperature is 21.875 degrees Celsius, 71.375 degrees
Fahrenheit.
Temperature is 21.687 degrees Celsius, 71.0366 degrees
Fahrenheit.
Temperature is 21.5 degrees Celsius, 70.7 degrees Fahrenheit.
Temperature is 21.187 degrees Celsius, 70.1366 degrees
Fahrenheit.
Temperature is 21.0 degrees Celsius, 69.8 degrees Fahrenheit.
```

If you get syntax errors, go back and check that you have entered every line exactly as shown in Listing 5-3. Python is really good at providing enough information to fix most syntax errors. If you encounter any, you see not only what the error is but also the line number of the file where the error occurs. Once you have fixed the error, try the script again until you see the correct output.

The next section explores a more complex project in which the Raspberry Pi communicates with a digital sensor that uses the I2C protocol.

For More Fun

To make this project a bit more fun, try connecting a second sensor (of the same type), and print out the data including the sensor from which the data was read. Hints: You can use the serial number embedded in the file to identify the sensor, and you should connect them in parallel. That is, each sensor connects to the same ground (pin 1) and power connections (pin 3). The data output (pin 2) of each sensor is wired to the same GPIO pin.

For extra-special fun, modify the code to detect when the sensor read has failed and print an appropriate error message. Can you spot where this is possible?[11] I'll give you a hint: what happens in the get_temp() method if t= is not found?

Project: Building a Raspberry Barometric Pressure Sensor Node

This project demonstrates how to use a different type of sensor—one that uses the I2C bus. For this, you need four wires to connect and facilities to communicate to the sensor. Fortunately, the Raspberry Pi has such a facility, but it takes a bit of work to make it available. You will use the BMP280 sensor module from Adafruit (www.adafruit.com/products/2651). Figure 5-16 shows the module from Adafruit.

---

[11]Hardcore code junkies and hackers alike love this stuff.

Figure 5-16. *BMP280 I2C sensor (courtesy of Adafruit)*

The I2C feature is disabled by default on the Raspberry Pi. Before you look at the hardware setup for this project, let's enable the I2C feature. You can do this easily by opening the Raspberry Pi configuration tool under the *Preferences* menu. Click the *Interfaces* tab and tick the I2C checkbox as shown in Figure 5-17.

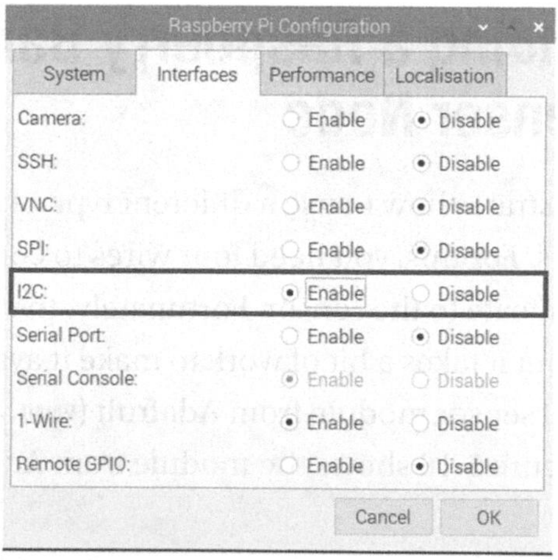

Figure 5-17. *Enable the I2C interface*

Next, we need to install the I2C tools and utilities. You can do so by opening a terminal and entering the following command:

```
$ sudo apt-get install i2ctools
```

That's it! You are now ready to begin connecting the hardware. The hardware portion of this project is easier than that in the previous project because there are fewer parts, but the code is more complex. Let's begin with the hardware setup.

Hardware Setup

The hardware needed for this project is a breadboard, a breakout board for the Raspberry Pi (such as Pi Cobbler+), a BMP280 sensor module, and some jumper wires. Insert your breakout board into the breadboard, aligning pin 1 (3.3V) to position 1 on the breadboard.

Connect the 5V pin on the Raspberry Pi Cobbler+ board to power on the sensor module. Connect the ground wire to the ground wire on the sensor. The I2C pins on the Raspberry Pi are pins GPIO 0 (SDA) and GPIO 1 (SCL). Connect wires from these pins to corresponding pins on the sensor module (SDA goes to SCK on the BMP280, SCL goes to SDI on the BMP280). Figure 5-18 shows the physical connections.

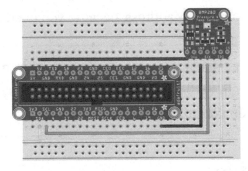

Figure 5-18. Connecting the BMP280 sensor to a Raspberry Pi

Testing the Hardware

Once you have double-checked your connections, go ahead and boot up your Raspberry Pi. When you have logged in, run the following command:

```
sudo i2cdetect -y 1
```

This command uses a utility to detect any sensors on the I2C bus. I say sensors because you can use the I2C protocol to connect multiple sensors. Each sensor has its own address. The following code shows the output of running the command:

```
$ sudo i2cdetect -y 1
     0  1  2  3  4  5  6  7  8  9  a  b  c  d  e  f
00:          -- -- -- -- -- -- -- -- -- -- -- -- --
10: 10 -- -- -- -- -- -- -- -- -- -- -- -- -- -- --
20: -- -- -- -- -- -- -- -- -- -- 2a -- -- -- -- --
40: -- -- -- 43 -- -- -- -- -- -- -- -- -- -- -- --
50: -- -- -- -- -- -- -- -- -- -- -- -- -- -- -- --
60: -- -- -- -- -- -- -- -- -- -- -- -- -- -- -- --
70: -- -- -- -- -- -- -- 77
```

Notice in the example that the graph shows data in column 7 for row 70 and a value of 77. This means the sensor is at address 0x77 (in hexadecimal). If other sensors were installed, they would appear in the graph as well. Remember this address, because you need it for the code.

Note   If you do not see any devices in the output from this command, try it with **-y 0** and see if this produces any output. For example, use **sudo i2cdetect -y 0**.

Software Setup

The software required for this project requires the Python libraries you installed earlier as well as a special library designed to communicate with the BMP280. You need a special module because the I2C protocol is bidirectional, and most I2C components are designed to respond to one or more commands to evoke data generation. In this case, you need a Python module that supports the BMP280 sensor module.

The library has been created by the nice people at Adafruit and is available for download from the Python package repository (PyPi[12]). You can find comprehensive documentation for the library at `https://readthedocs.org/projects/adafruit-circuitpython-bmp280/downloads/pdf/latest/`.

To download the module and install it, issue the `sudo pip3 install adafruit-circuitpython-bmp280` command in a terminal. This command will download and install the library and all of its dependent libraries for you. How cool is that? Note that `sudo` may not be needed for some Raspbian distributions. The following shows an excerpt of the installation.

```
$ sudo pip3 install adafruit-circuitpython-bmp280
Looking in indexes: https://pypi.org/simple, https://www.
piwheels.org/simple
Collecting adafruit-circuitpython-bmp280
  Downloading https://www.piwheels.org/simple/adafruit-
  circuitpython-bmp280/adafruit_circuitpython_bmp280-3.1.2-py3-
  none-any.whl
...
Successfully installed Adafruit-Blinka-3.9.0 Adafruit-
PlatformDetect-2.2.0 Adafruit-PureIO-1.0.4 adafruit-
circuitpython-bmp280-3.1.2 adafruit-circuitpython-
busdevice-4.1.4
```

---

[12]See `https://pypi.org/`.

I2C SENSOR LIBRARIES

A number of I2C sensor modules are available. However, corresponding Python (or other language) libraries have not been built for all of them. You should research the availability of a library to support the sensor prior to deciding to use it in your network. If you are a programmer, you may be able to adapt existing code (libraries) to add support for the new sensor by examining the datasheet and writing appropriate commands to interact with the sensor.

You will use the Adafruit_BMP280 code module to read data from the I2C bus. The Python module has support for a number of I2C modules, including the BMP280, and is based on the Adafruit_I2C module, which is also in this directory. To use the Adafruit_BMP280 library, you import the class for the BMP280 module and its dependencies as follows:

```
import board
import busio
import time
import adafruit_bmp280
```

Next, you need to initialize the class. In this case, you use the helper class named I2C from the busio module to configure use for the I2C interface. Next, we use that instance to initialize the BMP280 class as follows. You assign the instance to a variable so you can use it to make calls to the library later. The default address is 0x77. If you saw a different address from the i2cdetect utility, pass the address in hexadecimal with the parameter address=<hexadecimal> to the constructor for the BMP280 class.

```
i2c = busio.I2C(board.SCL, board.SDA)
bmp280 = adafruit_bmp280.Adafruit_BMP280_I2C(i2c)
```

There is one more option we may want to do: calibrate the module for use at our location. We do this by passing in the hPa value for our location. In this case, we use the standard for much of the United States (but may differ in some areas).

```
bmp280.sea_level_pressure = 1013.25
```

Once that is done, you only need to read the values using the attributes provided by the library and then print out the information. The major attributes you use are shown here:

```
bmp280.temperature
bmp280.pressure
bmp280.altitude
```

Now let's put it all together. Listing 5-4 shows the complete listing of the script. Open an editor, create a file named pi_bmp280.py, and enter the source code shown.

As you can see, with the help of the new library, your Python script becomes very short and very easy to write. This is a great example of how members of the Python community freely (well, most anyway) exchange ideas and share code for common and not-so-common tasks.

Listing 5-4. The pi_bmp280.py Script

```
#
# RasPi I2C Sensor - Beginning Sensor Networks 2nd Edition
#
# For this script, we connect to and read data from an
# I2C sensor. We use the BMP280 sensor module from Adafruit
# or Sparkfun to read barometric pressure and altitude
# using the Adafruit I2C Python code.
```

```
import board
import busio
import time

import adafruit_bmp280

# First, we configure the BMP280 class instance for our use.
i2c = busio.I2C(board.SCL, board.SDA)
bmp280 = adafruit_bmp280.Adafruit_BMP280_I2C(i2c)

# Calibrate the pressure (hPa) at sea level for our location
# in this case the East coast US
bmp280.sea_level_pressure = 1013.25

# Read data until cancelled
while True:
    try:
        # Read the data
        pressure = float(bmp280.pressure)
        altitude = bmp280.altitude

        # Display the data
        print("The barometric pressure at altitude {0:.2f} "
              "is {1:.2f} hPa.".format(pressure, altitude))

        # Wait for a bit to allow sensor to stabilize
        time.sleep(3)

    # Catch keyboard interrupt (CTRL-C) keypress
    except KeyboardInterrupt:
        break
```

Now that the software is written, let's see what it does.

Testing the Sensor

As in the previous project, you need to run the script as root using `python3` `./pi_bmp280.py`. When you do so, you may not see any output right away; but within a second or two, you should start seeing output like that shown here:

```
$ python3 ./pi_bmp280.py
The barometric pressure at altitude 1007.25 is 50.37 hPa.
The barometric pressure at altitude 1007.28 is 50.24 hPa.
The barometric pressure at altitude 1007.24 is 50.40 hPa.
The barometric pressure at altitude 1007.24 is 50.74 hPa.
The barometric pressure at altitude 1007.22 is 50.45 hPa.
The barometric pressure at altitude 1007.25 is 50.27 hPa.
The barometric pressure at altitude 1007.25 is 49.83 hPa.
The barometric pressure at altitude 1007.26 is 50.19 hPa.
The barometric pressure at altitude 1007.27 is 50.16 hPa.
```

The next section explores a more complex project in which the Raspberry Pi is a data collector (an aggregate node) hosting sensor data via an XBee wireless connection to a sensor node. You will reuse the sensor node created in Chapter 4. If you have not read through and succeeded in building the projects in Chapter 4, you may want to go back and complete the last project before proceeding.

For More Fun

The BMP280 sensor reads the barometric pressure, as you have seen, but it also reads temperature. Change the previous code to read the temperature data as well as the barometric pressure.

Project: Creating a Raspberry Pi Data Collector for XBee Sensor Nodes

This project combines what you have learned about the Raspberry Pi in this chapter and the XBee in Chapter 2 and the XBee sensor node from Chapter 4. More specifically, you use a Raspberry Pi and a remote sensor connecting the sensor with the Raspberry Pi using XBee modules. You know the basics from Chapter 4, so let's dive right in.

XBee Sensor Node

Follow the text from Chapter 4 to create the XBee sensor node. As a reminder, this node is constructed as shown in Figure 5-19.

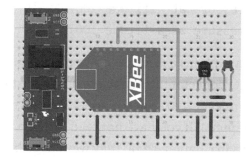

Figure 5-19. *XBee sensor node*

If you have not configured the sensor node from Chapter 4 or if you need to reset the module, you should begin by ensuring the latest firmware is loaded and use the settings shown in Table 5-1. Note that you do not need the *IR* setting from Chapter 4, but it's OK if you want to reuse the module you used in that chapter.

Table 5-1. *XBee Sensor Node Options and Values*

Code	Setting Name	Description	Value
D3	AD3/DIO3	Trigger analog or digital data recording	2—ADC
ID	PAN ID	Id for the network	8088
NI	Node Identifier	Name for the node	TMP36
V+	Supply Voltage Threshold	Supply voltage	FFFF (always send)

Tip   Be sure to use "TMP36" for the node id (NI). Your project will not return results unless the node id matches the value in the following code.

The coordinator node should be configured similarly with the latest firmware loaded and the settings shown in Table 5-2.

Table 5-2. *XBee Coordinator Options and Values*

Code	Setting Name	Description	Value
ID	PAN ID	Id for the network	8088
NI	Node Identifier	Name for the node	Coordinator

Hardware

The hardware setup for this project is very easy. All you need to do is use the serial interface that is part of the GPIO header to connect to the XBee's serial interface. It's that easy! Do not power on your Raspberry Pi or sensor node until after all hardware connections are complete and verified correct. I will tell you when to power up later in this section.

You need a breadboard and an XBee breadboard adapter like the one you used in Chapter 4; plug it into the breadboard. Then plug in your Raspberry Pi breadboard adapter. Now wire the 3.3V and ground to the pins on your XBee adapter. If you are using the XBee Explorer Regulated from SparkFun (`www.sparkfun.com/products/11373`), you can connect to the 5V power because the XBee Explorer can regulate the power (hence the name). The SparkFun board as shown has the serial interface pins arranged in a header on one side of the board. It also has onboard voltage regulation to protect the XBee in the event you accidentally connect the 5V pin instead of the 3.3V pin to the explorer.

Note   If you have soldered breadboard headers to the XBee adapter but have not soldered headers for the serial I/O header, take a moment to do that. You can connect the XBee via the other header, but the consolidated header makes it a bit easier.

Next, wire the TXD (output) pin GPIO 14 on the Raspberry Pi Cobber+ to the DIN pin on the XBee Explorer. Then wire the RXD (input) pin GPIO 15 on the Raspberry Pi Cobble+ to the DOUT pin on the XBee Explorer. Figure 5-20 shows the completed connections.

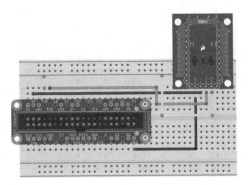

Figure 5-20. *Connecting an XBee to a Raspberry Pi*

If you are not using the SparkFun adapter, be sure to check the documentation on your adapter to make sure you are connecting the right pins. Take your coordinator XBee module and insert it into the XBee.

There is one more thing you need to do. The designers of the Raspberry Pi included the facility to connect a serial terminal to the Raspberry Pi at boot time. There is a setting in the preferences that allows you to enable this interface. It is disabled by default.

To turn on the serial interface, open a terminal and enter the command sudo raspi-config. This opens the Raspberry Pi configuration tool. To enable the serial interface, select the *Interfacing Options* in raspi-config. The easiest way is to use the arrow keys and highlight the selection and press *ENTER*.

On the next screen, choose the *Serial* option, then follow the next three screens to disable login shell over serial (choose *No*), enable the hardware serial port (choose *Yes*), and then press *ENTER* on the confirmation page.

When control returns to the main screen, use the *Tab* key to select *Finish* and then *Yes* to allow the Raspberry Pi to reboot. Figure 5-21 shows the sequence of screens and the options you should choose.

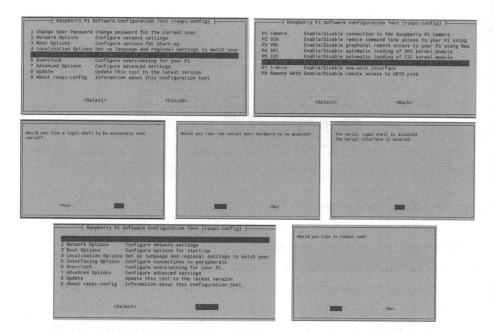

Figure 5-21. *Enabling the serial interface (raspi-config)*

After your machine reboots, we can install the software we need for the project.

Software

Before you can write your script, you need to download and install a special library. The software needed for this project is a special Python module provided by Digi and developed specifically to encapsulate (make it easy to use) the XBee protocols and frame-handling mechanisms. To install the module, issue the following command:

```
$ sudo pip3 install digi-xbee
Looking in indexes: https://pypi.org/simple, https://www.
piwheels.org/simple
Collecting digi-xbee
```

```
Downloading https://www.piwheels.org/simple/digi-xbee/digi_
xbee-1.3.0-py3-none-any.whl (224kB)
    100% |████████████████████████████████| 225kB 10kB/s
Collecting srp (from digi-xbee)
  Downloading https://www.piwheels.org/simple/srp/srp-1.0.15-
  py3-none-any.whl
Requirement already satisfied: pyserial>=3 in /usr/lib/python3/
dist-packages (from digi-xbee) (3.4)
Requirement already satisfied: six in /usr/lib/python3/dist-
packages (from srp->digi-xbee) (1.12.0)
Installing collected packages: srp, digi-xbee
Successfully installed digi-xbee-1.3.0 srp-1.0.15
```

This library has a host of classes used to work with XBee modules and has numerous examples you can use for your own projects. We are going to see just one of the ways you can use the library. For more details about other features in the library, you can download the Digi-Python Programmers Guide using the following URL: `https://xbplib.readthedocs.io/en/latest/getting_started_with_xbee_python_library.html`

If you want to see the code for the library itself, you can see it on GitHub at `https://github.com/digidotcom/xbee-python`.

Once the library is installed, you can start using it. For this example, we will use the basic XBeeDevice library along with the helper libraries IOLine and IOMode as follows:

```
from digi.xbee.devices import XBeeDevice
from digi.xbee.io import IOLine, IOMode
```

Before you instantiate those classes, let's make some definitions to make maintenance easier and improve readability of the source code. In this case, you create a reference to the serial port, baud rate, the name of the remote node (NI from sensor node setup), the analog line where the sensor is connected on the remote node, and the sampling rate:

```
SERIAL_PORT = "/dev/ttyS0"
BAUD_RATE = 9600
# Analog pin we want to monitor/request data
ANALOG_LINE = IOLine.DIO3_AD3
SAMPLING_RATE = 15
```

Note   If you have changed the baud rate of your XBee module, you must use that baud rate here.

Now you can instantiate the XBeeDevice class as follows. Pass in the serial port and baud rate we defined previously.

```
device = XBeeDevice(SERIAL_PORT, BAUD_RATE)
```

Now we're ready to get to the core of the program. We will use two techniques that you may not have seen before using methods. First, we will create a method to connect to the ZigBee network and retrieve an instance of the remote XBee module class that we can use to read data. Second, we will create a second method to be used to read data at the sampling rate. This is called a callback method since it is used by the libraries to "call back" to your program whenever the sampling rate dictates reading data.

The following code shows the method we use to set up the remote device named get_remote_device(). Here, we connect to the network and then ask the network to search for our remote node by node id (NI), and if found, we capture its address, request the analog line, and finally set the sampling rate. This should look familiar if you followed the samples in Chapter 4.

```
def get_remote_device():
    """Get the remote node from the network
    Returns:
    """
    # Request the network class and search the network for the
      remote node
    xbee_network = device.get_network()
    remote_device = xbee_network.discover_device(REMOTE_NODE_ID)
    if remote_device is None:
        print("ERROR: Remove node id {0} not found.".
        format(REMOVE_NODE_ID))
        exit(1)
    remote_device.set_dest_address(device.get_64bit_addr())
    remote_device.set_io_configuration(ANALOG_LINE, IOMode.ADC)
    remote_device.set_io_sampling_rate(SAMPLING_RATE)
```

The following shows the callback method named io_sample_callback(). In this method, we get the sample passed in a special format (see the following code) in the parameter named sample. We also get the instance of the remote node as remote and the time of the sample as time. So, you can not only see where the sample originated but also the date and time of the sample. Cool!

```
def io_sample_callback(sample, remote, time):
    print("Reading from {0} at {1}:".format(REMOTE_NODE_ID,
                                        remote.get_64bit_
                                        addr()))
    # Get the temperature in Celsius
```

```
temp_c = ((sample.get_analog_value(ANALOG_LINE) * 1200.0 /
          1024.0) - 500.0) / 10.0
# Calculate temperature in Fahrenheit
temp_f = ((temp_c * 9.0) / 5.0) + 32.0
print("\tTemperature is {0}C. {1}F".format(temp_c, temp_f))
# Calculate supply voltage
volts = (sample.power_supply_value * (1200.0 / 1024.0)) / 1000.0
print("\tSupply voltage = {0}v".format(volts))
```

Notice we also placed the code to decipher the data in this method. Specifically, we calculate the temperature in Celsius, convert it to Fahrenheit, and calculate the voltage at the node. I leave the details of the code as an exercise, but we've used the formulas in previous examples.

OK, now all that is left is putting everything together. We follow the pattern put forth in the Digi-Python examples by wrapping the code in a try...except block to capture errors. Inside the block, we simply open the device class instance (start the instance), get the remote device, and register the callback method. We use an infinite loop configuration and trap on the keyboard Ctrl+C command to exit the script.

```
try:
    print("Welcome to example of reading a remote TMP36 sensor!")

    device.open()  # Open the device class
    # Setup the remote device
    get_remote_device()
    # Register a listener to handle the samples received by the
      local device.
    device.add_io_sample_received_callback(io_sample_callback)
    while True:
        pass
```

```
except KeyboardInterrupt:
    if device is not None and device.is_open():
        device.close()
```

Before we look at the code as a single unit, let's discuss the format of the data returned in the parameter sample. Here, since we requested analog line DIO3_AD3, we see the sample is a tuple with two dictionaries: first the data sample and second the power supply voltage. If you simply print the value of the sample parameter, you will see how this is formed. The following code shows an example of some of the data returned in a test run:

```
> {[IOLine.DIO3_AD3: 563], [Power supply voltage: 3277]}
> {[IOLine.DIO3_AD3: 565], [Power supply voltage: 3269]}
> {[IOLine.DIO3_AD3: 565], [Power supply voltage: 3273]}
> {[IOLine.DIO3_AD3: 564], [Power supply voltage: 3272]}
> {[IOLine.DIO3_AD3: 563], [Power supply voltage: 3273]}
> {[IOLine.DIO3_AD3: 569], [Power supply voltage: 3269]}
> {[IOLine.DIO3_AD3: 566], [Power supply voltage: 3269]}
> {[IOLine.DIO3_AD3: 564], [Power supply voltage: 3268]}
```

Now let's put all that together and see what the completed code looks like. Open an editor, create the file pi_xbee.py, and enter the code from Listing 5-5.

Listing 5-5. Reading Data from an XBee Module

```
#
# Raspberry Pi Data Aggregator - Beginning Sensor Networks
Second Edition
#
# For this script. we read data from an XBee remote data mode
# from a ZigBee Coordinator connected to a Raspberry Pi via a
# serial interface.
```

```
#
# The data read includes an analog value from DIO3/AD3 and the
  current voltage value.
#
from digi.xbee.devices import XBeeDevice
from digi.xbee.io import IOLine, IOMode

# Serial port on Raspberry Pi
SERIAL_PORT = "/dev/ttyS0"
# BAUD rate for the XBee module connected to the Raspberry Pi
BAUD_RATE = 9600
# The name of the remote node (NI)
REMOTE_NODE_ID = "TMP36"
# Analog pin we want to monitor/request data
ANALOG_LINE = IOLine.DIO3_AD3
# Sampling rate
SAMPLING_RATE = 15

# Get an instance of the XBee device class
device = XBeeDevice(SERIAL_PORT, BAUD_RATE)

# Method to connect to the network and get the remote node by id
def get_remote_device():
    """Get the remote node from the network
    Returns:
    """
    # Request the network class and search the network for the
      remote node
    xbee_network = device.get_network()
    remote_device = xbee_network.discover_device(REMOTE_NODE_ID)
    if remote_device is None:
```

```python
        print("ERROR: Remove node id {0} not
        found.".format(REMOVE_NODE_ID))
        exit(1)
    remote_device.set_dest_address(device.get_64bit_addr())
    remote_device.set_io_configuration(ANALOG_LINE, IOMode.ADC)
    remote_device.set_io_sampling_rate(SAMPLING_RATE)

def io_sample_callback(sample, remote, time):
    print("Reading from {0} at {1}:".format(REMOTE_NODE_ID,
                                             remote.get_64bit_
                                             addr())))

    # Get the temperature in Celsius
    temp_c = ((sample.get_analog_value(ANALOG_LINE) * 1200.0 /
    1024.0) - 500.0) / 10.0

    # Calculate temperature in Fahrenheit
    temp_f = ((temp_c * 9.0) / 5.0) + 32.0
    print("\tTemperature is {0}C. {1}F".format(temp_c, temp_f))

    # Calculate supply voltage
    volts = (sample.power_supply_value * (1200.0 / 1024.0)) / 1000.0
    print("\tSupply voltage = {0}v".format(volts))

try:
    print("Welcome to example of reading a remote TMP36 sensor!")

    device.open()  # Open the device class

    # Setup the remote device
    get_remote_device()

    # Register a listener to handle the samples received by the
      local device.
```

```
        device.add_io_sample_received_callback(io_sample_callback)
        while True:
            pass
except KeyboardInterrupt:
    if device is not None and device.is_open():
        device.close()
```

Testing the Final Project

Now you can run your script and observe the output. Start the script with
python3 ./pi_xbee.py. Listing 5-6 shows sample output from the script.
To see the data change, I simply touched the sensor (careful not to short
the pins), allowing my body heat to increase the values read.

Listing 5-6. Output of the XBee Aggregate Node Script (pi_xbee.py)

```
$ python3 ./pi_xbee.py
Welcome to example of reading a remote TMP36 sensor!
Reading from TMP36 at 0013A2004192DB79:
    Temperature is 15.9765625C. 60.7578125F
    Supply voltage = 3.840234375v
Reading from TMP36 at 0013A2004192DB79:
    Temperature is 16.2109375C. 61.1796875F
    Supply voltage = 3.830859375v
Reading from TMP36 at 0013A2004192DB79:
    Temperature is 16.2109375C. 61.1796875F
    Supply voltage = 3.835546875v
Reading from TMP36 at 0013A2004192DB79:
    Temperature is 16.09375C. 60.96875F
    Supply voltage = 3.834375v
Reading from TMP36 at 0013A2004192DB79:
    Temperature is 15.9765625C. 60.7578125F
    Supply voltage = 3.835546875v
```

```
Reading from TMP36 at 0013A2004192DB79:
    Temperature is 16.6796875C. 62.0234375F
    Supply voltage = 3.830859375v
Reading from TMP36 at 0013A2004192DB79:
    Temperature is 16.328125C. 61.390625F
    Supply voltage = 3.830859375v
Reading from TMP36 at 0013A2004192DB79:
    Temperature is 16.09375C. 60.96875F
    Supply voltage = 3.8296875v
```

Did you see something similar? If so, you're doing great work and now have the knowledge needed to build sensor nodes and Raspberry Pi–based sensor data aggregators.

If you do not see any data at all, go back to Chapter 4 and follow the troubleshooting tips from the last project in the chapter. You can always plug the coordinator module into a USB explorer and use a terminal program on your personal computer to see if data is being received from the XBee sensor node.

Tip   If you don't see any data, power off your sensor node and Raspberry Pi. Remove the coordinator module from the Raspberry Pi, plug it into a USB XBee Explorer, plug that into your personal computer and connect a serial program to the port, and then power up your sensor node. After a few moments, you should see data being received on the coordinator node.

For More Fun

If you would like to expand the project, you can add a second XBee sensor node and modify the code to specify which node the data came from. For example, the script should record (write to standard output) the source of the data along with the sensor data from the XBee.

Component Shopping List

A number of components are needed to complete the projects in this chapter; they are listed in Table 5-3. Some of them, like the XBee modules and supporting hardware, are also included in the shopping list from Chapter 4.

Table 5-3. *Components Needed*

Item	Vendors	Est. Cost USD	Qty Needed
Raspberry Pi Model B	Most online stores such as Adafruit, SparkFun, and Mouser	$35.00 and up[13]	1
5V Power Supply (3A, 3B, 3B+)	www.pishop.us/product/ wall-adapter-power-supply- micro-usb-2-4a-5-25v/	$9.95	1
5V Power Supply (4B)	www.raspberrypi.org/ products/type-c-power- supply/	$8.00	1
HDMI or HDMI to DVI cable	Most online and retail stores	Varies	1
HDMI or DVI monitor	Most online and retail stores	Varies	1
USB keyboard	Most online and retail stores	Varies	1

(*continued*)

---

[13]I recommend shopping around to find the best deal. At the time of writing, demand for the Raspberry Pi 4B is still greater than the supply, so the cost is a bit higher.

Table 5-3. (*continued*)

Item	Vendors	Est. Cost USD	Qty Needed
USB Type A to micro-USB male	Most online and retail stores	Varies	1
SD card, 2GB or more	Most online and retail stores	Varies	1
Raspberry Pi Cobbler+ (you can also use the T-Cobbler+)	www.adafruit.com/ products/2028	$7.95	1
	www.adafruit.com/ products/2029		
150 Ohm Resistor	Most online and retail stores	Varies	1
0.10mF capacitor	Most online and retail stores	Varies	1
10K Ohm Resistor	Most online and retail stores	Varies	1
LED	Most online and retail stores	Varies	1
DS18B20 Digital Temperature Sensor	www.adafruit.com/ product/374	$3.95	1
Pushbutton	Most online and retail stores	Varies	1
BMP280 Sensor	www.adafruit.com/ products/2651	$9.95	1
Breadboard (not mini)	www.sparkfun.com/ products/9567	$5.95	2
	www.adafruit.com/ product/64		
XBee Explorer Regulated	www.sparkfun.com/ products/11373	$9.95	2

Summary

In this chapter, you explored the origins of the Raspberry Pi, including a tour of the hardware and a list of the available operating systems. You discovered how to create an SD boot image and learned how to start using the Raspberry Pi.

You also discovered how to use the GPIO header to illuminate an LED, read data from sensors, and read data via an XBee from an XBee sensor node. By executing these projects, you have learned far more about the Raspberry Pi than most.

By now, you should start to see the parts of building a sensor network coming together. You've explored XBee modules for wireless communication, host sensors with XBee and Raspberry Pi, and even how to build aggregate sensor nodes with both platforms.

We complete our tour of sensor nodes by examining the Arduino platform. In the next chapter, we will learn what the Arduino is and how to host sensors with it. Cool!

CHAPTER 6

Arduino-Based Sensor Nodes

One of the greatest advances in physical computing has been the proliferation of microcontrollers. A microcontroller consists of a processor with a small instruction set, memory, and programmable input/output circuitry contained on a single chip. Microcontrollers are usually packaged with supporting circuitry and connections on a small printed circuit board.

Microcontrollers are used in embedded systems where small software programs can be tailored to control and monitor hardware devices, making them ideal for use in sensor networks. One of the most successful and most popular microcontrollers is the Arduino platform.

In this chapter, you explore the Arduino platform with the goal of using the Arduino to manage sensor nodes. You see a short tutorial on the Arduino and several projects to help get you started working with the Arduino.

What Is an Arduino?

The Arduino is an open source hardware prototyping platform supported by an open source software environment. It was first introduced in 2005 and was designed with the goal of making the hardware and software easy to use and available to the widest audience possible. Thus, you do not have to be an electronics expert to use the Arduino.

© Charles Bell 2020
C. Bell, *Beginning Sensor Networks with XBee, Raspberry Pi, and Arduino*,
https://doi.org/10.1007/978-1-4842-5796-8_6

The original target audience included artists and hobbyists who needed a microcontroller to make their designs and creations more interesting. However, given its ease of use and versatility, the Arduino has quickly become the choice for a wider audience and a wider variety of projects.

This means you can use the Arduino for all manner of projects from reacting to environmental conditions to controlling complex robotic functions. The Arduino has also made learning electronics easier through practical applications.

Another aspect that has helped the rapid adoption of the Arduino platform is the growing community of contributors to a wealth of information made available through the official Arduino website (`http://arduino.cc/en/`). When you visit the website, you find an excellent "getting started" tutorial as well as a list of helpful project ideas and a full reference guide to the C-like language for writing the code to control the Arduino (called a sketch).

Arduino also provides an integrated development environment called the Arduino IDE. The IDE runs on your computer (called the host), where you can write and compile sketches and then upload them to the Arduino via USB connections. The IDE is available for Linux, Mac, and Windows. It is designed around a text editor especially designed for writing code and a set of limited functions designed to support compilation and loading of sketches.

Sketches are written in a special format consisting of only two required methods—one that executes when the Arduino is reset or powered on and another that executes continuously. Thus, your initialization code goes in `setup()` and your code to control the Arduino goes in `loop()`. The language is C-like, and you may define your own variables and functions. For a complete guide to writing sketches, see `http://arduino.cc/en/Tutorial/Sketch`.

You can expand the functionality of sketches and provide for reuse by writing libraries that encapsulate certain features such as networking, using memory cards, connecting to databases, doing mathematics, and the like.

The Arduino supports a number of analog and digital pins that you can use to connect to various devices and components and interact with them. The mainstream boards have specific pin layouts, or headers, that allow the use of expansion boards called shields. Shields let you add additional hardware capabilities such as Ethernet, Bluetooth, and XBee support to your Arduino. The physical layout of the Arduino and the shield allow you to stack shields. Thus, you can have an Ethernet shield as well as an XBee shield, because each uses different I/O pins. You learn the use of the pins and shields as you explore the application of Arduino to sensor networks.

The next sections examine the various Arduino boards and briefly describe their capabilities. I list the boards by when they became available, starting with the most recent models. Many more boards and variants are available, and a few new ones are likely to be out by the time this book is printed, but these are the ones that are typically used in a sensor network project.

Arduino Models

A growing number of Arduino boards are available. Some are configured for special applications, whereas others are designed with different processors and memory configurations. Some boards are considered official Arduino boards because they are branded and endorsed by Arduino.cc. Since the Arduino is licensed using a Creative Commons Attribution Share-Alike license, anyone can build Arduino-compatible boards if they adhere to the license. This section examines some of the more popular Arduino-branded boards.

The basic layout of an Arduino board consists of a USB connection, a power connector, a reset switch, LEDs for power and serial communication, and a standard spaced set of headers for attaching shields. The official boards sport a distinctive blue-colored PCB with white lettering. With the exception of one model, all the official boards can be mounted in a chassis (they have holes in the PCB for mounting screws). The exception is an Arduino designed for mounting on a breadboard.

Uno

The Uno board is the standard Arduino board that most new to the Arduino will choose. It features an ATmega328P processor; 14 digital I/O pins, of which 6 can be used as pulse-width modulation (PWM)[1] output; and 6 analog input pins. The Uno board has 32KB of flash memory and 2KB of SRAM.

The Uno is available either as a surface-mount device (SMD) or a standard IC socket. The IC socket version allows you to exchange processors should you desire to use an external IC programmer to build custom solutions. Details and a full datasheet are available at `https://store.arduino.cc/usa/arduino-uno-rev3`. It has a standard USB type B connector and supports all shields. Figure 6-1 shows the Arduino Uno board.

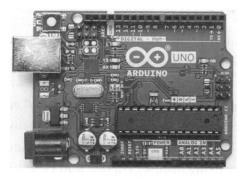

Figure 6-1. *Arduino Uno Rev3 (courtesy of Arduino.cc)*

---

[1]`https://en.wikipedia.org/wiki/Pulse-width_modulation`

There is also a version of this board that has a built-in Wi-Fi chip, making it possible for use in sensor networks or situations where using a Wi-Fi shield is problematic (lack of space, conflicts with other shields, etc.). While it is named the same, it differs from the standard Uno in several ways. Aside from the Wi-Fi chip, it has a different processor and one less PWM pin. You can read more about the Uno Wi-Fi board at `https://store.arduino.cc/usa/arduino-uno-WiFi-rev2`. Figure 6-2 shows the Arduino Uno Wi-Fi board.

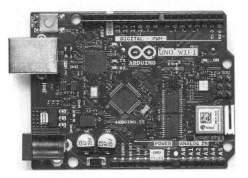

Figure 6-2. Arduino Uno Wi-Fi Rev2 (courtesy of Arduino.cc)

Leonardo

The Leonardo board represents another of the standard boards in the pantheon of Arduino platform. It is a little different in that, while it supports the standard header layout, it also has a USB controller that allows the board to appear as a USB device (e.g., mouse or keyboard) to the host computer. The board uses a newer ATmega32u4 processor with 20 digital I/O pins, of which 12 can be used as analog pins and 7 can be used as a pulse-width modulation (PWM) output. It has 32KB of flash memory and 2.5KB of SRAM.

The Leonardo has more digital pins than the Uno, but continues to support most shields. The USB connection uses a smaller USB connector. The board is also available with and without headers. Figure 6-3 depicts an official Leonardo board. Details and a full datasheet can be found at `https://store.arduino.cc/usa/leonardo`.

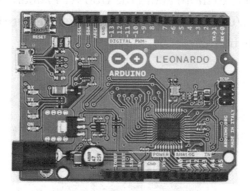

Figure 6-3. *Arduino Leonardo (courtesy of Arduino.cc)*

Due

The Arduino Due is a new, larger, and faster board based on the Atmel SAM3X8E ARM Cortex-M3 processor. The processor is a 32-bit processor, and the board supports a massive 54 digital I/O ports, of which 14 can be used for PWM output; 12 analog inputs; and 4 UART chips (serial ports) as well as 2 digital-to-analog (DAC) and 2 two-wire interface (TWI) pins. The new processor offers several advantages:

- 32-bit registers

- DMA controller (allows CPU-independent memory tasks)

- 512KB flash memory

- 96KB SRAM

- 84MHz clock

The Due has the larger form factor (called the mega footprint) but still supports the use of standard shields as well as mega format shields. The new board has one distinct limitation: unlike other boards that can accept up to 5V on the I/O pins, the Due is limited to 3.3V on the I/O pins. Details and a full datasheet can be found at https://store.arduino.cc/usa/due.

The Arduino Due is intended to be used for projects that require more processing power, more memory, and more I/O pins. Despite the significant capabilities of the new board, it remains open source and comparable in price to its predecessors. Look to the Due for your projects that require the maximum hardware performance. Figure 6-4 shows an Arduino Due board.

Figure 6-4. *Arduino Due (courtesy of Arduino.cc)*

Mega 2560

The Arduino Mega 2560 is an older form of the Due. It is based on the ATmega2560 processor (hence the name). Like the Due, the board supports a massive 54 digital I/O ports, of which 14 can be used as PWM output, 16 analog inputs, and 4 UARTs (hardware serial ports). It uses a 16MHz clock and has 256KB of flash memory. Details and a full datasheet can be found at https://store.arduino.cc/usa/mega-2560-r3.

The Mega 2560 is essentially a larger form of the standard Arduino Uno and Leonardo but supports the standard shields (as well as "mega" shields). Figure 6-5 shows the Arduino Mega 2560 board.

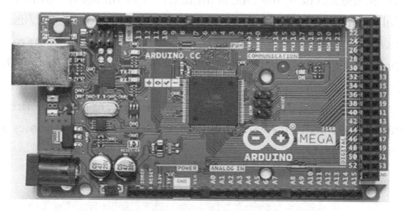

Figure 6-5. *Arduino Mega (courtesy of Arduino.cc)*

Interestingly, the Arduino Mega 256 is the board of choice for Prusa Mendel and similar 3D printers that require the use of a controller board named RepRap Arduino Mega Pololu Shield (RAMPS).

Tip Notice how much larger the Due is than the Uno. If you choose to incorporate a Due, Mega, or similar board, you may have to set aside more room to mount the board.

Micro

The Arduino Micro is a special form of the Leonardo board and uses the same processor with 20 digital I/O pins, of which 12 can be used as analog pins and 7 can be used as PWM output. It has 32KB of flash memory and 2.5KB of SRAM. Details and a full datasheet can be found at `https://store.arduino.cc/usa/arduino-micro`.

The Micro was made for use on breadboards in the same way as the Mini but in a newer, updated form. But unlike the Mini, the Micro is a full-featured board complete with USB connector. And like the Leonardo, it has built-in USB communication, allowing the board to connect to a computer as a mouse or keyboard. Figure 6-6 shows the Arduino Micro board.

Figure 6-6. *Arduino Micro (courtesy of Arduino.cc)*

Although branded as an official Arduino board, the Arduino Micro is produced in cooperation with Adafruit.

Nano

The Arduino Nano is an older form of the Arduino Micro. In this case, it is based on the functionality of the Duemilanove4 and has the ATmega328 processor (older models use the ATmega168) and 14 digital I/O pins, of which 6 can be used as PWM output and 8 analog inputs. The mini has 32KB of flash memory and uses a 16MHz clock. Details and a full datasheet can be found at `https://store.arduino.cc/usa/arduino-nano`.

Like the Micro, it has all the features needed for connecting to and programming via a USB connection. Figure 6-7 shows an Arduino Nano board.

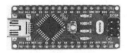

Figure 6-7. *Arduino Nano (courtesy of Arduino.cc)*

MKR-Series Boards

There is another form of Arduino called the MKR (for "maker") series. The MKR series includes a variety of boards based on the (now retired Zero) board that have various communication capabilities such as Wi-Fi, LoRa, LoRaWAN, and GSM.

They are based on the Atmel ATSAMW25 SoC (System on Chip) and designed for IoT projects and devices. It also supports cryptographic authentication. For those working on projects that require battery port, the MKR series of boards include a LiPo charging circuit for charging a LiPo battery while running on external power. Details and a full datasheet can be found at https://store.arduino.cc/usa/arduino-mkr1000.

The boards do not use the same pin layout as the Uno-compatible shield-based boards (but you can get an adapter). Rather, they are designed like the Nano and Mini (but a bit larger) to minimize the size of the board to make it easier to incorporate into your projects. In fact, they are one of the boards of choice for Internet of Things (IoT) projects and make an excellent choice for sensor network projects. Since they are relatively new and some have specialized communication options, most new to Arduino would be better served starting with the Arduino boards that support Uno-compatible shields.

Figure 6-8. *MKR1000 (courtesy of Arduino.cc)*

Caution   The MKR boards run on 3.3V power and have a maximum input on the GPIO pins of 3.3V.

Arduino Clones

A growing number of Arduino boards are available from a large number of sources. Because the Arduino is open hardware, it is not unusual or the least bit illicit to find Arduino boards made by vendors all over the world.

Although some would insist the only real Arduinos are those branded as such, the truth of the matter is that as long as the build quality is sound and the components are of high quality, the choice of using a branded vs. a copy, hence clone, is one of personal preference. I have sampled Arduino boards from a number of sources, and with few exceptions, they all perform their intended functions superbly.

Except for the Arduino Mini, the Arduino clone boards have a greater variety of hardware configurations. Some Arduinos are designed for use in embedded systems or on breadboards, and some are designed for prototyping. I examine a number of the more popular clone boards in the following sections.

Arduino Pro Mini

The Arduino Pro Mini is another board from SparkFun. It is based on the ATmega168 processor (older models use the ATmega168) and has 14 digital I/O pins, of which 6 can be used as PWM output, and 8 analog inputs. The Pro Mini has 16KB of flash memory and 1KB of SRAM, and it uses a 16MHz clock. Details and a full datasheet can be found at `www.sparkfun.com/products/11113`.

The Arduino Pro Mini is modeled on the Arduino Mini and is also intended for use on breadboards but does not come with headers. This makes the Arduino Pro Mini ideal for use in semi-permanent installations where the pins can be soldered to the components or circuitry and space is a premium. Figure 6-9 shows an Arduino Pro Mini board. It really is that tiny.

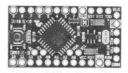

Figure 6-9. *Arduino Pro Mini (courtesy of SparkFun)*

Also, the Pro Mini does not include a USB connector and therefore must be connected to and programmed with a FTDI cable or similar breakout board. It comes as either a 3.3V model with an 8MHz clock or a 5V model with a 16MHz clock.

Fio

The Arduino Fio is yet another board made by SparkFun. It was designed for use in wireless projects. It is based on the ATmega32U4 processor with 14 digital I/O pins, of which 6 can be used as PWM outputs, and 8 analog pins. Details and a full datasheet can be found at www.sparkfun.com/products/11520.

The Fio requires a 3.3V power supply, which allows for use with a lithium polymer (LiPo) battery which can be recharged via the USB connector on the board.

Its wireless pedigree can be seen in the XBee socket on the bottom of the board. Although the USB connection lets you recharge the battery, you must use an FTDI cable or breakout adapter to connect to and program the Fio. Similar to the Pro models, the Fio does not come with headers, allowing the board to be used in semi-permanent installations where connections are soldered in place. Figure 6-10 shows an Arduino Fio board.

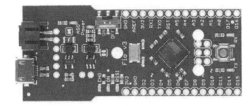

Figure 6-10. *Arduino Fio (courtesy of SparkFun)*

Seeeduino

The Seeeduino is an Arduino clone made by Seeed Studio
(www.seeedstudio.com). It is based on the ATmega328P processor and has
14 digital I/O pins, of which 6 can be used as PWM outputs, and 8 analog pins.
It has 32KB of flash memory and 2KB of SRAM. Details and a full datasheet
can be found at www.seeedstudio.com/Seeeduino-V4-2-p-2517.html.

The board has a footprint similar to the Arduino Uno and supports
all standard headers. It supports a number of enhancements such as I2C
and serial Grove connectors and a mini USB connector, and it uses SMD
components. It is also a striking red color with yellow headers. Figure 6-11
shows a Seeeduino board.

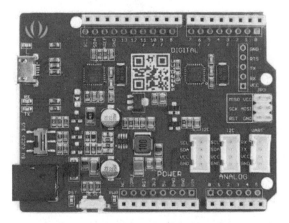

Figure 6-11. *Seeeduino (courtesy of Seeed Studio)*

Seeed Studio also makes a "mini" version of this board ().

Sippino

The Sippino from SpikenzieLabs (www.spikenzielabs.com) is designed to be used on a solder-less breadboard. It costs less because it has fewer components and a much smaller footprint. It comes unassembled and, if you are learning to solder, can make for a very enjoyable afternoon project.

It is based on the ATmega328 processor and has 14 digital I/O pins, of which 6 can be used as PWM output, and 6 analog input pins. The Sippino board has 32KB of flash memory and 2KB of SRAM. Details and a full datasheet can be found at www.spikenzielabs.com/Catalog/arduino/sippino-prototino-8482/sippino-kit?cPath=1&.

The Sippino does not have a USB connection, so you have to use an FTDI cable to program it. The good news is you need only one cable no matter how many Sippinos you have in your project. I have a number of Sippinos and use them in many of my Arduino projects where space is at a premium. Figure 6-12 shows a Sippino mounted on a breadboard.

Figure 6-12. *Sippino (courtesy of SpikenzieLabs)*

SpikenzieLabs also makes a version with a USB connector (www.spikenzielabs.com/Catalog/arduino/sippino-prototino-8482/sippino8482-usb-kit?cPath=1&).

While you cannot use normal shields with the Sippino, SpikenzieLabs also provides a special adapter called a shield dock that allows you to use a Sippino with standard Arduino shields. The shield dock is an amazing add-on that lets you use the Sippino as if it were a standard Uno or Duemilanove. Figure 6-13 shows a Sippino mounted on a shield dock. Details and a full datasheet can be found at `www.spikenzielabs.com/Catalog/spikenzielabs/the-shield-dock`.

Figure 6-13. *Sippino on a shield dock (courtesy of SpikenzieLabs)*

Prototino

The Prototino is another product of SpikenzieLabs. It has the same components as the Sippino, but instead of a breadboard-friendly layout, it is mounted on a PCB that includes a full prototyping area. Like the Sippino, it is based on the ATmega328 processor and has 14 digital I/O pins, of which 6 can be used as PWM output, and 6 analog input pins. The Prototino board has 32KB of flash memory and 2KB of SRAM. Details and a full datasheet can be found at `www.spikenzielabs.com/Catalog/arduino/sippino-prototino-8482/prototino?cPath=1&`.

The Prototino is ideal for building solutions that have supporting components and circuitry. In some ways, it is similar to the Nano, Mini, and similar boards, in that you can use it for permanent installations. But unlike those boards (and even the Arduino Pro), the Prototino provides a space for you to add your components directly to the board. I have used a number of Prototino boards for projects where I have added the components to the Prototino and install it in the chassis. This allowed me to create a solution using a single board and even build several copies quickly and easily.

Like the Sippino, the Prototino does not have a USB connection, so you have to use an FTDI cable to program it. Figure 6-14 shows a Prototino board.

Figure 6-14. *Prototino (courtesy of SpikenzieLabs)*

Metro from Adafruit

The Metro from Adafruit is a set of Arduino-compatible boards supporting a number of formats including several that support Arduino shields. The version I like as a balance of compatibility and cost is the Metro 328 (`www.adafruit.com/product/2488`). Figure 6-15 shows the Metro 328 board from Adafruit. The board uses the ATmega328P at 16MHz and host of minor improvements to make the Metro an excellent alternative to an Arduino Uno. Check out the product page for more details.

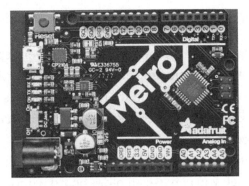

Figure 6-15. *Metro 328 (courtesy of Adafruit)*

Note   Adafruit also has several CircuitPython models. Some are smaller and thus may be an option if you need to minimize the footprint of your node. For more details, see www.adafruit.com/category/966.

THERE IS EVEN ONE MADE OF PAPER

Every now and then, you encounter something mundane that's made truly interesting by a change in medium. Such is the case of the PAPERduino created by Guilherme Martins. The PAPERduino is a minimal Arduino that uses a paper template in place of the PCB. All you need to do is download and print out the templates, purchase a small list of commonly available discrete components, and follow the connection diagram printed on the template to solder the components to short lengths of wire. You can find out more by visiting the following website: http://lab.guilhermemartins.net/2009/05/06/paperduino-prints/.

So, Which Do I Buy?

If you're wondering which Arduino to buy, the answer depends on what you want to do. For most of the projects in this book, any Arduino Uno or similar clone that supports the standard shield headers is fine. You need not buy the larger Due or its predecessors, since the added memory and I/O pins aren't needed.

I use the Arduino Uno, Uno Wi-Fi, or Leonardo for all the projects in this book. Although you can use an older board without issues, there are some issues with using the Leonardo board. I point these out as you encounter them. Most issues have to do with the relocated pins on the Leonardo board. For example, the SPI header pins (at upper left in Figure 6-3) have been moved on the Leonardo.

For future projects, there are some things you should consider before choosing the Arduino. For example, if your project is largely based on a breadboard or you want to keep the physical size of the project to a minimum, and you aren't going to use any shields, the Arduino Mini may be the better choice. Conversely, if you plan to do a lot of programming to implement complex algorithms for manipulating or analyzing data, you may want to consider the Due for its added processing power and memory.

The bottom line is that most of the time your choice will be based on physical characteristics (size, shield support, and so on) and seldom on processing power or memory. SparkFun has an excellent buyer's guide in which you can see the pros and cons of each choice. See www.sparkfun. com/pages/arduino_guide for more details.

Where to Buy

Due to the popularity of the Arduino platform, many vendors sell Arduino and Arduino clone boards, shields, and accessories. The Arduino.cc website (https://store.arduino.cc/usa) also has a page devoted to approved distributors. If none of the resources listed here are available to you, you may want to check this page for a retailer near you.

Online Retailers

There are a growing number of online retailers where you can buy Arduino boards and accessories. The following lists a few of the more popular sites:

- *SparkFun*: From discrete components to the company's own branded Arduino clones and shields, SparkFun has just about anything you could possibly want for the Arduino platform (www.sparkfun.com/).

- *Adafruit*: Carries a growing array of components, gadgets, and more. It has a growing number of products for the electronics hobbyist, including a full line of Arduino products. Adafruit also has an outstanding documentation library and wiki to support all the products it sells (www.adafruit.com/).

You can also visit the manufacturers of some of the clone boards. The following are the leading clone manufacturers and links to their storefronts:

- *SpikenzieLabs*: www.spikenzielabs.com/

- *Seeed Studio*: www.seeedstudio.com/

Retail Stores (United States)

There are also brick-and-mortar stores that carry Arduino products. Although there aren't as many as there are online retailers and their inventories are typically limited, if you need a new Arduino board quickly, you can find them at the following retailers. You may find additional retailers in your area. Look for popular hobby electronics stores:

- *Fry's*: An electronics superstore with a huge warehouse of electronics, components, microcontrollers, computer parts, and more available for order. Fry's carries Arduino-branded boards, shields, and accessories as well as products from Parallax, SparkFun, and many more (http://frys.com/).

- *Micro Center*: Micro Center is similar to Fry's, offering a huge inventory of products. However, most Micro Center stores have a smaller inventory of electronic components than Fry's (www.microcenter.com/).

Now that you have a better understanding of the hardware details and the variety of Arduino boards available, let's dive into how to use and program the Arduino. The next section provides a tutorial for installing the Arduino programming environment and programming the Arduino. Later sections present projects to build your skills for developing sensor networks.

Arduino Tutorial

This section is a short tutorial on getting started using an Arduino. It covers obtaining and installing the IDE and writing a sample sketch. Rather than duplicate the excellent works that precede this book, I cover the highlights and refer readers who are less familiar with the Arduino to online resources and other books that offer a much deeper introduction. Also, the Arduino IDE has many sample sketches that you can use to explore the Arduino on your own. Most have corresponding tutorials on the Arduino.cc site.

Learning Resources

A lot of information is available about the Arduino platform. If you are just getting started with the Arduino, Apress offers an impressive array of books covering all manner of topics concerning the Arduino, ranging from getting started using the microcontroller to learning the details of its design and implementation. The following is a list of the more popular books. Some are a little older than you may expect but still quite useful.

- *Beginning Arduino* by Michael McRoberts (Apress, 2010)

- *Practical Arduino: Cool Projects for Open Source Hardware (Technology in Action)* by Jonathan Oxer and Hugh Blemings (Apress, 2009)

- *Arduino Internals* by Dale Wheat (Apress, 2011)

There are also some excellent online resources for learning more about the Arduino, the Arduino libraries, and sample projects. The following are some of the best:

- *Arduino.cc*: http://arduino.cc/en/

- *Adafruit*: http://learn.adafruit.com/

- *SparkFun*: https://learn.sparkfun.com/

The Arduino IDE

The Arduino IDE is available for download for the Mac, Linux (32- and 64-bit versions), and Windows platforms. You can download the IDE from `http://arduino.cc/en/Main/Software`. There are links for each platform as well as a link to the source code if you need to compile the IDE for a different platform.

Tip   Interestingly, there is a web version of the IDE that you can use without installing it on your computer. This may be helpful if you want to use it on a PC where you don't want (or cannot) install the IDE.

Installing the IDE is straightforward. I omit the actual steps of installing the IDE for brevity, but if you require a walk-through of installing the IDE, you can see the Getting Started link on the download page or read more in *Beginning Arduino* by Michael McRoberts (Apress, 2010).

Once the IDE launches, you see a simple interface with a text editor area (a white background by default), a message area beneath the editor (a black background by default), and a *simple* button bar at the top. The buttons are (from left to right) *Compile, Compile and Upload, New, Open,* and *Save.* There is also a button to the right that opens the serial monitor. You use the serial monitor to view messages from the Arduino sent (or printed) via the Serial library. You see this in action in your first project. Figure 6-16 shows the Arduino IDE.

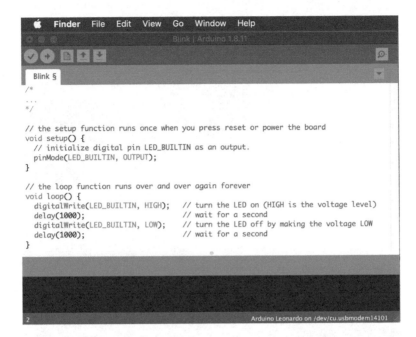

Figure 6-16. *The Arduino IDE*

Notice that in Figure 6-16 you see a sample sketch (called blink)
and the result of a successful compile operation. I loaded this sketch by
clicking *File ➤ Examples ➤ Basic ➤ Blink*. Notice also at the bottom that
it tells you that you are programming an Arduino Leonardo board on a
specific serial port.

Due to the differences in processor and supporting architecture, there
are some differences in how the compiler builds the program (and how the
IDE uploads it). Thus, one of the first things you should do when you start
the IDE is choose your board from the *Tools ➤ Board* menu. Figure 6-17
shows a sample of selecting the board on the Mac.

Figure 6-17. *Choosing the Arduino board*

Notice the number of boards available. Be sure to choose the one that matches your board. If you are using a clone board, check the manufacturer's site for the recommended setting to use. If you choose the wrong board, you typically get an error during upload, but it may not be obvious that you've chosen the wrong board. Because I have so many different boards, I've made it a habit to choose the board each time I launch the IDE.

The next thing you need to do is choose the serial port to which the Arduino board is connected. To connect to the board, use the *Tools* ➤ *Port* menu option. Figure 6-18 shows an example on the Mac. In this case, no serial ports are listed. This can happen if you haven't plugged your Arduino in to the computer's USB ports (or hub), you had it plugged in but disconnected it at some point, or you have not loaded the drivers for the Arduino (Windows). Typically, this can be remedied by simply unplugging the Arduino and plugging it back in and waiting until the computer recognizes the port.

Note   If you use a Mac, it doesn't matter which port you choose: either the one that starts with tty or the one that starts with cu will work.

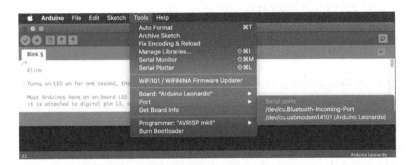

Figure 6-18. *Choosing the serial port*

Tip   See www.arduino.cc/en/Guide/HomePage?from=Guide. Howto if you need help installing the drivers on Windows.

OK, now that you have your Arduino IDE installed, you can connect your Arduino and set the board and serial port. You see the LEDs on the Arduino illuminate. This is because the Arduino is getting power from the USB. Thus, you do not need to provide an external power supply when the Arduino is connected to your computer. Next, you dive into a simple project to demonstrate the Arduino IDE and learn how basic sketches are built, compiled, and uploaded.

Project: Hardware "Hello, World!"

The ubiquitous "Hello, World!" project for the Arduino is the blinking light. The project uses an LED, a breadboard, and some jumper wires. The Arduino turns on and off through the course of the loop() iteration. That's a fine project for getting started, but it does not relate to how sensors could be used.

Thus, in this section, you expand on the blinking light project by adding a sensor. In this case, you still keep things simple by using what is arguably the most basic of sensors: a pushbutton. The goal is to illuminate the LED whenever the button is pushed.

Hardware Connections

Let's begin by assembling an Arduino. Be sure to disconnect (power down) the Arduino first. You can use any Arduino variant that has I/O pins. Place one LED and one pushbutton in the breadboard. Wire the 5V pin to the breadboard power rail and the ground pin to the ground rail, and place the pushbutton in the center of the breadboard. Place the LED to one side of the breadboard, as shown in Figure 6-19.

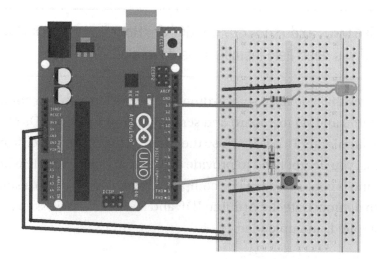

Figure 6-19. Diagram of an LED with a pushbutton

You're almost there. Now wire a jumper from the power rail to one side of the pushbutton, and wire the other side of the pushbutton to (DIGITAL) pin 2 on the Arduino (located on the side with the USB connector). Next, wire the LED to ground on the breadboard and a 150 Ohm resistor (colors: brown, green, brown, gold). The other side of the resistor should be wired to pin 13 on the Arduino. You also need a resistor to pull the button low when the button is not pressed. Place a 10K Ohm resistor (colors: brown, black, orange, gold) on the side of the button with the wire to pin 2 and ground.

The longest side of the LED is the positive side. The positive side should be the one connected to the resistor. It doesn't matter which direction you connect the resistor; it is used to limit the current to the LED. Check the drawing again to ensure that you have a similar setup.

Note   Most Arduino boards have an LED connected to pin 13. You reuse the pin to demonstrate how to use analog output. Thus, you may see a small LED near pin 13 illuminate at the same time as the LED on the breadboard.

COOL GADGET

One of the coolest gadgets for working with the Arduino is the Arduino mounting plate from Adafruit (www.adafruit.com/products/275). This small acrylic plate has space for a half-sized breadboard and an Arduino. It even has mounting holes for bolting the Arduino to the plate and small rubber feet to keep the plate off the work surface. The following illustration (courtesy of Adafruit) shows the mounting plate in action.

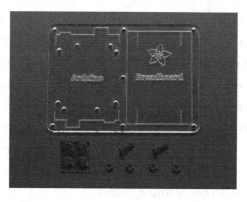

Although you can make your own Arduino mounting plate from Lexan or Plexiglas (I have), the Adafruit product is just a notch better than what you can make yourself. For about US$5.00, you can keep your Arduino and breadboard together and avoid scratches on your table (from the sharp prongs on the bottom of the Arduino)—and, better still, avoid the nasty side effects of accidentally placing a powered Arduino on a conductive surface (never a good idea).

Writing the Sketch

The sketch you need for this project uses two I/O pins on the Arduino: one output and one input. The output pin will be used to illuminate the LED, and the input pin will detect the pushbutton engagement. You connect positive voltage to one side of the pushbutton and the other side to the input pin. When you detect voltage on the input pin, you tell the Arduino processor to send positive voltage to the output pin. In this case, the positive side of the LED is connected to the output pin.

As you can see in the drawing in Figure 6-18, the input pin is pin 2 and the output pin is pin 13. Let's use a variable to store these numbers so you do not have to worry about repeating the hard-coded numbers (and risk getting them wrong). Use the pinMode() method to set the mode of each pin (INPUT, OUTPUT). You place the variable statements before the setup() method and set the pinMode() calls in the setup() method, as follows:

```
int led = 13;      // LED on pin 13
int button = 2;    // button on pin 2

void setup() {
  pinMode(led, OUTPUT);
  pinMode(button, INPUT);
}
```

In the loop() method, you place code to detect the button press. Use the digitalRead() method to read the status of the pin (LOW or HIGH), where LOW means there is no voltage on the pin and HIGH means positive voltage is detected on the pin.

You also place in the loop() method the code to turn on the LED when the input pin state is HIGH. In this case, you use the digitalWrite() method to set the output pin to HIGH when the input pin state is HIGH and similarly set the output pin to LOW when the input pin state is LOW. The following code shows the statements needed:

```
void loop() {
  int state = digitalRead(button);
  if (state == HIGH) {
    digitalWrite(led, HIGH);
  }
  else {
    digitalWrite(led, LOW);
  }
}
```

Now let's see the entire sketch, complete with proper documentation. Listing 6-1 shows the completed sketch.

Listing 6-1. Simple Sensor Sketch

```
/*
  Simple Sensor - Beginning Sensor Networks Second Edition
  For this sketch, we explore a simple sensor (a pushbutton) and
  a simple response to sensor input (a LED). When the sensor
  is activated (the button is pushed), the LED is illuminated.
*/
int led = 13; // LED on pin 13
int button = 2;    // button on pin 2
// the setup routine runs once when you press reset:
void setup() {
  // initialize pin 13 as an output.
  pinMode(led, OUTPUT);
  pinMode(button, INPUT);
}
// the loop routine runs over and over again forever:
void loop() {
  // read the state of the sensor
  int state = digitalRead(button);
  // if sensor engaged (button is pressed), turn on LED
  if (state == HIGH) {
    digitalWrite(led, HIGH);
  }
  // else turn off LED
  else {
    digitalWrite(led, LOW);
  }
}
```

When you've entered the sketch as written, you are ready to compile and run it. Name the sketch `basic_sensor.ino`.

Tip   Want to avoid typing all this by hand? You can find the source code on the Apress site for this book.

Compiling and Uploading

Once you have the sketch written, test the compilation using the *Compile* button in the upper-left corner of the IDE. Fix any compilation errors that appear in the message window. Typical errors include misspellings or case changes (the compiler is case sensitive) for variables or methods.

After you have fixed any compilation errors, click the *Upload* button. The IDE compiles the sketch and uploads the compiled sketch to the Arduino board. You can track the progress via the progress bar at lower right, above the message window. When the compiled sketch is uploaded, the progress bar disappears.

Testing the Sensor

Once the upload is complete, what do you see on your Arduino? If you've done everything right, the answer is nothing. It's just staring back at you with that one dark LED—almost mockingly. Now, press the pushbutton. Did the LED illuminate? If so, congratulations: you're an Arduino programmer!

If the LED did not illuminate, hold the button down for a second or two. If that does not work, check all of your connections to make sure you are plugged in to the correct runs on the breadboard and that your LED is properly seated with the longer leg connected to the resistor, which is connected to pin 13.

On the other hand, if the LED stays illuminated, try reorienting your pushbutton 90 degrees. You may have set the pushbutton in the wrong orientation.

Try out the project a few times until the elation passes. If you're an old hand at Arduino, that may be a very short period. If this is all new to you, go ahead and push that button and bask in the glory of having built your first sensor node!

The next section examines a more complicated sensor node, using a temperature and humidity sensor that sends digital data. As you will see, there is a lot more to do.

Hosting Sensors with Arduino

The digital and analog pins of the Arduino make it an ideal platform for hosting sensors. Since most sensors need very little in the way of supporting components, you can often host multiple sensors on one Arduino. For example, it is possible to host a temperature sensor or even multiple temperature sensors, barometric, humidity, and so on, for sampling weather conditions from a given site.

SparkFun and Adafruit have excellent websites that provide a great deal of information about the products they sell. Often the sensor product page includes links to examples and more information about using the sensor. If you are new to electronics, you should stick to sensors that provide examples of their use. It may sound like cheating, but unless you have a good knowledge of electronics, using a sensor incorrectly can get expensive as you burn your way through a few destroyed components before you get it right.

However, when there is another sensor you want to use, you should examine its datasheet. Most manufacturers and vendors supply the datasheet via a link on the product page. The datasheet provides all the information you need to use the sensor but may not have an actual example of its use. If you are familiar with electronics, this is all you are likely to need.

If you are more of a hobbyist or novice at electronics, check the wikis and forums on Arduino.cc, SparkFun, and Adafruit. These sites have a wealth of information and a great many examples, complete with sample code. If you cannot find any examples, you can try googling for one. Use terms like *"Arduino <sensor name> example".* If you cannot find any examples and are not an experienced electronics technician, you might want to reconsider using the sensor.

Another thing to consider is how you connect the sensor to the Arduino. Recall that there are a number of different physical layouts, depending on the Arduino you choose. Thus, you should be familiar with the pin layout of your Arduino when planning your Arduino-hosted sensor nodes. If you are hosting a single sensor with your Arduino, this may not be an issue. By way of example, Figure 6-20 shows an Arduino Leonardo board with the I/O pins highlighted. If you look carefully at your Arduino board, you see abbreviated text next to each pin to indicate its purpose. Some smaller-form-factor Arduino boards may not have room for the labels. In this case, consult the vendor's product page and print it out for future reference.

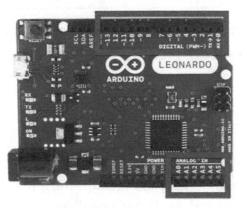

Figure 6-20. *Identifying the I/O pins on an Arduino board*

Now let's put the knowledge you've gained from learning about the Arduino to use in building a sensor node with an Arduino and a sensor.

Project: Building an Arduino Temperature Sensor

In this project, you build a more sophisticated Arduino-hosted sensor node. This project not only demonstrates how to host sensors with an Arduino but also provides an example of why you need a microcontroller to host certain types of sensors. In this case, the DHT22 sensor is a digital sensor that has its own protocol, which requires a bit of logic to interpret correctly, thereby making it more complicated to use with an XBee.[2] Later, you see an example of a simple analog sensor that you can connect directly to an XBee module.

This project uses a DHT22 temperature and humidity sensor connected to the Arduino via a breadboard. The DHT22 is a simple digital sensor that produces digital signals. It requires a single resistor to pull up from the data pin to voltage. Pull-up in this case makes sure the data value is "pulled up" to the voltage level to ensure a valid logic level on the wire.

Let's jump right in and connect the hardware.

Note   This example was adapted from an example on the Adafruit website (`http://learn.adafruit.com/dht`).

Hardware Setup

The hardware required for this project includes an Arduino, a DHT22 humidity and temperature sensor, a breadboard, a 4.7K Ohm resistor (colors: yellow, purple, red, gold), and breadboard jumper wires.

---

[2]At least, I have not found anyone who has done this successfully.

Tip   If you get stuck or want more information, there is an excellent tutorial on Adafruit's website.

Begin by placing your Arduino next to a breadboard. Plug the DHT22 sensor in to one side of the breadboard, as shown in Figure 6-21. Please refer to this figure often and double-check your connections before powering on your Arduino (or connecting it to your laptop). You want to avoid accidental experiments in electrical chaos theory.

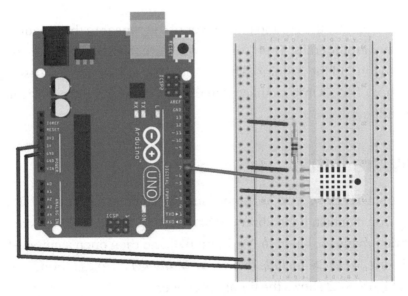

Figure 6-21. Wiring the DHT22

Next, connect the power from the Arduino to the breadboard. Use one jumper wire to connect the 5V pin on the Arduino to the breadboard power rail and another for the ground (GND) pin on the Arduino to the ground rail on the breadboard. With these wires in place, you are ready to wire the sensor. You use three of the four pins, as shown in Table 6-1.

Table 6-1. *DHT22 Connections*

Pin	Connected To
1	+5V, 4.7K resistor between the power supply and the data pin (strong pull-up)
2	Pin 7 on Arduino, 4.7K resistor
3	No connection
4	Ground

Next, connect the ground and power of the sensor to the breadboard power and ground rails. Then connect one wire from the data pin on the sensor to pin 7 of the Arduino. There is one last connection: you use a pull-up resistor of 4.7K Ohm connected to the data wire and the power rail of the breadboard.

Software Setup

To use the DHT22 with an Arduino, you need to have the latest DHT22 library. You can install the library right from the Arduino IDE by searching the library manager. Open the Arduino IDE and then open a new sketch and choose *Sketch* ➤ *Include Library* ➤ *Manage Libraries...* from the menu. Figure 6-22 shows the library manager.

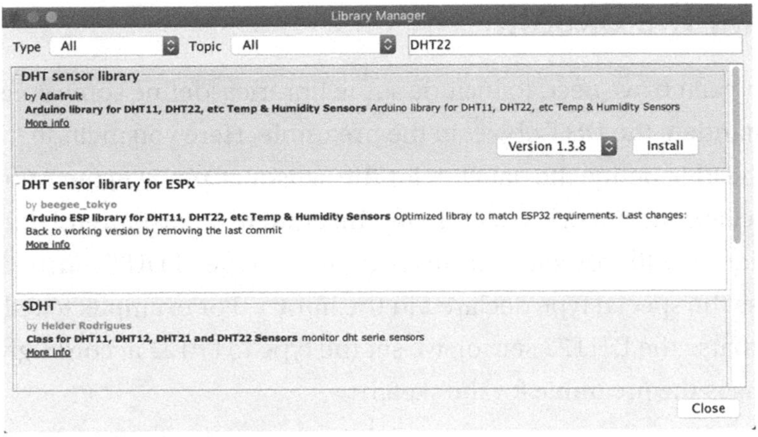

Figure 6-22. Library manager

It may take a moment for the library manager to connect to the server and download the latest catalog. When it is complete, you can type DHT22 into the text box in the upper right and press ENTER. This will search the library catalog for all of the libraries that match.

Choose the DHT sensor library from Adafruit and click Install. If you are prompted to install the supporting libraries, click Install all to ensure all prerequisites are installed as shown in Figure 6-23.

Figure 6-23. Install all libraries

Now that you have the hardware configured and the DHT22 library set up, let's write some code!

Writing the Sketch

Like any sketch, we need to include some libraries, define some constant, and instantiate the DHT object in the preamble. Here you include the DHT library header, define the data pin for the sensor as pin 7 on the Arduino, add a delay constant of 5 seconds, and instantiate an instance of the DHT class. Since the library supports more than one type of DHT sensor, we also must use the special type declared in the library. For example, to tell the library to use the DHT22 sensor, we set the type to DHT22 accordingly. The following is the preamble for the sketch:

```
#include "DHT.h"
#define DHTPIN 7          // DHT2 data is on pin 7
#define read_delay 5000   // 5 seconds
#define DHTTYPE DHT22     // DHT 22 (AM2302)
```

Next, we need to instantiate the DHT class. We do this by passing in the pin we want to use along with the DHT type.

```
DHT dht(DHTPIN, DHTTYPE);
```

The DHT22 has its own protocol for communicating data. Fortunately, the libraries from Adafruit make reading from the sensor easy. To read the data, you simply call the appropriate method as shown in Table 6-2 that returns the value so you can save it in a variable.

Table 6-2. *Data Methods from DHT Library*

Method	Description
dht.readHumidity()	Read the humidity
dht.readTemperature()	Read temperature in Celsius
dht.readTemperature(true)	Read temperature in Fahrenheit
dht.computeHeatIndex(temp_c, humidity, false)	Get heat index in Celsius
dht.computeHeatIndex(temp_c, humidity, true)	Get heat index in Fahrenheit

Knowing that, all we need to do to read the data is call these methods saving the data to variables and then print them out. To make the sketch easy and tidy, we can place this logic in a method named read_data(). Listing 6-2 shows the completed read_data() method.

Listing 6-2. The read_data() Method

```
void read_data() {
  // Read humidity
  float humidity = dht.readHumidity();
  // Read temperature as Celsius
  float temp_c = dht.readTemperature();
  // Read temperature as Fahrenheit (isFahrenheit = true)
  float temp_f = dht.readTemperature(true);

  // Check for errors and return if any variable has no value
  if (isnan(temp_c) || isnan(temp_f) || isnan(humidity)) {
    Serial.println("ERROR: Cannot read all data from DHT-22.");
    return;
  }
```

```
// Calculate heat index for Celsius
float hi_c = dht.computeHeatIndex(temp_c, humidity, false);
// Calculate heat index for temperature in Fahrenheit
float hi_f = dht.computeHeatIndex(temp_f, humidity, true);
Serial.print("Humidity: ");
Serial.print(humidity);
Serial.print("%, ");
Serial.print(temp_c);
Serial.print("C, ");
Serial.print(temp_f);
Serial.println("F ");
Serial.print("        Heat Index: ");
Serial.print(hi_c);
Serial.print("C, ");
Serial.print(hi_f);
Serial.println("F ");
}
```

Notice the code is pretty simple. We just read the values and then use the Serial.print() and Serial.println() methods to write the data to the serial monitor.

The only thing left is the setup() and loop() methods. The setup() method simply initializes the Serial and dht classes. The loop() method uses a delay and calls the read_data() method. Listing 6-3 shows the completed sketch.

Listing 6-3. Completed Sketch: Reading a DHT-22 Sensor

```
/*
  Beginning Sensor Networks Second Edition
  Sensor Networks Example Arduino Hosted Sensor Node
  This sensor node uses a DHT22 sensor to read temperature and
  humidity printing the results in the serial monitor.
```

```
*/
#include "DHT.h"

#define DHTPIN 7          // DHT2 data is on pin 7
#define read_delay 5000   // 5 seconds
#define DHTTYPE DHT22     // DHT 22 (AM2302)

DHT dht(DHTPIN, DHTTYPE);

void read_data() {
  // Read humidity
  float humidity = dht.readHumidity();
  // Read temperature as Celsius
  float temp_c = dht.readTemperature();
  // Read temperature as Fahrenheit (isFahrenheit = true)
  float temp_f = dht.readTemperature(true);

  // Check for errors and return if any variable has no value
  if (isnan(temp_c) || isnan(temp_f) || isnan(humidity)) {
    Serial.println("ERROR: Cannot read all data from DHT-22.");
    return;
  }
  // Calculate heat index for Celsius
  float hi_c = dht.computeHeatIndex(temp_c, humidity, false);
  // Calculate heat index for temperature in Fahrenheit
  float hi_f = dht.computeHeatIndex(temp_f, humidity, true);
  Serial.print("Humidity: ");
  Serial.print(humidity);
  Serial.print("%, ");
  Serial.print(temp_c);
  Serial.print("C, ");
  Serial.print(temp_f);
  Serial.println("F ");
```

```
  Serial.print("      Heat Index: ");
  Serial.print(hi_c);
  Serial.print("C, ");
  Serial.print(hi_f);
  Serial.println("F ");
}

void setup() {
  Serial.begin(115200);   // Set the serial port speed
  dht.begin();
  delay(1000);
  Serial.println("Welcome to the DHT-22 Arduino example!\n");
}

void loop() {
  delay(read_delay);
  read_data();
}
```

If you have not done so already, open a new Arduino sketch by clicking the *New menu* button or by choosing *File* ➤ *New*. Now you can compile, upload, and test the project. You can name it whatever you like such as dht22_example.ino.

Test Execution

Executing the sketch means uploading it to your Arduino and watching it run. If you haven't connected your Arduino, you can do that now.

I like to begin by compiling the sketch. Click the check mark on the left side of the Arduino application, and observe the output in the message screen at the bottom. If you see errors, fix them and retry the compile. Common errors include missing the DHT22 library (which may require restarting the Arduino application), typing errors, syntax errors, and the like. Once everything compiles correctly, you are ready to upload your sketch by clicking the *Upload* button on the toolbar.

Right after the upload completes, open the serial monitor by clicking the button at right on the toolbar. Observe the Arduino messages. Listing 6-4 shows the typical output you should see.

Listing 6-4. Output of the DHT22 Sensor Sketch

```
Welcome to the DHT-22 Arduino example!
Humidity: 48.00%, 18.20C, 64.76F
       Heat Index: 17.33C, 63.19F
Humidity: 50.00%, 18.30C, 64.94F
       Heat Index: 17.49C, 63.48F
Humidity: 51.80%, 19.10C, 66.38F
       Heat Index: 18.42C, 65.15F
Humidity: 53.60%, 20.20C, 68.36F
       Heat Index: 19.67C, 67.42F
Humidity: 53.20%, 21.40C, 70.52F
       Heat Index: 20.98C, 69.77F
Humidity: 51.50%, 22.10C, 71.78F
       Heat Index: 21.71C, 71.08F
Humidity: 50.00%, 22.50C, 72.50F
       Heat Index: 22.11C, 71.80F
Humidity: 48.50%, 22.60C, 72.68F
       Heat Index: 22.18C, 71.93F
```

If you see similar output, congratulations! You have just built your first Arduino-hosted sensor node. This is an important step in building your sensor network, as you now have the tools needed to start building more sophisticated, wireless sensor nodes and aggregate nodes for recording sensor data.

Let's take the Arduino sensor experience one step further and add XBee modules to enable the sensor to be placed away from the Arduino. This effectively demonstrates how an Arduino can remotely host a number of sensor nodes and thus become an aggregate node in a sensor network.

Project: Using an Arduino As a Data Collector for XBee Sensor Nodes

This project combines what you have learned about the Arduino in this chapter and the XBee in Chapters 2 and 4. More specifically, you use an Arduino and a remote sensor that connects the sensor with the Arduino using XBee modules. We will reuse the XBee sensor node from Chapter 4 and use the Arduino to read the data.

XBee Sensor Node

Follow the text from Chapter 4 to create the XBee sensor node. As a reminder, this node is constructed as shown in Figure 6-24.

Figure 6-24. *XBee sensor node*

If you have not configured the sensor node from Chapter 4 or if you need to reset the module, you should begin by ensuring the latest firmware is loaded and use the settings shown in Table 6-3. Note that you do not need the *IR* setting from Chapter 4, but it's OK if you want to reuse the module you used in that chapter.

Table 6-3. *XBee Sensor Node Options and Values*

Code	Setting Name	Description	Value
D3	AD3/DIO3	Trigger analog or digital data recording	2—ADC
ID	PAN ID	Id for the network	8088
IR	I/O Sampling Rate	Time to wait to send data	3A98—15,000ms
NI	Node Identifier	Name for the node	TMP36
V+	Supply Voltage Threshold	Supply voltage	FFFF (always send)

Notice unlike the project from Chapter 5, we must set up the I/O sampling rate. This is because the library we will be using does not have the same ability to search the ZigBee network for our remote node. Rather, in this project, the Arduino will poll until an IO sample is delivered to the coordinator node. Thus, we have seen two different ways to get data from a ZigBee network—requesting data directly from a node (Chapter 5) and polling for data sent from nodes (this chapter).

Coordinator Node

The coordinator node should be configured similarly with the latest firmware loaded and the settings shown in Table 6-4.

313

Table 6-4. *XBee Coordinator Options and Values*

Code	Setting Name	Description	Value
ID	PAN ID	Id for the network	8088
NI	Node Identifier	Name for the node	Coordinator

There is no need to install the XBee module just yet. You need to configure its settings. You do that in the next section.

Now, let's set up the Arduino and XBee.

Arduino with XBee Shield

You can use an Arduino to read the data from the XBee sensor node. This gives you an example of using an Arduino as a data aggregator (collector) of sensor data from XBee sensor nodes. Let's set up an Arduino with an XBee. This project demonstrates using an Arduino to receive data via XBee, but you can also send data via XBee.

Hardware Setup

The sample setup in this section uses a typical Arduino (Uno, Leonardo, etc.) that supports standard shields. Although it is not expressly necessary to use a shield designed to accept an XBee module, most XBee shields are designed to make the use of the XBee easier. In other words, you don't have to worry about how to wire the XBee to the Arduino. Figure 6-25 shows an Arduino with an XBee shield from SparkFun.

Figure 6-25. *Arduino XBee shield (courtesy of SparkFun)*

I use this shield to demonstrate how to communicate with an XBee module. If you decide to use another shield, be sure to check that shield's documentation for examples of how to use it and compare it with the code in this project. Make the appropriate modifications (hardware connections and changes to the sketch) so that your project will work correctly with your shield.

The shield lets you choose to communicate with the Arduino with the onboard serial circuitry (UART[3]) for the Arduino via digital pins 0 and 1. But these are also the pins used when communicating with the Arduino via USB from the Arduino IDE. Fortunately, the SparkFun XBee shield has a small switch that allows you to choose to use pins 2 and 3 instead. You use this option so that you can write a script to read data from the shield via the XBee and still connect to the Arduino IDE and use the serial monitor. But there is a catch: only one UART is available. You must use the

---

[3]http://en.wikipedia.org/wiki/Universal_asynchronous_receiver/
transmitter

software serial library to simulate a second serial connection. The software serial library is included in the Arduino IDE. You see how to do this in the "Software Setup" section.

Tip   If you are using a different XBee shield, you should consult the documentation on the shield and use the pins as instructed. Some shields are hard wired.

If you do not want to use a shield, you can wire your XBee to an Arduino as you did earlier. In this case, you use an XBee breakout board from SparkFun to mate to a breadboard. Figure 6-26 shows the wiring diagram for wiring the XBee Explorer Regulated breakout board to an Arduino. Notice that you use the 5V pin from the Arduino. If you are using a nonregulated breakout board, you should use the 3.3V pin instead. Always double-check the maximum voltage of any component you use before powering on the project.

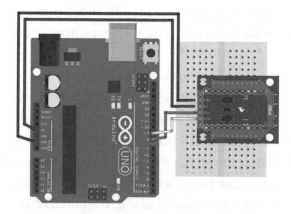

Figure 6-26. *Connecting an XBee to an Arduino via a SparkFun XBee breakout board*

Note   Either of these methods will work for this project.

Whichever method you choose, take the XBee coordinator module off your USB adapter and insert it into the XBee shield or the XBee Explorer Regulated breakout board. Now that the hardware is ready, let's set up your Arduino environment and write a sketch to read the data from the XBee sensor node.

Software Setup

Like most sensors, we need a library to connect to and read the data. Fortunately, there is a nice XBee serial library for Arduino. We install it like we did the DHT22 library by opening a new sketch and choose *Sketch ➤ Include Library ➤ Manage Libraries...* from the menu, then search for XBee, and install the library from Andrew Rapp. Figure 6-27 shows the library manager with the correct library chosen. Install it by clicking *Install*.

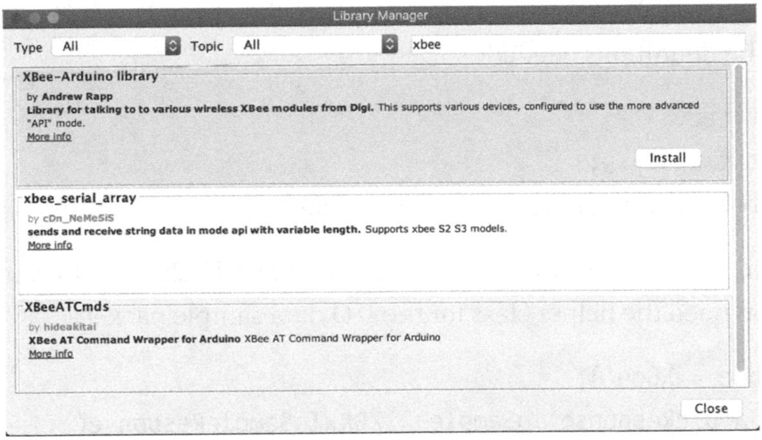

Figure 6-27. Loading the XBee Arduino library

Once the library is installed and you have restarted your Arduino IDE, you can write the script to read the data from the XBee. The library has classes for each of the popular XBee data packets to send and receive data to or from an XBee. This project uses the IO sample class because you know that is the only packet we are interested in using in this project.

You need to create several parts of the sketch. Using the XBee library is easier than writing your own communication methods, but the library has certain setup steps and methods you need to use to read the data packet.

To begin, let's include the library headers for the XBee and software serial libraries. Recall that the software serial library is part of the Arduino IDE:

```
#include <XBee.h>
#include <SoftwareSerial.h>
```

Now you must define the pins you use to communicate to the XBee module. You use the serial monitor as an output device, so you need to use alternative pins. In this case, you use pins 2 and 3 for the receive and transmit connections. You need to define these and initialize the software serial library and use that to communicate to the XBee. The following shows the definitions needed:

```
uint8_t recv = 8;
uint8_t trans = 9;
SoftwareSerial soft_serial(recv, trans);
```

Next, you must instantiate the XBee library and helper classes. In this case, you need the helper class for the I/O data sample packet:

```
XBee xbee = XBee();
ZBRxIoSampleResponse ioSample = ZBRxIoSampleResponse();
```

Now we are ready to write the startup code. For this project, you must initiate the software serial library and pass that to the XBee library for use in communicating with the XBee module. You also need to initialize the default serial class so that you can use print() statements to display the data read in a later portion of the code. The following shows the complete setup() method:

```
void setup() {
  Serial.begin(9600);
  while (!Serial);    // Leonardo boards need to wait for Serial
                          to start
  soft_serial.begin(9600);
  xbee.setSerial(soft_serial);
}
```

Notice the line with the while loop. You need to add this for use on Leonardo boards. If you omit this and run the sketch on a Leonardo board, the XBee may fail to work. Add this loop to allow the Leonardo time to start the Serial instance.

Now let's code the methods you use to read the data from the packet. You learn how to read the packet from the XBee a bit later. First, let's examine how to get the source address for the data packet. The following shows the code for doing so:

```
void get_address(ZBRxIoSampleResponse *ioSample) {
  Serial.print("Received data from address: ");
  Serial.print(ioSample->getRemoteAddress64().getMsb(), HEX);
  Serial.print(ioSample->getRemoteAddress64().getLsb(), HEX);
  Serial.println("");
}
```

Notice that you simply use the ioSample class instance and call the method getRemoteAddress64().getMsb(). Actually, this is a call to a subclass (RemoteAddress64) and its method getMsb(). This returns the most significant byte (high 16 bits) of the 64-bit address. You do the same for the least significant bit with the getRemoteAddress64().getLsb() call. You then print these values, specifying that you want to print them in hexadecimal. If you were reading data from multiple XBee nodes, it would be handy to apply a name to each address, such as "bedroom" or "living room". I leave that to you as an exercise.

Next, you want to read the data payload. In this case, you want to read the temperature data sent to the XBee coordinator from the XBee sensor node. The following shows the code needed to do this. You use the formulas discussed previously to convert the millivolt value read by the sensor to temperature in Celsius and then convert that to Fahrenheit.

```
void get_temperature(ZBRxIoSampleResponse *ioSample) {
  float adc_data = ioSample->getAnalog(3);
  Serial.print("Temperature is ");
  float temperatureC = ((adc_data * 1200.0 / 1024.0) - 500.0) / 10.0;
  Serial.print(temperatureC);
  Serial.print("c, ");
  float temperatureF = ((temperatureC * 9.0)/5.0) + 32.0;
  Serial.print(temperatureF);
  Serial.println("f");
}
```

Finally, you need to read the supply voltage from the data packet. In this case, the supply voltage appears after the data samples. Because you know there is only one data sample (via the analog sample mask), you know that the analog voltage appears right before the checksum. Sadly, there is no method currently to fetch that information from the I/O sample packet in the XBee library. However, all is not lost, because the author of the library stores the data in an array and has supplied a subclass for you to use to fetch the raw data. In this case, you want bytes 17 (most significant byte) and 18 (least significant byte) from the data. You know these are the indexes needed by counting from the byte following the frame type starting from zero. See Table 6-5 for details.

Like the temperature data, you must convert the value read to volts using the formula discussed previously. The following shows the code needed to read, convert, and display the supply voltage for the XBee sensor node. Notice that you shift the most significant byte 8 bits so that you can preserve the 16-byte floating-point value.

```
void get_supply_voltage() {
  Serial.print("Supply voltage is ");
  int ref = xbee.getResponse().getFrameData()[17] << 8;
  ref += xbee.getResponse().getFrameData()[18];
  float volts = (float(ref) * float(1200.0 / 1024.0))/1000.0;
  Serial.print(" = ");
  Serial.print(volts);
  Serial.println(" volts.");
}
```

Take some time to examine the calculations. In this example, you convert the voltage read and sent by the XBee sensor node to Celsius and then again to Fahrenheit. You also convert the supply voltage to volts for easier reading. All these values are sent to the serial monitor for feedback during testing.

Once you have those methods implemented, you place the code to read the data from the XBee in the loop() method, calling these methods to decipher the data and print it to the serial monitor.

Because this loop() method is called repeatedly, you use the XBee class method to read the packet and then determine if the packet is the I/O data sample packet. If it is, you read the data from the packet. If it is not, you add some simple error handling so that the Arduino can continue to read data rather than stop. The following shows the completed loop() method:

```
void loop() {
  xbee.readPacket();
  if (xbee.getResponse().isAvailable()) {
    if (xbee.getResponse().getApiId() == ZB_IO_SAMPLE_RESPONSE)
{
      xbee.getResponse().getZBRxIoSampleResponse(ioSample);
      // Read and display data
      get_address(&ioSample);
      get_temperature(&ioSample);
      get_supply_voltage();
    }
    else {
      Serial.print("Expected I/O Sample, but got ");
      Serial.print(xbee.getResponse().getApiId(), HEX);
    }
  } else if (xbee.getResponse().isError()) {
    Serial.print("Error reading packet.  Error code: ");
    Serial.println(xbee.getResponse().getErrorCode());
  }
}
```

Notice that in the code you check to see whether the packet is available; if it is, you read it. If the packet read is the right frame type, in this case ZB_IO_SAMPLE_RESPONSE, you read the data from the packet and display it. If it isn't the right packet, you print out to the serial monitor the frame type of the packet received. If there is an error reading the packet, you capture that in the last else and display the error to the serial monitor.

Notice the contents of the block of code for the ZB_IO_SAMPLE_ RESPONSE condition. You begin by initializing the I/O data sample class with the data read, then read the address of the XBee that sent the packet, and then perform the calculations for temperature and reference voltage.

Once you understand the code so far, start a new file and type the information into your new sketch window. Listing 6-5 shows the completed sketch for the Arduino XBee receiver project. This code is also available on the Apress site at the source code link for this book.

Listing 6-5. Arduino XBee Receiver

```
/**
   Beginning Sensor Networks Second Edition
   Sensor Networks Example Arduino Receiver Node

   This project demonstrates how to receive sensor data from
   an XBee sensor node. It uses an Arduino with an XBee shield
   with an XBee coordinator installed.

   Note: This sketch was adapted from the examples in the XBee
   library created by Andrew Rapp.
*/

#include <XBee.h>
#include <SoftwareSerial.h>

// Setup pin definitions for XBee shield
uint8_t recv = 2;
uint8_t trans = 3;
SoftwareSerial soft_serial(recv, trans);

// Instantiate an instance of the XBee library
XBee xbee = XBee();

// Instantiate an instance of the IO sample class
ZBRxIoSampleResponse ioSample = ZBRxIoSampleResponse();
```

```
void setup() {
  Serial.begin(9600);
  while (!Serial);    // Leonardo boards need to wait for Serial
                          to start
  soft_serial.begin(9600);
  xbee.setSerial(soft_serial);
  Serial.println("Hello. Welcome to the Arduino XBee Data
Aggregator.");
}

// Get address and print it
void get_address(ZBRxIoSampleResponse *ioSample) {
  Serial.print("Received data from address: ");
  Serial.print(ioSample->getRemoteAddress64().getMsb(), HEX);
  Serial.print(ioSample->getRemoteAddress64().getLsb(), HEX);
  Serial.println("");
}

// Get temperature and print it
void get_temperature(ZBRxIoSampleResponse *ioSample) {
  float adc_data = ioSample->getAnalog(3);

  Serial.print("Temperature is ");
  float temperatureC = ((adc_data * 1200.0 / 1024.0) - 500.0) / 10.0;
  Serial.print(temperatureC);
  Serial.print("c, ");
  float temperatureF = ((temperatureC * 9.0)/5.0) + 32.0;
  Serial.print(temperatureF);
  Serial.println("f");
}
```

```
// Get supply voltage and print it
void get_supply_voltage() {
  Serial.print("Supply voltage is ");
  int ref = xbee.getResponse().getFrameData()[17] << 8;
  ref += xbee.getResponse().getFrameData()[18];
  float volts = (float(ref) * float(1200.0 / 1024.0))/1000.0;
  Serial.print(" = ");
  Serial.print(volts);
  Serial.println(" volts.");
}

void loop() {
  //attempt to read a packet
  xbee.readPacket();

  if (xbee.getResponse().isAvailable()) {
    // got something

    if (xbee.getResponse().getApiId() == ZB_IO_SAMPLE_RESPONSE)
{

      // Get the packet
      xbee.getResponse().getZBRxIoSampleResponse(ioSample);

      // Read and display data
      get_address(&ioSample);
      get_temperature(&ioSample);
      get_supply_voltage();
    }
    else {
      Serial.print("Expected I/O Sample, but got ");
      Serial.print(xbee.getResponse().getApiId(), HEX);
    }
```

```
  } else if (xbee.getResponse().isError()) {
    Serial.print("Error reading packet.  Error code: ");
    Serial.println(xbee.getResponse().getErrorCode());
  }
}
```

Take some time to ensure that the sketch compiles before you upload it to your Arduino. Remember, once the sketch is uploaded, it begins to run. Save it as xbee_sensor.ino.

Testing the Final Project

To test the project, ensure that you start your Arduino first and then the XBee sensor node. Start the Arduino, upload the sketch, and then turn on the serial monitor. You should observe the link lights on the XBee regulated breakout board flicker as the XBee node is accepted by the coordinator on the Arduino and added to the network. Within about 5 seconds, the XBee sensor node begins sending data. When this occurs, the Arduino sketch should start printing statements to your serial monitor. Listing 6-6 shows an example of the output you should see in the serial monitor.

Listing 6-6. Sample Output of the XBee Arduino Sketch

```
Hello. Welcome to the Arduino XBee Data Aggregator.
Received data from address: 13A2004192DB79
Temperature is 12.46c, 54.43f
Supply voltage is  = 3.83 volts.
Received data from address: 13A2004192DB79
Temperature is 11.76c, 53.16f
Supply voltage is  = 3.83 volts.
Received data from address: 13A2004192DB79
```

```
Temperature is 12.46c, 54.43f
Supply voltage is  = 3.82 volts.
Received data from address: 13A2004192DB79
Temperature is 12.46c, 54.43f
Supply voltage is  = 3.83 volts.
Received data from address: 13A2004192DB79
Temperature is 12.34c, 54.22f
Supply voltage is  = 3.83 volts.
Received data from address: 13A2004192DB79
Temperature is 12.46c, 54.43f
Supply voltage is  = 3.82 volts.
Received data from address: 13A2004192DB79
Temperature is 12.46c, 54.43f
Supply voltage is  = 3.82 volts.
Received data from address: 13A2004192DB79
Temperature is 12.46c, 54.43f
Supply voltage is  = 3.82 volts.
Received data from address: 13A2004192DB79
Temperature is 12.46c, 54.43f
Supply voltage is  = 3.82 volts.
```

Did you see something similar? If so, you're doing great work and now have the rudimentary components to build sensor nodes and Arduino-based sensor data aggregators.

If you do not see any output in the serial monitor, do not panic. Instead, double-check that the XBee on your Arduino is plugged in correctly and that you are using the correct pins in the sketch that correspond to how the XBee shield you are using connects to the Arduino (not all shields use pins 2 and 3 like the SparkFun shield). Hint: Check the documentation for your shield.

If all that is correct, make sure you are using the coordinator API firmware on the XBee connected to the Arduino and the router API firmware on the XBee sensor node. If you are still having issues, step back to the previous project to ensure that the sensor node is still working.

You can also try turning off both the Arduino and the XBee sensor node; then turn on the Arduino, wait about 10 seconds, and turn the XBee sensor node back on. Sometimes the handshake process and network join can stall, and nothing happens for a while. Turning an XBee off and back on in this order ensures that it will reattempt to configure.

On the other hand, maybe you are getting data, but it is not correct—the temperature read is far too low for the actual environment. I had this happen once when the wire I was using to connect to the data pin on the TMP36 was accidentally removed. The bottom line is always check and recheck your wiring.

For More Fun

If you would like to expand the project, you can add a second XBee sensor node and modify the Arduino sketch to supply a location for each node. For example, you could label one node "office" and the other "kitchen". The sketch should record (write to the serial monitor) the location of the sensor along with the sensor data from the XBee.

Component Shopping List

A number of components are needed to complete the projects in this chapter. They are listed in Table 6-5.

Table 6-5. *Components Needed*

Item	Vendors	Est. Cost USD	Qty Needed
LED (any color)	www.sparkfun.com/products/9592	$0.35	1
Pushbutton (breadboard mount)	www.sparkfun.com/products/97	$0.35	1
Breadboard (not mini)	www.sparkfun.com/products/9567	$5.95	1
Breadboard jumper wires	www.sparkfun.com/products/8431 www.adafruit.com/product/758	$3.95	1
DHT22	www.sparkfun.com/products/10167 www.adafruit.com/products/385	$9.95	1
150 Ohm resistor	Most online and retail stores	Varies	1
4.7K Ohm resistor	Most online and retail stores	Varies	1
10K Ohm resistor	Most online and retail stores	Varies	1
Arduino XBee shield	www.sparkfun.com/products/10854	$24.95	1

(*continued*)

Table 6-5. (*continued*)

Item	Vendors	Est. Cost USD	Qty Needed
XBee-ZB (ZB) series 2, 2.5, or 3	www.sparkfun.com www.adafruit.com www.makershed.com	$25.00+	2
TMP36 sensor	www.sparkfun.com/products/10988 www.adafruit.com/products/165	$1.50	1
Breadboard power supply	www.sparkfun.com/products/10804	$14.95	1
Wall power supply (6V–12V)	www.sparkfun.com/products/15314	$5.95	1
0.10mF capacitor	www.sparkfun.com/products/8375	$0.25	1
XBee Explorer Regulated with headers	www.sparkfun.com/products/11373	$9.95	1
Breakaway male headers (optional)	www.adafruit.com/products/392	$4.95	1
Arduino Uno (any that supports shields)	Various	$25.00 and up	1

(*continued*)

Table 6-5. (*continued*)

Item	Vendors	Est. Cost USD	Qty Needed
SparkFun XBee shield	www.sparkfun.com/products/10854	$24.95	1
Soldering iron and solder (optional)	Most online and retail stores	Varies	1

Summary

This chapter covered a lot of ground. You explored the Arduino platform, including the many forms available and how to write sketches (programs) to control the Arduino. I also showed you how to host sensors with the Arduino by using a temperature and humidity sensor.

You applied the information you learned about the XBee in Chapters 2 and 4 to create an XBee sensor node to read temperature data. You then set up an Arduino with an XBee coordinator to receive the sensor data from the XBee sensor node and display it in the serial monitor.

In the next chapter, you will discover various mechanisms for storing sensor data either onboard or in the cloud.

CHAPTER 7

Methods for Storing Sensor Data

If you have had success with the projects thus far in the book, you have at your disposal several forms of sensor and data-aggregate nodes. In essence, you have the basic building blocks for constructing a sensor network to monitor and record temperature data. It would not take much more work to add nodes for other environmental sensors such as humidity or barometric pressure. Indeed, the basic sensor node you have built can host a variety of sensors.

If you have run the example projects and experimented with the challenges, no doubt you have noticed that a lot of data is being generated. What do you do with that data? Is it meaningful only at the instant it is generated, or do you think it is more likely that you would want to store the data and examine it later? For example, if you want to know the temperature range for your workshop on a monthly basis throughout the year, logically you need data from an entire year[1] to tabulate and average.

Arduino boards don't have built-in storage devices in general (but some specialized variants do). Raspberry Pi boards come with a secure digital (SD) drive and can accept USB-based storage devices where you can store data, but what do you do with the data from your Arduino-based nodes?

---

[1]Or at least the data from the time period in question.

© Charles Bell 2020

C. Bell, *Beginning Sensor Networks with XBee, Raspberry Pi, and Arduino*,
https://doi.org/10.1007/978-1-4842-5796-8_7

This chapter examines the available storage methods and gives examples of how to store data using those methods. Sample projects are provided to illustrate the mechanisms and code, but I omit the sensor-specific code for brevity.

Storage Methods

Sensor data can come in several forms. Sensors can produce numeric data consisting of floating-point numbers or sometimes integers. Some sensors produce more complex information that is grouped together and may contain several forms of data. Knowing how to interpret the values read is often the hardest part of using a sensor. In fact, you saw this in a number of the sensor node examples. For example, the temperature sensors produced values that had to be converted to scale to be meaningful.

Although it is possible to store all the data as text, if you want to use the data in another application or consume it for use in a spreadsheet or statistical application, you may need to consider storing it either in binary form or in a text form that can be easily converted. For example, most spreadsheet applications can easily convert a text string like "123.45" to a float, but they may not be able to convert "12E236" to a float. On the other hand, if you plan to write additional code for your Arduino sketches or Raspberry Pi Python scripts to process the data, you may want to store the data in binary form to avoid having to write costly (and potentially slow) conversion routines.

But that is only part of the problem. Where you store the data is a greater concern. You want to store the data in the form you need but also in a location (on a device) that you can retrieve it from and that won't be erased when the host is rebooted. For example, storing data in main memory on an Arduino is not a good idea. Not only does it consume valuable program space, but it is volatile and will be lost when the Arduino is powered off.

The Raspberry Pi offers better options. You can easily create a file and store the data on the root partition or in your home directory on the SD card. This is nonvolatile and does not affect the operation of the Raspberry Pi operating system. The only drawback is that it has the potential to result in too little disk space if the data grows significantly. But the data would have to grow to nearly two gigabytes (for a 2GB SD card) before it would threaten the stability of the operating system (although that can happen).

So, what are your options for storing data with Arduino? Are there any other possibilities with the Raspberry Pi? There are two types of storage to consider: local and remote. Local storage includes any method that results in the data being stored with the node, for example, storing data on the SD card on the Raspberry Pi. Remote storage includes any method where the data is stored on a device or medium that is not directly connected to the node, for example, storing data on a different node or even on a server connected to the Internet.

STORING DATE AND TIME WITH SAMPLES

Neither the Arduino nor the Raspberry Pi has a real-time clock (RTC) on board. If you want to store your sensor data locally, you have to either store the data with an approximate date and timestamp or use an RTC module to read an accurate date/time value.

Fortunately, there are RTC modules for use with an Arduino or the Raspberry Pi. If your Raspberry Pi is connected to the Internet and you have enabled the network time synchronization feature, you do not need the RTC module. However, if your Raspberry Pi is not connected to the Internet, and you want to store accurate time data, you should consider using the RTC module.

The following sections examine the various local and remote storage options available for the Arduino and Raspberry Pi.

Local Storage Options for the Arduino

Although it is true that the Arduino has no onboard storage devices, there are two ways you can store data locally for the Arduino. You can store data in a special form of nonvolatile memory or on an SD card hosted via either a special SD card shield or an Ethernet shield (most Ethernet shields have a built-in SD card drive).

If you are truly inventive (or perhaps unable to resist a challenge), you can use some of the communication protocols to send data to other devices. For example, you could use the serial interface to write data to a serial device.

The following sections discuss each option in greater detail. Later sections present small projects you can use to learn how to use these devices for storing data.

Nonvolatile Memory

The most common form of nonvolatile memory available to the Arduino is electrically erasable programmable read-only memory (EEPROM—pronounced "e-e-prom" or "double-e prom"). EEPROMs are packaged as chips (integrated circuits). As the name suggests, data can be written to the chip and is readable even after a power cycle but can be erased or overwritten.

Most Arduino boards have a small EEPROM where the sketch is stored and read during power-up. If you have ever wondered how the Arduino does that, now you know. You can write to the unused portion of this memory if you desire, but the amount of memory available is small (512KB for some boards). You can also use an EEPROM and wire it directly to the Arduino via the I2C protocol to overcome this limitation.

Writing to and reading from an EEPROM is supported via a special library that is included in the Arduino IDE. Due to the limited amount of memory available, storing data in the EEPROM memory is not ideal for most sensor nodes. You are likely to exceed the memory available if the data you are storing is large or there are many data items per sample.

You also have the issue of getting the data from the EEPROM for use in other applications. In this case, you would have to build not only a way to write the data but also a way to read the data and export it to some other medium (local or remote).

That is not to say that you should never use EEPROM to store data. Several possible reasons justify storing data in EEPROM. For example, if your sensor node is likely to be isolated, or connectivity to other nodes is limited, you may want to use an EEPROM to temporarily store data while the node is offline. In fact, you could build your sketch to detect when the node goes offline and switch to the EEPROM at that time. This way, your Arduino-based sensor node can continue to record sensor data. Once the node is back online, you can write your sketch to dump the contents of the EEPROM to another node (remote storage).

SD Card

You can also store (and retrieve) data on an SD card. The Arduino IDE has a library for interacting with an SD drive. In this case, you would use the library to access the SD drive via an SD shield or an Ethernet shield.

Storing data on an SD card is done via files. You open a file and write the data to it in whatever format is best for the next phase in your data analysis. Examples in the Arduino IDE and elsewhere demonstrate how to create a web server interface for your Arduino that displays the list of files available on the SD card.

Compared to EEPROMs, SD cards store many times more data. You can purchase high-density SD cards that exceed 128GB of storage space. That's a lot of sensor data!

You may choose to store data to an SD card in situations where your sensor node is designed as a remote sensor with no connectivity to other nodes, or you can use it as a backup-logging device in case your sensor node is disconnected or your data-aggregator node goes down. Because the card is removable and readable in other devices, you can read it on another device when you want to use the data.

Using an SD card means you can move the data from the sensor node to a computer simply by unplugging the card from the Arduino and plugging it in to the SD card reader in your computer.

Project: Saving Data in Nonvolatile Memory

Recall that you can use the local EEPROM on an Arduino to store data. There are some excellent examples in the Arduino IDE that I encourage you to experiment with at your leisure. They are located under the *Examples* menu under the EEPROM submenu. You need only an Arduino and your laptop to experiment with writing to and from the EEPROM on the Arduino.

Rather than rehash the example sketch for using the built-in EEPROM, this section outlines a project to use an external EEPROM to store data. Unlike the local EEPROM, which uses a dedicated library to interact with, an external EEPROM uses the I2C communication protocol.

Hardware Setup

The hardware for this project consists of a 24LC256 or 24LC512 EEPROM chip like those from SparkFun (www.sparkfun.com/products/525), a pushbutton, jumper wires, and an Arduino. Figure 7-1 shows a typical 24LC256 pin-mount EEPROM chip.

Figure 7-1. *I2C EEPROM chip (courtesy of SparkFun)*

The pushbutton will allow you to reset the memory on the chip. Doing so erases the data values stored, resetting the memory configuration for reuse. You will find this feature particularly handy when using the sketch for the first time, debugging problems, and reusing the chip once memory has been read and stored on another medium.

The chip communicates via an I2C bus. You can set the address for the chip by connecting ground or power to pins A0–A2, as shown in Figure 7-2. You can think of this as a binary number, where connecting ground to all three pins is the lowest address available (0x50) and power to all three pins is the highest address available (0x57). Table 7-1 shows the possible addresses and connections required. You use the lowest address (0x50) by connecting ground to all three pins.

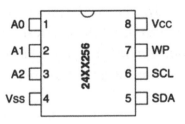

Figure 7-2. *Pinout of the I2C EEPROM*

Table 7-1. *Setting the Address of the I2C EEPROM*

Address	A0	A1	A2
0x50	Ground	Ground	Ground
0x51	Ground	Ground	+5V
0x52	Ground	+5V	Ground
0x53	Ground	+5V	+5V
0x54	+5V	Ground	Ground
0x55	+5V	Ground	+5V
0x56	+5V	+5V	Ground
0x57	+5V	+5V	+5V

Now that you understand how to address the chip, let's connect it to your Arduino. Begin by placing the chip in a breadboard with the half circle pointing to the left. This establishes pin 1 as the upper-right pin. Connect a ground wire to all four pins on the top side of the chip. These are pins 1–4, as shown in Figure 7-2.

Next, connect pin 5 (SDA) to pin 4 on the Arduino and pin 6 (SCL) to pin 5 on the Arduino. Connect a ground wire to pin 7. Then connect positive voltage (+5V) to pin 8. We also use 4.7K Ohm resistors on the I2C lines to reduce noise. Finally, connect the pushbutton to pin 2 on one side and power on the other. Use a 10K Ohm resistor to pull the button *HIGH* (connect it to positive voltage) as you did in a previous project. See Figure 7-3 for a detailed wiring diagram. Be sure to double-check your connections.

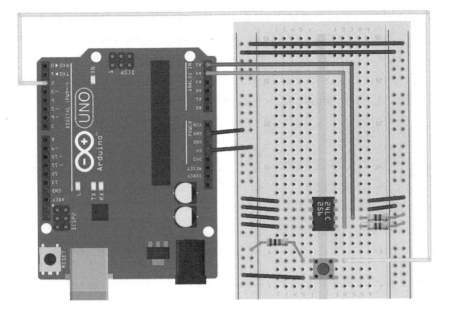

Figure 7-3. *Wiring the EEPROM to the Arduino*

Tip   If you are using the Leonardo board, you need to use the SDC and SCL pins located near the USB port. For the Uno board, they are located at A4 and A5 and on the Mega 2560, they are on pins 20 and 21. Check the hardware pinout for your board to ensure you use the correct I2C interface connections.

Software Setup

With the wiring in place, you are ready to start writing a sketch to read and write data. Rather than write a script to simply store data, in this example, you write a sketch to let you write data to and read it from the chip. You also include a reset operation to allow you to overwrite any memory.

You add the read methods so that you can create additional sketches to read data, should you wish to review the data, move the chip (data) to another Arduino, or use another sketch to process the data.

Let's get started. You use the I2C library (called Wire) to interact with the EEPROM. Open a new sketch, and enter the following:

```
#include <Wire.h>

#define FIRST_SAMPLE 0x02   // First position of first sample
#define MEM_ADDR 0x50       // EEPROM address
#define BUTTON_PIN 0x02     // Button pin
#define EEPROM_SIZE 32768   // Size of 24LC256
#define SAMPLE_BYTES 2      // Size of sample in bytes

int next_index = 0;         // Address of first sample
```

These statements include the Wire library and define a number of constants you use in the sketch. Notice that you have an address for the first sample (the position in memory on the chip), the address for the chip, a pin for the pushbutton, the maximum size (for the 256 chip), and the number of bytes per sample.

You need a number of methods. You need the ability to write a single byte to memory, store a sample, read a byte, and read a sample. Let's look at the simplest forms of these methods—the read byte method. In the following code, address refers to the address of the EEPROM chip, and index is the location in memory that you want to access:

```
byte read_byte(int address, unsigned int index)  {
  byte data = 0xFF;

  Wire.beginTransmission(address);
  Wire.write((int)(index >> 8));    // MSB
  Wire.write((int)(index & 0xFF)); // LSB
  Wire.endTransmission();

  Wire.requestFrom(address,1);
```

```
if (Wire.available()) {
    data = Wire.read();
  }
  return data;
}
```

Notice the process for communicating with the chip. First, you start a transmission with the chip, send the address that you intend to read, and then end the transmission. The address is a two-byte value, and the statements show you how to manipulate the bytes to form a word (two bytes). The next method, requestFrom( ), tells the chip you want to read a single byte. If the chip is ready, you read the data. Finally, you return the value to the caller.

You use the same format for every operation you wish to use with the chip. Let's look at the write method to write a single byte to the chip:

```
void write_byte(int address, unsigned int index, byte data) {
  Wire.beginTransmission(address);
  Wire.write((int)(index >> 8));    // MSB
  Wire.write((int)(index & 0xFF)); // LSB
  Wire.write(data);
  Wire.endTransmission();

  delay(5);
}
```

Notice that you have the same setup—you begin the transmission and set the value at the index specified. What differs is that you send the data (write it) before you end the transmission.

But how do you know what is written to which address (or index)? Rather than just write data willy-nilly or in some illogical order, let's use the first byte at index 0 to store the number of data samples (or rows) and the second byte to store how many bytes each sample consumes (or columns). In this way, you make the data easier to read because it is uniform and easier to manage on a reboot.

In fact, let's add a new method named sample_data() to write some data and display the contents of the data in the EEPROM on startup. Recall for the Arduino that if you want to execute a method once at startup, you place it in the setup() method. The following shows how you can use the existing read method to read data from the EEPROM and display the information in the serial monitor:

```
void sample_data(void) {
  int bytes_per_sample = SAMPLE_BYTES;
  byte buffer[SAMPLE_BYTES];

  next_index = read_byte(MEM_ADDR, 0);
  bytes_per_sample = read_byte(MEM_ADDR, 1);
  Serial.print("Byte pointer: ");
  Serial.println(next_index, DEC);
  Serial.print("Bytes per sample: ");
  Serial.println(bytes_per_sample, DEC);
  Serial.print("Number of samples:");
  Serial.println((next_index/bytes_per_sample)-1, DEC);

  // Add some sample data
  record_sample(MEM_ADDR, 6011);
  record_sample(MEM_ADDR, 8088);

  // Example of how to read sample data - read last 2 values
  read_sample(MEM_ADDR, next_index-(SAMPLE_BYTES * 2), buffer);
  Serial.print("First value: ");
  Serial.println((int)(buffer[0] << 8) + (int)buffer[1]);
  read_sample(MEM_ADDR, next_index-SAMPLE_BYTES, buffer);
  Serial.print("Second value: ");
  Serial.println((int)(buffer[0] << 8) + (int)buffer[1]);
}
```

This technique makes it easy to verify that the code is working by running the dump method on startup as shown as follows. In essence, you create a crude self-diagnostic mechanism that you can use to check the state of the data. If you see anything other than valid data at startup, you know something has gone wrong:

```
void setup(void) {
  Serial.begin(115200);
  while (!Serial);
  Wire.begin();
  Serial.println("Welcome to the Arduino external EEPROM
  project.");
  initialize(MEM_ADDR);
  sample_data();
}
```

But wait! What does this code do if you encounter an uninitialized EEPROM? In that case, you can create a special method to initialize the EEPROM. The following code shows the initialize() method:

```
void initialize(int address) {
  // Clear memory
  // NOTE: replace '10' with EEPROM_SIZE to erase all data
  for (int i = 0; i < 10; i++) {
    write_byte(address, i, 0xFF);
  }
  write_byte(address, 0, FIRST_SAMPLE);
  write_byte(address, 1, SAMPLE_BYTES);
  Serial.print("EEPROM at address 0x");
  Serial.print(address, HEX);
  Serial.println(" has been initialized.");
}
```

You use the write_byte() method to write 0 for the number of bytes and the constant defined earlier for the number of bytes per sample. The method begins by writing 0xff to the first 10 bytes to ensure that you have no data stored; then the number of bytes is written to index 0 and the number of bytes per sample to index 1. You add some print statements for feedback.

But how does this method get called? One way would be to put it in your setup() method as the first call after the call to initialize the Wire library, but that would mean you would have to comment out the other methods, load the sketch, execute it, remove the method, and reload. That seems like a lot of extra work. A better way is to trigger this method with a pushbutton. Code to do this is placed in the loop() method, as shown here:

```
if (digitalRead(BUTTON_PIN) == LOW) {
  initialize(MEM_ADDR);
  delay(500); // debounce
}
```

Now that you can read and write a byte and initialize the chip, you also need to be able to read a sample in case you want to use the chip in another sketch to process the data. The following code shows a method to read a sample:

```
void read_sample(int address, unsigned int index, byte *buffer) {
  Wire.beginTransmission(address);
  Wire.write((int)(index >> 8));    // MSB
  Wire.write((int)(index & 0xFF)); // LSB
  Wire.endTransmission();
  Wire.requestFrom(address, SAMPLE_BYTES);
```

```
for (int i = 0; i < SAMPLE_BYTES; i++) {
  if (Wire.available()) {
    buffer[i] = Wire.read();
  }
}
}
```

Notice that you form a sequence of events similar to read_byte(). But rather than read a single byte, you use a loop to read the number of bytes for a sample. You also need a method to store (write) a sample to the chip:

```
void write_sample(int address, unsigned int index, byte *data)
{
  Wire.beginTransmission(address);
  Wire.write((int)(index >> 8));     // MSB
  Wire.write((int)(index & 0xFF)); // LSB
  Serial.print("START: ");
  Serial.println(index);
  for (int i = 0; i < SAMPLE_BYTES; i++) {
    Wire.write(data[i]);
  }
  Wire.endTransmission();
  delay(5); // wait for chip to write data
}
```

Once again, the method is similar to the write_byte() method, but you use a loop to write the bytes for a sample. Notice that you include a debug statement to show the starting index used. You do this so that you can see the value increase if you run the sketch multiple times.

Note   You may have noticed that I duplicated the code among the *_byte() and *_sample() methods. I did so for clarity of the code, but it isn't strictly necessary. For example, you could consolidate the code if you changed the *_sample() methods to use an additional parameter indicating how many bytes to read/write. I leave this optimization to you as an exercise.

There is one more method to consider. Recall that you use a counter stored in index 0 to record the number of samples written. The write_sample() method simply writes a sample at a specific index. What you need is a method that manages the sample counter and stores the sample. Thus, you create a record_sample() method to handle the higher-level operation:

```
void record_sample(int address, int data) {
  byte sample[SAMPLE_BYTES];
  sample[0] = data >> 8;
  sample[1] = (byte)data;
  write_sample(address, next_index, sample);
  next_index += SAMPLE_BYTES;
  write_byte(address, 0, next_index);
}
```

Notice how you keep track of the number of samples and the next index for the next sample. You use the variable you created earlier and increment it by the number of bytes in the sample. This way, you always know what the next address is without reading the number of samples first and calculating the index. The last method updates the number of samples value.

Now that you have all the building blocks, Listing 7-1 shows the completed code for this sketch. Save the sketch as external_eeprom.ino. Notice that in the sketch you do not include any code to read from sensors.

I left this out for brevity and included some debug statements (shown in bold) in the setup() method instead to show how you record samples. Be sure to remove these statements when you modify the sketch for use with a sensor.

Listing 7-1. Storing and Retrieving Data on an External EEPROM

```
/**
  Beginning Sensor Networks Second Edition
  Sensor Networks Example Arduino External EEPROM data store

  This project demonstrates how to save and retrieve sensor data
  to/from an external EEPROM chip.
*/

#include <Wire.h>

#define FIRST_SAMPLE 0x02 // First position of fist sample
#define MEM_ADDR 0x50     // EEPROM address
#define BUTTON_PIN 0x02   // Button pin
#define EEPROM_SIZE 32768 // Size of 24LC256
#define SAMPLE_BYTES 2    // Size of sample in bytes

int next_index = 0;       // Address of first sample

/* Initialize the chip erasing data */
void initialize(int address) {
  // Clear memory
  // NOTE: replace '100' with EEPROM_SIZE to erase all data
  for (int i = 0; i < 100; i++) {
    write_byte(address, i, 0x00);
  }
  write_byte(address, 0, FIRST_SAMPLE);
```

```
  write_byte(address, 1, SAMPLE_BYTES);
  Serial.print("EEPROM at address 0x");
  Serial.print(address, HEX);
  Serial.println(" has been initialized.");
}

/* Write a sample to the chip. */
void write_sample(int address, unsigned int index, byte *data)
{
  Wire.beginTransmission(address);
  Wire.write((int)(index >> 8));    // MSB
  Wire.write((int)(index & 0xFF)); // LSB
  Serial.print("START: ");
  Serial.println(index);
  for (int i = 0; i < SAMPLE_BYTES; i++) {
    Wire.write(data[i]);
  }
  Wire.endTransmission();

  delay(5); // wait for chip to write data
}

/* Write a byte to the chip at specific index (offset). */
void write_byte(int address, unsigned int index, byte data) {
  Wire.beginTransmission(address);
  Wire.write((int)(index >> 8));    // MSB
  Wire.write((int)(index & 0xFF)); // LSB
  Wire.write(data);
  Wire.endTransmission();

  delay(5);
}

/* Read a sample from an index (offset). */
```

```
void read_sample(int address, unsigned int index, byte *buffer)
{
  Wire.beginTransmission(address);
  Wire.write((int)(index >> 8));   // MSB
  Wire.write((int)(index & 0xFF)); // LSB
  Wire.endTransmission();

  Wire.requestFrom(address, SAMPLE_BYTES);
  for (int i = 0; i < SAMPLE_BYTES; i++) {
    if (Wire.available()) {
      buffer[i] = Wire.read();
    }
  }
}

/* Read a byte from an index (offset). */
byte read_byte(int address, unsigned int index)  {
  byte data = 0xFF;

  Wire.beginTransmission(address);
  Wire.write((int)(index >> 8));   // MSB
  Wire.write((int)(index & 0xFF)); // LSB
  Wire.endTransmission();

  Wire.requestFrom(address,1);

  if (Wire.available()) {
    data = Wire.read();
  }
  return data;
}
/* Save a sample to the data chip and increment next address
counter. */
```

```
void record_sample(int address, int data) {
  byte sample[SAMPLE_BYTES];

  sample[0] = data >> 8;
  sample[1] = (byte)data;
  write_sample(address, next_index, sample);
  next_index += SAMPLE_BYTES;
  write_byte(address, 0, next_index);
}

/* Example write data sample */
void sample_data(void) {
  int bytes_per_sample = SAMPLE_BYTES;
  byte buffer[SAMPLE_BYTES];

  next_index = read_byte(MEM_ADDR, 0);
  bytes_per_sample = read_byte(MEM_ADDR, 1);
  Serial.print("Byte pointer: ");
  Serial.println(next_index, DEC);
  Serial.print("Bytes per sample: ");
  Serial.println(bytes_per_sample, DEC);
  Serial.print("Number of samples:");
  Serial.println((next_index/bytes_per_sample)-1, DEC);

  // Add some sample data
  record_sample(MEM_ADDR, 6011);
  record_sample(MEM_ADDR, 8088);

  // Example of how to read sample data - read last 2 values
  read_sample(MEM_ADDR, next_index-(SAMPLE_BYTES * 2), buffer);
  Serial.print("First value: ");
  Serial.println((int)(buffer[0] << 8) + (int)buffer[1]);
  read_sample(MEM_ADDR, next_index-SAMPLE_BYTES, buffer);
  Serial.print("Second value: ");
```

```
  Serial.println((int)(buffer[0] << 8) + (int)buffer[1]);
}

void setup(void) {
  Serial.begin(115200);
  while (!Serial);
  Wire.begin();
  Serial.println("Welcome to the Arduino external EEPROM
  project.");
  initialize(MEM_ADDR);
  sample_data();
}

void loop() {
  delay(2000);
  if (digitalRead(BUTTON_PIN) == LOW) {
    initialize(MEM_ADDR);
    delay(500); // debounce
  }
  //
  // Read sensor data and record sample here
  //
  sample_data();
}
```

Notice that you include some additional statements for communicating the progress of the sketch via the serial monitor. Take some time to examine these so that you are familiar with what to expect when the sketch runs.

Tip   If you want to write-protect the chip, disconnect the WP pin. Doing so makes the chip read-only.

Testing the Sketch

To test the sketch, be sure the code compiles and you have your hardware set up correctly. When you have a sketch that compiles, upload it to your Arduino and launch a serial monitor.

When the sketch is loaded for the first time, you need to press the button to initialize the EEPROM. This is because the values on the chip are uninitialized for a new chip. You only have to do this the first time you run the sketch. Once you've done that, you should see output similar to that in Listing 7-2.

Listing 7-2. Serial Monitor Output for EEPROM Example

```
Welcome to the Arduino external EEPROM project.
EEPROM at address 0x50 has been initialized.
Byte pointer: 2
Bytes per sample: 2
Number of samples: 0
START: 2
START: 4
First value: 6011
Second value: 8088
Byte pointer: 6
Bytes per sample: 2
Number of samples: 2
START: 6
START: 8
First value: 6011
Second value: 8088
Byte pointer: 10
Bytes per sample: 2
Number of samples: 4
START: 10
```

```
START: 12
First value: 6011
Second value: 8088
EEPROM at address 0x50 has been initialized.
Byte pointer: 2
Bytes per sample: 2
Number of samples: 0
START: 2
START: 4
First value: 6011
Second value: 8088
Byte pointer: 6
Bytes per sample: 2
Number of samples: 2
START: 6
START: 8
First value: 6011
Second value: 8088
```

Did you see something similar? If you run the sketch again (e.g., by pressing the *Reset* button), you should see the value for the start index (from the write_sample() method) increase. Go ahead and give it a try.

Once you've done it a few times Saving Data in Nonvolatile Memory, press the pushbutton and notice what happens. As you can see in Listing 7-2, the start index is reset, and the next samples are stored at the beginning of memory.

For More Fun

The sketch for this project has a lot of promise. No doubt you can think of a number of things you could do with this code. The following are some suggestions for improving the code and experimenting with using an external EEPROM:

- Add some visual aids for use in embedded projects (cases with no serial monitor capability). You can add an LED that illuminates when there is data on the chip. You can also add a set of seven-segment LEDs to display the number of data samples stored.

- Improve the code for reuse. Begin by removing the redundancy described earlier in the read and write methods, and then move the code to a class to make it easier to use the EEPROM in other sketches.

- Add a second EEPROM chip to expand the amount of storage available. Hint: You need to set each chip to a different address, but the methods used are the same.

- Perhaps a bit easier and more inline with the hardware-hacking element of Arduino is moving the EEPROM to another Arduino and reading all the values stored. This demonstrates the nonvolatile nature of EEPROM chips.

Caution   Use appropriate grounding to avoid electrostatic discharge (ESD) damage to the chip.

Project: Writing Data to an SD Card

Aside from an EEPROM chip, you can also store data locally on an Arduino by writing the data to an SD drive. The SD drive is a good choice for storing data because the data is stored in files, which other devices can read (and write to).

For example, although writing data to an EEPROM chip is not difficult, reading that chip on a personal computer requires writing a sketch for the Arduino to transfer the data. However, the SD card can be removed from the Arduino (once files are closed) and inserted in an SD drive connected to a personal computer, allowing you to read the files directly. Thus, the SD card makes a better choice for sensor networks where your sensor nodes are not connected via a network or other wireless connections.

There are several choices for adding an SD card reader to an Arduino. Two of the most popular are the Arduino Ethernet shield and the microSD shield from SparkFun (`www.sparkfun.com/categories/240`). If you use the Arduino Ethernet shield, you can use the networking capabilities and the SD card together. A number of similar devices are available from a variety of vendors.

Adafruit also has a Data Logging shield for Arduino with an onboard SD drive (`www.adafruit.com/product/1141`). The Data Logging shield also includes an RTC, making it possible to store date and time along with the sample. I discuss using an RTC in the next project.

Tip   Both the microSD shield and the Data Logging shield offer a prototyping area that you can use to mount your sensor components or even an XBee module.

An SD drive allows you to create a hybrid node where you store data locally as well as transmit it to another node in the network. This redundancy is one of the ways you can build durability in to your sensor network. For example, if a node loses its connection to another node via the network, it can still record its data locally. Although it is a manual process to recover the data (you must go get the SD card), the fact that the data is recoverable at all means the network can survive network failures without losing data.

It is possible to use an EEPROM as a local storage backup option, but an EEPROM is harder to use, is not as durable as an SD card, does not have the same storage capacity, and is not as easy to use in other devices.

There is one other very important thing to consider concerning building a durable sensor node. Having a local backup of the data may not be helpful if you do not know when the data was stored. The Arduino does not have any time-keeping capability beyond a limited accuracy cycle time. Thus, if you store data locally without a timestamp of any kind that you can relate to other data, the samples taken may not be meaningful beyond the sequence itself (the order of the values).

To mitigate this, you can add an RTC module to the Arduino. The RTC allows you to store the date and time a sample was taken. This information may be critical if you are trying to plot values over time or want to know when a spurious or otherwise interesting event took place.

Hardware Setup

The hardware for this project uses the Arduino Ethernet shield, the microSD shield from SparkFun (with an SD card installed), or the Data Logging shield from Adafruit. For simplicity, I used the Arduino Ethernet shield and show the code changes necessary to use the microSD shield or the Data Logging shield (via #define statements).

You also need the RTC module. There is an excellent product from Adafruit that performs very well and includes an onboard battery that powers the clock even when the Arduino is powered down. Adafruit's DS1307 Real-Time Clock breakout board kit (www.adafruit.com/product/3296) is an outstanding module to add to your project. Figure 7-4 shows the Adafruit RTC module.

Figure 7-4. *DS1307 Real-Time Clock breakout board (courtesy of Adafruit)*

SparkFun also has a product named Real-Time Clock module (www.sparkfun.com/products/99) that uses the same DS1307 chip and interface as the Adafruit offering. You can use either in this project.

Note   The Adafruit RTC module requires assembly. The RTC module from SparkFun does not.

The RTC module uses an I2C interface that is easy to connect to the Arduino. Simply connect 5V power to the 5V pin, ground to the GND pin, the SDA pin to pin 4 on the Arduino, and the SCL pin to pin 5 on the Arduino. Figure 7-5 shows the wiring diagram for connecting the RTC module.

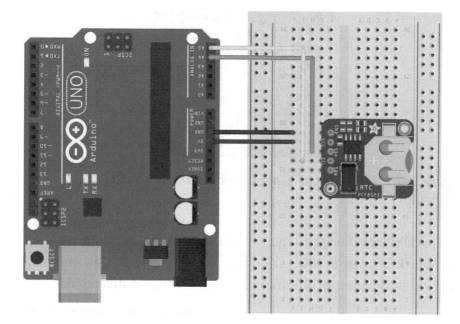

Figure 7-5. *Arduino with an Ethernet shield and RTC module*

Notice that the Ethernet shield is installed on the Arduino. Wiring connections would be the same if you were using the SparkFun microSD shield.

For this project, we will use the Adafruit Data Logging shield with an Arduino Uno Wi-Fi to keep the wiring to a minimum. In fact, all you need to do is plug the shield into your Uno and off you go! Figure 7-6 shows what the Data Logging shield looks like.

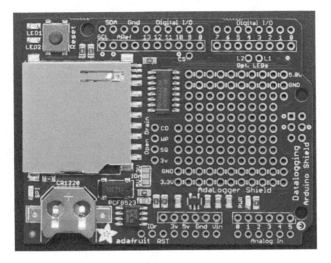

Figure 7-6. *Adafruit Data Logging shield (courtesy of Adafruit)*

Note   If you do not have a Data Logging shield, you can use the RTC module as described earlier.

Software Setup

With the Data Logging shield in place, you are ready to start writing a sketch to write data to the SD card. Be sure to insert a formatted SD card before you power on the board. But first, you must download and install the RTC library from Adafruit (https://github.com/adafruit/RTClib).

Recall, to install a library, we open the *Sketch* ➤ *Include Library* ➤ *Library Manager* and, once it has loaded all of the headers, type in RTCLib and select the library from Adafruit and click *Install* to install it. Figure 7-7 shows the library used for this project.

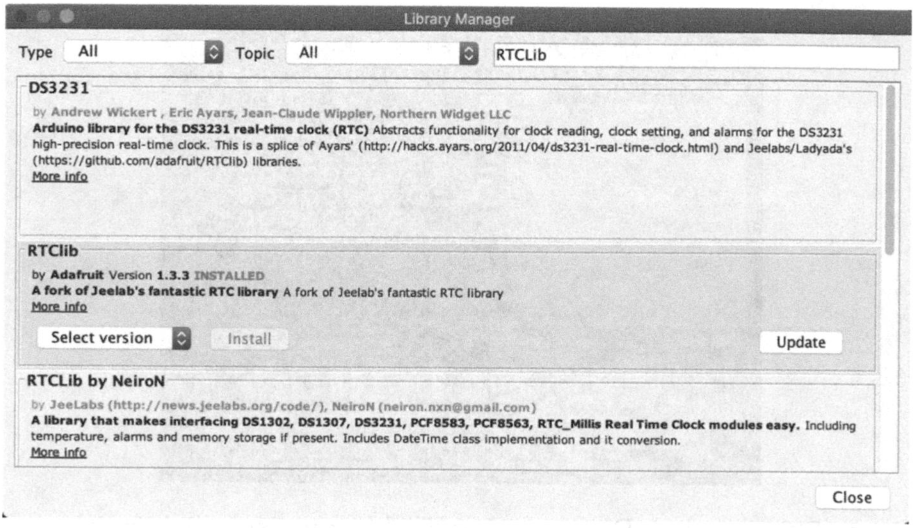

Figure 7-7. *Installing the Adafruit RTCLib in Library Manager*

Once the library is downloaded and installed (and you've restarted the Arduino IDE), you can begin a new sketch named `sd_file_example.ino`. Enter the following code to specify the modules you need to use in the sketch. You need the Wire, RTC, SD, and String libraries:

```
#include <Wire.h>
#include "RTClib.h"
#include <SD.h>
#include <String.h>
```

Next, you need to define the pin to use to communicate with the SD drive. The following are the definitions for all three SD drive options described earlier. I use the Ethernet shield in this example; but if you are not using the Ethernet shield, you can comment out that line and uncomment out the line that corresponds with the shield you are using.

You also include a definition for the name of the file you use to store samples. Note that we must use the 8.3 file name format when using the microSD formatted as FAT.[2]

```
// Pin assignment for Arduino Ethernet shield
// #define SD_PIN 4
// Pin assignment for SparkFun microSD shield
//#define SD_PIN 8
// Pin assignment for Adafruit Data Logging shield
#define SD_PIN 10
// Sensor data file - require 8.3 file name
#define SENSOR_DATA "sensdata.txt"
```

Now you declare some variables. You need one for the RTC module and one for the file you use on the SD drive. Notice I used the RTC_PCF8523 module since the Data Logging shield has that RTC module. Be sure to use the RTC module that matches your RTC chip.

```
RTC_PCF8523 rtc;
File sensor_data;
```

With the preliminaries complete, you need a method to save a sensor sample to the SD card. The method must read the date and time from the RTC module, accept the sample as a parameter, and store the data. In this example, you place the date and time first, followed by the sample value. Name this method record_sample().

Reading from the RTC module is easy with the RTC library. You simply use the library to get the current date and time with the now() method. From there, you can call methods to get the month, day, year, hour, and so

---

[2]This refers to the old FAT file system requirements for file naming, where you can have a maximum of eight characters for the file name and three for the extension (http://en.wikipedia.org/wiki/8.3_filename). Do you remember those days?

on. Forming the string to write to the file can be done in a variety of ways. I used the string class to construct the string. Feel free to use any other method you favor instead:

```
// Capture the date and time
DateTime now = rtc.now();
```

Writing to the file is very easy. You simply open the file in write mode (FILE_WRITE) that automatically permits any writes to be written to the end of the file (append). This is nice because you don't have to worry about seeking or finding out where a file pointer is in the file. Opening the file returns a file object instance, which you can use to write data. Writing to the file (once it is opened) requires only a single method call. The following code shows a simplified set of calls to open a file using the SD library and write data. I leave the details of the record_sample() method for you to explore in Listing 7-2:

```
// Open the file
sensor_data = SD.open(SENSOR_DATA, FILE_WRITE);
// Save the data
sensor_data.write(1234);
sensor_data.write("\n");
// Close the file
sensor_data.close();
```

Of course, you need a few things to properly set up the components and libraries. The setup() method should contain, at a minimum, initialization for the Serial, Wire, and RTC libraries (by calling their begin() methods) and a call to the SD library to start communication with the SD drive. The following is an excerpt of the code needed for these steps.

Notice that you also initialize the date and time for the RTC based on the last compiled date and time of the sketch (effectively, the date and time it was uploaded):

```
void setup () {
  Serial.begin(115200);
  while(!Serial);
  Wire.begin();
  rtc.begin();

  if (!rtc.initialized()) {
    Serial.println("RTC is NOT running!");
    // Set time to date and time of compilation
    rtc.adjust(DateTime(__DATE__, __TIME__));
  }

  // disable w5100 SPI (if needed)
  // pinMode(10,OUTPUT);
  // digitalWrite(10,HIGH);

  // Initialize the SD card.
  Serial.print("Initializing SD card...");
  if (!SD.begin(SD_PIN)) {
    Serial.println("initialization failed!");
    return;
  }
  Serial.println("initialization done.");
...
}
```

Notice that also you have code to turn off the Ethernet W5100 SPI interface. This is only necessary for the Ethernet shield and then only if you do not plan to use the networking capabilities.

There is one other thing you might want to add. You may want to check to see if you can read the file on the SD card. It is not enough to simply initialize the SD library. It is possible the SD drive will communicate properly, but you cannot open or create files on the card itself. Add the following code to the setup() method as an extra check. In this case, you check to see whether the file exists and, if it does not, attempt to create the file. You print a message if you get an error on the open call:

```
// Check for file. Create if not present
if (!SD.exists(SENSOR_DATA)) {
  Serial.print("Sensor data file does not exit. Creating
file...");
  sensor_data = SD.open(SENSOR_DATA, FILE_WRITE);
  if (!sensor_data) {
    Serial.println("ERROR: Cannot create file.");
  }
  else {
    sensor_data.close();
    Serial.println("done.");
  }
}
```

The loop() method is where you place calls to the record_sample() method. In this case, leave the loop() method empty for brevity. Feel free to add your own code to read sensors here and call the record_sample() method for each.

Listing 7-3 shows the complete code for this project. Although the explanation thus far has been about the key parts of the sketch, notice that the listing adds additional error-handing code to make sure the SD drive is initialized properly and the file exists and can be written.

Listing 7-3. Storing Data on an SD Card

```
/**
  Beginning Sensor Networks Second Edition
  Sensor Networks Example Arduino SD card data store

  This project demonstrates how to save sensor data to a
  microSD card.
*/

#include <Wire.h>
#include "RTClib.h"
#include <SD.h>
#include <String.h>

// Pin assignment for Arduino Ethernet shield
//#define SD_PIN 4
// Pin assignment for SparkFun microSD shield
//#define SD_PIN 8
// Pin assignment for Adafruit Data Logging shield
#define SD_PIN 10

// Sensor data file - require 8.3 file name
#define SENSOR_DATA "sensdata.txt"

RTC_PCF8523 rtc;
File sensor_data;

void record_sample(int data) {
  // Open the file
  sensor_data = SD.open(SENSOR_DATA, FILE_WRITE);
  if (!sensor_data) {
    Serial.println("ERROR: Cannot open file. Data not saved!");
    return;
  }
```

```
  // Capture the date and time
  DateTime now = rtc.now();

  String timestamp(now.month(), DEC);
  timestamp += ("/");
  timestamp += now.day();
  timestamp += ("/");
  timestamp += now.year();
  timestamp += (" ");
  timestamp += now.hour();
  timestamp += (":");
  timestamp += now.minute();
  timestamp += (":");
  timestamp += now.second();
  timestamp += (" ");

  // Save the sensor data
  sensor_data.write(&timestamp[0]);

  String sample(data, DEC);
  sensor_data.write(&sample[0]);
  sensor_data.write("\n");

  // Echo the data
  Serial.print("Sample: ");
  Serial.print(timestamp);
  Serial.print(data, DEC);
  Serial.println();

  // Close the file
  sensor_data.close();
}

void setup () {
  Serial.begin(115200);
  while(!Serial);
```

```
Wire.begin();
rtc.begin();

if (!rtc.initialized()) {
  Serial.println("RTC is NOT running!");
  // Set time to date and time of compilation
  rtc.adjust(DateTime(__DATE__, __TIME__));
}

// disable w5100 SPI
// pinMode(10,OUTPUT);
// digitalWrite(10,HIGH);

// Initialize the SD card.
Serial.print("Initializing SD card...");
if (!SD.begin(SD_PIN)) {
  Serial.println("initialization failed!");
  return;
}
Serial.println("initialization done.");

// Check for file. Create if not present
if (!SD.exists(SENSOR_DATA)) {
  Serial.print("Sensor data file does not exit. Creating
  file...");
  sensor_data = SD.open(SENSOR_DATA, FILE_WRITE);
  if (!sensor_data) {
    Serial.println("ERROR: Cannot create file.");
  }
  else {
    sensor_data.close();
    Serial.println("done.");
  }
}
```

```
  // Record some test samples.
  record_sample(1);
  record_sample(2);
  record_sample(3);
}

void loop () {
  // Read sensor data here and record with record_sample()
}
```

I added debug statements to the setup() method for illustration purposes and to make sure the sketch works. Placing these calls in the setup() method permits you to load the sketch (or reboot the Arduino) and check the contents of the SD card to see if the code worked. If you place the statements in the loop() method, then depending on when you turn off your Arduino (unplug it), you may not know how many lines were added or even if the file were closed properly. Placing the record_sample() statements in the setup() method means you have expected output to check.

Tip   If you get SD drive initialization errors, check the pin assignment used in the definition section to make sure you are using the correct pin for your SD drive/shield.

If you encounter file write or open errors, make sure the SD card is formatted as a FAT partition, the SD card is not write protected, and you can create and read files on the drive using your personal computer.

Testing the Sketch

To test the sketch, be sure the code compiles and you have your hardware set up correctly. Once you have a sketch that compiles, upload it to your Arduino and launch a serial monitor. The following code shows the expected output in the serial monitor:

```
Initializing SD card...initialization done.
Sample: 2/29/2020 16:34:27 1
Sample: 2/29/2020 16:34:27 2
Sample: 2/29/2020 16:34:28 3
```

Note   The first time you run the sketch, you may see a message about initializing the SD card and creating the file. This is normal. Subsequent runs (restarts of the Arduino) may not show the messages.

If you run the sketch a number of times as it is written, it will insert three rows at the end of the file each time the sketch is initialized. This is because you placed sample calls to record_sample() in the setup() method for debugging purposes. These calls would naturally be placed in the loop() method after you read your sensors. The following code shows an example of the file contents after running the sketch (starting the Arduino) four times:

```
2/29/2020 16:31:8 1
2/29/2020 16:31:8 2
2/29/2020 16:31:8 3
2/29/2020 16:34:27 1
2/29/2020 16:34:27 2
2/29/2020 16:34:28 3
```

If you examine the file and find more sets of entries than you expect, try deleting the data from the file, starting your Arduino, and then pressing the *Reset* button twice. When you look at the contents, you should see exactly three sets of entries (one for the initial start because the sketch was in memory to begin with and one for each time you restarted the Arduino).

If you see only partial sets (fewer than three rows for each set), check to ensure that you are allowing the Arduino to start before powering it off. It is best to use the serial monitor and wait until all three statements are echoed to the monitor before shutting down the Arduino.

Should the case arise that your sketch compiles and no errors are shown in the serial monitor but the data file is empty, check to make sure the card is usable and not corrupt. Try reformatting the card with the FAT file format.

HANDLE WITH CARE

MicroSD cards are very fragile. They can be damaged easily if handled improperly or subjected to ESD or magnetic fields. If your card does not work properly and you cannot reformat it, it is possible that it is damaged beyond use. You can try using a formatting program from sdcard.org, but if it fails, your card is no longer viable. So far, this has happened to me only once.

Now that you have examined two primary methods for storing data locally on an Arduino, let's look at the options available for the Raspberry Pi.

Local Storage Options for the Raspberry Pi

Because the Raspberry Pi is a personal computer, it has the capability to create, read, and write files. Although it may be possible to use an EEPROM connected via the GPIO header, why would you do that? Given the ease of programming and the convenience of using files, there is very little need for another form of storage.

You also know the Raspberry Pi can be programmed in a number of ways and with one of the most popular languages, Python.[3] Working with files in Python is very easy and is native to the default libraries. This means there is nothing that you need to add to use files.

The following project demonstrates the ease of working with files in Python. The online Python documentation explains reading and writing files in detail (`https://docs.python.org/2/tutorial/inputoutput.html#reading-and-writing-files`).

One thing you will notice is that it doesn't matter where the file is located—on the SD card or an attached USB drive. You only need to know the path to the location (folder) where you want to store data and pass that to the open() method.

Savvy Python programmers[4] know that the Python library contains additional libraries and classes for manipulating folders, navigating paths, and much more. For more information, examine the Python documentation for the OS and Sys libraries. For example, look for normpath() and the Path[5] class.

Project: Writing Data to Files

This project demonstrates how easy it is to use files on the Raspberry Pi with Python. Because no additional hardware or software libraries are needed, I can skip those sections and jump directly into the code.

Start your Raspberry Pi, and log in. Open a new file with the following command (or similar):

```
nano file_io_example.py
```

---

[3]Ni! (With apologies to Monty Python.)
[4]Called Pythonistas.
[5]A path! A path! (More apologies to Monty Python.)

You name the file with a .py extension to indicate that it is a Python script. Enter the following code in the file:

```
import datetime
with open("/home/pi/sample_data.txt", "a+") as my_file:
    my_file.write("{0} {1}\n".format(datetime.datetime.now(), 101))
```

In this example, you first import the datetime library. You use the datetime to capture the current date and time. Next, you open the file (notice that you are using the Pi users' home directory) using the newer with clause and write a row to the file (you do not need to close the file—that is done for you when execute leaves the scope of the with clause). If you feel better using the explicit open and close, feel free to do so.

Notice the open() method. It takes two parameters—the file path and name and a mode to open the file. You use "a+" to append to the file (a) and create the file if it does not exist (+). Other values include r for reading and w for writing. Some of these can be combined: for example, "rw+" creates the file if it does not exist and allows for both reading and writing data.

Note   Using write mode truncates the file. For most cases in which you want to store sensor samples, you use append mode.

For each execution, you should see one row with a slightly different time value corresponding to when the script was run. To execute the file, use the following command:

```
python ./file_io_example.py
```

Go ahead and try to run the script. If you get errors, check the code and correct any syntax errors. If you encounter problems opening the file (you see I/O errors when you run the script), try checking the permissions for the folder you are using. Try running the script a number of times, and then display the contents of the file. The following code shows the complete sequence of commands for this project:

```
$ nano file_io_example.py
$ python ./file_io_example.py
$ python ./file_io_example.py
$ python ./file_io_example.py
$ python ./file_io_example.py
$ python ./file_io_example.py
$ python ./file_io_example.py
$ python ./file_io_example.py
$ more sample_data.txt
2020-02-29 16:50:34.076657 101
2020-02-29 16:53:23.252384 101
2020-02-29 16:53:24.078429 101
2020-02-29 16:53:24.680599 101
2020-02-29 16:53:25.676225 101
2020-02-29 16:53:26.324482 101
```

Did you get similar results? If not, correct any errors and try again until you do. As you can see from this simple example, it is very easy to write data to files using Python on the Raspberry Pi.

Remote Storage Options

Remote storage means the data is sent to another node or system for recording. This normally requires some form of communication or network connectivity to the remote system. Sensor networks by nature are connected and thus can take advantage of remote storage.

To give you an idea of what I am discussing, consider an Arduino sensor node with an XBee module connected to a Raspberry Pi–based node. Suppose also that you want to write your sample data to files. Rather than using an SD card on the Arduino node to store data, you could send that data to the Raspberry Pi–based node and store the data in a file there. The main motivation is that it is much easier to use files via Python on the Raspberry Pi. If you also factor in the possibility of having multiple Arduino sensor nodes with XBee modules, you can use the Raspberry Pi–based node as a data aggregate, storing all the data in a single file.

SINGLE FILE OR MULTIPLE FILES?

I sometimes get this question when discussing storing aggregate data. If your data is similar (e.g., temperature), you can consider storing data from like sensors to the same file. However, if the data differs (such as temperature from one node and humidity from another), you should consider using different files. This makes reading the files easier because you don't have to write code (or use tools) to separate the data.

But are you really talking about only storing data in files? The answer is no. There are a number of mechanisms for storing data remotely. Although storing data in files is the easiest form, you can also store data in the cloud or even on a remote database server.

If you are experienced with using databases for storing and retrieving data, this method will appeal to you—especially if you plan to use other tools to process the data later. For example, you may want to perform statistical analyses or create charts that track the samples over time. Because working with databases is a complex topic, I examine this form of remote storage in the next couple of chapters.

You have already seen how easy it is to use files, but what about storing data in the cloud? What is that about? Simply stated, storing data in the cloud involves using a cloud-based data storage service to receive your data and host it in some way. The most popular form presents the data for others on the Internet to view or consume for their own use.

The following section discusses storing sample data in the cloud using a popular, easy to use, cloud-based IoT data-hosting service from MathWorks called ThingSpeak (`www.thingspeak.com`). You will see example projects for using ThingSpeak on both the Arduino and the Raspberry Pi.

Storing Data in the Cloud

Unless you live in a very isolated location, you have likely been bombarded with talk about the cloud and IoT. Perhaps you've seen advertisements in magazines and on television, or read about it in other books, or attended a seminar or conference. Unless you've spent time learning what cloud means, you are probably wondering what all the fuss is about.

Simply stated,[6] the cloud is a name tagged to services available via the Internet. These can be servers you can access (running as a virtual machine on a larger server), systems that provide access to a specific software or environment, or resources such as disks or IP addresses that you can attach to other resources. The technologies behind the cloud include grid computing (distributed processing), virtualization, and networking. The correct scientific term is cloud computing. Although a deep dive into cloud computing is beyond the scope of this book, it is enough to understand that you can use cloud computing services to store your sensor data.

---

[6]Experienced cloud researchers will tell you there is a lot more to learn about the cloud.

There are a number of IoT cloud vendors that offer all manner of products, capacities, and features to match just about anything you can conjure for an IoT project. With so many vendors offering IoT solutions, it can be difficult to choose one. The following is a short list of the more popular IoT offerings from the top vendors in the cloud industry:

- *Oracle IoT*: `www.oracle.com/internet-of-things/`

- *Microsoft Azure IoT Hub*: `https://azure.microsoft.com/en-us/product-categories/iot/`

- *Google IoT Core*: `https://cloud.google.com/iot-core`

- *IBM IoT*: `www.ibm.com/internet-of-things`

- *Arduino IoT Cloud*: `www.arduino.cc/en/IoT/HomePage`

- *MathWorks ThingSpeak*: `https://thingspeak.com/`

Most of the vendors offer commercial products, but a few like Google, Azure, Arduino, and ThingSpeak offer limited free accounts. As you may surmise, some of the offerings are complex solutions with steep learning curve, but the Arduino and ThingSpeak offerings are simple and easy to use. Since we want a solution that supports Arduino and Raspberry Pi (and other platforms), we will use ThingSpeak in this chapter as an example of what is possible when storing data in the cloud.

Tip   If you want or need to use one of the other vendors, be sure to read all of the tutorials thoroughly before jumping into your code.

ThingSpeak offers a free account for non-commercial projects that generate fewer than 3 million messages (or data elements) per year or around 8000 messages per day. Free accounts are also limited to seven channels (a channel is equivalent to a project and can save up to eight data items). If you need to store or process more data than that, you can purchase a commercial license in one of four categories, each with specific products, features, and limitations: Standard, Academic, Student, and Home. See `https://thingspeak.com/prices` and click each of the license options to learn more about the features and pricing.

Note   Unless you use a work or school account, you may need to pay to use some of the products such as MatLab.

ThingSpeak works by receiving messages from devices that contain the data you want to save or plot. There are libraries available that you can use for certain platforms or programming languages such as Arduino or Python. That is by far the easiest way to connect to ThingSpeak and transmit data.

However, you can also use a machine-to-machine (M2M) connectivity protocol (called MQTT[7]) or representational state transfer (REST[8]) API designed as a request-response model that communicates over HTTP to send data to or read data from ThingSpeak. Yes, you can even read your data from other devices.

Tip   See `www.mathworks.com/help/thingspeak/channels-and-charts-api.html` for more details about the ThingSpeak MQTT and REST API.

When you want to read or write a ThingSpeak channel, you can either publish MQTT messages, send requests via HTTP to the REST API, or use one of the platform-specific libraries that encapsulate these mechanisms

---

[7]`http://mqtt.org/`
[8]`https://en.wikipedia.org/wiki/Representational_state_transfer`

for you. A channel can have up to eight data fields represented as a string or numeric data. You can also process the numeric data using several sophisticated procedures such as summing, average, rounding, and more.

We won't get too far into the details of these protocols; rather, we will see how to use ThingSpeak as a quick-start guide. MathWorks provides a complete set of tutorials, documentation, and examples. So, if you need more information about how ThingSpeak works, check out the documentation at www.mathworks.com/help/thingspeak/.

THE CLOUD: ISN'T THAT JUST MARKETING HYPE?

Don't believe all the hype or sales talk about any product that includes "cloud" in its name. Cloud computing services and resources should be accessible via the Internet from anywhere, available to you via subscription (fee or for free), and permit you to consume or produce and share the data involved. Also, consider the fact that you must have access to the cloud to get to your data. Thus, you have no alternative if the service is unreachable (or down).

Getting Started with ThingSpeak

To use ThingSpeak, you must first sign up for an account. Fortunately, they provide the option for a free account. In fact, you get a free account to start with and add (purchase) a license later. To create a free account, visit https://thingspeak.com/users/sign_up and fill in your email address, location (general geographic), and first and last name and then click *Continue*. You will then be sent a validation email. Open that and follow instructions to verify your email and complete your free account by choosing a password and completing a short questionnaire.

Creating a Channel

Once you log in to ThingSpeak, you can create a channel to hold your data. Recall, each channel can have up to eight data items (fields). From your login home page, click *New Channel* as shown in Figure 7-8.

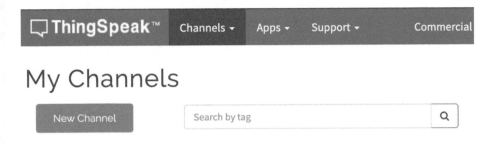

Figure 7-8. *Creating a channel in ThingSpeak*

You will be presented with a really long form that has a lot of fields that you can fill out. Figure 7-9 shows an example of the form.

Figure 7-9. *New Channel form*

At a minimum, you need only name the channel, enter a description (not strictly required but recommended), and then select (tick) one or more fields naming each. That's it. Click *Save Channel* to complete the process.

So, what are all those channel settings? The following gives a brief overview of each. As you work with ThingSpeak, you may want to start using some of these fields:

- *Percentage complete*: A calculated field based on the completion of the name, description, location, URL, video, and tags in your channel.

- *Channel Name*: Unique name for the channel.

- *Description*: Description of the channel.

- *Field#*: Tick each box to enable the field.

- *Metadata*: Additional data for the channel in JSON, XML, or CSV format.

- *Tags*: A comma-separated list of keywords for searching.

- *Link to External Site*: If you have a website about your project, you can provide the URL here to publish on the channel.

- *Show Channel Location*: Tick this box to include the following fields:

  - *Latitude*: Latitude of the sensor(s) for the project or source of the data

  - *Longitude*: Longitude of the sensor(s) for the project or source of the data

  - *Elevation*: Elevation in meters for use with projects affected by elevation

- *Video URL*: If you have a video associated with your project, you can provide the URL here to be published on the channel.

- *Link to GitHub*: If your project is hosted in GitHub, you can provide the URL to be published on the channel.

Wow, that's a lot of stuff for free! As you will see, this isn't a simple toy or severely limited product. You can accomplish quite a lot with these settings. Notice there are places to put links to video, website, and GitHub. This is because channels can be either private (only your login or API KEY as we will see can access) or public. Making a channel public allows you to share the data with anyone and thus those URL fields may be handy to document your project. Cool.

Once you create your channel, it is time to write some data. There are two pieces of information you will need for most projects: the API Key for the channel and for some libraries the channel number (the integer value shown on the channel page). There are libraries available for many platforms, and on some platforms, there may be several ways (libraries or techniques) to write data to a ThingSpeak channel.

You can find the API Key on the channel page by clicking the *API Keys* tab. When you create a new channel, you will have one write and one read API Key. You can add more keys if you need them so that you can use one key per device, location, customer, and so on. Figure 7-10 shows the *API Keys* tab for the channel created previously in Figure 7-9.

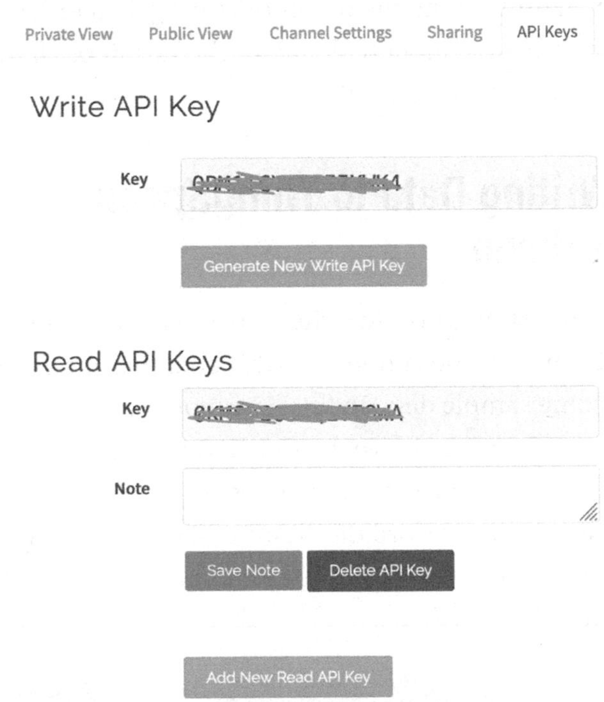

Private View   Public View   Channel Settings   Sharing   API Keys

Write API Key

Key   ~~ODM~~ ~~JK4~~

Generate New Write API Key

Read API Keys

Key   ~~QAM~~ ~~SQNA~~

Note

Save Note   Delete API Key

Add New Read API Key

Figure 7-10. *API Keys for a ThingSpeak channel*

Notice I masked out the keys. If you make your channel public, do not share the write key with anyone you don't want to allow to write to your channel. You can create new keys by clicking the *Generate New Write API Key* or *Add New Read API Key* buttons. You can delete read keys by clicking the *Delete API Key* button.

We use the key in our code to allow the device to connect to and write data to the channel. So, we typically copy this string from the channel page and paste it into our code as a string. Recall, we may use a library that encapsulates the HTTP or MQTT mechanism or, in the case of the Raspberry Pi Python library, we use a Python library and the HTTP protocol. We will see both in the upcoming sample projects for Arduino and Raspberry Pi.

Now that you understand the basics of writing data to ThingSpeak, let's take a look at how to do it in more detail for the Arduino. This is followed by an example for the Raspberry Pi.

Project: Writing Data to ThingSpeak with an Arduino

This project demonstrates how to write sensor data to a ThingSpeak channel. Unlike the previous projects in this chapter, you use a sensor and generate some sample data. In this case, you monitor temperature on an Arduino MKR1000 and save the Celsius and Fahrenheit values to your ThingSpeak. If you have not yet created a ThingSpeak channel for the Arduino, do that now and record the channel ID and API key generated. Use the following data for the channel and name it MKR1000_TMP36 as shown in Figure 7-11.

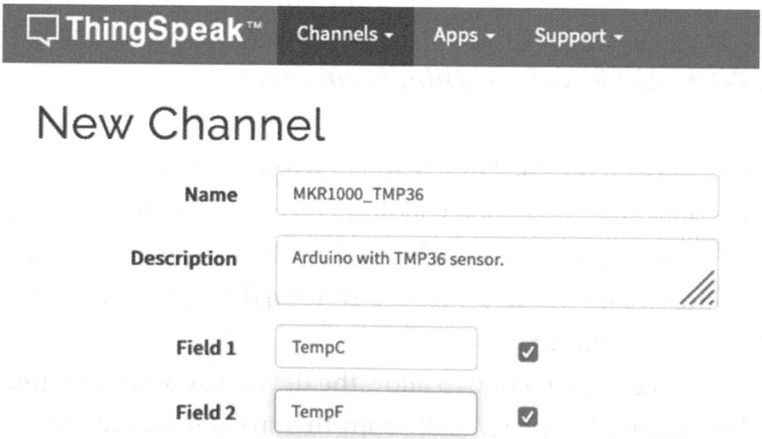

Figure 7-11. *Set up a channel for the MKR1000 and TMP36 sensor*

Click the *Save Channel* button to create the channel. Then, on the *API Key* tab, copy the write key and paste it a new file for later use.

Now that we have a channel created, let's set up the hardware.

Hardware Setup

The hardware for this project is an Arduino MKR1000, a breadboard, breadboard wires, a TMP36 temperature sensor, and a 0.10uF capacitor. Wire the sensor and the capacitor as shown in Figure 7-12. Attach pin 1 of the sensor to the 5V pin on the Arduino, pin 2 of the sensor to the A1 pin on the MKR1000, and pin 3 to ground on the MKR1000. The capacitor is also attached to pins 1 and 3 of the sensor (orientation does not matter).

Tip   You can use the newer MKR models, provided they are of the Wi-Fi variety.

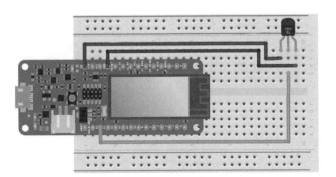

Figure 7-12. *Wiring setup for the ThingSpeak temperature feed for the Arduino*

To use connect to the Internet, you will also need a Wi-Fi access point or router to connect. You will need the SSID and password for the connection.

Now, let's see how we set up the software and the sketch for the project.

Configuring the Arduino IDE

We will need to set up several things in our Arduino IDE in order to create the sketch. We will need to ensure the MKR boards are supported and the ThingSpeak and the Wi-Fi 101 libraries are installed. Let's begin with the MKR board support.

In the Arduino IDE, open a new sketch and click *Tools* ➤ *Board XXXX* ➤ *Boards Manager...* (the *XXXX* represents the board you used last). When the form loads, type Arduino&MKR1000 into the search box and install the Arduino SAMD support as shown in Figure 7-13.

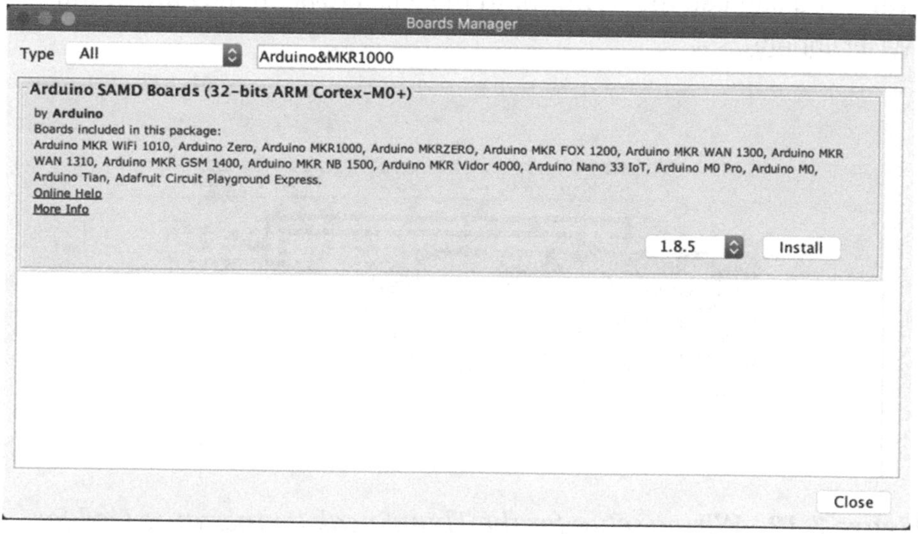

Figure 7-13. Installing the SAMD Boards support

Click the *Install* button to install the board support module. On some PC platforms, the Arduino IDE may prompt you to install the board support when you start the IDE for the first time with the board connected to your PC.

388

Now, let's install the two libraries we need. You can do them in either order. In the Arduino IDE, choose *Sketch* ➤ *Include Library...* ➤ *Manage Libraries*. Enter ThingSpeak in the search box and then click the *Install* button as shown in Figure 7-14. Once again, click *Install* to install the library.

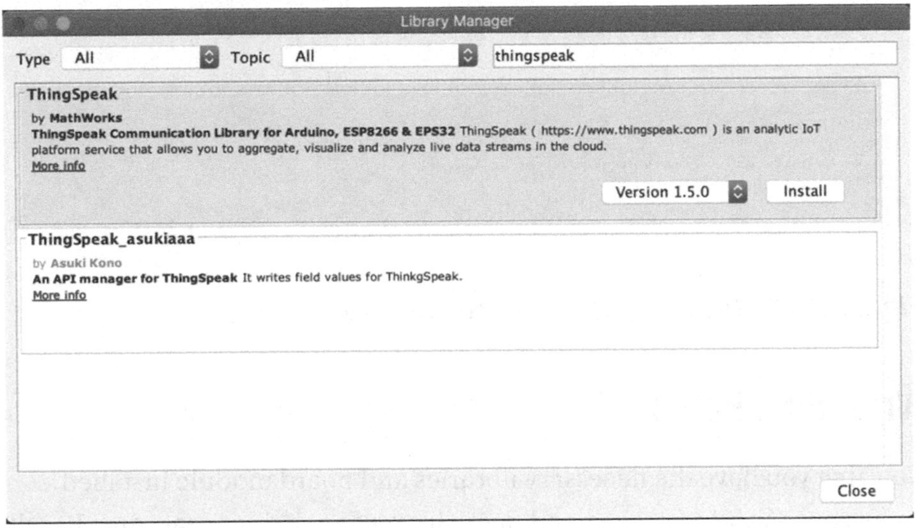

Figure 7-14. *Installing the ThingSpeak library*

We also need the Wi-Fi 101 library to permit use to communicate with the Internet. In the Arduino IDE, choose *Sketch* ➤ *Include Library...* ➤ *Manage Libraries*. Enter Wi-Fi 101 in the search box and then click the *Install* button as shown in Figure 7-15. Once again, click *Install* to install the library.

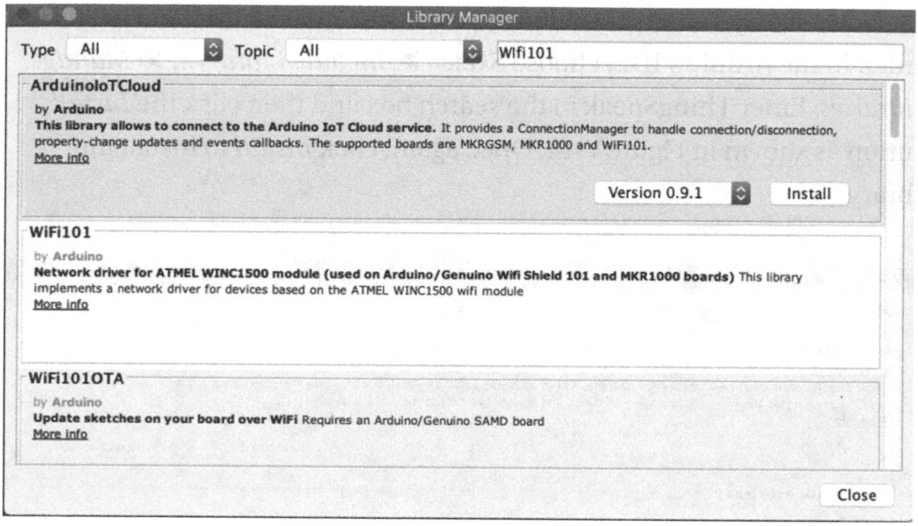

Figure 7-15. *Installing the WiFi 101 library*

Write the Sketch

Now that you have the necessary libraries and board module installed, open a new Arduino project and name it arduino_thingspeak.ino. Recall, we will use a TMP36 and read the values from pin A1 on the MKR1000. We have seen code to read the TMP36 in Chapter 6, so we will skip the explanation and dive into how to interact with ThingSpeak.

In this example, we will see how to store our API Key and other critical data in a separate header (.h) file, which will be part of the sketch and saved in the same folder. To add a header file, click the *small down arrow* button to the right of the sketch and select *New Tab* as shown in Figure 7-16. In the prompt, enter secrets.h and press *Enter*. This will open a *new* tab. Click that tab to open the file.

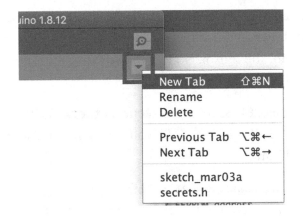

Figure 7-16. *Add New Tab*

We will place the Wi-Fi and our ThingSpeak channel data in this file. Use the #define directive to create new strings that we will use in the main sketch. The following code shows the lines and data you need for the file. Type these in and save the file.

```
#define SECRET_SSID "YOUR_SSID"                     // SSID
#define SECRET_PASS "SSID_PASS"                     // WiFi
                                                       Password
#define SECRET_CH_ID 0000000000                     // Channel
                                                       number
#define SECRET_WRITE_APIKEY "ABCDEFGHIJKLMNOP"      // Write API
                                                       Key
```

Now, return to the *main sketch* tab. Begin the sketch with the following includes. You need the ThingSpeak.h, WiFi101.h, and the secrets.h file we just created.

```
#include "ThingSpeak.h"
#include <WiFi101.h>
#include "secrets.h"
```

Next, we need to declare several variables as well as instantiate the Wi-Fi client as shown in the following code. We also add a variable to store the pin number for the sensor. Notice we use those #defines we stored in the secrets.h file.

```
char ssid[] = SECRET_SSID;    // your network SSID (name)
char pass[] = SECRET_PASS;    // your network password
WiFiClient  client;

unsigned long myChannelNumber = SECRET_CH_ID;
const char * myWriteAPIKey = SECRET_WRITE_APIKEY;

int SENSOR_PIN = 1;
```

To use the Ethernet shield, you must also declare a MAC address. The IP address for the Ethernet shield is requested via DHCP. You define the MAC address as an array. This can be a random set of values, provided they are in the range 0x00–0xff. You can use what is shown here:

```
byte mac_addr[] = { 0xDE, 0xAD, 0xBE, 0xEF, 0xFE, 0xED };
```

Next, you define your ThingSpeak API key and feed ID. You also define the pin number for your TMP36 sensor. This example uses pin 0. You can choose whatever pin you want to use—just change this define, and the rest of the code will point to the correct pin:

```
char ThingSpeakKey[] = "<YOUR_KEY_HERE>";
#define FEED_NUMBER <YOUR_FEED_HERE>
#define SENSOR_PIN 0
```

Now we are ready to write the setup() method. You must initialize the serial class (so you can use the serial monitor) and initialize the Wi-Fi and ThingSpeak client. You use the begin() method for each of these operations. For the Wi-Fi class, you pass in the SSID and password defined earlier. The complete setup() method is as follows:

```
void setup() {
  Serial.begin(115200);        // Initialize serial
  while (!Serial);
  // Connect to WiFi
  Serial.println("Welcome to the MKR1000 + TMP36 ThingSpeak
  Example!");
  while(WiFi.status() != WL_CONNECTED){
    WiFi.begin(ssid, pass);
    delay(5000);
  }
  Serial.println(" Connected.");
  ThingSpeak.begin(client);  // Initialize ThingSpeak
}
```

Finally, the loop() method contains the code to read the sensor, calculate the temperature in Celsius and Fahrenheit, and send those data to our ThingSpeak channel. To do so, we first call the setField() method for the ThingSpeak library to set each field we want to update (field numbers start at 1). We then use the writeFields() method to send the data to ThingSpeak. We can check the result of that call to ensure the code returned is 200, which means success (OK). A simplified version of the loop() method is shown here:

```
void loop() {
  // Read TMP36 here

  // Set the fields with the values
  ThingSpeak.setField(1, temperatureC);
  ThingSpeak.setField(2, temperatureF);

  // Write to the ThingSpeak channel
  int res = ThingSpeak.writeFields(myChannelNumber, myWriteAPIKey);
  if (res == 200) {
    Serial.println("Channel update successful.");
```

```
  } else {
    Serial.print("Problem updating channel. HTTP error code ");
    Serial.println(res);
  }
  Serial.println("sleeping...");
  delay(20000); // Wait 20 seconds to update the channel again
}
```

Notice we display the actual result if it does not return a code of 200. Notice also we add a sleep (delay()) at the end to sleep for 20 seconds. We do this because the ThingSpeak free account is limited to updates once every 15 seconds.

Now that you understand the flow and contents of the sketch, you can complete the missing pieces and start testing. Listing 7-4 shows the complete sketch for this project.

Listing 7-4. Arduino-Based ThingSpeak Channel Write

```
/**
  Beginning Sensor Networks Second Edition
  Sensor Networks Arduino ThingSpeak Write Example

  This project demonstrates how to write data to a ThingSpeak
  channel.
*/

#include "ThingSpeak.h"
#include <WiFi101.h>
#include "secrets.h"

char ssid[] = SECRET_SSID;   // your network SSID (name)
char pass[] = SECRET_PASS;   // your network password
WiFiClient  client;
```

```
unsigned long myChannelNumber = SECRET_CH_ID;
const char * myWriteAPIKey = SECRET_WRITE_APIKEY;

int SENSOR_PIN = 1;

void setup() {
  Serial.begin(115200);        // Initialize serial
  while (!Serial);
  // Connect to WiFi
  Serial.println("Welcome to the MKR1000 + TMP36 ThingSpeak
  Example!");
  Serial.print("Attempting to connect to SSID: ");
  Serial.print(SECRET_SSID);
  Serial.print(" ");
  while(WiFi.status() != WL_CONNECTED){
    WiFi.begin(ssid, pass);
    Serial.print(".");
    delay(5000);
  }
  Serial.println(" Connected.");
  ThingSpeak.begin(client);  // Initialize ThingSpeak
}

void loop() {
  // Read TMP36
  float adc_data = analogRead(A1);
  float voltage = adc_data *  (3.3 / 1024.0);
  Serial.print("Temperature is ");
  float temperatureC = (voltage - 0.525) / 0.01;
  Serial.print(temperatureC);
  Serial.print("C, ");
  float temperatureF = ((temperatureC * 9.0)/5.0) + 32.0;
```

```
Serial.print(temperatureF);
Serial.println("F");

// Set the fields with the values
ThingSpeak.setField(1, temperatureC);
ThingSpeak.setField(2, temperatureF);

// Write to the ThingSpeak channel
int res = ThingSpeak.writeFields(myChannelNumber, myWriteAPIKey);
if (res == 200) {
  Serial.println("Channel update successful.");
} else {
  Serial.print("Problem updating channel. HTTP error code ");
  Serial.println(res);
}
Serial.println("sleeping...");
delay(20000); // Wait 20 seconds to update the channel again
}
```

Note   Be sure to substitute your API key and channel number in the `secrets.h` file. Failure to do so will result in compilation errors.

Take some time to make sure you have all the code entered correctly and that the sketch compiles without errors. Once you reach this stage, you can upload the sketch and try it out.

Testing the Sketch

To test the sketch, be sure the code compiles and you have your hardware set up correctly. Once you have a sketch that compiles, upload it to your Arduino MKR1000 and launch a serial monitor. The following code shows an example of the output you should see:

```
Attempting to connect to SSID: ATT-WiFi-0059 . Connected.
Temperature is 15.50C, 59.90F
Channel update successful.
sleeping...
Temperature is 16.14C, 61.06F
Channel update successful.
sleeping...
Temperature is 15.82C, 60.48F
Channel update successful.
sleeping...
Temperature is 16.14C, 61.06F
Channel update successful.
sleeping...
Temperature is 16.46C, 61.64F
Channel update successful.
sleeping...
```

Did you see similar output? If you did not, check the return code as displayed in the serial monitor. You should be seeing a return code of 200 (meaning success). If the return code was a single digit (1, 2, 3, and so on), you are likely encountering issues connecting to ThingSpeak. If this occurs, connect your laptop to the same network cable, and try to access ThingSpeak.

If the connection is very slow, you could encounter a situation in which you get an error code other than 200 every other or every N attempts. If this is the case, you can increase the timeout in the loop() method to delay processing further. This may help for some very slow connections, but it is not a cure for a bad or intermittent connection.

Let the sketch run for about 3 minutes before you visit ThingSpeak. Once the sketch has run for some time, navigate to ThingSpeak, log in, and click your channel page. You should see results similar to those shown in Figure 7-17.

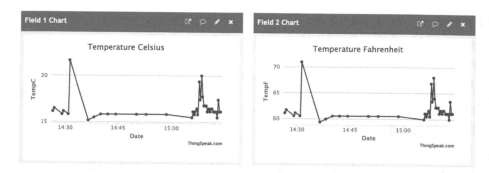

Figure 7-17. *Example channel data (MKR1000_TMP36)*

Notice the peaks near the beginning and end of the graph. I simulated a spike in the data by pressing a warm object device on the TMP36 (my finger). If you try this, be careful not to touch any of the wires!

For More Fun

You can have a lot of fun with this script. Try connecting other sensors and creating other channels in ThingSpeak. You can also experiment with reading the data you saved in ThingSpeak.

Now that you know how to save data to ThingSpeak on the Arduino, let's explore how to do the same on the Raspberry Pi.

Project: Writing Data to ThingSpeak with a Raspberry Pi

This project demonstrates the ease of using the ThingSpeak REST API via HTTP on the Raspberry Pi to write sensor data to a ThingSpeak channel. Recall, to read the analog temperature sensor (TMP36), you use an I2C module that provides 12-bit precision for reading values.

Tip   This example demonstrates how to use the HTTP interface to write data to ThingSpeak. However, this is also a ThingSpeak Python library you can use if you want. You can install it with the `pip3 install thingspeak` command. Documentation for the ThingSpeak Python library can be found at `https://thingspeak.readthedocs.io/en/latest/`.

If you have not yet created a ThingSpeak channel for the Raspberry Pi, do that now and record the channel ID and API key generated. Use the following data for the channel and name it `RASPI_TMP36` as shown in Figure 7-18.

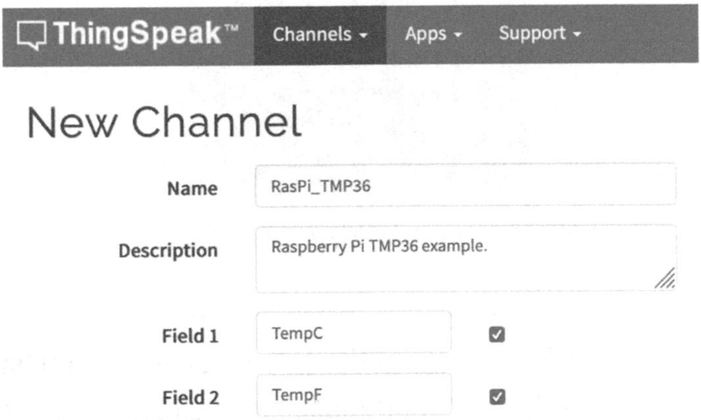

Figure 7-18. Set up a channel for the Raspberry Pi and TMP36 sensor

Click the *Save Channel* button to create the channel. Then, on the *API Key* tab, copy the write key and paste it a new file for later use.

Now that we have a channel created, let's set up the hardware.

Hardware Setup

The hardware for this project consists of a Raspberry Pi, a Raspberry Pi Cobbler+ (optional), a breadboard, the TMP36 sensor, jumper wires, and an ADC module.

I mentioned the Raspberry Pi does not include any ADCs, so you cannot use an analog sensor. In this project, you explore how to use a multichannel ADC with the Raspberry Pi to enable the use of the TMP36 analog temperature sensor. Figure 7-19 shows the 12-bit ADC from Adafruit (www.adafruit.com/products/1083). This module supports up to four sensors (channels). In the figure, you can see pins A0–A3; these are the pins used for each of the channels supported.

Figure 7-19. *12-bit ADC module (courtesy of Adafruit)*

Tip   You are exploring the use of the ADC module with a Raspberry Pi, because it supports the I2C protocol, but you can use the module with the Arduino too. See http://learn.adafruit.com/adafruit-4-channel-adc-breakouts for more details.

You also require connectivity to the Internet via a network connection on the Raspberry Pi. The Internet connection can be via a wired Ethernet connection or via a wireless connection. There are no specific requirements for connectivity as there are with an Arduino.

Figure 7-20 shows the connections you need to make. Most of these should be familiar to you if you have completed the projects in previous chapters. For the TMP36, connect pin 1 to the same 5V connection as the ADC module and pin 3 to the GND connection on the ADC module. Pin 2 on the sensor connects to the A0 pin on the ADC module.

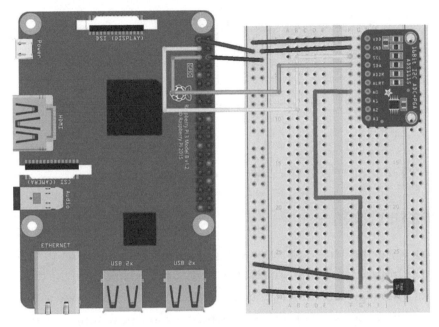

Figure 7-20. *Wiring the TMP36 and ADC to the Raspberry Pi*

Connect the TMP36 sensor as follows (again, see Figure 7-20).

Caution   Be sure to double-check your connections and compare them to Figure 7-20. Failure to connect things properly on the Raspberry Pi can lead to a damaged board.

Once you have made these connections, power on your Raspberry Pi and issue the following command:

```
$ sudo i2cdetect -y 1
```

You should see the ADC module appear as address 0x48 in the output, as shown in Figure 7-21.

```
pi@raspberrypi ~ $ sudo i2cdetect -y 1
     0  1  2  3  4  5  6  7  8  9  a  b  c  d  e  f
00:          -- -- -- -- -- -- -- -- -- -- -- -- --
10: -- -- -- -- -- -- -- -- -- -- -- -- -- -- -- --
20: -- -- -- -- -- -- -- -- -- -- -- -- -- -- -- --
30: -- -- -- -- -- -- -- -- -- -- -- -- -- -- -- --
40: -- -- -- -- -- -- -- -- 48 -- -- -- -- -- -- --
50: -- -- -- -- -- -- -- -- -- -- -- -- -- -- -- --
60: -- -- -- -- -- -- -- -- -- -- -- -- -- -- -- --
70: -- -- -- -- -- -- -- --
```

Figure 7-21. *Verifying the ADC module*

Write the Code

Now that you have the libraries you need, it is time to write a script to read samples from a TMP36 sensor (via the ADC module) and save the data to your ThingSpeak channel. Since we have already written code to read the TMP36 sensor, we will concentrate on the code for writing data to ThingSpeak.

Begin by opening a new file on your Raspberry Pi named raspi_ tmp36.py. You can use the Thonny IDE or a text editor or nano in a terminal to create the file.

Let's begin with the imports. We need to import the http.client, time, urllib, board, busio, and the Adafruit libraries for the ADC module as shown here:

```
import http.client
import time
import urllib
```

```
# import the Raspberry Pi libraries
import board
import busio

# Import the ADC Adafruit libraries
import adafruit_ads1x15.ads1115 as ADS
from adafruit_ads1x15.analog_in import AnalogIn
```

Next, we need to declare a variable for our API Key and instantiate the I2C interface as shown here:

```
# API KEY
THINGSPEAK_APIKEY = 'YOUR_API_KEY'

# Instantiate (start/configure the I2C protocol)
i2c = busio.I2C(board.SCL, board.SDA)
# Instantiate the ADS1115 ADC board
ads = ADS.ADS1115(i2c)
# Setup the channel from Pin 0 on the ADS1115
channel0 = AnalogIn(ads, ADS.P0)
```

Next is the core code for the script. We will use a try…except block to capture the keyboard interrupt (*Ctrl+C*). Inside that, we prepare a special URL to encode the field data for our channel and then open the URL.

More specifically, we encode the data in the form of a dictionary containing the field data using the urllib.parse class urlencode() method. This ensures the strings created are valid for use in a URL. Next, we create a header dictionary and pass that to the http.client class HttpConnection() method to open a connection to ThingSpeak. Finally, we send the data to ThingSpeak in the form of a POST command to the update REST API endpoint. Wow! The following code shows the steps. Take a moment to read through them. They should be easy to comprehend. Remember, you can.

```
params = urllib.parse.urlencode(
    {
        'field1': temp_c,
        'field2': temp_f,
        'key': THINGSPEAK_APIKEY,
    }
)
# Create the header
headers = {
    "Content-type": "application/x-www-form-urlencoded",
    'Accept': "text/plain"
}
# Create a connection over HTTP
conn = http.client.HTTPConnection("api.thingspeak.com:80")
# Execute the post (or update) request to upload the data
conn.request("POST", "/update", params, headers)
```

Listing 7-5 shows the complete code for the script for this project. You will notice we skipped the print() statements and error handling code, but it is all things we have seen in previous projects. Be sure to read through the code before you run it so you can see how it all works. Also, rather than type all of this code in, you can download it from the book website.

Listing 7-5. Complete Code for the raspi_thingspeak.py Script

```
#
# Beginning Sensor Networks Second Edition
#
# IoT Example - Publish temperature data from a Raspberry Pi
# with TMP36 and ADC.
#
# Dr. Charles A. Bell
```

```python
# March 2020
#
from __future__ import print_function

# Python imports
import http.client
import time
import urllib

# import the Raspberry Pi libraries
import board
import busio

# Import the ADC Adafruit libraries
import adafruit_ads1x15.ads1115 as ADS
from adafruit_ads1x15.analog_in import AnalogIn

# API KEY
THINGSPEAK_APIKEY = 'YOUR_API_KEY'

# Instantiate (start/configure the I2C protocol)
i2c = busio.I2C(board.SCL, board.SDA)
# Instantiate the ADS1115 ADC board
ads = ADS.ADS1115(i2c)
# Setup the channel from Pin 0 on the ADS1115
channel0 = AnalogIn(ads, ADS.P0)

# Run the program to upload temperature data to ThingSpeak
print("Welcome to the ThingSpeak Raspberry Pi temperature
sensor! Press CTRL+C to stop.")
try:
    while 1:
        # Get temperature in Celsius
        temp_c = ((channel0.voltage * 3.30) - 0.5) * 10
```

```python
# Calculate temperature in Fahrenheit
temp_f = (temp_c * 9.0 / 5.0) + 32.0
# Display the results for diagnostics
print("Uploading {0:.2f} C, {1:.2f} F"
      "".format(temp_c, temp_f), end=' ... ')
# Setup the data to send in a JSON (dictionary)
params = urllib.parse.urlencode(
    {
        'field1': temp_c,
        'field2': temp_f,
        'key': THINGSPEAK_APIKEY,
    }
)
# Create the header
headers = {
    "Content-type": "application/x-www-form-urlencoded",
    'Accept': "text/plain"
}
# Create a connection over HTTP
conn = http.client.HTTPConnection("api.thingspeak.com:80")
try:
    # Execute the post (or update) request to upload
      the data
    conn.request("POST", "/update", params, headers)
    # Check response from server (200 is success)
    response = conn.getresponse()
    # Display response (should be 200)
    print("Response: {0} {1}".format(response.status,
                                    response.reason))
    # Read the data for diagnostics
    data = response.read()
    conn.close()
```

```
    except Exception as err:
        print("WARNING: ThingSpeak connection failed: {0}, "
            "data: {1}".format(err, data))

    # Sleep for 20 seconds
    time.sleep(20)
except KeyboardInterrupt:
    print("Thanks, bye!")
exit(0)
```

Note   Be sure to substitute your API key in the location marked.
Failure to do so will result in runtime errors.

Now that you have all the code entered, let's test the script and see
if it works.

Testing the Script

Python scripts are interpreted programs. Although there is a fair amount of
syntax checking at the start of a script, logic errors are not discovered until
the statement is executed. Thus, you may encounter errors or exceptions
if the script was not entered correctly (e.g., if you misspelled a method
or variable name). This may also happen if you failed to replace the
placeholder for the API key and feed number.

To run the script, enter the following command. Let the script run for
several iterations before using *Ctrl+C* to break the main loop.

```
$ python3 ./raspi_thingspeak.py
```

The following code shows an example of the output you should see:

```
Welcome to the ThingSpeak Raspberry Pi temperature sensor!
Press CTRL+C to stop.
Uploading 18.46 C, 65.23 F ... Response: 200 OK
Uploading 18.49 C, 65.28 F ... Response: 200 OK
Uploading 19.20 C, 66.56 F ... Response: 200 OK
Uploading 18.41 C, 65.13 F ... Response: 200 OK
Uploading 18.24 C, 64.83 F ... Response: 200 OK
Uploading 18.25 C, 64.85 F ... Response: 200 OK
Uploading 18.31 C, 64.96 F ... Response: 200 OK
Uploading 18.32 C, 64.97 F ... Response: 200 OK
Uploading 18.29 C, 64.93 F ... Response: 200 OK
Uploading 18.35 C, 65.03 F ... Response: 200 OK
Uploading 18.24 C, 64.83 F ... Response: 200 OK
Uploading 18.39 C, 65.09 F ... Response: 200 OK
Uploading 18.25 C, 64.84 F ... Response: 200 OK
Thanks, bye!
```

Let the script run for 3 minutes or so, and then navigate to your
Raspberry Pi channel on ThingSpeak. You should see your sensor data
displayed, similar to that shown in Figure 7-22.

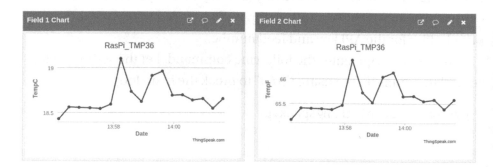

Figure 7-22. *Sample ThingSpeak feed for the Raspberry Pi*

If you do not see similar data, go back and check the return codes as discussed in the last project. You should see return codes of 200 (success). Check and correct any errors in network connectivity or syntax or logic errors in your script until it runs successfully for several iterations (all samples stored return code 200).

If you see similar data, congratulations! You now know how to generate data and save it to the cloud using two different platforms.

For More Fun

You can have a lot of fun with this script. Try connecting other sensors and creating other channels for them in ThingSpeak. You can also experiment with reading the data you saved in ThingSpeak.

Storing Sensor Data in a Database

As you may have surmised, it is possible to store sensor data to a database on a Raspberry Pi. You can use MySQL as your database server and the Connector/Python library to write Python scripts that read sensor data and store the data in tables for later processing. Because there is a lot more involved than a few dozen lines of code (like setting up MySQL on the Raspberry Pi), you explore this topic in greater detail in Chapters 8 and 9.

Component Shopping List

A number of components are needed to complete the projects in this chapter, as listed in Table 7-2. Some of them, like the XBee modules and supporting hardware, are also included in the shopping list from other chapters. These are shown in Table 7-3.

Table 7-2. *Components Needed*

Item	Vendors	Est. Cost USD	Qty Needed
I2C EEPROM	www.sparkfun.com/products/525	$1.95	1
Arduino Ethernet Shield	www.sparkfun.com/products/9026	$24.95	1*
microSD Shield	www.sparkfun.com/products/9802	$14.95	*
Data Logging shield for Arduino	www.adafruit.com/products/1141	$19.95	*
DS1307 Real-Time Clock breakout board	www.adafruit.com/product/3296	$7.50	1**
Real-Time Clock module	www.sparkfun.com/products/99	$14.95	**
12-bit ADC module	www.adafruit.com/products/1083	$9.95	1

*You need only one of these options.
**Either of these will work.

Table 7-3. *Components Reused from Previous Chapters*

Item	Vendors	Est. Cost USD	Qty Needed
Pushbutton	www.sparkfun.com/products/97	$0.35	1
Breadboard (not mini)	www.sparkfun.com/products/9567	$4.95	1

(*continued*)

Table 7-3. (*continued*)

Item	Vendors	Est. Cost USD	Qty Needed
Breadboard jumper wires	www.sparkfun.com/products/8431	$3.95	1
TMP36 sensor	www.sparkfun.com/products/10988 www.adafruit.com/products/165	$1.50	1
0.10uF capacitor	www.sparkfun.com/products/8375	$0.25	1
Raspberry Pi 3B, 3B+, or 4B	Most online and retail stores	$35 and up	1
HDMI or HDMI to DVI cable	Most online and retail stores	Varies	1
HDMI or DVI monitor	Most online and retail stores	Varies	1
USB keyboard	Most online and retail stores	Varies	1
USB power supply	Most online and retail stores	Varies	1
USB Type A to USB micro male	Most online and retail stores	Varies	1
SD card, 2GB or more	Most online and retail stores	Varies	1
Cobbler+	www.adafruit.com/products/914	$7.95	1
10K Ohm Resistor	Most online and retail stores	Varies	1
4.7K Ohm Resistor	Most online and retail stores	Varies	2

Summary

This chapter explored the local storage options for the Arduino and Raspberry Pi. You completed a number of small projects demonstrating each of the possible storage options. I also discussed storing sensor data in the cloud using the ThingSpeak IoT site from MathWorks. There, we learned how to create channels and send data to the channel.

In the next two chapters, I take a break from this exploration of sensor projects and begin discussing another form of remote storage: a database server. Chapter 8 focuses on setting up a MySQL server, and Chapter 9 focuses on using the MySQL server with the Arduino via a special database connector (library) written for the Arduino.

CHAPTER 8

Turning Your Raspberry Pi into a Database Server

Now that you know what sensor networks are and even how to build sensor nodes using an Arduino and a Raspberry Pi, it's time to do something really cool with your Raspberry Pi. The last chapter discussed the various ways you can store data from your sensors. One of the most reliable and the most versatile is storing your sensor data in a database. This chapter explores using a Raspberry Pi as a database server.

While this has always been an option with the Raspberry Pi starting from the older version 2B boards, it is even more an option now that the Raspberry Pi 4B boards are out. They have more than enough processing power and (now, thankfully) more memory for heavier database work. Cool!

You begin with a short introduction to MySQL and then jump into getting MySQL up and running on a Raspberry Pi.[1] If you have experience with installing and using MySQL, you may want to skip ahead to the "Building a Raspberry Pi MySQL Server" section.

---

[1]Note that the Raspberry Pi (which uses the ARM architecture rather than x86 or SPARC) is not a supported platform for MySQL at the time of writing—but you can make it work!

© Charles Bell 2020

C. Bell, *Beginning Sensor Networks with XBee, Raspberry Pi, and Arduino*, https://doi.org/10.1007/978-1-4842-5796-8_8

What Is MySQL?

MySQL is the world's most popular open source database system for many excellent reasons. First and foremost, it is open source, which means anyone can use it for a wide variety of tasks for free.[2] Best of all, MySQL is included in many platform repositories, making it easy to get and install. If your platform doesn't include MySQL in the repository (such as aptitude), you can download it from the MySQL website (http://dev.mysql.com).

Oracle Corporation owns MySQL. Oracle obtained MySQL through an acquisition of Sun Microsystems, which acquired MySQL from its original owners, MySQL AB. Despite fears to the contrary, Oracle has shown excellent stewardship of MySQL by continuing to invest in the evolution and development of new features as well as faithfully maintaining its open source heritage. Although Oracle also offers commercial licenses of MySQL—just as its prior owners did in the past—MySQL is still open source and available to everyone.

WHAT IS OPEN SOURCE? IS IT REALLY FREE?

Open source software grew from a conscious resistance to the corporate-property mindset. While working for MIT, Richard Stallman, the father of the free software movement, resisted the trend of making software private (closed) and left MIT to start the GNU (GNU's Not Unix) project and the Free Software Foundation (FSF).

---

[2]According to GNU (www.gnu.org/philosophy/free-sw.html), "free software is a matter of liberty, not price. To understand the concept, you should think of 'free' as in 'free speech,' not as in 'free beer.'"

Stallman's goal was to reestablish a cooperating community of developers. He had the foresight, however, to realize that the system needed a copyright license that guaranteed certain freedoms. (Some have called Stallman's take on copyright "copyleft," because it guarantees freedom rather than restricts it.) To solve this, Stallman created the GNU Public License (GPL). The GPL, a clever work of legal permissions that permits the code to be copied and modified without restriction, states that derivative works (the modified copies) must be distributed under the same license as the original version without any additional restrictions.

There was one problem with the free software movement. The term free was intended to guarantee freedom to use, modify, and distribute; it was not intended to mean "no cost" or "free to a good home." To counter this misconception, the Open Source Initiative (OSI) formed and later adopted and promoted the phrase open source to describe the freedoms guaranteed by the GPL license. For more information about open source software, visit www.opensource.org.

MySQL runs as a background process (or as a foreground process if you launch it from the command line[3]) on your system. Like most database systems, MySQL supports Structured Query Language (SQL). You can use SQL to create databases and objects (using data definition language [DDL]), write or change data (using data manipulation language [DML]), and execute various commands for managing the server.

To issue these commands, you must first connect to the database server. MySQL provides a client application that enables you to connect to and run commands on the server. The application is named MySQL Shell (mysqlsh) and has many improvements over the older client including a better interface as well as SQL, Python, and JavaScript modes. If you have

---

[3]And use the --console command-line option on Windows systems.

used MySQL in the past, you may be familiar with the older MySQL client (mysql), which you can also use, but MySQL Shell is much easier to use. Please see the online reference manual for MySQL Shell (https://dev. mysql.com/doc/mysql-shell/8.0/en/) to learn more about how to use it, but those who've used the older client or who are following along in the tutorial will take to it quickly.

Tip   It is best to use the older mysql client when working on the Raspberry Pi because it requires one less compilation and installation step, but you can build and install the MySQL Shell on Raspberry Pi.

If you don't already have the MySQL Shell installed, visit https://dev. mysql.com/downloads/shell/ and download it and then install it on your system. For macOS and Linux, follow the platform-specific installation procedures that you use for any other software. For Windows, you can download a separate MySQL Shell installation (.msi) or you can download the Windows Installer, which contains all MySQL applications, tools, and drivers. In that case, you simply select the components you want at the start of the installation.

Of course, you will also need to have access to a MySQL server running some place. The good news is you can install it on your PC! Just download the correct installer from the website (community edition) https://dev. mysql.com/downloads/mysql/, and install it on your system. It is very easy to install, but if you want a step-by-step instruction, see the online reference manual for help (https://dev.mysql.com/doc/refman/8.0/en/).

Once MySQL Shell is installed on your system, you can launch it as shown in Listing 8-1, which shows examples of each type of command discussed earlier in action. Note that these commands will work the same way in the older client.

Listing 8-1. Commands Using the MySQL Shell

```
$ mysqlsh --uri root@localhost:33060
Please provide the password for 'root@localhost:33060':
Save password for 'root@localhost:33060'? [Y]es/[N]o/Ne[v]er
(default No): y
MySQL Shell 8.0.18

Copyright (c) 2016, 2019, Oracle and/or its affiliates. All
rights reserved.
Oracle is a registered trademark of Oracle Corporation and/or
its affiliates.
Other names may be trademarks of their respective owners.

Type '\help' or '\?' for help; '\quit' to exit.
Creating a session to 'root@localhost:33060'
Fetching schema names for autocompletion... Press ^C to stop.
Your MySQL connection id is 8 (X protocol)
Server version: 8.0.18 MySQL Community Server - GPL
> CREATE DATABASE testme;
Query OK, 1 row affected (0.0012 sec)

> CREATE TABLE testme.table1 (sensor_node char(30), sensor_
value int, sensor_event timestamp);
Query OK, 0 rows affected (0.0059 sec)

> INSERT INTO testme.table1 VALUES ('living room', 23, NULL);
Query OK, 1 row affected (0.0051 sec)
```

```
> SELECT * FROM testme.table1;
+-------------+--------------+--------------+
| sensor_node | sensor_value | sensor_event |
+-------------+--------------+--------------+
| living room |           23 | NULL         |
+-------------+--------------+--------------+
1 row in set (0.0003 sec)

> SET @@global.server_id = 111;
Query OK, 0 rows affected (0.0002 sec)

> \q
Bye!
```

If you've not used the MySQL Shell yet, take a look at how I started the shell. Notice I typed in the user credentials in a different format, which is quite intuitive and a bit easier than separate options. Notice also the shell permits me to save the password for faster subsequent logins. Nice!

In this example, you see DML in the form of the CREATE DATABASE and CREATE TABLE statements, DDL in the form of the INSERT and SELECT statements, and a simple administrative command to set a global server variable. Next, you see the creation of a database and a table to store the data, the addition of a row in the table, and finally retrieval of the data in the table.

A great many commands are available in MySQL. Fortunately, you need master only a few of the more common ones. The following are the commands you will use most often. The portions enclosed in <> indicate user-supplied components of the command, and [...] indicates that additional options are needed:

Tip   You must terminate each command with a semicolon (;) or \G.

- CREATE DATABASE <database_name>: Creates a database

- USE <database>: Sets the default database

- CREATE TABLE <table_name> [...]: Creates a table or structure to store data

- INSERT INTO <table_name> [...]: Adds data to a table

- UPDATE [...]: Changes one or more values for a specific row

- DELETE FROM <table_name> [...]: Removes data from a table

- SELECT [...]: Retrieves data (rows) from the table

Although this list is only a short introduction and nothing like a complete syntax guide, there is an excellent online reference manual that explains each and every command (and much more) in great detail. You should refer to the online reference manual whenever you have a question about anything in MySQL. You can find it at https://dev.mysql.com/doc/refman/8.0/en/.

If you are thinking that there is a lot more to MySQL than a few simple commands, you are absolutely correct. Despite its ease of use and fast startup time, MySQL is a full-fledged relational database management system (RDBMS). There is much more to it than you've seen here. For more information about MySQL, including all the advanced features, see the reference manual.

MYSQL—WHAT DOES IT MEAN?

The name MySQL is a combination of a proper name and an acronym. SQL is Structured Query Language. The My part isn't the possessive form—it is a name. In this case, My is the name of one of the founder's daughter. As for pronunciation, MySQL experts pronounce it "My-S-Q-L" and not "my sequel." Indeed, the mark of a savvy MySQL user is in their correct pronunciation of the product.

Getting Started with MySQL

Now that you know what MySQL is and how it is used, you need to know a bit more about RDBMSs and MySQL in particular before you start building your first database server. This section discusses how MySQL stores data (and where it is stored), how it communicates with other systems, and some basic administration tasks required in order to manage your new MySQL server.

Note   I present this information as a tutorial or primer on MySQL. You install MySQL on the Raspberry Pi in a later section.

But first, let's review what a relational database system is and why it matters.

What's a Relational Database Management System?

An RDBMS is a data storage-and-retrieval service based on the relational model of data as proposed by E. F. Codd in 1970. These systems are the standard storage mechanism for structured data. A great deal of research is devoted to refining the essential model proposed by Codd, as discussed by C. J. Date in *The Database Relational Model: A Retrospective Review and Analysis*.[4] This evolution of theory and practice is best documented in The Third Manifesto.[5]

The relational model is an intuitive concept of a storage repository (database) that can be easily queried by using a mechanism called a query language to retrieve, update, and insert data. The relational model has been implemented by many vendors because it has a sound systematic theory, a firm mathematical foundation, and a simple structure. The most commonly used query mechanism is SQL, which resembles natural language. Although SQL is not included in the relational model, it provides an integral part of the practical application of the relational model in RDBMSs.

The data are represented as related pieces of information (attributes or columns) about a certain event or entity. The set of values for the attributes is formed as a tuple (sometimes called a record or row). Tuples are stored in tables that have the same set of attributes. Tables can then be related to other tables through constraints on keys, attributes, and tuples.

Tables can have special mappings of columns called indexes that permit you to read the data in a specific order. Indexes are also very useful for fast retrieval of rows that match the value(s) of the indexed columns.

Now that we know a bit about the theory, let's see how MySQL works to store our data.

---

[4]C. J. Date, *The Database Relational Model: A Retrospective Review and Analysis* (Reading, MA: Addison-Wesley, 2001).

[5]C. J. Date and H. Darwen, *Foundation for Future Database Systems: The Third Manifesto* (Reading, MA: Addison-Wesley, 2000).

How and Where MySQL Stores Data

The MySQL database system stores data via an interesting mechanism of programmatic isolation called a storage engine that is governed by the handler interface. The handler interface permits the use of interchangeable storage components in the MySQL server so that the parser, the optimizer, and all manner of components can interact in storing data on disk using a common mechanism. This is also referred to as a pluggable storage engine.[6] While MySQL supports several storage engines, the default storage engine is called the InnoDB, which is a transactional storage engine.

What does this mean to you? It means you have the choice of different mechanisms for storing data, but for most application, you won't need to change the storage engine. If you do want to change the storage engine, you can specify the storage engine in the CREATE TABLE statement shown in the following code sample. Notice the last line in the command: this is how a storage engine is specified. Leaving off this clause results in MySQL using the default storage engine (InnoDB).

```
CREATE TABLE `books` (
  `ISBN` varchar(15) DEFAULT NULL,
  `Title` varchar(125) DEFAULT NULL,
  `Authors` varchar(100) DEFAULT NULL,
  `Quantity` int(11) DEFAULT NULL,
  `Slot` int(11) DEFAULT NULL,
  `Thumbnail` varchar(100) DEFAULT NULL,
  `Description` text
) ENGINE=MyISAM;
```

---

[6]If you would like to know more about storage engines and what makes them tick, see my book, *Expert MySQL Second Edition* (Apress).

Great! Now, what storage engines exist on MySQL? You can discover which storage engines are supported by issuing the following command. As you see, there are a lot to choose from. I cover a few that may be pertinent to planning sensor networks.

```
> SELECT engine, support, transactions FROM information_schema.
engines;
+--------------------+---------+--------------+
| engine             | support | transactions |
+--------------------+---------+--------------+
| ARCHIVE            | YES     | NO           |
| BLACKHOLE          | YES     | NO           |
| MRG_MYISAM         | YES     | NO           |
| FEDERATED          | NO      | NULL         |
| MyISAM             | YES     | NO           |
| PERFORMANCE_SCHEMA | YES     | NO           |
| InnoDB             | DEFAULT | YES          |
| MEMORY             | YES     | NO           |
| CSV                | YES     | NO           |
+--------------------+---------+--------------+
9 rows in set (0.0005 sec)
```

Common Storage Engines

As of version 5.6, MySQL uses the InnoDB storage engine by default. Previous versions used MyISAM as the default. InnoDB is a fully transactional, ACID[7] storage engine. A transaction is a batch of statements that must all succeed before any changes are written to disk. The classic example is a bank transfer. If you consider a system that requires deducting

---

[7]http://en.wikipedia.org/wiki/ACID

an amount from one account and then crediting that amount to another account to complete the act of moving funds, you would not want the first to succeed and the second to fail or vice versa!

Wrapping the statements in a transaction ensures that no data is written to disk until and unless all statements are completed without errors. Transactions in this case are designated with a BEGIN statement and concluded with either a COMMIT to save the changes or a ROLLBACK to undo the changes. InnoDB stores its data in a single file (with some additional files for managing indexes and transactions).

The MyISAM storage engine is optimized for reads. MyISAM has been the default for some time and was one of the first storage engines available. In fact, a large portion of the server is dedicated to supporting MyISAM. It differs from InnoDB in that it does not support transactions and stores its data in an indexed sequential access method format. This means it supports fast indexing. You would choose MyISAM over InnoDB if you did not need transactions and you wanted to be able to move or back up individual tables.

Another storage engine that you may want to consider, especially for sensor networks, is Archive. This engine does not support deletes (but you can drop entire tables) and is optimized for minimal storage on disk. Clearly, if you are running MySQL on a small system like a Raspberry Pi, minimizing disk usage may be a goal. The inability to delete data may limit more advanced applications, but most sensor networks merely store data and rarely delete it. In this case, you can consider using the Archive storage engine.

There is also the CSV storage engine (where CSV stands for comma-separated values). This storage engine creates text files to store the data in plain text that can be read by other applications such as a spreadsheet application. If you use your sensor data for statistical analysis, the CSV storage engine may make the process of ingesting the data easier.

424

Where Is My Data Stored?

So where is all this data? If you query the MySQL server and issue the command SHOW VARIABLES LIKE 'datadir';, you see the path to the location on disk that all storage engines use to store data. In the case of InnoDB, this is a single file on disk located in the data directory. InnoDB also creates a few administrative files, but the data is stored in the single file. For most other storage engines except NDB and MEMORY, the data for the tables is stored in a folder with the name of the database under the data directory. Listing 8-2 shows an example. The database folders are shown in bold. Some files omitted for brevity.

Tip   When you use sudo for the first time, you are required to enter the password for the root user.

Listing 8-2. Finding Where Your Data Is Located

```
> SHOW VARIABLES LIKE 'datadir';
+---------------+----------------------+
| Variable_name | Value                |
+---------------+----------------------+
| datadir       | /usr/local/mysql/data/ |
+---------------+----------------------+
1 row in set (0.0037 sec)
> \q
Bye!

$ sudo ls -lsa /usr/local/mysql/data
total 336248
```

```
   0 drwxr-x---   12 _mysql   _mysql        384 Nov
4 16:28 #innodb_temp
   0 drwxr-x---   30 _mysql   _mysql        960 Nov
4 17:05 .
   0 drwxr-xr-x   17 root     wheel         544 Nov
4 16:28 ..
   8 -rw-r-----    1 _mysql   _mysql         56 Nov
4 16:28 auto.cnf
   8 -rw-r-----    1 _mysql   _mysql        665 Nov
4 16:28 binlog.000001
 264 -rw-r-----    1 _mysql   _mysql      84608 Nov
4 17:05 binlog.000002
   8 -rw-r-----    1 _mysql   _mysql         32 Nov
4 16:28 binlog.index
   0 drwxr-x---    8 _mysql   _mysql        256 Nov
4 17:05 bvm
   8 -rw-r-----    1 _mysql   _mysql       3513 Nov
4 16:28 ib_buffer_pool
98304 -rw-r-----    1 _mysql   _mysql   50331648 Nov
4 17:05 ib_logfile0
98304 -rw-r-----    1 _mysql   _mysql   50331648 Nov
4 16:28 ib_logfile1
24576 -rw-r-----    1 _mysql   _mysql   12582912 Nov
4 17:05 ibdata1
24576 -rw-r-----    1 _mysql   _mysql   12582912 Nov
4 16:28 ibtmp1
   0 drwxr-x---    8 _mysql   _mysql        256 Nov
4 16:28 mysql
49152 -rw-r-----    1 _mysql   _mysql   25165824 Nov
4 17:05 mysql.ibd
```

```
    8 -rw-r-----   1 _mysql  _mysql        739 Nov
 4 16:28 mysqld.local.err
    8 -rw-r-----   1 _mysql  _mysql          5 Nov
 4 16:28 mysqld.local.pid
    0 drwxr-x--- 105 _mysql  _mysql       3360 Nov
 4 16:28 performance_schema
    0 drwxr-x---   3 _mysql  _mysql         96 Nov
 4 16:28 sys
    0 drwxr-x---   3 _mysql  _mysql         96 Nov
 4 16:36 testme
20480 -rw-r-----   1 _mysql  _mysql   10485760 Nov
 4 17:05 undo_001
20480 -rw-r-----   1 _mysql  _mysql   10485760 Nov
 4 17:05 undo_002
$ sudo ls -lsa /usr/local/mysql/data/bvm
total 64
    0 drwxr-x---   8 _mysql  _mysql    256 Nov  4 17:05 .
    0 drwxr-x---  30 _mysql  _mysql    960 Nov  4 17:05 ..
   16 -rw-r-----   1 _mysql  _mysql   5324 Nov  4 17:05 books.MYD
    8 -rw-r-----   1 _mysql  _mysql   1024 Nov  4 17:05 books.MYI
   16 -rw-r-----   1 _mysql  _mysql   8012 Nov  4 17:05 books_354.sdi
    8 -rw-r-----   1 _mysql  _mysql    281 Nov  4 17:05 settings.MYD
    8 -rw-r-----   1 _mysql  _mysql   1024 Nov  4 17:05 settings.MYI
    8 -rw-r-----   1 _mysql  _mysql   2250 Nov  4 17:05 settings_355.sdi
```

This example first queries the database server for the location of the
data directory (it is in a protected folder on this machine). If you issue a
listing command, you can see the InnoDB files identified by the ib and
ibd prefixes. You also see a number of directories, all of which are the

databases on this server. Below that is a listing of one of the database folders. Notice the files with the extension .MY?: these are MyISAM files (data and index).

For more information about storage engines and the choices and features of each, please see the online MySQL reference manual section "Storage Engines" (https://dev.mysql.com/doc/refman/8.0/en/storage-engines.html).

The MySQL Configuration File

The MySQL server can be configured using a configuration file, similar to the way you configure the Raspberry Pi. On the Raspberry Pi, the MySQL configuration file is located in the /etc/mysql folder and is named my.cnf. This file contains several sections, one of which is labeled [mysqld]. The items in this list are key-value pairs: the name on the left of the equal sign is the option and its value on the right. The following is a typical configuration file (with many lines suppressed for brevity):

```
[mysqld]
port = 3306
basedir = /usr/local/mysql
datadir = /usr/local/mysql/data
server_id = 5
general_log
```

As you can see, this is a simple way to configure a system. This example sets the TCP port, base directory (the root of the MySQL installation including the data as well as binary and auxiliary files), data directory, and server ID (used for replication, as discussed shortly) and turns on the general log (when the Boolean switch is included, it turns on the log). There are many such variables you can set for MySQL. See the online MySQL reference manual for details concerning using the configuration file. You will change this file when you set up MySQL on the Raspberry Pi.

How to Start, Stop, and Restart MySQL

While working with your databases and configuring MySQL on your Raspberry Pi, you may need to control the startup and shutdown of the MySQL server. The default mode for installing MySQL is to automatically start on boot and stop on shutdown, but you may want to change that, or you may need to stop and start the server after changing a parameter. In addition, when you change the configuration file, you need to restart the server to see the effect of your changes.

You can start, stop, and restart the MySQL server with the script located in /etc/init.d/mysql. Here is a list of its options:

```
$ /etc/init.d/mysql --help
Usage: mysql.server  {start|stop|restart|reload|force-
reload|status}  [ MySQL server options ]
```

The script can start, stop, and restart the server as well as get its status. You can also pass configuration (such as startup) options to the server. This can be useful for turning on a feature for temporary use as an alternative to modifying the configuration file. For example, if you want to turn on the general log for a period of time, you can use these commands:

```
/etc/init.d/mysql restart --general-log
/etc/init.d/mysql restart
```

The first restart restarts the server with the general logon, and the second restarts the server without the log enabled (assuming it isn't in the configuration file). It's probably a good idea to make sure no one is using the server when you restart it.

However, the better way to start and stop MySQL on the latest release of Raspbian is with the systemctl command as follows. You can use either method.

- *Start*: sudo systemctl start mysqld

- *Stop*: sudo systemctl stop mysqld

- *Restart*: sudo systemctl restart mysqld

- *Status*: sudo systemctl status mysqld

SHUTTING DOWN CORRECTLY

You may be tempted to just power down your Raspberry Pi database server like you do your Arduino sensor nodes, but you should avoid that temptation. The Raspberry Pi is a real computer with active file systems that require a synchronized shutdown. You should always execute a controlled shutdown before powering down.

To shut down the Raspberry Pi, recall that you issue the sudo shutdown -h now command. To reboot, you can use the sudo shutdown -r now command.

Creating Users and Granting Access

You need to know about two additional administrative operations before working with MySQL: creating user accounts and granting access to databases. MySQL can perform both of these with the CREATE USER and one or more GRANT statements. For example, the following shows the creation of a user named sensor1 and grants the user access to the database room_temp:

```
CREATE USER 'sensor1'@'%' IDENTIFIED BY 'secret';
GRANT SELECT, INSERT, UPDATE ON room_temp.* TO 'sensor1'@'%';
```

The first command creates the user named sensor1, but the name also has an @ followed by another string. This second string is the hostname of the machine with which the user is associated. That is, each user in MySQL

has both a user and a hostname, in the form user@host, to uniquely
identify them. That means the user and host sensor1@10.0.1.16 and
the user and host sensor1@10.0.1.17 are not the same. However, the %
symbol can be used as a wildcard to associate the user with any host. The
IDENTIFIED BY clause sets the password for the user.

A NOTE ABOUT SECURITY

It is always a good idea to create a user for your application that does not
have full access to the MySQL system. This is so you can minimize any
accidental changes and also to prevent exploitation. For sensor networks, it
is recommended that you create a user with access only to those databases
where you store (or retrieve) data. You can change MySQL user passwords
with the following command:

```
ALTER USER sensor1@"%" IDENTIFIED BY 'super_secret';
```

Also be careful about using the wildcard % for the host. Although it makes it
easier to create a single user and let the user access the database server from
any host, it also makes it much easier for someone bent on malice to access
your server (once they discover the password).

Another consideration is connectivity. As with the Raspberry Pi, if you connect
a database to your network and the network is in turn connected to the
Internet, it may be possible for other users on your network or the Internet to
gain access to the database. Don't make it easy for them—change your root
user password, and create users for your applications.

The second command allows access to databases. There are many
privileges that you can give a user. The example shows the most likely
set that you would want to give a user of a sensor network database: read

(SELECT),[8] add data (INSERT), and change data (UPDATE). See the online reference manual for more information about security and account access privileges.

The command also specifies a database and objects to which to grant the privilege. Thus, it is possible to give a user read (SELECT) privileges to some tables and write (INSERT, UPDATE) privileges to other tables. This example gives the user access to all objects (tables, views, and so on) in the room_temp database.

Now that you've had a short (and perhaps a bit terse) introduction to MySQL, let's get started on your MySQL Raspberry Pi database server.

Building a Raspberry Pi MySQL Server

It is time to get your hands dirty and work some magic on your unsuspecting Raspberry Pi! Let's begin by adding a USB drive to it. A flash drive with fast read/write speeds can work especially well considering it does not need as much power as a traditional external hard drive. Depending on the size of your data, you may want to seriously consider doing this.

If your data will be small (never more than a few megabytes), you may be fine using MySQL from your boot image SD card. However, if you want to ensure that you do not run out of space and keep your data separate from your boot image, you should mount a USB drive that automatically connects on boot. This section explains how to do this in detail.

If you plan to use an external hard drive, be sure you use a good-quality powered USB hub to host your external drive. This is especially important if you are using a traditional spindle drive, because it consumes

---

[8]Although most sensor nodes only write data, it is possible that some sensor data might need to be combined with other known data (via a lookup table) to be relevant.

a lot more power. Connecting your external drive directly to the Raspberry Pi may rob it of power and cause untold frustration. Symptoms include random reboot (always a pleasant surprise), failed commands, data loss, and so on. Always be sure you have plenty of power for your peripherals as well as your Raspberry Pi.

The choice of what disk to use is up to you. You can use a USB flash drive, which should work fine if it has plenty of space and is of sufficient speed (most newer models are fast). You can also use a solid-state drive (SSD) if you have an extra one or want to keep power usage and heat to a minimum. On the other hand, you may have an extra hard drive lying around that can be pressed into service. This section's example uses a surplus 250GB laptop hard drive mounted in a typical USB hard drive enclosure.

Tip   Using an external hard drive—either an SSD or traditional spindle drive—is much faster than accessing data on a flash drive. It is also typically cheaper per unit (gigabyte) or, as I mentioned, can be easily obtained from surplus.

Partitioning and Formatting the Drive

Before you can use a new or an existing drive with a file system incompatible with the Raspberry Pi, you must partition and format the drive. Because the surplus drive in this example had an old Windows partition on it, I had to follow these steps. Your Raspberry OS may be able to read the format of your old drive, but you should use the ext4 file system for optimal performance. This section shows you how to partition and format your drive.

Begin by connecting the drive to the Raspberry Pi. Then determine what drives are attached by using the fdisk command as shown:

```
$ sudo fdisk -1
...
Disk /dev/sda: 59.2 GiB, 63518539776 bytes, 124059648 sectors
Disk model: Cruzer Fit
Units: sectors of 1 * 512 = 512 bytes
Sector size (logical/physical): 512 bytes / 512 bytes
I/O size (minimum/optimal): 512 bytes / 512 bytes
Disklabel type: dos
Disk identifier: 0xde217a25
```

Device	Boot	Start	End	Sectors	Size	Id	Type
/dev/sda1	*	64	6691199	6691136	3.2G	17	Hidden HPFS/NTFS
/dev/sda2		6691200	6692671	1472	736K	1	FAT12

What you see here are all the devices attached to the Raspberry Pi. If you are new to Linux or partitioning drives, this may look like a lot of nonsense. I've highlighted the interesting rows in bold. Notice that the output identifies a 64GB drive located on a device designated as /dev/sda. All the interesting data about the drive is shown as well.

As I mentioned, there is already a partition on this drive, indicated by the row with the name of the device plus the number of the partition. Thus, /dev/sda1 is the one and only partition on this drive. Let's delete that partition and create a new one. You execute both operations using the fdisk application as shown in Listing 8-3.

Caution   If you have a partition on your drive that has data you want to keep, abort now and copy the data to another drive first. The following steps erase all data on the drive!

Listing 8-3. Partitioning the USB Drive

```
$ sudo fdisk /dev/sda

Welcome to fdisk (util-linux 2.33.1).
Changes will remain in memory only, until you decide to write
them.
Be careful before using the write command.

Command (m for help): p

Disk /dev/sda: 59.2 GiB, 63518539776 bytes, 124059648 sectors
Disk model: Cruzer Fit
Units: sectors of 1 * 512 = 512 bytes
Sector size (logical/physical): 512 bytes / 512 bytes
I/O size (minimum/optimal): 512 bytes / 512 bytes
Disklabel type: dos
Disk identifier: 0xde217a25

Device     Boot    Start      End Sectors  Size Id Type
/dev/sda1  *          64  6691199 6691136  3.2G 17 Hidden HPFS/NTFS
/dev/sda2         6691200  6692671    1472  736K  1 FAT12

Command (m for help): d
Partition number (1,2, default 2):

Partition 2 has been deleted.

Command (m for help): d
Selected partition 1
Partition 1 has been deleted.

Command (m for help): n
Partition type
   p   primary (0 primary, 0 extended, 4 free)
   e   extended (container for logical partitions)
```

```
Select (default p): p
Partition number (1-4, default 1):
First sector (2048-124059647, default 2048):
Last sector, +/-sectors or +/-size{K,M,G,T,P} (2048-124059647,
default 124059647):

Created a new partition 1 of type 'Linux' and of size 59.2 GiB.

Command (m for help): w
The partition table has been altered.
Calling ioctl() to re-read partition table.
Syncing disks.
```

The first command, d, deletes a partition. In this case, there was only one partition, so you select it by entering 1. You then create a new partition using the command n and accept the defaults to use all the free space. To check your work, you can use the p command to print the device partition table and metadata. It shows (and confirms) the new partition.

If you are worried that you may have made a mistake, do not panic! The great thing about fdisk is that it doesn't write or change the disk until you tell it to with the w or write command. In the example, you issue the w command to write the partition table. To see a full list of the commands available, you can use the h command or run man fdisk.

Tip   For all Linux commands, you can view the manual file by using the command man <application>.

The next step is to format the drive with the ext4 file system. This is easy and requires only one command: mkfs (make file system). You pass it the device name. If you recall, this is /dev/sda1. Even though you created a new partition, it is still the first partition because there is only one on the drive.

If you are attempting to use a different partition, be sure to use the correct number! The command may take a few minutes to run, depending on the size of your drive. Listing 8-4 shows the command in action.

Listing 8-4. Formatting the Drive

```
$ sudo mkfs.ext4 /dev/sda
mke2fs 1.44.5 (15-Dec-2018)
/dev/sda contains an iso9660 file system labelled 'Backup'
Proceed anyway? (y,N) y
Creating filesystem with 15507456 4k blocks and 3883008 inodes
Filesystem UUID: d370c755-18be-4c7f-bf66-4dd666ade676
Superblock backups stored on blocks:
    32768, 98304, 163840, 229376, 294912, 819200, 884736,
    1605632, 2654208, 4096000, 7962624, 11239424

Allocating group tables: done
Writing inode tables: done
Creating journal (65536 blocks): done
Writing superblocks and filesystem accounting information: done
```

Now you have a new partition, and it has been properly formatted. The next step is associating the drive with a mount point on the boot image and then connecting that drive on boot, so you don't have to do anything to use the drive each time you start your Raspberry Pi.

Setting Up Automatic Drive Mounting

External drives in Linux are connected (mounted) with mount and disconnected (unmounted) with umount. Unlike with some operating systems, it is generally a bad idea to unplug your USB drive without unmounting it first. Likewise, you must mount the drive before you can use it. This section shows the steps needed to mount the drive and to make the drive mount automatically on each boot.

I begin with a discussion of the preliminary steps to get the drive mounted and ready for automatic mounting. These include creating a folder under the /media folder to mount the drive (called a mount point), changing permissions to the folder to allow access, and executing some optional steps to tune the drive:

```
$ sudo mkdir /media/mysql
$ sudo chmod 755 /media/mysql
$ sudo tune2fs -m 0 /dev/sda
tune2fs 1.44.5 (15-Dec-2018)
Setting reserved blocks percentage to 0% (0 blocks)
$ sudo tune2fs -L MySQL /dev/sda
tune2fs 1.44.5 (15-Dec-2018)
$ sudo mount /dev/sda /media/mysql
$ sudo ls -lsa /media/mysql
total 24
 4 drwxr-xr-x 3 root root  4096 Nov 27 13:44 .
 4 drwxr-xr-x 4 root root  4096 Nov 27 13:55 ..
16 drwx------ 2 root root 16384 Nov 27 13:44 lost+found
```

These commands are easy to discern and are basic file and folder commands. However, the tuning steps using tune2fs (tune file system) are used to first reset the number of blocks used for privileged access (which saves a bit of space) and then label the drive as MYSQL. Again, these are optional, and you may skip them if you like.

Tip   You can unmount the drive with sudo umount /dev/sda1.

At this point, the drive is accessible and ready to be used. You can change to the /media/HDD folder and create files or do whatever you'd like. Now let's complete the task of setting up the drive for automatic mounting.

The best way to do this is to refer to the drive by its universally unique identifier (UUID). This is assigned to this drive and only this drive. You can tell the operating system to mount the drive with a specific UUID to a specific mount point (/media/HDD).

Remember the /dev/sda device name from earlier? If you plugged your drive into another hub port—or, better still, if there are other drives connected to your device and you unmount and then mount them—the device name may not be the same the next time you boot! The UUID helps you determine which drive is your data drive, frees you from having to keep the drive plugged in to a specific port, and allows you to use other drives without fear of breaking your MySQL installation if the drive is given a different device name.

To get the UUID, use the blkid (block ID) application:

```
$ sudo blkid
...
/dev/sda: LABEL="MySQL" UUID="d370c755-18be-4c7f-bf66-
4dd666ade676" TYPE="ext4"
...
```

Notice the line in bold. Wow! That's a big string. A UUID is a 128-byte (character) string. Copy it for the next step.

To set up automatic drive mapping, you use a feature called static information about the file system (fstab). This consists of a file located in the /etc folder on your system. You can edit the file however you like. If you are from the old school of Linux or Unix, you may choose to use vi.[9] The resulting file is as follows:

```
$ sudo nano /etc/fstab
proc    /proc    proc    defaults  0        0
/dev/mmcblk0p1  /boot   vfat    defaults  0        0
/dev/mmcblk0p2  /       ext4    defaults,noatime  0        0
UUID= d370c755-18be-4c7f-bf66-4dd666ade676 /media/
mysql   ext4    defaults,noatime    0   0
```

The line you add is shown in bold. Here you simply add the UUID, mount point, file system, and options. That's it! You can reboot your Raspberry Pi using the following command and watch the screen as the messages scroll. Eventually, you see that the drive is mounted. If there is ever an error, you can see it in the boot-up sequence:

```
$ sudo shutdown -r now
```

Now you are ready to build a MySQL database server! The following section details the steps needed to do this using your Raspberry Pi.

---

[9]What does vi mean? If you've ever had the pleasure of trying to learn it for the first time, you may think it means "virtually impossible," because the commands are terse (by design) and difficult to remember. But seriously, vi is short for vim or Vi Improved text editor. The name suggests that the original editor may very well have been completely impossible to use!

440

Project: Installing MySQL Server on a Raspberry Pi

Turning a Raspberry Pi into a MySQL database server is easy. Well, almost. The latest version of MySQL (8.0) is not available for the Raspberry Pi.[10] However, since MySQL is open source, we can build (compile and link) MySQL from source on our Raspberry Pi. How cool is that? This section shows you how to acquire the source code for MySQL, build, and install it. We then learn how to move its default data directory from your boot image to the new external drive you connected in the previous section.

WHAT ABOUT OTHER MYSQL VARIANTS?

Savvy readers may already be aware of variants of MySQL that are available from other vendors. While most claim to be 100% compatible with Oracle's MySQL (owners of the source code), there are some differences that can make development more difficult. For example, the MySQL database connector for Arduino (called Connector/Arduino) is known to have issues with some versions of some variants. Thus, it is this author's opinion you should always use Oracle's release of MySQL rather than variants.

In this section, we will use Raspberry Pi computers rather than more expensive mainstream server hardware. If you would like to follow along and use more traditional server hardware, you can do, but remember that some of the commands used on the Raspberry Pi are very similar to those you would use on typical Linux-based platforms. You may need to substitute platform-specific versions to use the following on your PC.

---

[10]Older versions of MySQL are available for the Raspberry Pi, but beware! Some of these releases are not distributed or maintained by Oracle. It is highly recommended to use Oracle's current release of MySQL even though it does require a bit more work to run in on the Raspberry Pi.

Recall, since MySQL is open source, we can download the source code, compile, and install it ourselves. In fact, we will do just that in this walk-through. The following lists the steps necessary to prepare a Raspberry Pi computer for use with MySQL:

- Build MySQL.

- Install MySQL manually.

- Configure MySQL.

This list is like the process you would use to set up MySQL on commodity hardware, but the build and configuration steps are required to make MySQL work on Raspbian (because there are no installation packages). It is important to note that these extra steps are not unique to Raspbian.

In fact, building, installing, and configuring MySQL from source is a viable alternative to using installation packages. You can find instructions on building MySQL for various platforms in the section entitled "Installing MySQL from Source" in the online reference manual (`https://dev.mysql.com/doc/refman/8.0/en/source-installation.html`).

The process is straightforward involving a few minor system configuration items to prepare our system and two commands: `cmake` and `make`. This section will walk you through all those steps with ample examples and every step documented.

The task of building MySQL from source code may seem daunting to those who have never programmed or for those who haven't written a program in a while, but do not despair. The hardest part of compiling MySQL on the Raspberry Pi is waiting for the process to complete. That is, it may take an hour or so to compile everything. But that is a small price to pay for being able to use Raspberry Pi computers to experiment with MySQL!

Let's dive into compiling MySQL on Raspbian starting with the prerequisites.

Prerequisites

There are several things you need to install to prepare your Raspberry Pi to compile MySQL including hardware and software prerequisites MySQL.

The hardware requirement is that the latest version of MySQL (8.0.18 at the time of this writing) requires using a Raspberry Pi 4B with 2GB or 4GB (4GB is faster) board. Thus, you should consider whether you want to build MySQL on the same Raspberry Pi 4B where you want to install it. Why is this important? It is important because you may want to run MySQL on older Raspberry Pi boards. More specifically, while it is best to compile MySQL on the 4B, you can install and run it on the 3B+ without any issues. We will see how to do this later. The reason we need to use the 4B is largely due to memory. MySQL simply requires more than the 1GB of RAM found on the 3B boards.[11]

Beyond requiring a Raspberry Pi 4B, the software prerequisites include the following software:

- You need to install Curses 5 (`libncurses5-dev`).

- You need to install Bison.

- You need to install OpenSSL (`libssl-dev`).

- You need to install CMake.

To install all these libraries at one time, use the following command in a terminal window. This will download the necessary files and install them. Notice we must use elevated privileges to install the library.

```
$ sudo apt-get install libncurses5-dev bison libssl-dev cmake
```

---

[11]While you may be able to create a larger swap file to compensate, compilation with a large swap file could take more than 12 hours to complete due to the slow performance of swapping with disk.

The only other prerequisite is we must download the MySQL Server source code. Go to `https://dev.mysql.com/downloads/mysql/`, select *Source Code* in the *Select Operating System* drop-down box, *Generic Linux* from the *Select OS Version* drop-down box, and then click the Generic Linux (Architecture Independent), Compressed TAR Archive Includes Boost Headers download link at the bottom of the list as shown in Figure 8-1. This file contains another library that we need (boost) as well as the server source code. It is the easiest of the downloads to start from to build. Once you've downloaded the file, copy it to your Raspberry Pi.

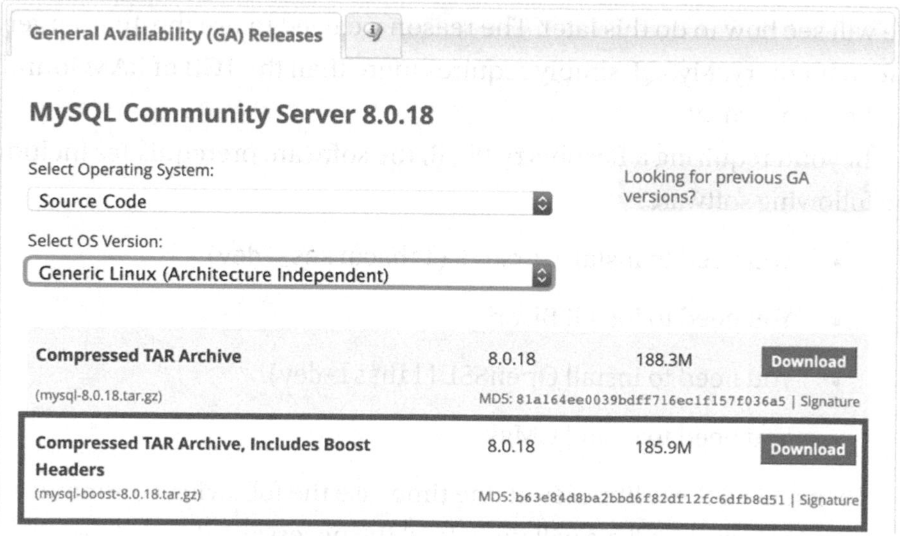

Figure 8-1. *Download MySQL server source code*

OK, now we're ready to build the MySQL server.

Building MySQL Server

There are just three steps to building MySQL on Raspberry Pi. We first run the preprocessor called CMake, then build the code with make, and finally build an installation package with the make package command. We can use this package to install MySQL on another Raspberry Pi. Let's see the details of each of these steps beginning with CMake.

CMake (cmake.org) is another open source product used to build, test, and package software. Recall, we installed CMake in the previous section. There are many variations of options you can use to build software and many that apply to MySQL. In fact, you can spend a lot of time customizing the CMake command options to build for almost any platform. Since we downloaded the MySQL source code for generic Linux with the Boost libraries, we've got everything we need.

Thus, the command options we need to use with CMake are minimal and include the following. Each of these will be explained in a bit more detail here:

- You should set -DWITH_UNIT_TESTS=OFF to save compile time (not needed).

- You should set the PREFIX to set the installation path to make it easy to install.

- We need to turn off the "gold" linker.

- We must build with the release code (debug requires too much memory for the Raspberry Pi).

- We must add additional compiling and build flags to ensure the code builds properly on ARM32.

Running CMake (Preparing to Compile)

The first thing we're going to do is extract the TAR file that we downloaded. You can do so with the following commands. This will create a folder named mysql-8.0.18. It is recommended that you unpack this file in a folder in the root user's home folder, for example, /home/pi/source. The unpack process will take a few minutes as it contains a lot of code.

```
$ cd /home/pi
$ mkdir source
$ cd source
$ cp ~/Downloads/mysql-boost-8.0.18.tar.gz .
$ tar -xvf mysql-boost-8.0.18.tar.gz
```

Next, we will make a directory to store all the compiled code using the following commands. This helps prevent accidents when compiling and preserves the source code.

```
$ cd mysql-8.0.18
$ mkdir build
$ cd build
```

Now we can run the CMake command. Listing 8-5 shows the complete command you need to use from within the build folder. Notice the command has many options specified including (in order of appearance) using Unix makefiles, setting the build to release code (rather than debug), ignoring AIO checking, setting the boost folder (included in the TAR file we downloaded), turning off the unit tests, and setting some arcane settings for compiling on ARM32.

Listing 8-5. Running the CMake Command (ARM32)

```
$ cmake -G "Unix Makefiles" -DCMAKE_BUILD_TYPE=release -DBUILD_
CONFIG=mysql_release -DDEBUG_EXTNAME=OFF -DIGNORE_AIO_CHECK=1
-DWITH_UNIT_TESTS=OFF -DCMAKE_C_LINK_FLAGS="-Wl,--no-keep-
memory,-latomic" -DCMAKE_CXX_LINK_FLAGS="-Wl,--no-keep-memory,-
latomic" -DCMAKE_C_FLAGS_RELEASE="-fPIC" -DCMAKE_CXX_FLAGS_
RELEASE="-fPIC" -DCMAKE_INSTALL_PREFIX="/usr/local/mysql"
-DUSE_LD_GOLD=OFF -DWITH_BOOST="../boost" ..
-- Running cmake version 3.13.4
-- Found Git: /usr/bin/git (found version "2.20.1")
-- MySQL 8.0.18
-- Source directory /media/pi/source/mysql-8.0.18
-- Binary directory /media/pi/source/mysql-8.0.18/build
-- CMAKE_GENERATOR: Unix Makefiles
...
-- CMAKE_C_FLAGS: -fno-omit-frame-pointer  -Wall -Wextra
-Wformat-security -Wvla -Wundef -Wwrite-strings -Wjump-misses-
init
-- CMAKE_CXX_FLAGS: -std=c++14 -fno-omit-frame-pointer  -Wall
-Wextra -Wformat-security -Wvla -Wundef -Woverloaded-virtual
-Wcast-qual -Wimplicit-fallthrough=2 -Wlogical-op
-- CMAKE_CXX_FLAGS_DEBUG: -DSAFE_MUTEX -DENABLED_DEBUG_SYNC -g
-- CMAKE_CXX_FLAGS_RELWITHDEBINFO: -DDBUG_OFF -ffunction-
sections -fdata-sections -O2 -g -DNDEBUG
-- CMAKE_CXX_FLAGS_RELEASE: -DDBUG_OFF -ffunction-sections
-fdata-sections -fPIC
-- CMAKE_CXX_FLAGS_MINSIZEREL: -DDBUG_OFF -ffunction-sections
-fdata-sections -Os -DNDEBUG
-- CMAKE_C_LINK_FLAGS: -Wl,--no-keep-memory,-latomic
-- CMAKE_CXX_LINK_FLAGS: -Wl,--no-keep-memory,-latomic
-- CMAKE_EXE_LINKER_FLAGS
```

```
-- CMAKE_MODULE_LINKER_FLAGS
-- CMAKE_SHARED_LINKER_FLAGS
-- Configuring done
-- Generating done
```

Don't worry if this command looks strange, and it is not necessary to understand all the special settings we've used for the compile and link phases. However, if you do want to learn more about these options, you can see the documentation on the GNU compiler (http://gcc.gnu.org/onlinedocs/gcc/Option-Summary.html) and linker (https://gcc.gnu.org/onlinedocs/gcc/Link-Options.html) options.

The command could take a few minutes to run. Be sure there are no errors and that the last lines indicate the build files have been written to the build folder. Pay special attention to the LINK_FLAGS messages at the end. The options in the CMake command do not include spaces. If you accidentally added spaces, the comma-separated list would show them in the CMake output. Be sure there are no spaces. If there are spaces, you may get an error stating --icf=safe (or other) options are invalid. If that happens, run the command again without the spaces.

If you've gotten this far without errors, you can almost relax. The next step, compiling the code is easy, but it can take a while to run on a Raspberry Pi 4B (at least 1–2 hours).

Running Make (Compiling)

The next step is to compile the code. This is done simply with the make command. This command allows us to specify how many parallel threads we want to use. For the Raspberry Pi 4B and a total of four CPU cores, it is safe to use three cores for compiling. If you have a watcher for CPU usage running, you will see those three and possibly at times all four cores running at 100%. If your Raspberry Pi is mounted in a case, make sure you have adequate ventilation or a fan blowing over the board.

Listing 8-6 shows the compilation step of the MySQL server code using the command make -j3. The listing is an excerpt of the messages you will likely see (there will be thousands of lines), but the important ones to note are the last several. These ensure the code has compiled without errors.

Tip   You may see minor warnings flow past when the code is compiling, which you can ignore. However, you should not see any compilation errors. If you do, go back and check your CMake command and rerun it if necessary. If all else fails, delete the build directory and start over.

Listing 8-6. Compiling MySQL Server

```
$ make -j3
[  0%] Built target INFO_SRC
[  0%] Built target INFO_BIN
[  0%] Building C object extra/zlib/CMakeFiles/zlib_objlib.dir/
       gzread.o
[  0%] Building C object extra/zstd/CMakeFiles/zstd_objlib.dir/
       lib/common/threading.c.o
[  0%] Building C object extra/zstd/CMakeFiles/zstd_objlib.dir/
       lib/common/xxhash.c.o
[  0%] Building C object extra/zlib/CMakeFiles/zlib_objlib.dir/
       gzwrite.o
...
[100%] Building CXX object storage/innobase/CMakeFiles/
       innobase.dir/os/os0thread.cc.o
[100%] Building CXX object storage/innobase/CMakeFiles/
       innobase.dir/page/zipdecompress.cc.o
```

```
[100%] Building CXX object storage/innobase/CMakeFiles/
       innobase.dir/rem/rec.cc.o
[100%] Building CXX object storage/innobase/CMakeFiles/
       innobase.dir/ut/crc32.cc.o
[100%] Building CXX object storage/innobase/CMakeFiles/
       innobase.dir/ut/ut.cc.o
[100%] Linking CXX static library libinnobase.a
[100%] Built target innobase
       Scanning dependencies of target mysqld
[100%] Building CXX object sql/CMakeFiles/mysqld.dir/main.cc.o
[100%] Linking CXX executable ../runtime_output_directory/
       mysqld
[100%] Built target mysqld
```

Once the compilation is complete, the next step is to build a package (TAR file) we can use to install MySQL on our server.

Making the Package

The last thing we need to do is build the installation package. In this case, we will build a compress TAR file that we will be able to copy to our initial server and install. We do this with the make package command as shown in Listing 8-7.

Listing 8-7. Building the TAR Package

```
$ make package
[  0%] Built target abi_check
[  0%] Built target INFO_SRC
[  0%] Built target INFO_BIN
[  1%] Built target zlib_objlib
[  1%] Built target zlib
[  2%] Built target zstd_objlib
```

```
[  2%] Built target zstd
[  3%] Built target edit
[  4%] Built target event_core
...
[100%] Built target routing
[100%] Built target rest_routing
[100%] Built target mysqlrouter
[100%] Built target mysqlrouter_keyring
Run CPack packaging tool...
CPack: Create package using TGZ
CPack: Install projects
CPack: - Run preinstall target for: MySQL
CPack: - Install project: MySQL
CPack: Create package
CPack: - package: /home/pi/source/mysql-8.0.18/build/mysql-
8.0.18-linux-armv7l.tar.gz generated.
```

That's it! We've built MySQL on the Raspberry Pi! That wasn't so bad, was it? Now, let's see how to install and test MySQL on our server.

Installing MySQL Server

If we built MySQL on a different Raspberry Pi, we need to copy the TAR file to a removable drive to copy the file to the target Raspberry Pi.

Once the server is booted, log in and change to the /usr/local directory and create a new folder named mysql. Then, change to the new folder and copy the TAR file to that folder. Finally, unpack the file using the following commands. There are a lot of files, so it could take a few minutes to unpack.

```
$ cd /usr/local/
$ mkdir mysql
$ cd mysql
```

```
$ sudo cp ~/source/mysql-8.0.11/build/mysql-8.0.18-linux-
armv7l.tar.gz .
$ sudo tar -xvf mysql-8.0.11-linux-armv7l.tar.gz --strip-
components=1
```

Notice the last command uses an option to strip one component (the first folder—mysql-8.0.18-linux-armv71) from the extracted file directories. This ensures the MySQL files get copied to /usr/local/mysql.

However, there is one more command we need to run. Since we are space conscience, we do not need the MySQL test files, so we can delete them with the following command. Once we're done with the TAR file, we can delete that too as shown here:

```
$ sudo rm -rf mysql-test
$ sudo rm mysql-8.0.18-linux-armv71.tar.gz
```

Installing from the TAR file requires more steps than installing from a typical platform-specific package. This is because installation packages typically take care of several required configuration steps, all of which are detailed in the online reference manual section entitled "Installing MySQL on Unix/Linux Using Generic Binaries" (https://dev.mysql.com/doc/refman/8.0/en/binary-installation.html).

Configuring MySQL Server

Now that we have the files copied, we can finish the setup. The process is not tedious but does involve several commands run from a terminal, so some patience is needed to ensure all the commands are entered correctly.

We begin by creating a new group named mysql, then add a user named mysql, then create a folder for MySQL to use, and grant access to the folder to the mysql user. The following code shows the commands needed. Run these from a terminal (there will be no output from any of the commands).

```
$ sudo groupadd mysql
$ sudo useradd -r -g mysql -s /bin/false mysql
$ cd /usr/local/mysql
$ sudo mkdir mysql-files
$ sudo chown mysql:mysql mysql-files
$ sudo chmod 750 mysql-files
```

We can initialize the data directory easily with the `--initialize` option as shown in the following code. Notice we run the command with elevated privileges and specify the user to use (mysql). The following code shows an example of the output with the successful messages highlighted. If you see errors, consult the online reference manual to resolve the errors. Notice the output contains the initial root user password. You will need that for the next step. Note that this step can take a few moments to run.

```
$ sudo ./bin/mysqld --initialize --user=mysql
2019-11-17T02:02:41.118355Z 0 [System] [MY-013169] [Server]
/usr/local/mysql/bin/mysqld (mysqld 8.0.18) initializing of
server in progress as process 7704
2019-11-17T02:05:04.757386Z 5 [Note] [MY-010454] [Server] A
temporary password is generated for root@localhost: VPw&eFjU-0z#
```

Next, we create a configuration file using our favorite editor as shown here:

```
$ sudo vi /etc/my /etc/my.cnf
```

Add the following lines to the configuration file and save it (press *Esc* then :, then *w*, and then *q*). We will use this configuration file to start the server in the next step.

```
[mysqld]
basedir=/usr/local/mysql/
datadir=/usr/local/mysql/data
```

OK, we are now ready to start MySQL for the first time. Use the `mysqld` command to start MySQL from the command line. We use this command instead of the `/etc/init.d/mysql start` command so we can check the output for errors. If there are no errors, you should see output like those shown here:

```
$ sudo bin/mysqld --defaults-file=/etc/my.cnf --user=mysql &
[1] 8745
$ 2019-11-17T02:09:41.429418Z 0 [Warning] [MY-011037]
[Server] The CYCLE timer is not available. WAIT events in the
performance_schema will not be timed.
2019-11-17T02:09:42.191155Z 0 [System] [MY-010116] [Server]
/usr/local/mysql/bin/mysqld (mysqld 8.0.18) starting as process 8750
2019-11-17T02:09:58.600980Z 0 [Warning] [MY-010068] [Server] CA
certificate ca.pem is self signed.
2019-11-17T02:09:59.167758Z 0 [System] [MY-010931] [Server]
/usr/local/mysql/bin/mysqld: ready for connections. Version:
'8.0.18'  socket: '/tmp/mysql.sock'  port: 3306  Source
distribution.
2019-11-17T02:09:59.378833Z 0 [System] [MY-011323] [Server] X
Plugin ready for connections. Socket: '/tmp/mysqlx.sock' bind-
address: '::' port: 33060
```

Now we can test our MySQL server with the mysql client using the following command. Be sure to use the password displayed when you initialized the data directory. Listing 8-8 shows an example of using the `mysql` client to connect to the server for the first time. We will first display the version and then change the root user password. Notice we also shut down the server with the shutdown SQL command.

Listing 8-8. Connecting to MySQL for the First Time

```
$ bin/mysql -uroot -p
Enter password:
Welcome to the MySQL monitor.   Commands end with ; or \g.
Your MySQL connection id is 8
Server version: 8.0.18

Copyright (c) 2000, 2019, Oracle and/or its affiliates. All
rights reserved.

Oracle is a registered trademark of Oracle Corporation and/or its
affiliates. Other names may be trademarks of their respective
owners.

Type 'help;' or '\h' for help. Type '\c' to clear the current
input statement.

mysql> SELECT @@version;
+-----------+
| @@version |
+-----------+
| 8.0.18    |
+-----------+
1 row in set (0.00 sec)

mysql> ALTER USER 'root'@'localhost' IDENTIFIED BY 'secret';
Query OK, 0 rows affected (0.11 sec)

mysql> shutdown;
Query OK, 0 rows affected (0.00 sec)

mysql> \q
```

Next, we must add the path to the MySQL binaries. We can do this easily by editing our Bash resource file using the command nano ~/.bashrc. When the file opens, add the following line to the bottom of the file. The next time you open a terminal, you can execute the MySQL applications and tools without specifying the path.

```
export PATH=${PATH}:/usr/local/mysql/bin
```

There is one final step needed—we must copy the startup and shutdown script (service) to allow us to automatically start MySQL at boot. To do so, copy the mysql.server file from the support-files folder from the build to the /etc/init.d/mysql file as shown in Listing 8-9. We will also test the server connection again and then shut it down with the sudo systemctl daemon-reload command to refresh the list of daemons and the sudo systemctl start or sudo systemctl stop commands to start or stop MySQL. You can also use sudo systemctl status command to see the status of MySQL. This can be helpful if you encounter errors or want to check to see if MySQL is running. Note that you may be prompted for a password when using the command. Also, you want to copy the mysql.server file from the build directory, not the root of the source code directory.

Listing 8-9. Starting MySQL Automatically or Manually with systemctl

```
$ sudo cp ./support-files/mysql.server /etc/init.d/mysql
$ sudo chmod 0755 /etc/init.d/mysql
$ sudo systemctl daemon-reload
$ sudo systemctl start mysql
$ sudo systemctl status mysql
● mysql.service - LSB: start and stop MySQL
    Loaded: loaded (/etc/init.d/mysql; generated)
    Active: active (running) since Sat 2019-11-16 21:22:44 EST;
    6s ago
```

```
    Docs: man:systemd-sysv-generator(8)
 Process: 11023 ExecStart=/etc/init.d/mysql start
 (code=exited, status=0/SUCCESS)
   Tasks: 40 (limit: 2200)
  Memory: 350.5M
  CGroup: /system.slice/mysql.service
          ├─11037 /bin/sh /usr/local/mysql//bin/mysqld_safe
          --datadir=/usr/local/mysql/data --
          └─11148 /usr/local/mysql/bin/mysqld --basedir=/usr/
          local/mysql/ --datadir=/usr/local
...
Nov 16 21:22:44 raspberrypi systemd[1]: Started LSB: start and
stop MySQL.

$ mysql -uroot -p -e "select @@version"
Enter password:
+-----------+
| @@version |
+-----------+
| 8.0.18    |
+-----------+
$ sudo systemctl stop mysql
$ sudo systemctl status mysql
...
Nov 16 21:23:02 raspberrypi systemd[1]: Stopped LSB: start and
stop MySQL.
```

That's it! We've installed MySQL server and tested that is works. It would also be a good idea to install the MySQL Shell on each server. In the next section, you tell MySQL to use the external drive instead for storing your databases and data.

Moving the Data Directory to the External Drive

Recall that you want to use MySQL to store your sensor data. As such, the sensor data may grow in volume and over time may consume a lot of space. Rather than risk filling up your boot image SD, which is normally only a few gigabytes, you can use an external drive to save the data. This section shows you how to tell MySQL to change its default location for saving data.

The steps involved require stopping the MySQL server, changing its configuration, and then restarting the server. Finally, you test the change to ensure that all new data is being saved in the new location. Begin by stopping the MySQL server:

```
$ sudo systemctl stop mysql
```

You must create a folder for the new data directory:

```
$ sudo mkdir /media/mysql/mysql_data
```

Now you copy the existing data directory and its contents to the new folder. Notice that you copy only the data and not the entire MySQL installation, which is unnecessary:

```
$ sudo cp -R /usr/local/mysql/data  /media/mysql/mysql_data
$ chown -R mysql mysql /media/mysql/mysql_data
```

Note   If you get permission errors, try changing the owner of the /media/mysql folder to mysql:mysql.

Next, you edit the configuration file for MySQL. In this case, you change the datadir line to read datadir = /media/mysql. It is also a good idea to comment out the bind-address line to permit access to MySQL from other systems on the network:

```
$ sudo vi /etc/mysql/my.cnf
```

There is one last step. You must change the owner and group to the MySQL user that was created on installation. Here is the correct command:

```
$ sudo chown -R mysql:mysql /media/mysql/mysql_data
```

Now you restart MySQL:

```
$ sudo systemctl start mysql
```

You can determine whether the changes worked by connecting to MySQL, creating a new database, and then checking to see if the new folder was created on the external drive, as shown in Listing 8-10.

Listing 8-10. Testing the New Data Directory

```
$ ./bin/mysql -uroot -p
Enter password:
Welcome to the MySQL monitor.  Commands end with ; or \g.
Your MySQL connection id is 9
Server version: 8.0.18 Source distribution

Copyright (c) 2000, 2019, Oracle and/or its affiliates. All
rights reserved.

Oracle is a registered trademark of Oracle Corporation and/or its
affiliates. Other names may be trademarks of their respective
owners.

Type 'help;' or '\h' for help. Type '\c' to clear the current
input statement.
```

```
mysql> SHOW VARIABLES LIKE 'datadir';
+---------------+-----------------------------------+
| Variable_name | Value                             |
+---------------+-----------------------------------+
| datadir       | /media/pi/mysql/mysql_data/data/  |
+---------------+-----------------------------------+
1 row in set (0.08 sec)

mysql> CREATE DATABASE testme;
Query OK, 1 row affected (0.08 sec)

mysql> SHOW DATABASES;
+--------------------+
| Database           |
+--------------------+
| information_schema |
| mysql              |
| performance_schema |
| sys                |
| testme             |
+--------------------+
5 rows in set (0.06 sec)

mysql> \q
Bye
pi@raspberrypi:/usr/local/mysql $ sudo ls -lsa /media/pi/mysql/
mysql_data/data
total 168024
    4 drwxr-x--- 7 mysql mysql     4096 Nov 27 15:09 .
    4 drwxr-xr-x 3 mysql mysql     4096 Nov 27 15:03 ..
    4 -rw-r----- 1 mysql mysql       56 Nov 27 15:03 auto.cnf
    4 -rw-r----- 1 mysql mysql      499 Nov 27 15:03 binlog.
                                                     000001
```

```
    4 -rw-r----- 1 mysql mysql      178 Nov 27 15:03  binlog.
                                                       000002
    4 -rw-r----- 1 mysql mysql      346 Nov 27 15:09  binlog.
                                                       000003
    4 -rw-r----- 1 mysql mysql       48 Nov 27 15:06  binlog.
                                                       index
...
    4 -rw-r----- 1 mysql mysql     3344 Nov 27 15:03  ib_buffer_
                                                       pool
12288 -rw-r----- 1 mysql mysql 12582912 Nov 27 15:09  ibdata1
49152 -rw-r----- 1 mysql mysql 50331648 Nov 27 15:09  ib_
                                                       logfile0
49152 -rw-r----- 1 mysql mysql 50331648 Nov 27 15:03  ib_
                                                       logfile1
12288 -rw-r----- 1 mysql mysql 12582912 Nov 27 15:06  ibtmp1
...
    4 drwxr-x--- 2 mysql mysql     4096 Nov 27 15:09  testme
```

In the output, the new database name is represented as the folder testme.

Well, there you have it—a new MySQL database server running on a Raspberry Pi!

If you are curious about what more you can do with your new database server, read on. In the next section, you tackle a very popular feature of MySQL called replication. It permits two or more servers to have copies of databases. For your purposes, it may be handy to use the copies as a backup, so you don't have to do any manual file copying from your Raspberry Pi.

Advanced Project: Using MySQL Replication to Back Up Your Sensor Data

One of the nicest things about using an external drive to save your MySQL data is that at any point you can shut down your server, disconnect the drive, plug it in to another system, and copy the data. That may sound great if your Raspberry Pi database server is in a location that makes it easy to get to (physically) and if there are periods when it is OK to shut down the server.

However, this may not be the case for some sensor networks. One of the benefits of using a Raspberry Pi for a database server is that the server can reside in close proximity to the sensor nodes. If the sensor network is in an isolated area, you can collect and store data by putting the Raspberry Pi in the same location. But this may mean trudging out to a barn or pond or walking several football field lengths into the bowels of a factory to get to the hardware if there is no network to connect to your database server.

But if your Raspberry Pi is connected to a network, you can use an advanced feature of MySQL called replication to make a live, up-to-the-minute copy of your data. Not only does this mean you can have a backup, but it also means you can query the server that maintains the copy and therefore unburden your Raspberry Pi of complex or long-running queries. The Raspberry Pi is a very cool small-footprint computer, but a data warehouse it is not.

What Is Replication, and How Does It Work?

MySQL replication is an easy-to-use feature and yet a very complex and major component of the MySQL server. This section presents a bird's-eye view of replication for the purpose of explaining how it works and how to set up a simple replication topology. For more information about replication and its many features and commands, see the online MySQL reference manual (http://dev.mysql.com/doc/refman/5.5/en/replication.html).

Replication requires two or more servers. One server must be designated as the origin or master. The master role means all data changes (writes) to the data are sent to the master and only the master. All other servers in the topology maintain a copy of the master data and are by design and requirement read-only servers. Thus, when your sensors send data for storage, they send it to the master. Applications you write to use the sensor data can read it from the slaves.

The copy mechanism works using a technology called the binary log that stores the changes in a special format, thereby keeping a record of all the changes. These changes are then shipped to the slaves and re-executed there. Thus, once the slave re-executes the changes (called events), the slave has an exact copy of the data.

The master maintains a binary log of the changes, and the slave maintains a copy of that binary log called the relay log. When a slave requests data changes from the master, it reads the events from the master and writes them to its relay log; then another thread in the slave executes those events from the relay log. As you can imagine, there is a slight delay from the time a change is made on the master to the time it is made on the slave. Fortunately, this delay is almost unnoticeable except in topologies with very high traffic (lots of changes). For your purposes, it is likely when you read the data from the slave, it is up to date. You can check the slave's progress using the command SHOW SLAVE STATUS; among many other things, it shows you how far behind the master the slave is. You see this command in action in a later section.

Now that you have a little knowledge of replication and how it works, let's see how to set it up. The next section discusses how to set up replication with the Raspberry Pi as the master and a desktop computer as the slave.

How to Set Up Replication

This section demonstrates how to set up replication from a Raspberry Pi (master) to a desktop computer (slave). The steps include preparing the master by enabling binary logging and creating a user account for reading the binary log, preparing the slave by connecting it to the master, and starting the slave processes. You conclude with a test of the replication system.

Preparing the Master

Replication requires the master to have binary logging enabled. It is not turned on by default, so you must edit the configuration file and turn it on. Edit the configuration file with sudo vi /etc/mysql/my.cnf, and turn on binary logging by uncommenting and changing the following lines:

```
server-id = 1
log_bin = /media/mysql/mysql_data/mysql-bin.log
```

The first line sets the server ID of the master. In basic replication (what you have for version 5.5), each server must have a unique server ID. In this case, you assign 1 to the master; the slave will have some other value, such as 2. Imaginative, yes?

The next line sets the location and name of the binary log file. You save it to your external drive because, like the data itself, the binary log can grow over time. Fortunately, MySQL is designed to keep the file to a reasonable size and has commands that allow you to truncate it and start a new file (a process called rotating). See the online reference manual (https://dev.mysql.com/doc/refman/8.0/en/replication.html) for more information about managing binary log files. Once the edits are saved, you can restart the MySQL server (or simply stop and then start).

Next, you must create a user to be used by the slave to connect to the master and read the binary log. There is a special privilege for this named REPLICATION SLAVE. The following code shows the correct GRANT statement to create the user and add the privilege. Remember the user and password you use here—you need it for the slave:

```
mysql> CREATE USER 'rpl'@'%' IDENTIFIED BY 'secret'
Query OK, 0 rows affected (0.01 sec)
mysql> GRANT REPLICATION SLAVE ON *.* TO 'rpl'@'%';
Query OK, 0 rows affected (0.01 sec)
```

But one more piece of information is needed for the slave. The slave needs to know the name of the binary log to read and what position in the file to start reading events. You can determine this with the SHOW MASTER STATUS command:

```
mysql> SHOW MASTER STATUS;
+---------------+----------+--------------+------------------+...
| File          | Position | Binlog_Do_DB | Binlog_Ignore_DB |...
+---------------+----------+--------------+------------------+...
| binlog.000003 |      878 |              |                  |...
+---------------+----------+--------------+------------------+...
1 row in set (0.00 sec)
```

Now that you have the master's binary log file name and position as well as the replication user and password, you can visit your slave and connect it to the master. You also need to know the hostname or IP address of the Raspberry Pi as well as the port on which MySQL is running. By default, the port is 3306; but if you changed that, you should note the new value. Jot down all the information in Table 8-1.

Table 8-1. *Information Needed from the Master for Replication*

Item from Master	Value
IP Address or Hostname	
Port	
Binary log file	
Binary log file position	
Replication user ID	
Replication user password	

The MySQL server you want to use as a slave should be the same version as the server on the Raspberry Pi or at least a server that is compatible. The online reference manual specifies which MySQL versions work well together. Fortunately, the list of versions with issues is very short. In this section, you should have a server installed on your desktop or server computer and ensure that it is configured correctly.

The steps needed to connect a slave to a master include issuing a CHANGE MASTER command to connect to the master and a START SLAVE command to initiate the slave role on the server. Yes, it is that easy! Recall that you need the information from the master to complete these commands. The following commands show a slave being connected to a master running on a Raspberry Pi. Let's begin with the CHANGE MASTER command as shown here:

```
mysql> CHANGE MASTER TO MASTER_HOST='10.0.1.17', MASTER_
PORT=3306, MASTER_LOG_FILE='mysql-bin.000003', MASTER_LOG_
POS=878, MASTER_USER='rpl', MASTER_PASSWORD='secret';
Query OK, 0 rows affected (0.22 sec)
```

This example uses the IP address of the Raspberry Pi, the port number (3306 is the default), the log file and position from the SHOW MASTER STATUS command, and the user and password for the replication user. If you typed the command correctly, it should return without errors. If there are errors or warnings, use the SHOW WARNINGS command to read the warnings and correct any problems.

The next step is to start the slave processes. This command is simply START SLAVE. It normally does not report any errors; you must use SHOW SLAVE STATUS to see them. Here are both of these commands in action as shown in Listing 8-11.

Tip   For wide results, use the \G option to see the columns as rows (called vertical format).

Listing 8-11. Starting the Slave

```
mysql> start slave;
Query OK, 0 rows affected (0.00 sec)

mysql> show slave status \G
*************************** 1. row
***************************
        Slave_IO_State: Waiting for master to send event
  Master_Host: 10.0.1.17
  Master_User: rpl
  Master_Port: 3306
Connect_Retry: 60
      Master_Log_File: mysql-bin.000003
  Read_Master_Log_Pos: 107
        Relay_Log_File: clone-relay-bin.000003
```

```
              Relay_Log_Pos: 4
      Relay_Master_Log_File: mysql-bin.000001
           Slave_IO_Running: Yes
          Slave_SQL_Running: Yes
            Replicate_Do_DB:
        Replicate_Ignore_DB:
         Replicate_Do_Table:
             Replicate_Ignore_Table:
             Replicate_Wild_Do_Table:
        Replicate_Wild_Ignore_Table:
          Last_Errno: 0
          Last_Error:
       Skip_Counter: 0
        Exec_Master_Log_Pos: 107
            Relay_Log_Space: 555
            Until_Condition: None
             Until_Log_File:
Until_Log_Pos: 0
          Master_SSL_Allowed: No
          Master_SSL_CA_File:
          Master_SSL_CA_Path:
             Master_SSL_Cert:
           Master_SSL_Cipher:
             Master_SSL_Key:
      Seconds_Behind_Master: 0
Master_SSL_Verify_Server_Cert: No
Last_IO_Errno: 0
Last_IO_Error:
             Last_SQL_Errno: 0
             Last_SQL_Error:
```

```
Replicate_Ignore_Server_Ids:
    Master_Server_Id: 1
1 row in set (0.00 sec)

mysql>
```

Take a moment to slog through all these rows. There are several key
fields you need to pay attention to. These include anything with error in
the name and the state columns. For example, the first row (Slave_IO_
State) shows the textual message indicating the state of the slave's I/O
thread. The I/O thread is responsible for reading events from the master's
binary log. There is also a SQL thread that is responsible for reading events
from the relay log and executing them.

For this example, you just need to ensure that both threads are running
(YES) and there are no errors. For detailed explanations of all the fields
in the SHOW SLAVE STATUS command, see the online MySQL reference
manual (https://dev.mysql.com/doc/refman/8.0/en/replication-
configuration.html).

Now that the slave is connected and running, let's check for that
testme database on it:

```
mysql> show databases;
+--------------------+
| Database           |
+--------------------+
| information_schema |
| mysql              |
| performance_schema |
+--------------------+
3 rows in set (0.00 sec)

mysql>
```

Wait! Where did it go? Wasn't this example supposed to replicate everything? Well, yes and no. It is true that your slave is connected to the master and will replicate anything that changes on the master from this point on. Recall that you used the SHOW MASTER STATUS command to get the binary log file and position. These values are the coordinates for the location of the next event, not any previous events. Aha: you set up replication after the testme database was created.

How do you fix this? That depends. If you really wanted the testme database replicated, you would have to stop replication, fix the master, and then reconnect the slave. I won't go into these steps, but I list them here as an outline for you to experiment on your own:

1. Stop the slave.

2. Go to the master and drop the database.

3. Get the new SHOW MASTER STATUS data.

4. Reconnect the slave.

5. Start the slave.

Got that? Good. If not, it is a good exercise to go back and try these steps on your own.

Once you get the master cleaned and replication restarted, go ahead and try to create a database on the master and observe the result on the slave. The following are the commands. I used a different database name in case you elected to not try the previous challenge as shown here:

```
mysql> create database testme_again;
Query OK, 1 row affected (0.00 sec)
```

```
mysql> show databases;
+--------------------+
| Database           |
+--------------------+
| information_schema |
| mysql              |
| performance_schema |
| testme             |
| testme_again       |
+--------------------+
4 rows in set (0.01 sec)

mysql>
```

Returning to the slave, check to see what databases are listed there as shown here:

```
mysql> show databases;
+--------------------+
| Database           |
+--------------------+
| information_schema |
| mysql              |
| performance_schema |
| testme_again       |
+--------------------+
4 rows in set (0.00 sec)

mysql>
```

Success! Now your Raspberry Pi database server is being backed up by your desktop computer.

Component Shopping List

The only new component you need for this chapter is a surplus USB hard drive, which is listed in Table 8-2. Table 8-3 shows a list of the supporting hardware that is included in the shopping list from other chapters.

Table 8-2. *Components Needed*

Item	Vendors	Est. Cost USD	Qty Needed
Surplus hard drive	Any USB hard drive (surplus or purchased)	Varies	1

Table 8-3. *Components Reused from Previous Chapters*

Item	Vendors	Est. Cost USD	Qty Needed
Raspberry Pi Model 4B 2GB or 4GB RAM	sparkfun.com, adafruit.com, thepithut.com	$50 and up	1
Mini-HDMI cable	Most online and retail stores	Varies	1
HDMI or DVI monitor	Most online and retail stores	Varies	1
USB keyboard	Most online and retail stores	Varies	1
USB-C power supply	Most online and retail stores	Varies	1
SD card, 32GB or more	Most online and retail stores	Varies	1

Summary

This chapter introduced MySQL and gave you a crash course on how to use it. You also compiled and installed MySQL on a Raspberry Pi and saw how to use more advanced features of MySQL, like replication.

472

Although it does not have nearly the sophistication of a high-availability, five-nines uptime (99.999%) database server, the low-cost Raspberry Pi with an attached USB hard drive makes for a very small-footprint database server that you can put just about anywhere.

This is great because sensor networks, by nature and often by necessity, need to be small and low cost. Having to build an expensive database server is not usually the level of investment desired.

Furthermore, depending on your choice of host for the sensor, saving data is difficult. If you choose an Arduino as the host, saving the data to a database requires a connection to the Internet and reliance on another service to store your data. This is fine for cases where you can actually connect the sensor nodes to the Internet[12] (or the sensor network's aggregator node); but if you cannot or do not want to connect to the Internet, it is difficult to get data into a database server from the Arduino.

That is, it was until recently. As you will see, there is indeed a way to save sensor data from a sensor node. In the next chapter, you build a sensor node that saves its data in your new database server—directly from an Arduino!

---

[12]Having sensor nodes connected to the Internet is one of the building blocks for the Internet of Things (IoT).

CHAPTER 9

MySQL and Arduino: United at Last!

In previous chapters, I discussed several methods you can use to store sensor data. One of those methods is storing the data in a database located on your network. If you recall, this has several advantages, not the least of which is that you do not have to connect your sensor network to the Internet to enable this capability.

This is not difficult to achieve if your sensor nodes are connected to a Raspberry Pi, but how do you do this if your sensor nodes are connected to an Arduino? The Arduino could be a sensor node itself, with one or more sensors connected directly to the Arduino I/O ports; or the Arduino could be a data aggregator, collecting data from other sensor nodes via a ZigBee wireless network using XBee modules as you saw in Chapter 6. But how do you insert data into MySQL without using a third-party application or cloud-based solution?

This chapter introduces a new database connector library that enables you to send sensor data from your Arduino to a MySQL database.

© Charles Bell 2020
C. Bell, *Beginning Sensor Networks with XBee, Raspberry Pi, and Arduino*,
https://doi.org/10.1007/978-1-4842-5796-8_9

Introducing Connector/Arduino

Congratulations! You have just entered a new world of Arduino projects. With a new database connector made specifically for the Arduino, you can connect your Arduino project directly to a MySQL server without using an intermediate computer or a web-based service.

Having direct access to a database server means you can store data acquired from your project in a database. You can also check values stored in tables on the server. The connector allows you to keep your sensor network local to your facility—it can even be disconnected from the Internet or any other external network.

If you have used some of the other methods of storing data from an Arduino, such as writing data to flash memory (e.g., a secure digital card) or an EEPROM device, you can eliminate the manual data copy and extraction methods altogether. Similarly, if your project is such that you cannot or do not want to connect to the Internet to save your data, the ability to write to a local database server solves that problem as well.

Saving your data in a database not only preserves the data for analysis at a later time but also means your project can feed data to more complex applications. Better still, if you have projects that use large data volumes for calculations or lookups, you can store the data on the server and retrieve only the data you need for the calculation or operation—all without taking up large blocks of memory on your Arduino. Clearly, this opens a whole new avenue of Arduino projects!

The database connector is named Connector/Arduino. It implements the MySQL client communication protocol (called a database connector) in a library built for the Arduino platform. Henceforth, I refer to Connector/Arduino when discussing general concepts and features and refer to the actual source code as the Connector/Arduino library, the connector, or simply the library.

Sketches (programs) written to use the library permit you to encode SQL statements to insert data and run small queries to return data from the database (e.g., using a lookup table).

You may be wondering how a microcontroller with limited memory and processing power can possibly support the code to insert data into a MySQL server. You can do this because the protocol for communicating with a MySQL server is not only well known and documented but also specifically designed to be lightweight. This is one of the small details that make MySQL attractive to embedded developers.

In order to communicate with MySQL, the Arduino must be connected to the MySQL server via a network. To do so, the Arduino must use an Ethernet or WiFi shield and be connected to a network or subnet that can connect to the database server (you can even connect across the Internet). The library is compatible with most new Arduino Ethernet, WiFi, and compatible clone shields that support the standard Ethernet library.

Caution   If you are using WiFi or Ethernet shields or modules that are not 100% compatible Arduino, you may run into issues using the connector. Be sure you choose shields and modules that use the standard Ethernet set of classes from Arduino. If they come with their own libraries, chances are they may not be compatible with Connector/Arduino or, worst case, you may need to make changes to the connector code in order to use it.

Hardware Requirements

Connector/Arduino requires an Arduino or Arduino clone with at least 32KB of memory. If you are using an older Arduino like the Duemilanove, be sure you have the version that uses the ATmega328P processor. Figures 9-1 and 9-2 depict two of the most common Arduino boards.

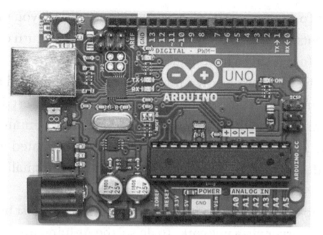

Figure 9-1. *Arduino Uno (courtesy of arduino.cc)*

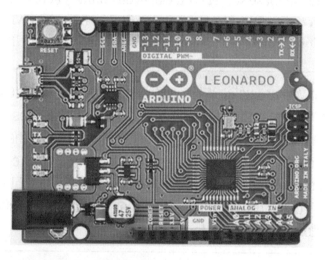

Figure 9-2. *Arduino Leonardo (courtesy of arduino.cc)*

Notice that the headers are different on the Leonardo as compared to the Uno. You may not see the subtle differences in the boards, but the Leonardo has built-in USB communication capabilities that enable the use of a mouse and keyboard, four additional digital pins, six more analog pins, and one more pulse-width modulation (PWM) pin. For more information about the differences and new features, see www.arduino.cc/ en/Guide/ArduinoLeonardoMicro?from=Guide.ArduinoLeonardo.

Connector/Arduino also requires the Arduino Ethernet or WiFi shield or equivalent. This is because the library references the Ethernet library written for the Ethernet shield. If you have some other form of Ethernet shield or if the Ethernet shield you are using requires a different library, you have to make a slight modification to the library to use it. You see this in a later section. Figure 9-3 shows the Arduino Ethernet Shield 2, and Figure 9-4 shows the Arduino WiFi shield.

Note   While the WiFi shield is listed as retired on the Arduino site, you can still find them on most online retailer sites. There are also a variety of Arduino clone WiFi shields that may be used. Be sure to find one that is compatible with the Ethernet libraries from Arduino.

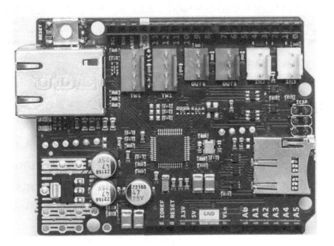

Figure 9-3.   *Arduino Ethernet Shield 2 (courtesy of arduino.cc)*

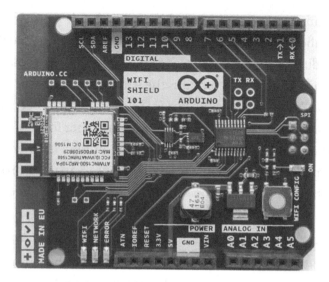

Figure 9-4. Arduino WiFi 101 shield (courtesy of arduino.cc)

WHAT ABOUT THE DUE?

The connector has been tested and works with the Due and similar clone boards. If you have a Due, you can use an Arduino Ethernet shield[1] with the connector.

What About Memory?

Connector/Arduino is implemented as an Arduino library. Although the protocol is lightweight, the library does consume some memory. In fact, the library requires about 28KB of flash memory to load. Thus, it requires the ATmega328 or similar (or later) processor with 32KB of flash memory.

---

[1]I was unable to get the WiFi shield to work with the Due. The WiFi library needs some work in this area, because it results in compilation errors. Check the WiFi guide page for the latest concerning using the WiFi shield with the Due.

That may seem like there isn't a lot of space for programming your sensor node, but as it turns out you really don't need that much for most sensors. If you do, you can always step up to a new Arduino with more memory. For example, the latest Arduino, the Due, has 512KB of memory for program code. Based on that, a mere 28KB is an insignificant amount of overhead.

Installing MySQL Connector/Arduino

To start using the library, you simply install it from the Arduino IDE like we've done in other projects. Recall, we need to open a new sketch, then choose Sketch ➤ Include Library ➤ Manage Libraries..., and, when the dialog opens, enter MySQL in the search box. Then, install the MySQL Connector/Arduino by clicking the *Install* button as shown in Figure 9-5.

The library is open source, licensed as GPLv2, and owned by Oracle Corporation. Thus, any modifications to the library that you intend to share must meet the GPLv2 license. Although it is not an officially supported product of Oracle or MySQL, you can use the library under the GPLv2.

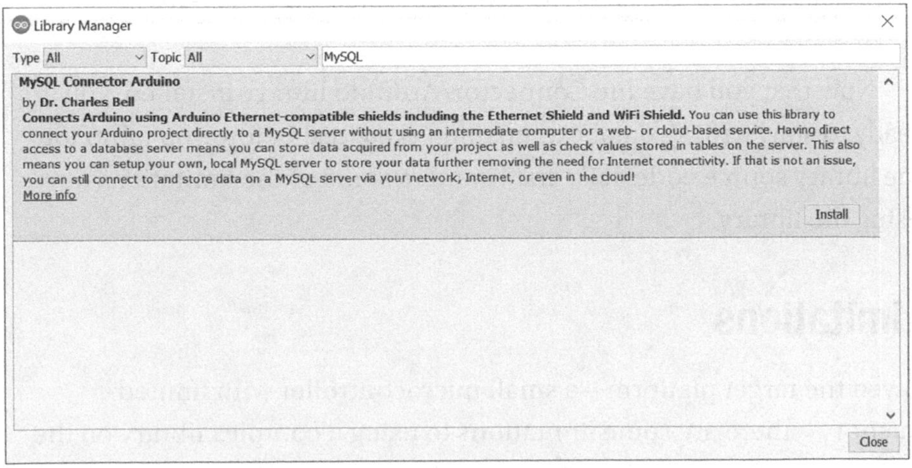

Figure 9-5. Installing MySQL Connector/Arduino

DATABASE CONNECTORS FOR MYSQL

There are many database connectors for MySQL. Oracle supplies a number of database connectors for a variety of languages including the following. You can find the connectors at `http://dev.mysql.com/downloads/connector/`.

- *Connector/ODBC*: Standard ODBC compliant

- *Connector/Net*: Windows .Net platforms

- *Connector/J*: Java applications

- *Connector/Python*: Python applications

- *Connector/C++*: Standardized C++ applications

- *Connector/Node.js*: JavaScript applications

- *MySQL native driver for PHP* (mysqlnd): PHP connector

As you can see, there is a connector for just about any programming language you are likely to encounter—and now there is even one for the Arduino!

Now that you have the Connector/Arduino library installed, you are ready to start writing database-enabled sketches! Before you jump into the library source code, let's first examine some of the limitations of using the library.

Limitations

Given the target platform—a small microcontroller with limited memory—there are some limitations to using a complex library on the Arduino platform. The first thing you should know about Connector/

Arduino is that it isn't a small library: it can consume a lot of memory. Although the library uses dynamic memory to keep memory use to a minimum, how much memory is required depends on how you use the connector.

More specifically, you need to limit how many string constants you create. If you are issuing simple data-insertion commands (INSERT INTO), an easy way to calculate this is that the connector uses a bit more than the sum of the length of all of your strings. If you are querying the server for data, the connector uses a bit more than the cumulative size of a row of data returned.

If you are using the latest Arduino Due or similar board with a lot of memory, this may not be an issue. But there are other considerations. The following are the known limitations of the Connector/Arduino:

- Query strings (the SQL statements) must fit into memory. This is because the class uses an internal buffer for building data packets to send to the server. It is suggested that long strings be stored in program memory using PROGMEM (see cmd_query_P). See www.arduino.cc/reference/en/language/variables/utilities/progmem/ for more information.

- Result sets are read one row at a time and one field at a time.

- The combined length of a row in a result set must fit into memory.

- Server error responses are processed immediately. The connector prints the error code and message to the serial monitor.

Now that you know how the connector works on a high level, what hardware is required, and how to download and install the connector, let's dive into using the connector to write sketches that insert data into a MySQL server.

There is one other limitation that bears mentioning. The connector is written to support the current and recent releases of MySQL from Oracle Corporation. There are other variants maintained by other vendors, but most of these have some modification that introduces subtle incompatibilities. For example, there is at least one variant that is known to cause problems working with the connector.[2] Should you encounter strange errors or issues using the connector with your MySQL server, ensure you are using the server binaries distributed by Oracle. Switching to the base or "original" source of MySQL can solve a host of small issues and incompatibilities.

Tip   If you would like the latest information about the connector including upcoming releases or if you need help with an issue with the connector, visit the GitHub repository for the connector at `https://github.com/ChuckBell/MySQL_Connector_Arduino/wiki`.

WHAT ABOUT THE ESP8266?

Due to the popularity of the small and affordable ESP like of microcontrollers and WiFi modules, you may encounter these as you plan your sensor networks. It is perfectly fine to use these as they can be programmed using the Arduino IDE. However, you should take care and read the documentation for the connector because it requires some minor changes to your script to enable use with the ESP modules. There is even a sample sketch you can view for ideas.

---

[2]Yes, I am saying categorically and against what marketing materials may suggest that not all MySQL variants are 100% compatible. Some have minor changes to the client protocol, which causes the connector to behave in unexpected ways and, in some cases, fail.

Building Connector/Arduino-Enabled Sketches

Let's begin with a simple sketch designed to insert a single row into a table in MySQL. You are creating a "hello, world!" sketch (but saved in a database table). All database-enabled sketches share the same common building blocks. These include setting up a database to use, creating a sketch with a specific set of include files, connecting to the database server, and executing queries. This section walks through the basic steps needed to create and execute a database-enabled sketch.

Database Setup

The first thing you need is a database server! You can use your desktop or laptop computer if you'd prefer to limit the unknowns (always a good practice when experimenting with embedded systems). I used a laptop running MySQL to keep the example simple. However, if you built a Raspberry Pi MySQL database server in the previous chapter, feel free to use your shiny new Raspberry Pi database server instead.

I also keep the example simple by using only the setup() method to connect to the MySQL server and issue the query. This simplifies things because the setup() method is called only once. Feel free to move the INSERT statement to the loop() method if you want to see what happens when multiple INSERT statements are issued. Be sure to include the delay() call to allow the library sufficient time to execute and negotiate the protocol. Attempting to issue too many queries too quickly can be a source of strange errors or missing rows.

You begin by creating a database and a table to use to store the data. For this experiment, you create a simple table with two columns: a text column (char) to store a message and a TIMESTAMP column to record the date and time the row was saved. I find the TIMESTAMP data type to be an excellent choice for storing sensor data. It is rare that you would not want to know when the sample was taken! Best of all, MySQL makes it very easy to use. In fact, you don't even need to pass a token NULL value to the server because it generates and stores the current timestamp itself.[3]

Listing 9-1 shows a MySQL client (named mysql) session that creates the database and the table and inserts a row into the table manually. The sketch will execute a similar INSERT statement from your Arduino. By issuing a SELECT command, you can see each time the table was updated.

Note   I am using the MySQL Shell for the examples in this chapter, but you can use the older mysql client if you prefer.

Listing 9-1. Creating the Test Database

```
> mysqlsh --sql --uri root@localhost:33060
MySQL Shell 8.0.19

Copyright (c) 2016, 2019, Oracle and/or its affiliates. All
rights reserved.
Oracle is a registered trademark of Oracle Corporation and/or
its affiliates.
Other names may be trademarks of their respective owners.

Type '\help' or '\?' for help; '\quit' to exit.
Creating a session to 'root@localhost:33060'
Fetching schema names for autocompletion... Press ^C to stop.
Your MySQL connection id is 18 (X protocol)
Server version: 8.0.19 MySQL Community Server - GPL
No default schema selected; type \use <schema> to set one.
> CREATE DATABASE test_arduino;
```

---

[3]Older versions of MySQL (prior to 8.0) may require passing NULL as the value for a TIMESTAMP column.

```
Query OK, 1 row affected (0.0190 sec)
> USE test_arduino;
Default schema set to `test_arduino`.
Fetching table and column names from `test_arduino` for auto-
completion... Press ^C to stop.
> CREATE TABLE hello (source char(20), event_date timestamp
DEFAULT CURRENT_TIMESTAMP ON UPDATE CURRENT_TIMESTAMP);
Query OK, 0 rows affected (0.0503 sec)
> CREATE USER 'arduino_user'@'%' IDENTIFIED WITH mysql_native_
password BY 'secret';
Query OK, 0 rows affected (0.0126 sec)
> GRANT ALL ON *.* to 'arduino_user'@'%';
Query OK, 0 rows affected (0.0108 sec)
> INSERT INTO hello (source) VALUES ('From Laptop');
Query OK, 1 row affected (0.0080 sec)
> SELECT * FROM hello;
+-------------+---------------------+
| source      | event_date          |
+-------------+---------------------+
| From Laptop | 2020-03-04 13:24:14 |
+-------------+---------------------+
```

Notice here I created the database as well as a user for accessing that database. You may notice a new phrase in the CREATE USER command. The IDENTIFIED WITH mysql_native_password clause tells MySQL to use the native password plugin instead of the newer sha256_password plugin. If you have an older version of the MySQL server (5.7 and prior), you do not need this clause as it may generate and error.

Tip Be sure to enable the mysql_native_password plugin for your MySQL server if you have connection issues or use the preceding clause when creating users you want to use to connect from your Arduino.

Notice I also created a simple table with a timestamp column for recording the date and time of the event. This is a very simple example, but you can use these techniques to help make your database easier to use. That is, you don't have to calculate the date and time for a row—just insert the data and let the database handle it. Cool.

DESIGNING TABLES FOR STORING SENSOR DATA

When designing tables for your sensor networks, be sure to select the correct data type and length (if applicable) carefully. It would be a tragedy to learn months later that your painstakingly constructed sensor network has had its data truncated as a consequence of choosing the wrong data type. Similarly, if you run into problems with your sensor nodes or aggregate nodes failing when saving data, check the length of your character and other fields to ensure that you are not overrunning the allocated size (length).

Setting Up the Arduino

The hardware you need for this example is one Arduino or shield-compatible clone and an Arduino Ethernet shield. There are various forms of the Ethernet shield, but I prefer the Arduino-branded shields because they tend to be more reliable.

BUYER BEWARE: CHECK COMPATIBILITY

For the most part, Arduino clones described as "shield compatible" are safe to use, but you should always check. I failed to do this once, thinking I had found a great deal on an Ethernet shield that was "100% compatible," only to discover it had an annoying flaw that required me to remove the shield in order to upload sketches. Although the shield works and I use it regularly, it is *not* 100% compatible.

I like to mount my Arduino on a platform in order to make it easier to handle and less likely that I will accidentally set it down on a surface or object that conducts electricity—or, perhaps worse, that it will accidentally scratch my desk! Go ahead and mount the Ethernet shield to your Arduino. Be sure all the pins are seated. Figure 9-6 shows my Arduino and Ethernet shield mounted on a platform[4] with a handy small breadboard nearby.

Figure 9-6. *Arduino with Ethernet shield*

Starting a New Sketch

It is time to start writing your sketch. Open your Arduino environment, and create a new sketch named hello_mysql.ino. The following sections detail the parts of a typical MySQL database-enabled sketch. You begin with the required include files.

---

[4]Breadboard and mounting plate by Adafruit (www.adafruit.com/products/275).

Include Files

To use the Connector/Arduino library, recall that it requires an Ethernet shield and therefore the Ethernet library. We also need to include the connector headers for making a connection and issuing a query. The following shows all the library header files you need to include at a bare minimum for a MySQL database-enabled sketch. Go ahead and enter these now:

```
#include <Ethernet.h>
#include <MySQL_Connection.h>
#include <MySQL_Cursor.h>
```

Note   Including the Ethernet.h header is not needed for the examples in this book, but it is OK to include it if you get compilation errors.

Preliminary Setup

With the include files set up, you next must take care of some preliminary declarations. These include declarations for the Ethernet library and Connector/Arduino.

The Ethernet library requires you to set up a MAC address and the IP address of the server. The MAC address is a string of hexadecimal digits and need not be anything special, but it should be unique among the machines on your network. It uses Dynamic Host Control Protocol (DHCP) to get an IP address, DNS, and gateway information. The IP address of the server is defined using the IPAddress class (which stores the value as an array of four integers, just as you would expect).

On the other hand, the Ethernet class also permits you to supply an IP address for the Arduino. If you assign an IP address for the Arduino, it must be unique for the network segment to which it is attached. Be sure to use an IP scanner to make sure your choice of IP address isn't already in use.

The following shows what these statements would look like for a node on a 10.0.1.X network:

```
byte mac_addr[] = { 0xDE, 0xAD, 0xBE, 0xEF, 0xFE, 0xED };
IPAddress server_addr(10,0,1,35);   // IP of the MySQL *server*
here
```

Next, you need to set up some variables for Connector/Arduino. You need to define a reference to the library and some strings to use for the data you use in the sketch. At a minimum, these include a string for the user ID, another for the password, and one for the query you use. This last string is optional because you can just use the literal string directly in the query call, but it is good practice to make strings for the query statements. It is also the best way to make queries parameterized for reuse.

The following is an example of the statements needed to complete the declarations for your sketch:

```
EthernetClient client;
MySQL_Connection conn((Client *)&client);

char user[] = "arduino_user";       // MySQL user login username
char password[] = "secret";         // MySQL user login password
char INSERT_SQL[] = "INSERT INTO test_arduino.hello (source)
VALUES ('Hello from Arduino!')";
```

Notice the INSERT statement. You include a string to indicate that you are running the query from your Arduino.

Connecting to a MySQL Server

That concludes the preliminaries; let's get some code written! Next, you change the setup() method. This is where the code for connecting to the MySQL server should be placed. Recall that this method is called only once each time the Arduino is booted. Listing 9-2 shows the code needed.

Listing 9-2. Setup() Method

```
void setup() {
  Serial.begin(115200);
  while (!Serial); // wait for serial port to connect
  Ethernet.begin(mac_addr);
  Serial.println("Connecting...");
  if (conn.connect(server_addr, 3306, user, password)) {
    delay(1000);
    // insert query here //
  }
  else
    Serial.println("Connection failed.");
}
```

The code begins with a call to the Ethernet library to initialize the network connection. Recall that when you use the Ethernet.begin() method, passing only the MAC address as shown in the example, it causes the Ethernet library to use DHCP to obtain an IP address. If you want to assign an IP address manually, see the Ethernet.begin() method documentation at http://arduino.cc/en/Reference/EthernetBegin.

Next is a call to serial monitor. Although not completely necessary, it is a good idea to include it so you can see the messages written by Connector/Arduino. If you have problems with connecting or running queries, be sure to use the serial monitor so you can see the messages sent by the library.

Now comes a call to the delay() method. You issue this wait of one second to ensure that you have time to start the serial monitor and not miss the debug statements. Feel free to experiment with changing this value if you need more time to start the serial monitor.

After the delay, you print a statement to the serial monitor to indicate that you are attempting to connect to the server. Connecting to the server is a single call to the Connector/Arduino class we created earlier with the method named connect(). You pass the IP address of the MySQL database server, the port the server is listening on, and the user name and password. If this call passes, the code drops to the next delay() method call.

This delay is needed to slow execution before issuing additional MySQL commands. Like the previous delay, depending on your hardware and network latency, you may not need this delay. You should experiment if you have strong feelings against using delays to avoid latency issues. On the other hand, should the connection fail, the code falls through to the print statement to tell you the connection has failed.

Notice the commented line, // insert query here //. This is where we would place our example query so that the Arduino sends the data once to MySQL. If we place this in the loop() method, it will send the data many times, and for this example, that isn't what we want.

Running a Query

Now it is time to run the query. Place this code in the branch that is executed after a successful connection. Listing 9-3 shows the section of code we will use to run the INSERT query. Take a moment to read through it. Notice we create a new instance of the MySQL_Cursor class, execute the query, and then check the result for errors (false means it failed). At the end, we simply delete the instance as we don't need it anymore.

Listing 9-3. Connecting and Running a Query

```
Serial.print("Recording hello message...");
// Initiate the query class instance
MySQL_Cursor *cur_mem = new MySQL_Cursor(&conn);
// Execute the query
int res = cur_mem->execute(INSERT_SQL);
if (!res) {
  Serial.println("Query failed.");
} else {
  Serial.println("Ok.");
}
// Note: since there are no results, we do not need to read any
data
// Deleting the cursor also frees up memory used
delete cur_mem;
```

Notice that you simply invoke a method named cur_mem->execute() and pass it the query you defined earlier. Yes, it is that easy!

Finally, the loop() method is empty for this example as we aren't doing anything more than the one query on start.

```
void loop() {
}
```

One More Thing...

At this point, you've got everything you need to set up and run a basic sketch with the connector. However, there are two things you may want to consider when developing your sketches. First, you should enable debug mode so that you can see more information when there are errors. Second, if you plan to execute SELECT queries, enable the select code. Both of these modes are turned off by default in order to save a few bytes by disabling parts of the code.

For example, the many debug print statements to the serial monitor consume a bit more space than you may have. Similarly, the code for processing data from the server for SELECT queries takes up a bit of space for that code. When working with small devices like the Arduino, sometimes saving a few bytes may make the sketch stable and successful.

To turn on debug mode, navigate to the MySQL_Packet.h file in your Arduino library directory under the MySQL_Connector_Arduino/src folder. Add the following line of code (shown in bold) immediately after the version line. This will enable printing of additional diagnostic data when there are errors.

```
#define MYSQL_OK_PACKET     0x00
#define MYSQL_EOF_PACKET    0xfe
#define MYSQL_ERROR_PACKET  0xff
#define MYSQL_VERSION_STR   "1.2.0"
#define DEBUG
```

Tip   Always enable debug mode when starting a new sketch. You can remove it later once you've got it working correctly.

To enable the select mode, add the following line of code (shown in bold) after the version line. This will enable the sections of code that support SELECT queries.

```
#define MYSQL_OK_PACKET     0x00
#define MYSQL_EOF_PACKET    0xfe
#define MYSQL_ERROR_PACKET  0xff
#define MYSQL_VERSION_STR   "1.2.0"
#define WITH_SELECT
```

Testing the Sketch

You now have all the code needed to complete the sketch except for the loop() method. In this case, you make it an empty method because you are not doing anything repetitive. Listing 9-4 shows the completed sketch.

Tip   If you are having problems getting the connector working, see the "Troubleshooting Connector/Arduino" section and then return to this project.

Listing 9-4. "Hello, MySQL!" Sketch

```
/**
 * Beginning Sensor Networks Second Edition
 * Example: Hello, MySQL!
 *
 * This code module demonstrates how to create a simple
   database-enabled
 * sketch.
 *
 * Dr. Charles Bell 2020
 */
#include <MySQL_Connection.h>
#include <MySQL_Cursor.h>

byte mac_addr[] = { 0xDE, 0xAD, 0xBE, 0xEF, 0xFE, 0xED };

IPAddress server_addr(10,0,1,35);   // IP of the MySQL *server*
                                        here
char user[] = "arduino_user";       // MySQL user login username
char password[] = "secret";         // MySQL user login password
```

```
// Sample query
char INSERT_SQL[] = "INSERT INTO test_arduino.hello (source)
VALUES ('Hello, Arduino!')";

EthernetClient client;
MySQL_Connection conn((Client *)&client);

void setup() {
  Serial.begin(115200);
  while (!Serial); // wait for serial port to connect
  Ethernet.begin(mac_addr);
  Serial.print("My local IP is: ");
  Serial.println(Ethernet.localIP());
  Serial.println("Connecting...");
  if (conn.connect(server_addr, 3306, user, password)) {
    delay(1000);
    Serial.print("Recording hello message...");
    // Initiate the query class instance
    MySQL_Cursor *cur_mem = new MySQL_Cursor(&conn);
    // Execute the query
    int res = cur_mem->execute(INSERT_SQL);
    if (!res) {
      Serial.println("Query failed.");
    } else {
      Serial.println("Ok.");
    }
    // Note: since there are no results, we do not need to read
      any data
    // Deleting the cursor also frees up memory used
    delete cur_mem;
  }
```

```
  else
    Serial.println("Connection failed.");
}

void loop() {
}
```

Before you press the button to compile and upload the sketch, let's discuss a couple of errors that could occur. If you have the wrong IP address or the wrong user name and password for the MySQL server, you could see a connection failure in the serial monitor like that shown as follows. Notice here it tells us what to look for; the user id and password are incorrect.

```
My local IP is: 192.168.42.12
Connecting...
...trying...
Error: 84 = Access denied for user 'arduino_user'@'192.168.42.12'
(using password: YES).
Connection failed.
```

If your Arduino connects to the MySQL server but the query fails, you see an error in the serial monitor like the one shown as follows. Notice it tells us what to look for; the table name is wrong (doesn't exist).

```
My local IP is: 192.168.42.12
Connecting...
...trying...
Connected to server version: 8.0.18
Recording hello message...Error: 60 = Table 'test_arduino.
hello_arduino' doesn't exist.
Query failed.
```

Be sure to double-check the source code and the IP address of your MySQL server as well as the username and password chosen. If you are still encountering problems connecting, see the "Troubleshooting Connector/Arduino" section for a list of things to test to ensure that your MySQL server is configured correctly.

Once you have double-checked the server installation and the information in the sketch, compile and upload the sketch to your Arduino. Then start the serial monitor and observe the process of connecting to the MySQL server. The following shows a completed and successful execution of the code:

```
My local IP is: 192.168.42.12
Connecting...
...trying...
Connected to server version: 8.0.18
Recording hello message...Ok.
```

Wow, is that it? Not very interesting, is it? If you see the statements in your serial monitor as shown earlier, rest assured that the Arduino has connected to and issued a query to the MySQL server. To check, simply return to the mysql client or MySQL shell and issue a SELECT on the table. But first, run the sketch a number of times to issue several inserts in the table.

You can do this in two ways.

First, you can press *RESET* on your Arduino. If you leave your serial monitor running, the Arduino presents the messages in order, as shown as follows. Second, you can upload the sketch again. In this case, the serial monitor closes, and you have to reopen it. The advantage of this method is you can change the query statement each time, thereby inserting different rows into the database. Go ahead and try that now, and check your database for the changes.

```
My local IP is: 192.168.42.12
Connecting...
```

```
...trying...
Connected to server version: 8.0.18
Recording hello message...Ok.
My local IP is: 192.168.42.12
Connecting...
...trying...
Connected to server version: 8.0.18
Recording hello message...Ok.
My local IP is: 192.168.42.12
Connecting...
...trying...
Connected to server version: 8.0.18
Recording hello message...Ok.
```

Let's check the results of the test runs. To do so, you connect to the database server with the mysql client and issue a SELECT query. Listing 9-5 shows the results of the three runs from the example. Notice the different timestamp for each run. As you can see, I ran it once, then waited a few minutes and ran it again (I used the *RESET* button on my Arduino Ethernet shield), and then ran it again right away. Very cool, isn't it?

Listing 9-5. Verifying the Connection

```
$ mysqlsh --uri root@localhost:33060 --sql
MySQL Shell 8.0.18

Copyright (c) 2016, 2019, Oracle and/or its affiliates. All
rights reserved.
Oracle is a registered trademark of Oracle Corporation and/or
its affiliates.
Other names may be trademarks of their respective owners.
```

```
Type '\help' or '\?' for help; '\quit' to exit.
Creating a session to 'root@localhost:33060'
Fetching schema names for autocompletion... Press ^C to stop.
Your MySQL connection id is 37 (X protocol)
Server version: 8.0.18 MySQL Community Server - GPL
No default schema selected; type \use <schema> to set one.
 MySQL  localhost:33060+ ssl  SQL > SELECT * FROM test_arduino.
 hello;
+-----------------+---------------------+
| source          | event_date          |
+-----------------+---------------------+
| From Laptop     | 2020-03-10 14:21:21 |
| Hello, Arduino! | 2020-03-10 14:48:11 |
| Hello, Arduino! | 2020-03-10 14:54:24 |
| Hello, Arduino! | 2020-03-10 14:54:41 |
| Hello, Arduino! | 2020-03-10 14:54:56 |
+-----------------+---------------------+
5 rows in set (0.0003 sec)
```

What About the Ethernet Shield 2?

If you are planning to use the Ethernet Shield 2, you do not need to change anything. The connector and the example sketch will work without modification.

What About the WiFi Shield?

If you are planning to use the WiFi shield, you need to make a few minor changes to enable the WiFi-specific code in the connector.[5] Changing the connector code is very simple. Open the MySQL_Packet.h file and add the following line of code replacing (or commenting out) the #include <Ethernet.h> line:

```
#ifdef ARDUINO_ARCH_ESP32
    #include <Arduino.h>
#elif ARDUINO_ARCH_ESP8266
    #include <ESP8266WiFi.h>
#else
    #include <WiFi.h>
//     #include <Ethernet.h>
#endif
```

You need to use one of the available WiFi connection mechanisms and comment out the Ethernet.begin() call. An example setup() method with changes is shown here:

```
// WiFi card example
char ssid[] = "my_lonely_ssid";
char pass[] = "horse_with_silly_name";

Connector my_conn;          // The Connector/Arduino reference

void setup() {
  Serial.begin(115200);
  while (!Serial);          // wait for serial port to connect.
                            Leonardo only
```

---

[5]Assuming you have downloaded and installed the WiFi shield library from https://github.com/arduino/wifishield.

```
// WiFi section
int status = WiFi.begin(ssid, pass);
// if you're not connected, stop here:
if ( status != WL_CONNECTED) {
  Serial.println("Couldn't get a WiFi connection!");
  while(true);
}
// if you are connected, print out info about the connection:
else {
  Serial.println("Connected to network");
  IPAddress ip = WiFi.localIP();
  Serial.print("My IP address is: ");
  Serial.println(ip);
}
...
```

See http://arduino.cc/en/Guide/ArduinoWiFiShield for more examples of how to use a connection method to connect your WiFi shield to your access point.

If you plan to use the WiFi shield with an Arduino that is older than an Arduino Uno Rev3, you need to use a jumper on the IOREF pin, as shown here (courtesy of arduino.cc) for the WiFi shield to work properly. The WiFi shield page has this and a host of other very important information for using the WiFi shield in your project.

What About the WiFi 101 Shield?

The newer WiFi 101 shield can also be used. You must modify the MySQL_ Packet.h file similar to the WiFi shield as shown here:

```
#ifdef ARDUINO_ARCH_ESP32
    #include <Arduino.h>
```

```
#elif ARDUINO_ARCH_ESP8266
    #include <ESP8266WiFi.h>
#else
    #include <WiFi101.h>
//    #include <Ethernet.h>
#endif
```

Tip   If your board has WiFi capabilities, be sure to check which WiFi library it requires and change the connector accordingly.

Troubleshooting Connector/Arduino

Setting up and using Connector/Arduino as described usually results in success. However, there are cases when the setup does not go quite right and the examples in this chapter simply won't work. Many problems can be attributed to your choice of Arduino hardware, networking environment setup, and even MySQL server configuration.

For example, if your Arduino hardware is not an official Arduino product, if it is newer than the examples used in the book, or if your Ethernet shield is a clone or something other than a wired network shield, you may encounter problems getting everything to work.

If this happens to you, don't give up![6] This section is designed to give you tips and techniques for figuring out what is wrong with your hardware, software, network, and operating system that may be preventing the connector from working.

---

[6]As satisfying as it may be, please refrain from giving your tiny Arduino skeet-shooting lessons. All is not lost, and most issues can be resolved with a little patience and the techniques described here.

Rather than include an exhaustive description of all the procedures needed for all cases,[7] I present a taxonomy that you can use to diagnose and solve your issues. There are several categories of problem areas. I discuss each of these in turn:

- MySQL server configuration

- MySQL user account problems

- Networking configuration

- Connector installation

- Others

The following sections explain the issue and suggest a cause and solution. It may be that one or more of these issues are causing your sketch to fail. The best way to use this section is to read through it from start to finish, checking your system along the way. Each section builds on the previous section, ensuring that all possible issues are solved in an orderly manner. I am certain you can get your sketch working using this technique.

Tip   The Arduino site has a very good troubleshooting section for general Arduino help. You should consult this page in addition to following the advice in this section. See `http://arduino.cc/en/ Guide/troubleshooting`.

---

[7]An impossible feat for mere mortals.

MySQL Server Configuration

One of the most common issues that can cause your MySQL sketch to fail or not work properly has to do with how the MySQL server is configured. In general, you are likely to see errors connecting to the server in the serial monitor. This section contains a number of causes for this problem.

Server Is Not Using Networking

The MySQL server can be configured to disable networking with the --skip-networking option. In this case, you may be able to connect to your MySQL server on your local machine (on the machine where MySQL is installed) by using the mysql client, but accessing the machine from another host fails.

The best way to check this without using a second computer (which is also a viable test) is to use the mysql client as follows. To test local connection to the server, run this command (substituting your username and password):

```
$ mysql -uroot -psecret
```

If this works, then your server is alive and accepting connections. If this does not work, refer to the MySQL online reference manual to check your configuration and other ways to ensure that MySQL is running properly.

Now, let's attempt to connect via the network. This is triggered whenever you use the host option as shown next. Notice that it is almost the same command, but in this case, you supply the IP address of the server (your machine) and the port for MySQL:

```
$ mysql -uroot -psecret -h 10.0.1.23 --port 3306
```

This simulates how the Arduino connects to the MySQL server. If it works, it verifies that your MySQL server is alive and accepting network connections using the IP and port supplied. Be sure to use these settings in your sketch.

If the command fails, locate your `mysql.cnf` file (`mysql.ini` for some Windows installations), and remove the skip-networking option. You can disable it by placing a # in the first column of the line. Once you have done this, be sure to restart your MySQL server to make the changes take effect, and then try the previous test again.

Cannot Connect, and Correct IP Address Is Used

Another issue that is closely related to the `--skip-networking` option is the `--bind-address` option. This option ensures that MySQL listens and communicates on a specific IP address. It is used mainly for multi-homed systems (computers with multiple network adapters). If this option is enabled and it is not set to the same IP address as the host on which it is installed, the MySQL server will exhibit behavior similar to the previous problem.

Testing this problem uses the same test as the previous example. The resolution is simply to comment out the bind-address option in the MySQL configuration file. Remember to restart your MySQL server if you change the configuration file.

I Can Connect Locally but Not Remotely

If the previous issues do not resolve the problem or if your MySQL server is configured correctly and you still cannot connect, it is possible that your computer is running a firewall or similar port-blocking application. The best way to test this is to use a second computer and the `mysql` client application to try to connect to the server. If you get errors related to the server not responding or similar, the server could be blocking connections. Again, the command to use from the remote computer is

```
$ mysql -uroot -psecret -- 10.0.1.23 --port 3306
```

To resolve the issue, you must change your firewall or port-blocking application. MySQL uses port 3306 by default. Be sure to check your firewall application to ensure that it permits connections (inbound and outbound) through port 3306. If it does not, enable this port and try your sketch again.

Tip   For more information about setting up the MySQL server for network access and platform-specific installation steps, see the online MySQL reference manual.

MySQL User Account Problems

Another very common source of issues concerns how the MySQL user is created. More specifically, it has to do with the choice of hostname in the CREATE USER or GRANT statement. For example, if you issued the following commands, you could have problems connecting from your Arduino or a second computer:

```
> CREATE USER 'joe'@'10.0.1.23' IDENTIFIED BY 'secret';
Query OK, 0 rows affected (0.01 sec)
> GRANT SELECT ON test_arduino.* TO 'joe'@'10.0.1.24';
Query OK, 0 rows affected (0.01 sec)
```

Do you see the problems (there are three)? First, you created a user with a specific host (10.0.1.23), but later you granted SELECT privileges to the test_arduino database to the same user—or did you?

Note   The GRANT statement shown in the example may fail for newer versions of the MySQL server.

This is the second problem. In the GRANT statement, you used the host 10.0.1.24, which means when user joe connects from 10.0.1.24, he can see the test_arduino database.

The third problem arises from the second. Because you did not reference an existing user and host combination, MySQL does not require joe to use a password when connecting from host 10.0.1.24. You can see that this is the case by querying the mysql.user table:

```
> SELECT user, host, password from mysql.user WHERE user = 'joe';
+------+-----------+-------------------------------------------+
| user | host      | password                                  |
+------+-----------+-------------------------------------------+
| joe  | 10.0.1.23 | *14E65567ABDB5135D0CFD9A70B3032C179A49EE7 |
| joe  | 10.0.1.24 |                                           |
+------+-----------+-------------------------------------------+
2 rows in set (0.00 sec)
```

Aha, you say. Aha indeed. The lesson here is always make sure your choice of user and host match the IP (or hostname) of the machine from which you want to connect.

But you may be thinking, "What about DHCP?" If you use DHCP, as do most sketches and examples, then you may not know what IP address your Arduino has been assigned. What do you do then?

One of the ways to reduce hostname and permissions problems is to use wildcards. Consider this alternative to the previous commands:

```
> CREATE USER 'joe'@'10.0.1.%' IDENTIFIED BY 'secret';
Query OK, 0 rows affected (0.00 sec)
> GRANT SELECT ON test_arduino.* TO 'joe'@'10.0.1.%';
Query OK, 0 rows affected (0.00 sec)
> SELECT user, host, password from mysql.user WHERE user = 'joe';
```

```
+------+----------+-----------------------------------------+
| user | host     | password                                |
+------+----------+-----------------------------------------+
| joe  | 10.0.1.% | *14E65567ABDB5135D0CFD9A70B3032C179A49EE7 |
+------+----------+-----------------------------------------+
1 row in set (0.00 sec)
```

Notice that here you use a % for the last portion of the IP address. This effectively permits the user to connect from any computer on that subnet. Cool! Notice also that your problem of two user accounts has been resolved.

Other issues related to user accounts are cases where you've forgotten the password, misspelled it, or used caps (or not caps) when you assigned the password. All these user account issues can be tested with the mysql client application. I recommend trying the connection locally and remotely from a second computer. If it works remotely, you know the account is set up correctly. Be sure to do a SELECT or two when you are connected with your Arduino user account, just to make sure the permissions are set correctly.

There is one other issue that can cause connection issues. Recall we discussed the mysql_native_password plugin. If you are using a recent version of MySQL, you will need to either set this for each user when you create them or set the password plugin default.

To enable the mysql_native_password plugin for each user, add the clause as shown here:

```
CREATE USER 'user'@'%' IDENTIFIED WITH mysql_native_password BY 'secret';
```

If you have already created users, you can use the ALTER USER command to change the password plugin.

```
ALTER USER 'user'@'%' IDENTIFIED WITH mysql_native_password;
```

To make the native password plugin the default for all users, add the following to the configuration file and restart MySQL:

```
[mysqld]
...
default-authentication-plugin=mysql_native_password
...
```

Networking Configuration

When networking problems occur, it isn't always obvious what is wrong. Rather than listing a number of common error conditions or specific examples, I discuss things you need to check to make sure things are working.

When there are networking issues, you are likely to encounter or observe an inability to connect to your MySQL server. Yes, you probably see the same problems as described previously in almost the same ways.

The best way to check whether you are having networking issues is to connect a second computer to the same network cable that you are using for your Arduino and try to connect with your friend the mysql client. Be sure to check that the computer is set up to get its IP address from DHCP and all other networking settings are the same as your Arduino (no static DNS, and so on).

This is very important because if your computer is configured with a static IP and the Arduino sketch is using DHCP (or vice versa), this can mask the problem! For example, if no DHCP server is available, Arduino sketches configured to get the IP address dynamically will fail.

If you connect a second computer to your network using the same cable as the Arduino, and it works but the sketch still does not work, you should consider the possibility that your Ethernet shield is faulty or incompatible with your hardware. Check the vendor's or manufacturer's website for any limitations or compatibility workarounds. I have seen this on at least one occasion. Another possibility is that the shield has malfunctioned (rare, but it does happen).

Now, if your computer fails to connect to your MySQL server, check the following items to ensure that your networking is configured correctly. Some of these may seem a little dumb, but I can assure you that I've personally encountered each of these at least once:

- Is the router/switch turned on?[8]

- Are you using the correct subnet?

- Are you using the correct options in the proper order for Ethernet.begin()? See the online Arduino library reference page (http://arduino.cc/en/Reference/EthernetBegin) for more details.

- If you are trying to use DHCP, is there a DHCP server on your network?

- Is the network cable plugged in to the switch/router?[9]

- Check the lights on the switch/router. Does it show that the cable is connected? If not, you may have a bad cable.

Once again, check and fix all of these issues, go back to the second computer, and try the connection. When it is working, your sketch should connect to the MySQL server.

---

[8]You will be surprised how often this happens—and how humble you feel when you discover that it works great once it has proper power supplied.

[9]Been there, done that. Twice. You know it's got two ends, right?

Note   A complete tutorial or overview of networking is beyond the scope of this book. However, a few well-typed key phrases in a Google search will give you a host of good advice for diagnosing networking problems.

Another thing to try is to load one of the example sketches for the Ethernet shield. For example, load, compile, and run the *WebClient* sketch. What you should see is a mass of data returned from a search request to google.com. If this works, you can be sure that your Ethernet shield is working properly and that you still have issues with either your database server or your sketch.

Connector Installation

The last major area of potential issues has to do with how the connector is installed. If you have gotten this far and your sketch compiles and uploads correctly, you do not have any problems related to the connector installation. I describe the most common installation problems in the following sections.

Compilation Errors Related to "No Module Named"

If you encounter compilation errors complaining that there is no module named Connector or similar errors, you do not have the libraries installed in the proper location. Go back to the "Installing MySQL Connector/ Arduino" section earlier in this chapter, and ensure that you have installed the library.

If you downloaded the library from GitHub, you must ensure you have the library files placed in the correct location. In fact, it is possible that your libraries folder is not where you think it is. Be sure to check the Preferences dialog to find the default location. The libraries folder should be a subfolder of the sketchbook location.

The best indicator that you have the connecter copied correctly is that you can see the *MySQL Connector Arduino* submenu in the *File ➤ Examples* menu.

Compilation Errors Related to Include File

Errors like this can be caused by the use of quotes vs. brackets in the `#include <MySQL***.h>` statements. If you are using quotes and the files are not copied to your project folder or a subfolder thereof, you may see compilation errors. The correct method is to use brackets with the connector files located in the `libraries` folder.

Others

There are also some other issues you could encounter that do not fall into the previous categories.

Strange Characters Appear in the Serial Monitor

If you see garbage or strange characters in your serial monitor output, it could be that your setting for the `Serial.begin()` method does not match the serial monitor setting. Choose the appropriate speed from the drop-down list in the serial monitor, and try your sketch again.

No Output in the Serial Monitor

This one is a lot harder to diagnose. Sometimes the Arduino is hung, or there is a hardware issue like a shield not being fully seated, insufficient power, or even a sketch that is too big to fit in memory (see the next section). When this occurs, check your hardware carefully for proper seating of all components, and make sure your Arduino IDE settings for the serial port and board are correct.

My Sketch Is Too Big

Because the connector uses a lot of program memory, it is possible to run out of space when compiling your sketch. When this occurs, you may get an error like this:

```
Binary sketch size: 32510 bytes (of a 32256 byte maximum).
```

If this happens, try removing all the unnecessary variables, strings, include files, and code that you can. The troubleshooting section on the Arduino site has several entries for suggestions on reducing sketch size.

In the extreme case, you can edit the source files for the connector itself and remove unneeded features. In this case, you want to remove any methods you are not using by commenting them out.

Note   In some versions of the IDE, modifying the files may require reloading your sketch to activate the changes in the IDE.

None of These Solved My Problem—What Next?

If you have tried the suggestions in the previous sections and you are still having issues, go back to the top and work through the solutions again. If that does not solve the problem, try a different Arduino (such as an Uno) and a different Ethernet shield. The tests and diagnoses should have eliminated all other issues, leaving only the Arduino hardware as the suspect.

Now that you know the basics of what a MySQL database-enabled sketch requires, let's take a short tour of the Connector/Arduino library to learn what methods are available for your use.

A Tour of the MySQL Connector/ Arduino Code

Before you embark on a project, let's take a moment to tour the source code for the library. This section examines the library and its supporting methods in more detail. If you never intend to extend or otherwise modify the library, you can skip ahead to the project section.

Library Files

The *MySQL Connector Arduino* folder contains a number of files and a directory. The following list describes each of the files:

- *examples*: A directory containing example code for using the library

- *extras*: A directory containing documentation and usage notes

- *src*: A directory containing the source code for the library

- keywords.txt: The list of keywords reserved for the library

- library.properties: A file containing the Arduino properties for the library

- README.md: Introductory documentation

The source code is spread across several source files each with its own purpose. The following lists the source code module (header .h and source .cpp file) and its purpose:

- MySQL_Connection: Handles initial handshake and general client/server connection

- MySQL_Cursor: Handles execution of queries and their result sets

- MySQL_Encrypt_Sha1: Implements the SHA1 encryption for the connection handshake

- MySQL_Packet: Handles low-level packet format, transmit, and receive for the client/server connection

If you need to change the connector, you can concentrate your changes in the appropriate module. For example, if you need to adjust the way the connector makes the connection to the server, look in MySQL_Connection.h/.cpp.

Field Structure

The library uses a number of structures when communicating with the server. There is one structure that you use frequently when returning result sets. It is called field_struct and is shown in the following. You can find this in MySQL_Cursor.h.

```
// Structure for retrieving a field (minimal implementation).
typedef struct {
  char *db;
  char *table;
  char *name;
} field_struct;
```

The field structure is used to retrieve the metadata for a field. Notice that you get the database, table, and field name. This permits you to determine which table a field is derived from in the case of queries involving joins. The method used to populate this field structure, get_field(), creates the strings in memory. It is your responsibility to free this memory—the strings—when you are finished reading or operating on the data.

There are also two structures for working with result sets: column_ names and row_values. I discuss these in more detail in the next section but include them here for completeness. Use column_names for getting column information and row_values for getting row values in a result set. You can also find these in MySQL_Cursor.h.

```
// Structure for storing result set metadata.
typedef struct {
  int num_fields;     // actual number of fields
  field_struct *fields[MAX_FIELDS];
} column_names;

// Structure for storing row data.
typedef struct {
  char *values[MAX_FIELDS];
} row_values;
```

Now that you understand the structures involved with working with the library methods, let's examine the methods available to you for communicating with a MySQL server.

Public Methods

Libraries—or, more specifically, classes—typically have one or more public methods that can be used by any caller (program) via an instantiation of the class. Classes also have some parts that are private, which are typically helper methods to do something internal for the class. The methods can abstract portions of the class or simply hide data and operations that do not need to be accessed by the caller (think abstract data types). The public methods and attributes are therefore the things the designer permits the caller to access.

The Connector/Arduino library has a number of public methods that define the library's capabilities. There are methods for connecting, executing queries, and returning results (rows) from the database. Each of which is declared in the appropriate code module. I demonstrate how to use most of these methods in later sections.

We will look at the public methods for the three most commonly used modules. The SHA1 module has no methods applicable to MySQL-enabled sketches.

MySQL_Connection

The following shows the method declarations for the public methods for the MySQL_Connection class in the MySQL_Connection.h file. I discuss the details of each in the following paragraphs.

```
boolean connect(IPAddress server, int port, char *user, char
*password,
                char *db=NULL);
int connected() { return client->connected(); }
const char *version() { return MYSQL_VERSION_STR; }
void close();
```

The connect() method, as you have seen, is the method you must call to connect to a MySQL database server. This method must be called after the initialization of the Ethernet class and before any other method from the library. It requires the IP address of the server, the port for the server, and the username and password to use to connect. You can also specify a default database so that you do not have to specify the database in your SQL commands.

It returns a Boolean, where true indicates success and false means there was some error in connecting to the server. If you encounter problems connecting to the server, you should attempt to connect from another machine on your network using the mysql client and the IP, port, user, and password defined in your sketch, to ensure connectivity and that there are no user or password issues.

The connected() method returns true if the Arduino is connected to the server or false if not. You can use this method to test connectivity if or when there are long periods of inactivity or errors.

The version() method returns the server version to which you connected. It is only valid once the connection is successful.

The close() method disconnects from the server and closes the connection. Always call this method if you connect and disconnect periodically.

MySQL_Cursor

The following shows the method declarations for the public methods for the MySQL_Cursor class in the MySQL_Cursor.h file. I discuss the details of each in the following paragraphs.

```
boolean execute(const char *query, boolean progmem=false);
void show_results();
void close();
column_names *get_columns();
row_values *get_next_row();
int get_rows_affected() { return rows_affected; }
int get_last_insert_id() { return last_insert_id; }
```

The execute() method is the method you can use to execute a query (SQL statement). The method takes a constant string reference that contains the query you wish to execute. You can also pass the string passed if it is defined using program space. In this case, you set the progmem parameter to true. For more information about using program space (called PROGMEM), see the Arduino online reference (www.arduino.cc/en/Reference/PROGMEM). Basically, if you need more space for data but can afford to use program space for data, you should use this method to execute strings from program space.

The show_results() method is both an example of how to retrieve data from the database for SELECT queries and a method you can use as is to execute after issuing the execute() call. The method reads one row at a time and sends it to the serial monitor. It can be handy for testing queries and for experimenting with new sketches.

On the other hand, if you want to read rows from a database and process the data, you can write your own method to do this. You must first execute the query with execute(); then, if there is a result set, read the column headers (the server always sends the column headers first) using get_columns() and read the rows with the iterator get_next_row().

If you want to retrieve the number of rows affected for SQL commands that return such, you can use the get_rows_affected() method after executing the query to get that value. Similarly, you can get the last inserted auto-increment value with get_last_insert_id(), but that is only valid when using auto increment.

MySQL_Packet

This module isn't used that much for most sketches, but there is one method that bears mentioning. The print_packet() method can be used in the cursor or connector classes to write the packet data to the serial monitor. If you are experimenting with modifying the connector for use with a different board or client/server protocol, you can place this method in key locations to display the data in the packet. Be sure to turn on debug mode before using the method.

Example Uses

Besides connecting to a database server, the two uses of the library are issuing queries that do not return results (like INSERT) and returning rows from queries that return result sets (like SELECT or SHOW VARIABLES). The following sections demonstrate each of these options.

Queries Without Results

You have seen how to issue queries without result sets in the "Hello, MySQL!" example. Recall that this is simply a call to execute() with the query passed as a string. The following shows an example of a query that returns no results:

```
MySQL_Cursor *cur_mem = new MySQL_Cursor(&conn);
int res = cur_mem->execute(INSERT_SQL);
if (!res) {
  Serial.println("Query failed.");
} else {
  Serial.println("Ok.");
}
delete cur_mem;
```

Queries Returning Results

Returning results (rows) from the server is a bit more complicated but not overly so. To read a result set from the server, you must first read the result set header and the field packets and then the data rows. Specifically, you must anticipate, read, and parse the following packets:

- *Result-set header packet*: Number of columns

- *Field packets*: Column descriptors

- *EOF packet*: Marker: end-of-field packets

- *Row data packets*: Row contents

- *EOF packet*: marker: End-of-data packets

This means the MySQL server first sends the number of fields and a list of the fields (columns) that you must read, and then the row data appears in one or more packets until there are no more rows. The algorithm for reading a result set is as follows:

1. Read result set header for number of columns.

2. Read fields until EOF.

3. Read rows until EOF.

Let's take a look at the contents of the show_results() method; see Listing 9-6.

Listing 9-6. Displaying Result Sets

```
void MySQL_Cursor::show_results() {
  column_names *cols;
  int rows = 0;

  // Get the columns
  cols = get_columns();
  if (cols == NULL) {
    return;
  }

  for (int f = 0; f < columns.num_fields; f++) {
    Serial.print(columns.fields[f]->name);
    if (f < columns.num_fields-1)
      Serial.print(',');
  }
  Serial.println();
```

```
  // Read the rows
  while (get_next_row()) {
    rows++;
    for (int f = 0; f < columns.num_fields; f++) {
      Serial.print(row.values[f]);
      if (f < columns.num_fields-1)
        Serial.print(',');
    }
    free_row_buffer();
    Serial.println();
  }

  // Report how many rows were read
  Serial.print(rows);
  conn->show_error(ROWS, true);
  free_columns_buffer();

  // Free any post-query messages in queue for stored procedures
  clear_ok_packet();
}
```

So what's going on here? Notice how the code is structured to execute the query; if there are results (execute() does not return NULL), you read the column headers. The return from the get_columns() method is a structure that contains an array of field structures. The structure is shown next:

```
// Structure for retrieving a field (minimal implementation).
Typedef struct {
  char *db;
  char *table;
  char *name;
} field_struct;
```

```
// Structure for storing result set metadata.
Typedef struct {
  int num_fields; // actual number of fields
  field_struct *fields[MAX_FIELDS];
} column_names;
```

Notice that the column_names structure has a fields array. Use that array to get information about each field in the form of the field_struct (shown earlier). In that structure, you can get the database name, table name, and column name. In the code, you simply print out the column names and a comma after each.

Next, you read the rows using a special iterator named get_next_row(), which returns a pointer to a row structure that contains an array of the field values:

```
// Structure for storing row data.
typedef struct {
  char *values[MAX_FIELDS];
} row_values;
```

In this case, while get_next_row() returns a valid pointer (not NULL), you read each field and print out the values.

You may be wondering what MAX_FIELDS is. Well, it is an easy way to make sure you limit your array of columns (fields). This is defined in MySQL_Cursor.h and is set to 32 (0x20). If you want to save a few bytes, you can change that value to something lower, but beware: if you exceed that value, your code will wander off into wonkyville[10] (unreferenced pointer). So tread lightly.

---

[10]A state of wonkiness where wonky is the norm.

Notice also the calls to `free_row_buffer()` and `free_columns_buffer()`. These are memory-cleanup methods needed to free any memory allocated when reading columns and row values (hey—you have to put it somewhere!). You call the `free_row_buffer()` after you are finished processing the row and the `free_columns_buffer()` at the end of the method. If you fail to add these to your own query handler method, you will run out of memory quickly.

Why is it manual? Well, like the `MAX_FIELDS` setting, I wanted to keep it simple and therefore save as much space as possible. Automatic garbage collection would have added a significant amount of code.

You can use this method as a template to build your own custom query handler. For example, instead of printing the data to the serial monitor, you could display it in an LCD or perhaps use the information in another part of your sketch.

As an exercise, you can change the library to display the bar and dash output (called a grid). This isn't especially difficult but requires more than a few bytes of code (which is why I left it out of the library). If you'd like a hint for how to know how many dashes to print for each field, recall that you read the fields first (which includes the size of each field). The challenge is to print the bar and dashes so that they line up in the display area.

Now that you are more familiar with the Connector/Arduino library, let's reexamine the Arduino sensor node from Chapter 6—but this time, you add the code to save the sensor data to a MySQL server.

ADJUSTING THE SPEED OF QUERY RESULTS

The library contains a delay in the `wait_for_client()` method (in `mysql.cpp`) that can be adjusted to improve the speed of query results returned. It is currently set at a modest delay. Depending on your network latency and proximity to the database server (as in, no network hops), you can reduce this value considerably. It was originally added to help prevent issues with slower wireless networks.

Project: Building a MySQL Arduino Client

In the previous sections, you learned what Connector/Arduino is and how to use it to make an Arduino MySQL client update a table in a MySQL database server. In this section, you revisit the sensor node example from an earlier chapter and make it save the data to the database instead of the serial monitor. In this case, we will use a WiFi shield since that is a more common way to connect Arduino boards to your network.

You proceed at a faster pace because all examples of using the Connector/Arduino library are the same. Also, rather than use the XBee modules, you wire the sensor to the Arduino to further simplify the example. Let's begin with the hardware setup.

Note   I repeat the steps from Chapter 6 to provide a complete explanation and walk-through. I skip the details of the code for reading the DHT22 because that part is the same.

Hardware Setup

The hardware required for this project includes an Arduino, a WiFi shield, a DHT22 humidity and temperature sensor, a breadboard, a 4.7K Ohm resistor (colors: yellow, purple, red, gold), and breadboard jumper wires. With the exception of the WiFi shield, this is the same setup as the project from Chapter 6.

Tip   If you get stuck or want more information, there is an excellent tutorial on Adafruit's website. See `http://learn.adafruit.com/dht`.

Begin by placing your Arduino next to a breadboard. If you have not already done so, install the WiFi shield on your Arduino. Be sure that all pins are seated in their sockets before proceeding.

Plug the DHT22 sensor into one side of the breadboard, as shown in Figure 9-7. Please refer to this often and double-check your connections before powering on your Arduino (or connecting it to your laptop). You want to avoid accidental experiments in electrical chaos theory.

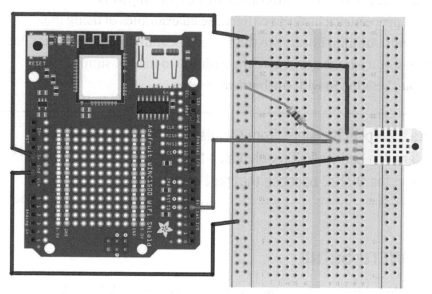

fritzing

Figure 9-7. Wiring the DHT22

Next, connect the power from the Arduino to the breadboard. Use one jumper wire to connect the 5V pin on the Arduino to the breadboard power rail and another to connect the ground (GND) pin on the Arduino to the ground rail on the breadboard. With these wires in place, you are ready to wire the sensor. You use three of the four pins, as shown in Table 9-1.

Table 9-1. *DHT22 Connections*

Pin	Connected To
1	+5V
2	Pin 4 on Arduino, 4.7K Ohm resistor between VCC and the data pin (strong pull-up)
3	No connection
4	Ground

Note   We use pin 4 for the DHT22 because some WiFi shields use pin 7.

Software Setup

To use the DHT22 with an Arduino, you need to have the latest DHT22 library. You can install the library right from the Arduino IDE by searching the library manager. Open the Arduino IDE, then open a new sketch, and choose *Sketch ➤ Include Library ➤ Manage Libraries...* from the menu. Figure 9-8 shows the library manager.

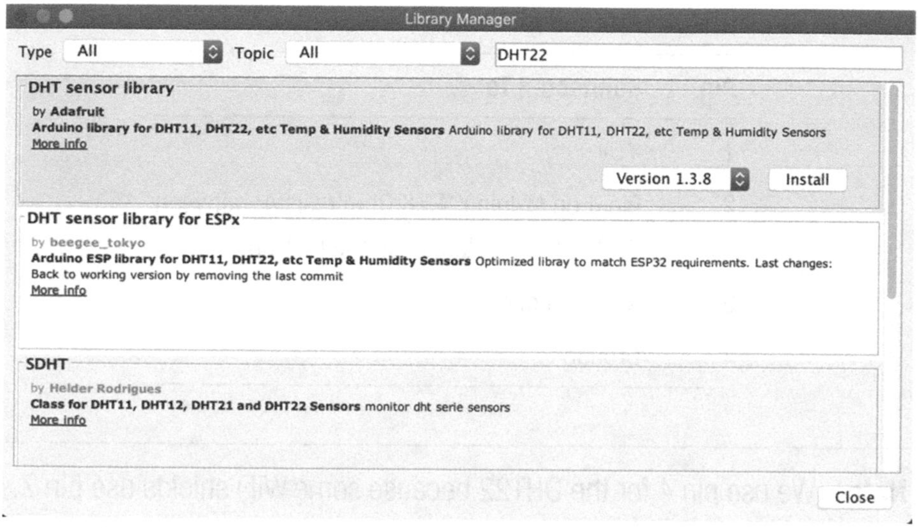

Figure 9-8. *Library manager*

It may take a moment for the library manager to connect to the server and download the latest catalog. When it is complete, you can type DHT22 into the text box in the upper right and press ENTER. This will search the library catalog for all of the libraries that match.

Choose the DHT sensor library from Adafruit and click Install. If you are prompted to install the supporting libraries, click Install all to ensure all prerequisites are installed as shown in Figure 9-9.

Figure 9-9. *Install all libraries*

Setting Up the Sensor Database

You also need to create a table on your MySQL server. The following shows the SQL statements needed to create the test database and the table. Use the mysql client of the MySQL Shell to execute these commands.

```
CREATE DATABASE dht22_test;
CREATE TABLE dht22_test.temp_humid (
  `id` int(11) NOT NULL AUTO_INCREMENT,
  `temp_c` float DEFAULT NULL,
  `rel_humid` float DEFAULT NULL,
  PRIMARY KEY (`id`)
);
```

Now that you have the hardware configured and the database set up, let's write some code!

Tip   Be sure to add #include <WiFi.h> to the MySQL_ Packet.h file for use with the WiFi shield.

Writing the Code

The code is very similar to the project from Chapter 6, except that you add the code needed to connect to the MySQL server and insert the sensor data. This code module demonstrates a basic data-collection node in the form of a temperature and humidity sensor node. It uses the common DHT22 sensor connected to an Arduino with WiFi shield.

In this project, we will also see two of the newest features of the connector: connecting with a default database specified and retrieving the rows affected and last insert id. We will also see examples of how to organize the code to make it a bit easier to read.[11]

More specifically, we will move reading the sensor and writing the data to MySQL into its own method named read_data(). We also move the connection code to connect to MySQL to a method named connect_to_mysql().

Rather than walk through each of nuance of the code, we will present the code in a single listing focusing on the MySQL portions. Open a new sketch and name it dht22_mysql.ino. Or, download the sample code from the book website. Listing 9-7 shows the complete source code.

Listing 9-7. Reading a DHT22 Sensor

```
/*
  Beginning Sensor Networks Second Edition
  Example: Arduino Hosted Sensor Node

  This sensor node uses a DHT22 sensor to read temperature and
  humidity
  printing the results in the serial monitor.
*/
#include "DHT.h"
#include <WiFi.h>
#include <MySQL_Connection.h>
#include <MySQL_Cursor.h>
```

---

[11]There are many ways one can organize code. This is by no means the only or perhaps best way.

```
#define DHTPIN 4              // DHT22 data is on pin 4
#define read_delay 5000       // 5 seconds
#define DHTTYPE DHT22         // DHT22 (AM2302)

byte mac_addr[] = { 0xDE, 0xAD, 0xBE, 0xEF, 0xFE, 0xED };

IPAddress server_addr(192,168,42,8);  // IP of the MySQL
                                      *server* here
char user[] = "arduino_user";        // MySQL user login username
char password[] = "secret";          // MySQL user login password

// Sample query
char INSERT_DATA[] = "INSERT INTO temp_humid (temp_c,
rel_humid) VALUES (%s, %s)";
char DEFAULT_DATABASE = "dht22_test";
char ssid[] = "SSID";
char pass[] = "PASSWORD";

WiFiClient client;
MySQL_Connection conn((Client *)&client);

DHT dht(DHTPIN, DHTTYPE);

/*
 * Read the data from the sensor and save it in the database.
 */
void read_data() {
  char query_buf[128];
  char temp_str[20];
  char humidity_str[20];
  int rows_affected;
  int last_insert_id;
```

```
// Read humidity
float humidity = dht.readHumidity();
// Read temperature as Celsius
float temp_c = dht.readTemperature();

// Check for errors and return if any variable has no value
if (isnan(temp_c) || isnan(humidity)) {
  Serial.println("ERROR: Cannot read all data from DHT-22.");
  return;
}

// Convert values to strings for the string buffer
dtostrf(temp_c, 7, 2, temp_str);
dtostrf(humidity, 7, 2, humidity_str);
sprintf(query_buf, INSERT_DATA, temp_str, humidity_str);

Serial.print("Humidity: ");
Serial.print(humidity);
Serial.print("%, ");
Serial.print(temp_c);
Serial.print("C ... ");

// Initiate the query class instance
MySQL_Cursor *cur_mem = new MySQL_Cursor(&conn);
// Execute the query
int res = cur_mem->execute(query_buf);
if (!res) {
  Serial.println("Query failed.");
} else {
  Serial.println("Ok.");
}
// Get the last insert id and rows affected
rows_affected = cur_mem->get_rows_affected();
last_insert_id = cur_mem->get_last_insert_id();
```

```
  Serial.print(rows_affected);
  Serial.print(" rows affected, last insert id = ");
  Serial.println(last_insert_id);

  delete cur_mem;
}
/*
 * Connect to MySQL
 */
void connect_to_mysql() {
  // Now connect to MySQL
  Serial.println("Connecting...");
  if (conn.connect(server_addr, 3306, user, password, DEFAULT_
  DATABASE)) {
    delay(1000);
  } else {
    Serial.println("Connection failed.");
  }
}

void setup() {
  Serial.begin(115200);
  while (!Serial); // wait for serial port to connect
  Serial.println("Welcome to the DHT-22 Arduino MySQL example!");
  // WiFi section
  Serial.println("Starting WiFi.");
  int status = WiFi.begin(ssid, pass);
  // if you're not connected, stop here:
  if (status != WL_CONNECTED) {
    Serial.println("Couldn't get a WiFi connection!");
    while(true);
  }
```

```
  // if you are connected, print out info about the connection:
  else {
    Serial.println("Connected to network");
    IPAddress ip = WiFi.localIP();
    Serial.print("My IP address is: ");
    Serial.println(ip);
  }
  dht.begin();
  Serial.println("Starting Sensor Data Collection:");
  connect_to_mysql();
}

void loop() {
  delay(read_delay);
  if (conn.connected()) {
    read_data();
  } else {
    conn.close();
    Serial.println("Retrying connection.");
    connect_to_mysql();
  }
}
```

Notice that the setup() method has the same code as in the previous example, except that in this case you connect to the WiFi, connect to MySQL, set up the DHT library, and exit. The code to insert the data into the MySQL database is in the read_data() method. Let's look at the code for forming the query string. I repeat the code as an excerpt here for clarity:

```
char INSERT_DATA[] = "INSERT INTO temp_humid (temp_c, rel_
humid) VALUES (%s, %s)";
...
char query_buf[128];
```

```
char temp_str[20];
char humidity_str[20];
...
float humidity = dht.readHumidity();
float temp_c = dht.readTemperature();
...
// Convert values to strings for the string buffer
dtostrf(temp_c, 7, 2, temp_str);
dtostrf(humidity, 7, 2, humidity_str);
sprintf(query_buf, INSERT_DATA, temp_str, humidity_str);
...
```

There is one peculiarity on the Arduino platform concerning float to string conversion. You must use the dtostrf() method to convert a float to a string using a character buffer. You can specify the size and precision in the process. We then use these strings to build a string from a static buffer of size 128 using the sprintf()[12] method to format and populate the values for the table.

Caution   Watch out for array sizes! If you intend to save character string data returned by sensor nodes, be sure your query will fit into memory.

If you have a different network than what is depicted here, you can change the IPAddress variable accordingly. Likewise, if your user and password are different, be sure to change those values as well. Finally, if you want to slow the sample rate, you can adjust read_delay accordingly.

---

[12]See the sprintf() documentation at www.cplusplus.com/reference/cstdio/ sprintf/ for more details.

Once you have all the code entered into your Arduino environment and your Arduino is ready to go, it is time to try it out. If you have problems, refer to the earlier sections for common errors.

Test Execution

Executing the sketch means uploading it to your Arduino and watching it run. If you haven't connected your Arduino, you can do that now. I like to begin by compiling the sketch. Click the check mark on the left side of the Arduino application, and observe the output in the message screen at the bottom. If you see errors, fix them and retry the compile. Common errors include missing the DHT22 library (which may require restarting the Arduino application), typing errors, syntax errors, and the like. Once everything compiles correctly, you are ready to upload your sketch by clicking the *Upload* button on the toolbar.

As soon as the upload completes, open the serial monitor by clicking the button at the right on the toolbar. Observe the Arduino connecting to the MySQL server and the message printed each time the sensor data is recorded. Let this run a few times to generate some data. Listing 9-8 shows the typical output you should see.

Listing 9-8. Example Execution of the DHT22 MySQL Example

```
Welcome to the DHT-22 Arduino MySQL example!
Starting WiFi.
Connected to network
My IP address is: 192.168.42.13
Connecting...
...trying...
Connected to server version 8.0.18
Deleting all rows from table ... Ok.
18 rows affected.
Starting Sensor Data Collection:
```

```
Humidity: 39.80%, 23.20C ... Ok.
1 rows affected, last insert id = 462
Humidity: 39.70%, 23.20C ... Ok.
1 rows affected, last insert id = 463
Humidity: 39.70%, 23.20C ... Ok.
1 rows affected, last insert id = 464
Humidity: 39.70%, 23.20C ... Ok.
1 rows affected, last insert id = 465
Humidity: 39.70%, 23.20C ... Ok.
1 rows affected, last insert id = 466
Humidity: 39.70%, 23.20C ... Ok.
1 rows affected, last insert id = 467
```

Tip   If you get "ACK Timeout" errors, try unplugging the sensor and plugging it back in, or disconnect and reconnect the power lead while the sketch is running. Be very careful to avoid ESD!

Once the thrill of watching your Arduino spin is over, stop the Arduino by disconnecting the USB cable. You can now check the database to ensure that the sensor data was recorded. Listing 9-9 shows the steps needed. All you do here is issue a SELECT command on the table. You should see one row for each time your Arduino recorded its data.

Listing 9-9. Example Data Collected

```
> select * from dht22_test.temp_humid;
+-----+--------+-----------+
| id  | temp_c | rel_humid |
+-----+--------+-----------+
| 535 |   23.5 |      39.6 |
| 536 |   23.5 |      39.6 |
```

```
| 537 |    23.5 |      39.6 |
| 538 |    23.5 |      39.6 |
| 539 |    23.5 |      39.6 |
| 540 |    23.5 |      39.6 |
| 541 |    23.5 |      39.6 |
| 542 |    23.5 |      39.7 |
| 543 |    23.5 |      39.6 |
| 544 |    23.5 |      39.6 |
| 545 |    23.5 |      39.6 |
| 546 |    23.5 |      39.6 |
| 547 |    23.5 |      39.6 |
| 548 |    23.5 |      39.6 |
+-----+--------+-----------+
14 rows in set (0.0004 sec)
```

If you see similar output, congratulations! You have just built your first database-enabled Arduino-based sensor node. This is an important step in building your sensor network, because you now have the tools needed to start building more sophisticated wireless sensor nodes and aggregate nodes for inserting sensor data into the database.

For More Fun

Once you are comfortable testing and experimenting with the project, if you have an inquisitive mind like me, you will probably start to see things that you can do to improve the code and the project. I list a few here for you to consider on your own. Don't be afraid to tweak and modify—that's one of the greatest joys of working with the Arduino!

- Change the code to store the temperature in Fahrenheit.

- Change the sampling rate to once every 15 minutes or once every hour.

- Change the table to add a new column, and use a trigger to automatically convert the temperature to Fahrenheit. Hint: `ALTER TABLE dht22_test.temp_humid ADD COLUMN temp_f float AFTER temp_c`.

- For experts: rather than split the data from the DHT22 and store two values in the database, store the raw value in the database and use a view to split the values.

Do you see a trend here? The last two bullets suggest moving some of the logic from the Arduino to the database. This is a very good practice and one you should hone by learning more about features such as views, functions, triggers, and events provided by the MySQL server.

Because the Arduino platform is a small device with limited capability, moving data manipulation to the database server not only saves on processing power but also saves memory usage. Having the database server do the heavy work of data conversion may also permit you to take more frequent sensor readings.

To read more about triggers, views, and events, see the online MySQL reference manual.

The next two sections present some examples of how to use the connector in your sketches. These are not complete projects; rather, they are intended to be used as templates for writing your own sketches using the connector.

Project Example: Inserting Data from Variables

When writing the connector, I discovered a number of posts on my blog from people unfamiliar with C programming or those new to programming in general. This is great because it means the Arduino is reaching some of its target audience!

One of the questions that kept arising was how to do an INSERT query supplying values from sensors or how to construct an INSERT statement with values stored in variables. We saw this earlier in the DHT22 example by using strings. But what if you want to insert integers? Well, simply put, everything you want to add must be converted to a string.

The trick then is knowing which format specifier to use. For example, we use one for strings, a different one for integers, and so on. The following lists a few of the more commonly used format specifiers available. See the sprintf() documentation for more options. One such location is www.tutorialspoint.com/c_standard_library/c_function_sprintf.htm.

- %c: Character

- %i: Integer

- %s: A string of characters

- %x: Number in hexadecimal (base 16)

Now, let's see a segment of code to do some of the preceding formatting. Listing 9-10 shows an example sketch that demonstrates how to take a value (presumably read from a sensor or such) and create an INSERT statement. This happens to show an INSERT statement, but the technique also works for populating the WHERE clause for other statements.

Listing 9-10. SQL String Formatting

```
/*
  Beginning Sensor Networks Second Edition
  Example: Formatting data for SQL statements.
*/
void setup() {
  Serial.begin(115200);
  while (!Serial); // wait for serial port to connect
  Serial.println("Welcome to the SQL string format example!");
```

```
// SQL command formatting string
const char INSERT_DATA[] = "INSERT INTO test_arduino.temps
VALUES (%s, %i, '0x%x')";
// Buffers for strings
char query[128];
char temp_buff[10];
// Some variables
float float_val = 26.9;
int int_val = 13;
int hex_val = 251;
// Convert float to string
dtostrf(float_val, 1, 1, temp_buff);
// Format the string
sprintf(query, INSERT_DATA, temp_buff, int_val, hex_val);
// Show the result
Serial.println(query);
}

void loop() {
}
```

If you want to try this out yourself, you can. Just open a new sketch and place the code in the setup() method and run it. I named the example in the sql_format.ino. You should see the following output:

```
Welcome to the SQL string format example!
INSERT INTO test_arduino.temps VALUES (26.9, 13, '0xfb')
```

In this example, I also show you how to deal with floating-point values. Recall, floating-point values are not supported by the Arduino sprintf() method, so you have to first convert the floating-point value to a string and then use that string in your sprintf() method. The method you use to convert the floating-point value is dtostrf().

If you read through the code example, you see how this new string is formed. This resulting string could be sent to the database and the values inserted into the database.

Project Example: How to Perform SELECT Queries

There are times when you need to get information out of your database server to be used in calculations or for displaying (or transmitting) labels. For example, suppose you have a sensor that requires calibration or conversion using a formula that depends on other data. Rather than code all of those things (there could be dozens or hundreds), consuming a lot of memory in the process, why not store that information in a database table and query it when you need to look up the value?

Similarly, suppose you have text strings that you would like to display in an LCD or perhaps even in the serial monitor, but the strings depend on the sensor being read. That is, you could have sensors located in different locations. Rather than code all of those strings and thereby consume a lot of space, you can save that space by putting those strings in a table and getting them when needed.

In this section, I demonstrate several examples of how to use the connector to return data from the database.

Tip   The library contains a number of methods useful for querying a database and consuming the data in your sketch. It also includes helpful methods for displaying the data, should you wish to see it in the serial monitor. Note that this code does add about 2KB more to your compiled sketch size. Depending on the memory size of your

Arduino, if you add more than a few queries to your sketch, you could run out of space. See the troubleshooting section "My Sketch Is Too Big" for suggestions on reducing the size of your sketch.

Displaying a Result Set in the Serial Monitor

If you want to run a query and display the results in the serial monitor, you can use the built-in method show_results(). This method prints the column names separated by commas and then iterates over the result set and prints the values separated by commas.

The code is very simple. You need only call execute(), passing it the query string, and then call the show_results() method. Of course, the serial monitor must be open for you to see the results. The following shows an example of a method named show_data() that demonstrates the technique:

```
void show_data() {
  Serial.print("Getting all rows from the table ... ");

  MySQL_Cursor *cur_mem = new MySQL_Cursor(&conn);
  // Execute the query
  int res = cur_mem->execute(SELECT_SQL);
  if (!res) {
    Serial.println("Query failed.");
  } else {
    Serial.println("Ok.");
  }
  cur_mem->show_results();
  delete cur_mem;
}
```

Provided you executed the preceding DHT22 project, when you run this code, you will get results similar to the following. Note that you can use the DHT22 code as a base stripping the DHT-specific portions or you can download the sample code for the book and open the sketch named select_mysql.ino.

```
Welcome to the MySQL SELECT example!
Starting WiFi.
Connected to network
My IP address is: 192.168.42.13
Connecting...
...trying...
Connected to server version 8.0.18
Getting all rows from the table:Ok.
id,temp_c,rel_humid
540,23.5,39.6
541,23.5,39.6
542,23.5,39.7
543,23.5,39.6
544,23.5,39.6
545,23.5,39.6
546,23.5,39.6
547,23.5,39.6
548,23.5,39.6
14 rows in result.
```

Writing Your Own Display Method

There are cases where you may want to build your own iterator to read the result set from a query. For example, you may want to display the results in an LCD or send them to another node in your network. Fortunately, you can do so by writing your own version of show_results() using a number of helper methods. I discussed how to use the show_results() method in a previous section, but I discuss the methods used in that method for writing your own method. As you will see, the helper methods are already there for your use and are named to make it easier to see how the code works.

These include get_columns() for retrieving the column names; get_next_row(), which is an iterator to read rows; and memory-cleanup methods free_columns_buffer() and free_row_buffer(). You call the free_row_buffer() method after processing the data for the row and the free_columns_buffer() once all the rows are read.

Listing 9-11 shows a modified version of the previous show_data() method to show all of the steps to read take the query passed as a parameter, execute the query, and then read the columns and rows. We will embellish it a bit to make things a bit more interesting. This code can be found in the sample code for the book in the custom_results.ino sketch.

Listing 9-11. Custom Query Results Method

```
/*
 * Custom show results example
 */
void show_data(char *query) {
  column_names *cols;
  int rows = 0;
  char buffer[24];

  Serial.print("Getting all rows from the table ... ");

  // Execute the query
  MySQL_Cursor *cur_mem = new MySQL_Cursor(&conn);
  int res = cur_mem->execute(query);
```

```
  if (!res) {
    Serial.println("Query failed.");
    return;
  } else {
    Serial.println("Ok.\n");
  }

  // Fetch the columns and print them
  cols = cur_mem->get_columns();
  for (int f = 0; f < cols->num_fields; f++) {
    sprintf(buffer, COL_FORMAT, cols->fields[f]->name);
    Serial.print(buffer);
  }
  Serial.println();

  // Print a separator
  for (int f = 0; f < cols->num_fields; f++) {
    Serial.print("---------- ");
  }
  Serial.println();

  // Read the rows and print them
  row_values *row = NULL;
  do {
    row = cur_mem->get_next_row();
    if (row != NULL) {
      for (int f = 0; f < cols->num_fields; f++) {
        sprintf(buffer, COL_FORMAT, row->values[f]);
        Serial.print(buffer);
      }
```

```
      Serial.println();
    }
  } while (row != NULL);

  delete cur_mem;
}
```

Notice that you first must read the columns. This is because MySQL always sends the column names before any rows. Once you have read the columns, you can then read the rows using the iterator helper method until there are no rows returned.

The get_columns() method returns a pointer to a special structure that contains the number of fields and an array of fields that is also a special structure. Both structures are shown next; you can see how they are used in Listing 9-11.

```
// Structure for retrieving a field (minimal implementation).
typedef struct {
  char *db;
  char *table;
  char *name;
} field_struct;
```

```
// Structure for storing result set metadata.
typedef struct {
  int num_fields; // actual number of fields
  field_struct *fields[MAX_FIELDS];
} column_names;
```

The method get_next_row() returns a pointer to a similar structure that contains an array of strings. This is because all data (rows) returned from the server are returned as character strings. It is up to you to convert the values to other data types if you need to do so.

Here is the second structure:

```
// Structure for storing row data.
typedef struct {
  char *values[MAX_FIELDS];
} row_values;
```

You may be wondering why you have to do the memory-cleanup bits. Simply put, in order to make the connector as lightweight as possible, some of the convenience routines have been intentionally omitted. A case in point is clearing (freeing) memory allocated during the reads of the columns and row data. The previous example shows the proper location for these calls.

Caution   Failure to free the memory as shown will result in a rapid deterioration of your sketch's execution and an eventual freeze or hang.

Once you have created a method like this, you can use it elsewhere in your sketch to execute and process query results as follows:

```
const char TEST_SELECT_QUERY[] = "SELECT * FROM world.city
LIMIT 10";
show_data(TEST_SELECT_QUERY);
```

If you plan to write a method like this to send the data elsewhere, take care in the amount of code you use and eliminate any unnecessary strings and conversions (floating-point conversion requires a library named dtostf() that can add up to 2KB to your compiled sketch size).

If you executed this code after the DHT22 example, you'd see something like the following code for output in the serial monitor:

```
Welcome to the MySQL Custom SELECT example!
Starting WiFi.
Connected to network
My IP address is: 192.168.42.13
Connecting...
...trying...
Connected to server version 8.0.18
Getting all rows from the table ... Ok.
```

id	temp_c	rel_humid
540	23.5	39.6
541	23.5	39.6
542	23.5	39.7
543	23.5	39.6
544	23.5	39.6
545	23.5	39.6
546	23.5	39.6
547	23.5	39.6
548	23.5	39.6

Example: Getting a Lookup Value from the Database

Although the previous examples show you how to process result sets of multiple rows for displaying lots of data, the more common reason to query a database is to return a specific value or set of values for use in the sketch. Typically, this is done using a query that is designed to return a single row. For example, it could return a specific value from a lookup table.

As in the previous example, you must process the result set in order starting with the column data. You don't need it for this type of query, so you simply ignore it. You also still need to iterate over the rows, because the result set terminates with a special packet and the get_next_row() method reads that packet and returns NULL if it is encountered (signaling no more rows). Listing 9-12 shows the code you need to read a single value from the database and use it. This example can be made into a separate method if it will be called multiple times or from several places in your sketch.

Listing 9-12. Getting a Lookup Value

```
int get_data() {
  row_values *row = NULL;
  long head_count = 0;

  // Initiate the query class instance
  MySQL_Cursor *cur_mem = new MySQL_Cursor(&conn);
  // Execute the query
  cur_mem->execute(SELECT_SQL);
  // Fetch the columns (required) but we don't use them.
  column_names *columns = cur_mem->get_columns();

  // Read the row (we are only expecting the one)
  do {
    row = cur_mem->get_next_row();
    if (row != NULL) {
      head_count = atol(row->values[0]);
    }
  } while (row != NULL);
  // Deleting the cursor also frees up memory used
  delete cur_mem;

  return head_count;
}
```

```
...
void setup() {
...
  connect_to_mysql();
  int count = get_data();
  // Show the result
  Serial.print("NYC pop = ");
  Serial.println(count);
}
```

As you can see, the library supports the capability to process queries that return result sets. These include SELECT, SHOW, and similar commands.

If you execute this example, you should see the following output or similar:

```
Welcome to the MySQL lookup table example!
Starting WiFi.
Connected to network
My IP address is: 192.168.42.13
Connecting...
...trying...
Connected to server version 8.0.18
NYC pop = 12886
```

However, note (again) that the Arduino platform is very limited in the amount of memory available. Constructing a sketch with several complex queries that return large result sets is likely to exhaust the memory on Arduino boards such as the Uno and Leonardo. If your sketch is large, you may want to consider moving to the Due board.

Component Shopping List

A number of components are needed to complete the projects in this chapter. All of these components were used in previous chapters. They're listed in Table 9-2.

Table 9-2. *Components Needed*

Item	Vendors	Est. Cost USD	Qty Needed
Arduino Uno, Leonardo (any that supports shields)	Various	$25.00 and up	1
Arduino Ethernet Shield 2	www.sparkfun.com/ products/ 11166	$24.95 and up	1
Arduino WiFi Shield	www.sparkfun.com/ products/13287	$16.95	1
Breadboard	www.sparkfun.com/ products/9567	$5.95	1
Breadboard jumper wires	www.sparkfun.com/ products/8431	$3.95	1
DHT22	www.sparkfun.com/ products/10167 www.adafruit.com/ products/385	$9.95	1
150 Ohm resistor	Various	Varies	1

Summary

With the Connector/Arduino library, you can make your sensor nodes quite a bit more sophisticated. By enabling your sensor nodes to save data in a MySQL database, you also enhance your monitoring solutions by making the data much easier to access and stored in a very reliable place (a database server).

In this chapter, you discovered how to write database-enabled Arduino sketches and took a detailed tour of the Connector/Arduino library. Armed with this knowledge, you are ready to move on to creating a real sensor network. In the next chapter, you put the accumulated knowledge of the previous chapters to use in creating your first sensor network with a MySQL database server, an Arduino aggregate node, and wireless sensor nodes.

CHAPTER 10

Building Your Network: Arduino Wireless Aggregator + Wireless Sensor Node + Raspberry Pi Server

With the information you have learned thus far in the book, and especially in Chapters 8 and 9, it is time to put it all together and build your first sensor network with a MySQL database server.

In this chapter, you put all the components together and build a working sensor network that features your Raspberry Pi MySQL server as the data repository, a data-aggregate node (you see examples of both Arduino and Raspberry Pi), and a number of sensor nodes connected via XBee modules. These are the building blocks you built in previous chapters, now combined to demonstrate how you can build low-cost sensor networks.

© Charles Bell 2020

C. Bell, *Beginning Sensor Networks with XBee, Raspberry Pi, and Arduino*,
https://doi.org/10.1007/978-1-4842-5796-8_10

Data-Aggregate Nodes

Recall that a data aggregator is a special node designed to receive information from multiple sources (sensors) and store the results. The source data can originate from multiple sensors on the node itself, but more often the data-aggregate node receives information from multiple sensor nodes that are not attached directly to the aggregate node (they connect via XBee modules).

Most often, these sensors are hosted by other nodes and placed in other locations, and the data-aggregate node is connected to the sensor nodes via a wired or wireless connection. For example, you may have a sensor hosted on a low-power Arduino in one location and another sensor hosted on a Raspberry Pi in another location, both connected to your data-aggregate node using XBee modules. Except for the limitations of the network medium chosen, you can have dozens of nodes feeding sensor data to a data-aggregate node.

The use of data-aggregate nodes has several advantages. If you are using a wireless technology such as ZigBee with XBee modules, data-aggregate nodes can permit you to extend the range of the network by placing the data-aggregate nodes nearest the sensors. The data-aggregate nodes can then transmit the data to another node such as a database server via a more reliable medium.

For example, you may want to place a data-aggregate node in an outbuilding that has power and an Ethernet connection to collect data from remote sensor nodes located in various other buildings. A case to consider is monitoring temperature in one or more rooms or even external storage buildings. These buildings may or may not have power but most likely are not wired for Ethernet. The data-aggregate node therefore could be placed in the closest building that has power and an Ethernet port.

Note   In this case, I mean the closest point to the sensor nodes that is still within range of the wireless transmission media (such as XBee).

Data-aggregate nodes can also permit you to move the logic to process a set of sensors to a more powerful node. For example, if you use sensors that require code to process the values (such as the TMP36), you can use a data-aggregate node to receive the raw data from those sensors, store it, and calculate the values at a later time. Not only does this ensure that you have code in only one location, but it also allows you to use less sophisticated (less powerful) hosts for the remote sensors. That is, you could use less expensive or older Arduino boards for the sensors and a more powerful Arduino for the data-aggregate node. This has the added advantage that if a remote sensor is destroyed, it is not costly to replace.

Recall also that you have to decide where you want to store your sensor data. Data-aggregate nodes either can store the data locally on removable media or an onboard storage device (local storage) or can transmit the data to another node for storage (remote storage). The choice of which to use is often based on how the data will be consumed or viewed.

For example, if you want to store only the last values read from the sensors, you may want to consider some form of visual display or remote-access mechanism. In this case, it may be more cost-effective and less complicated to use local storage storing only the latest values.

On the other hand, if you require data values recorded over time for later processing, you should consider storing the data on another node so that the data can be accessed without affecting the sensor network. That is, you can store the data on a more robust system (say, a personal computer, server, or cloud-based service) and further reduce the risk of losing data should the aggregate node fail.

The following sections explore examples of each form of data
aggregator based on the examples from previous chapters. I keep these
sections brief to provide a frame of reference and to help you build
knowledge for the projects discussed later in this chapter.

Local-Storage Data Aggregator

A local-storage data aggregator is a node designed to receive sensor data
from one or more sensors or sensor nodes and store the data on a device
that is built in to or attached to the node. Recall that for Arduino-based
nodes this is typically EEPROM (memory) or an SD drive via either the
Arduino Ethernet shield or another SD card shield. Recall that for the
Raspberry Pi this could be the SD boot drive, a USB drive, or an EEPROM
connected via the general-purpose input/output (GPIO) pins.

The nature of the local storage is a limiting factor in what you can do
with a local-storage data-aggregate node. That is, if you want to process
the data at a later time, you would choose a medium that permits you
to retrieve the data and move it to another computer. As mentioned in
Chapter 7, the EEPROM is an unlikely choice due to its volatility and
difficulty in connecting to a personal computer. This leaves the SD card
or a removable drive as the only reasonable alternatives. But if the sensor
data is used primarily for displaying data, you can use the EEPROM to
store the latest values or a short list of values for display on demand.

This does not mean the local-storage data aggregator is a useless
concept. Let's consider the case where you want to monitor temperature in
several outbuildings. You are not using the data for any analysis but merely
want to be able to read the values when it is convenient (or required).

One possible solution is to design the local-storage data-aggregate
node with a visual display. For example, you can use an LCD to display the
sensor data. Of course, this means the data-aggregate node must be in a
location where you can get to it easily.

But let's consider the case where your data-aggregate node is also in a remote location. Perhaps it too is in another outbuilding, but you spend the majority of your time in a different location. In this case, a remote-access solution would be best.

Fortunately, you can provide such a mechanism with very little work. Consider the Ethernet library for the Arduino. There are sample sketches that show you how to host a lightweight web server on the Arduino. For the case where you simply want to access the sensor data for viewing from a remote location, a web server is the perfect solution. You point your browser to your data-aggregate node and view the data.

The design of such a data-aggregate node would require storing the latest values locally, say, in memory or EEPROM, and, when a client connects, displaying the data. This is a simple and elegant solution for a local-storage data-aggregate node. The following project demonstrates these techniques.

Project: Data-Aggregate Node with Local Storage

If you have not built the components from the previous projects or had problems getting one or more to work, you may want to go back and revisit those chapters. I discuss each of the components needed, but not to the level of detail in the previous chapters. If you find you need a refresher for some of the components, please refer to those chapters cited.

With that stated, it's time to build your first sensor network with a local-storage data-aggregate node. Savvy readers will realize you've already built examples of all the sensor components in the previous chapters. What is new is the choice of local storage and the mechanism for displaying the data.

In this project, you build a data-aggregate node that can be accessed via an Ethernet network and that supports a lightweight web server to display the last values read from each of several sensors. The sensor nodes are networked with XBee modules to the data-aggregate node. Except for the web server portion and the choice of using the onboard EEPROM for storing data, the code for the data-aggregate node is similar to the code you have used in previous projects.

Hardware

The hardware for this project consists of several XBee-based temperature sensor nodes communicating to an Arduino-based node that will be your data-aggregate node. I discussed XBee modules in Chapters 2 and 4 and the XBee temperature sensor node in Chapter 4.

Data-Aggregate Node

Because you want to use a web server, the data-aggregate node requires an Arduino Ethernet shield as well as an XBee shield (or equivalent). If you use both shields with your Arduino, you may need to use a stackable header kit (www.sparkfun.com/products/11417) to ensure that the Ethernet shield does not prohibit the pins from the XBee shield to seat properly.

Figure 10-1 shows one form of data-aggregate node I use for my projects. The Arduino shield is mounted on the Arduino board, and headers are used to raise the height of the connections so that the XBee shield can be mounted securely. Although this makes for a rather tall stack of boards, it is still a compact form.

Figure 10-1. *Arduino-based data-aggregate node*

If you are using XBee modules that have an on-chip antenna or another
form of antenna that does not protrude from the top of the XBee module,
you may be able to place the XBee shield on the Arduino first and the
Ethernet shield on top. In this case, you would not need the additional risers.

The stackable header kit is a handy accessory to have because it
permits you to raise the height of shields so that you can access or in some
cases view components on the Arduino board (like the LEDs and *various*
buttons or switches common to some shields). You can find stackable
header kits at SparkFun, Adafruit, and most vendors that stock Arduino
boards and shields.

You also need a way to power your data-aggregate node. If you plan
to execute the project as an experiment and leave the node connected to
your laptop via a USB cable, then you are fine and need nothing more. But
if you plan to deploy the node, you need to power the Arduino via a typical
wall wart power supply. A 9V power supply should be sufficient, or you can
use a 9V battery connected via a barrel connector. Figure 10-2 shows a wall
wart power supply from SparkFun. Figure 10-3 shows a 9V battery carrier
from SparkFun.

Figure 10-2. *Wall wart power supply (courtesy of SparkFun)*

Figure 10-3. *9V battery carrier (courtesy of SparkFun)*

Be sure to use an XBee module configured with the *COORDINATOR API* firmware for the data-aggregate node. Please refer to Chapters 2 and 4 for details on how to configure your XBee modules.

Sensor Nodes

Recall from Chapter 4 that the hardware for the XBee sensor node
consists of a breadboard, some jumper wires, a breadboard power
supply, a power supply (a typical 5–9V wall wart will do nicely), a TMP36
temperature sensor, and a 0.10uF capacitor. You also need an XBee
breakout board with male headers (0.1" spacing for breadboards) like
those available from Adafruit or SparkFun. Power for the temperature
sensor nodes can be via a 9V battery or, if power is available, a 9V wall
wart power supply.

I repeat the wiring diagram from Chapter 4 in Figure 10-4 for
convenience. You need to build at least two of these temperature sensor
nodes, but three would make for a better test project.

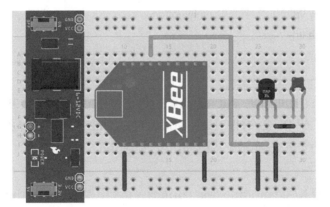

Figure 10-4. Wiring the TMP sensor node

Note   It may be possible to use lower voltage power supplies.
Consult the documentation for your breadboard power supply for
more information.

565

Be sure to use an XBee module configured with the *END DEVICE* or *ROUTER API* firmware for each sensor node. Please refer to Chapters 2 and 4 for details on how to configure your XBee modules. The settings for each sensor node are repeated in Table 10-1.

Table 10-1. *XBee Sensor Node Options and Values*

Code	Setting Name	Description	Value
D3	AD3/DIO3	Trigger analog or digital data recording	2—ADC
ID	PAN ID	Id for the network	8088
IR	I/O Sampling Rate	Time to wait to send data	3A98—15,000ms
NI	Node Identifier	Name for the node	TMP36_*
V+	Supply Voltage Threshold	Supply voltage	FFFF (always send)

Note   You should give each XBee a unique node id such as TMP36_1, TMP36_2, TMP36_3, and so on. This will be essential for the Raspberry Pi example later in this chapter.

Recall, the XBee module that connects to the Arduino is the *COORDINATOR* role using the following settings shown in Table 10-2.

Table 10-2. *XBee Coordinator Options and Values*

Code	Setting Name	Description	Value
ID	PAN ID	Id for the network	8088
NI	Node identifier	Name for the node	Coordinator

Go ahead and build your temperature sensor nodes. Wire them up, and double-check the power settings for your breadboard power supply. Be sure it is set to 3.3V. Once you have all of your temperature sensor nodes wired, don't power them on yet. You need to wait until you have finished writing and uploading the sketch to the data-aggregate node before powering on the sensor nodes. I discuss the sketch in the next section.

Tip   While you are working with this project—and, indeed, the first few times you power up the network—you should test everything at the same location. For example, set up the sensor nodes and the data-aggregate node on the same table or workbench, and debug the network until everything works correctly. Only then can you safely deploy the sensor nodes to their remote locations.[1]

Software

The software for this project does not require any additional special libraries or similar downloads that you haven't already loaded in previous chapters. I present an overview of the sketch first and then discuss the new portions in more detail. I skip some of the code used in previous projects, for brevity. Please refer to the complete code in Listing 10-4 for more details, and be sure you understand how the code works.

---

[1]Within XBee range, of course.

Overview

The sketch you use is a combination of the web server example in the Arduino IDE as well as the code from previous projects. You rearrange things a bit because there is less need for writing data to the serial monitor. In fact, you don't really need to write anything to the serial monitor. But you do leave in a few statements for debugging purposes.

If you have not experimented with the web server examples in the Arduino IDE (see *File ➤ Examples ➤ Ethernet* or *File ➤ Examples ➤ WiFi*), you may want to do so if you find the code for this sketch challenging (or if you want to just have fun with your Arduino and its Ethernet or WiFi shield).

Tip   If the sketch does not work as you expect, consider adding additional print statements to print debug information to the serial monitor. This is a very common practice for writing and debugging large or complex sketches.

The web server portion of this sketch is not complicated nor difficult to follow. Essentially, you use the `EthernetServer` library to listen for a connection; and once a connection is made, you write HTML code back to the client via an instance of `EthernetClient`.

Or, if you decide to use the WiFi shield, you use the `WiFiServer` library to listen for a connection; and once a connection is made, you write HTML code back to the client via an instance of `WiFiClient`. We will explore a WiFi version of the sketch in this section.

As stated previously, you're storing the last values from each sensor node for display in the web server. Storing these values presents a problem when using the Arduino, as described in Chapter 7. Your choices are limited to using the SD drive on the Arduino Ethernet shield or the onboard EEPROM.

Although you experimented with an external EEPROM in Chapter 7, you use the onboard EEPROM instead for simplicity. The onboard EEPROM varies in size among the choices of Arduino boards, but in most cases, it is large enough to store a dozen or so bytes for each sensor node.

To use the onboard EEPROM, simply include the EEPROM.h file in your sketch. Reading from and writing to the onboard EEPROM is very easy and is done one byte at a time. You call EEPROM.read(), passing in the address for the byte you want to read. Writing to EEPROM is similar. You call EEPROM.write(), passing in the address where you want to store the byte and the value of the data (byte) you want to store. Examples of using this library can be found in the Arduino IDE.

Now let's get into the code! The following sections present the major components of the sketch—web server, local storage, and reading from the sensor nodes. I omit the code for manipulating the sensor data because that is a direct copy of the code from Chapter 4, and I skip some of the mundane operations for brevity. Open a new sketch in the Arduino IDE, and name it Arduino_Web_Aggregate.ino.

Lightweight Web Server

The code for the lightweight web server was taken from an example in the Arduino IDE. You modify the example by moving the code to send the data to the client into a separate function.

To build a web server, you first must include the correct library and declare a few variables. The following excerpt shows the code needed (with code from other components omitted for clarity):

```
#include <WiFi.h>
...
byte mac[] = {0xDE, 0xAD, 0xBE, 0xEF, 0xFE, 0xED};
IPAddress ip(10, 0, 1, 111);

// Start Ethernet Server class with port 80 (default for HTTP)
WiFiServer server(80);
...
```

Notice that you include the WiFi (or Ethernet) and SPI headers. You also declare two variables: a MAC address and an IP address. In previous projects, you allowed the Ethernet library to use DHCP to assign the IP address; but in this case, you need to know the IP address, and therefore you must use a static IP address. Be sure to choose one that is valid for the network segment where your data-aggregate node will be attached.

Finally, you initialize an instance of the WiFiServer class, passing it in port 80 (which is the default for an HTTP service). You can choose another port number, but it may require adding it to your URL in order to access the web server. For example, if you choose 3303, you would use http://10.0.1.111:3303.

Now comes the really fun part. The web server you build is a simplified service that returns only a small amount of HTTP code to the client. Aside from the include files and variables, you also need to initialize the Ethernet classes in the setup() method. The following code shows what is needed. Essentially, you initialize the Serial library, then the WiFi library (omitted for brevity), and finally the server instance. Please refer to the WiFi examples in Chapters 6, 7, and 9 for more details on setting up the WiFi section.

```
void setup() {
  Serial.begin(115200);
  while (!Serial); // wait for serial port to connect

  // WiFi section
...
  server.begin();
...
}
```

To make the web server respond when a client attaches, you add a new
method named `listener()` to the sketch. The following code shows where
this method is called—from the `loop()` method. In this case, you first
check for a response from the sensors; and if no sensor data is available,
you check to see if a client has attached and respond to the call:

```
void loop() {
  if [...]

  } else {
    // Listen for client and respond.
    listener();
  }
}
```

As for the listener portion, what you need to do is check to see if a
client has connected via the `server.available()` method. The return
of this method is an instance of the `EthernetClient` class. If the variable
is not NULL (a client has connected), you then check to see whether the
client is available via the `client.available()` method. If so, you send the
data for each response requested until a newline is detected.

You begin by sending HTTP headers via the `client.print()` and
`client.println()` methods. You also send a banner welcoming the user. If
sensor data is stored locally, you send the data for each sensor node stored
(via a loop); otherwise, you send a status banner stating there is no data.

The sending of the sensor data is via a new method named `send_
sensor_data()`. This method uses the `client.print()` and `client.
println()` methods[2] of the client instance to write the data in text form

---

[2]Since you pass the client variable by reference, you dereference the pointer using
`->` instead of a period.

and the ending HTTP tags for each block of data. In this case, you send the
address of the sensor node, the temperature in Celsius, the temperature
again in Fahrenheit, and the reference voltage from the sensor node.

Listing 10-1 shows the code needed to listen for a client and send the
response. I show an excerpt of the client code to send data: the setup()
and loop() code, for brevity. Refer to Listing 10-4 for the complete code
needed.

Listing 10-1. The Web Server Code

```
...
void send_sensor_data(EthernetClient *client, int num_sample) {
  unsigned int address;
  float temp_c;
  float temp_f;
  float volts;

  // Read sensor data from memory and display it.
  read_sample(num_sample, &address, &temp_c, &temp_f, &volts);

  client->println("<br />");
  client->print("Node Address: ");
  client->print(address, HEX);
  client->print(".");
...
}

void listener() {
  // listen for incoming clients
  EthernetClient client = server.available();
  if (client) {
    Serial.println("Got a connection!");
    // an http request ends with a blank line
    boolean currentLineIsBlank = true;
```

```
while (client.connected()) {
  if (client.available()) {
    char c = client.read();
    // if you've gotten to the end of the line (received a
      newline
    // character) and the line is blank, the http request
      has ended,
    // so you can send a reply
    if (c == '\n' && currentLineIsBlank) {
      // send a standard http response header
      client.println("HTTP/1.1 200 OK");
      client.println("Content-Type: text/html");
      client.println();

      // Print header
      client.println("Welcome to the Arduino Data Aggregate
      Node!");
      client.println("<br />");

      // read sensor data
      byte num_samples = EEPROM.read(0);
      for (int i = 0; i < num_samples; i++) {
        send_sensor_data(&client, i);
      }
      // if no data, say so!
      if (num_samples == 0) {
        client.print("No samples to display.");
        client.println("<br />");
      }
      break;
    }
```

```
      if (c == '\n') {
        currentLineIsBlank = true;
      }
      else if (c != '\r') {
        currentLineIsBlank = false;
      }
    }
  }
  // give the web browser time to receive the data
  delay(1);
  // close the connection:
  client.stop();
  }
}
...
```

Now that you understand how the web server component works, let's
examine the local-storage component.

Local Storage Using the Onboard EEPROM

The local-storage component uses the onboard EEPROM to store and
retrieve the sensor data. In the overview section, I discussed how easy it is
to use the library. In this section, I discuss the specifics of how you store
and retrieve the sensor data.

Because you're storing only the last values (samples) from each sensor
node and you may have more than one sensor node communicating, you
need a simple mechanism to keep the data organized. You use something
similar to the external EEPROM project from Chapter 7.

You use the first byte of EEPROM memory (address 0) to store the number of samples present and a block of 10 bytes for each sample. Rather than store the entire 64-bit address for each sensor node (the XBee 64-bit network address), you store the last 2 bytes, which will display four hexadecimal digits when converted to hexadecimal and displayed as text.[3] You also store only the raw sensor data, which is a float (4 bytes), and the reference voltage, which is also a float (4 bytes). Thus, you need 10 bytes to store a sample.

Because you store only the raw data from the sensor, you must perform the temperature calculations as you did in Chapter 4 at a later time. I leave this for you to explore in Listing 10-4.

You also add code to the setup() method to initialize the EEPROM on the initial start. In this case, writing a 0 to address 0 means there are no samples stored. This ensures that you can restart from scratch simply by resetting (or powering off and then on) the data-aggregate node. If you find you need to make the values persistent, take the following code out of the setup() method after it has executed at least once:

```
void setup() {
  ...
  // Initialize the EEPROM
  EEPROM.write(0, 0);
}
```

To make things a bit easier, you create four new methods for reading and writing from and to the EEPROM. Listing 10-2 shows the complete methods. Notice that you have two sets of methods, one for integers (2 bytes) and one for float variables (4 bytes).

---

[3]Why only four digits (characters)? Won't there be collisions? No, not necessarily. Most XBee modules you can purchase do not have 64-bit addresses where the last four digits are the same. It is possible, but unlikely. If you find this is the case for your XBee modules, consider using the last eight characters instead.

Listing 10-2. EEPROM Helper Methods

```
...
// Read an integer from EEPROM
int read_int(byte position) {
  int value = 0;
  byte* p = (byte*)(void*)&value;
  for (int i = 0; i < sizeof(value); i++)
      *p++ = EEPROM.read(position++);
  return value;
}

// Read a float from EEPROM
float read_float(byte position) {
  float value = 0;
  byte* p = (byte*)(void*)&value;
  for (int i = 0; i < sizeof(value); i++)
      *p++ = EEPROM.read(position++);
  return value;
}

// Write an integer to EEPROM
void write_int(byte position, int value) {
  const byte *p = (const byte *)(const void *)&value;
  for (int i = 0; i < sizeof(value); i++)
      EEPROM.write(position++, *p++);
}

// Write a float to EEPROM
void write_float(byte position, float value) {
  const byte *p = (const byte *)(const void *)&value;
  for (int i = 0; i < sizeof(value); i++)
      EEPROM.write(position++, *p++);
}
...
```

Notice that in the code you use some pointer trickery to turn the integer and float into an array of bytes. This is not uncommon for code written by advanced C and C++ programmers. Although it is possible to use other methods (such as shifting bytes) to break the values into bytes, I wanted to include this advanced technique to get you thinking about how pointers work. Much of what you are likely to encounter in more complex sketches will involve manipulating pointer in similar ways.

Tip   For those of you who simply cannot leave things alone (you know who you are), no doubt you can see some room for optimization here. Notice that the methods are very similar. The only thing that really changes is the type. So how would you optimize this code even further? Hint: Consider a template[4] (`http://playground. arduino.cc/Code/EEPROMWriteAnything`).

Now that you understand how to store and retrieve samples to and from the EEPROM, let's examine how this fits into the code for reading data from the sensor nodes.

---

[4]I did not use templates here because I do not want to make the code too complex. As it is, unless you are familiar with pointers, you may think this code is illegible and won't compile or that it mysteriously "just works." In that case, you have to take my word that it does. How much more mysterious can someone make their code for those new to Arduino programming than by using templates? I know some very good C++ programmers who find using templates a challenge.

Reading Data from Sensor Nodes via XBee

The code for reading data from multiple XBee modules is unchanged
from the project in Chapter 4. Indeed, the code you wrote for that sketch
can and does support connections to multiple sensor nodes. Recall that
this is possible because your data-aggregate node uses an XBee module
configured as the coordinator, and your sensor nodes use XBee modules
configured as routers.

Because the initialization code is unchanged from the project in
Chapter 4, I omit those details here. But the code for storing the sensor
data is different. In this case, you need to store the sample in memory
(EEPROM). Because you want to store only the latest value, you must look
for the sample in memory first by address. If you find a match, you save the
data in the same location. If you do not find a match among the samples
stored, you add it to the end and increment the number of samples stored.
You name this method the same as before—record_sample().

But you do not end there. You also need methods to read and write
the sample data. You break these into separate methods so that you can
make the record_sample() method smaller and easier to read. Thus, you
create read_sample() and write_sample() methods that use the EEPROM
helper methods described previously to store and retrieve the samples.

Listing 10-3 shows the major portions of the new code for storing
sensor data and the completed code for the loop() method. Notice how it
precludes the listener() call.

Listing 10-3. Reading from XBee Sensor Nodes

```
// Read a sample from EEPROM
void read_sample(byte index, unsigned int *address, float *temp_f,
                 float *temp_c, float *volts) {
  float temp;
  byte position = (index * bytes_per_sample) + 1;
```

```
  *address = read_int(position);

  temp = read_float(position + 2);

  *temp_c = ((temp * 1200.0 / 1024.0) - 500.0) / 10.0;
  *temp_f = ((*temp_c * 9.0)/5.0) + 32.0;

  *volts = read_float(position + 6);
}

// Write sample to EEPROM
void write_sample(byte index) {
  byte position =  (index * bytes_per_sample) + 1;

  write_int(position, address);
  write_float(position + 2, temperature);
  write_float(position + 6, voltage);
}

void record_sample(ZBRxIoSampleResponse *ioSample) {
  int saved_addr;

  // Get sample data from XBee
  get_sample_data(ioSample);

  // See if already in memory. If not, add it.
  byte num_samples = EEPROM.read(0);
  boolean found = false;
  for (byte i = 0; i < num_samples; i++) {
    byte position = (i * bytes_per_sample) + 1;
```

```
      // get address
      saved_addr = read_int(position);
      if (saved_addr == address) {
        write_sample(i);
        found = true;
      }
    }
    if (!found) {
      // Save sample
      write_sample(num_samples);

      // Update number of sensors
      num_samples++;
      EEPROM.write(0, num_samples);
    }
  }

...

void loop() {
  //attempt to read a packet
  xbee.readPacket();

  if (xbee.getResponse().isAvailable()) {
    // got something

    if (xbee.getResponse().getApiId() == ZB_IO_SAMPLE_RESPONSE) {

      // Get the packet
      xbee.getResponse().getZBRxIoSampleResponse(ioSample);

      // Get and store the data locally (in memory)
      record_sample(&ioSample);
    }
```

```
    else {
      Serial.print("Expected I/O Sample, but got ");
      Serial.print(xbee.getResponse().getApiId(), HEX);
    }
  } else if (xbee.getResponse().isError()) {
    Serial.print("Error reading packet.  Error code: ");
    Serial.println(xbee.getResponse().getErrorCode());
  } else {
    // Listen for client and respond.
    listener();
  }
}
```

This completes the discussion of the new components for this sketch. The following section includes the entire sketch with all of these components in their proper context. Be sure to take your time reading through the code. It is by far the largest sketch (code) you have worked with in this book.

Putting It All Together

Now that you understand the workings of the major components of the sketch, let's examine the completed sketch in more detail. Listing 10-4 shows the completed code for the sketch. Recall, we named the file Arduino_Web_Aggregate.ino.

Tip   If you are using a Leonardo, check the notes on the software serial page (www.arduino.cc/en/Reference/SoftwareSerial) code regarding the pins for the XBee shield. Depending on which shield you are using with your Leonardo, you may need to change these.

Listing 10-4. Local-Storage Data-Aggregate Node

```
/**
   Beginning Sensor Networks Second Edition
   Example Arduino Data Aggregate Node

   This project demonstrates how to receive sensor data from
   multiple XBee sensor nodes, save the samples in the onboard
   EEPROM and present them as a web page. It uses an Arduino
   with an XBee shield with an XBee coordinator installed.

   Note: This sketch was adapted from the examples in the XBee
   library created by Andrew Rapp.
*/

#include <XBee.h>
#include <SoftwareSerial.h>
#include <WiFi.h>
#include <EEPROM.h>

byte bytes_per_sample = 10; // address (2), temp (4), volts (4)

// Setup pin definitions for XBee shield
uint8_t recv = 8;
uint8_t trans = 9;
SoftwareSerial soft_serial(recv, trans);

// assign a MAC address and IP address for the Arduino
byte mac_addr[] = { 0xDE, 0xAD, 0xBE, 0xEF, 0xFE, 0xED };

IPAddress server_addr(192,168,42,8);  // IP of the MySQL
*server* here
char user[] = "arduino_user";              // MySQL user login username
char password[] = "secret";                // MySQL user login password
char ssid[] = "SSID";
char pass[] = "PASSWORD";
```

```
// Start WiFi Server class with port 80
WiFiServer server(80);

// Instantiate an instance of the XBee library
XBee xbee = XBee();

// Instantiate an instance of the IO sample class
ZBRxIoSampleResponse ioSample = ZBRxIoSampleResponse();

// Sample data values
unsigned int address;    // Last 4 digits of XBee address
float temperature;       // Raw temperature value
float voltage;           // Reference voltage

// Get sample data
void get_sample_data(ZBRxIoSampleResponse *ioSample) {
  Serial.print("Received data from address: ");
  address = (ioSample->getRemoteAddress64().getMsb() << 8) +
             ioSample->getRemoteAddress64().getLsb();
  Serial.print(ioSample->getRemoteAddress64().getMsb(), HEX);
  Serial.println(ioSample->getRemoteAddress64().getLsb(), HEX);
  temperature = ioSample->getAnalog(3);
  int ref = xbee.getResponse().getFrameData()[17] << 8;
  ref += xbee.getResponse().getFrameData()[18];
  voltage = (float(ref) * float(1200.0 / 1024.0))/1000.0;
}

// Read an integer from EEPROM
int read_int(byte position) {
  int value = 0;
  byte* p = (byte*)(void*)&value;
  for (int i = 0; i < sizeof(value); i++)
      *p++ = EEPROM.read(position++);
  return value;
}
```

583

```
// Read a float from EEPROM
float read_float(byte position) {
  float value = 0;
  byte* p = (byte*)(void*)&value;
  for (int i = 0; i < sizeof(value); i++)
      *p++ = EEPROM.read(position++);
  return value;
}

// Write an integer to EEPROM
void write_int(byte position, int value) {
  const byte *p = (const byte *)(const void *)&value;
  for (int i = 0; i < sizeof(value); i++)
      EEPROM.write(position++, *p++);
}

// Write a float to EEPROM
void write_float(byte position, float value) {
  const byte *p = (const byte *)(const void *)&value;
  for (int i = 0; i < sizeof(value); i++)
      EEPROM.write(position++, *p++);
}

// Read a sample from EEPROM
void read_sample(byte index, unsigned int *address, float *temp_c,
                float *temp_f, float *volts) {
  float temp;
  byte position =  (index * bytes_per_sample) + 1;

  *address = read_int(position);

  temp = read_float(position + 2);
```

```
  *temp_c = ((temp * 1200.0 / 1024.0) - 500.0) / 10.0;
  *temp_f = ((*temp_c * 9.0)/5.0) + 32.0;

  *volts = read_float(position + 6);
}

// Write sample to EEPROM
void write_sample(byte index) {
  byte position =  (index * bytes_per_sample) + 1;

  write_int(position, address);
  write_float(position + 2, temperature);
  write_float(position + 6, voltage);
}

// Record a sample
void record_sample(ZBRxIoSampleResponse *ioSample) {
  int saved_addr;

  // Get sample data from XBee
  get_sample_data(ioSample);

  // See if already in memory. If not, add it.
  byte num_samples = EEPROM.read(0);
  boolean found = false;
  for (byte i = 0; i < num_samples; i++) {
    byte position = (i * bytes_per_sample) + 1;

    // get address
    saved_addr = read_int(position);
    if (saved_addr == address) {
      write_sample(i);
      found = true;
    }
  }
```

```
  if (!found) {
    // Save sample
    write_sample(num_samples);

    // Update number of sensors
    num_samples++;
    EEPROM.write(0, num_samples);
  }
}

void send_sensor_data(WiFiClient *client, int num_sample) {
  unsigned int address;
  float temp_c;
  float temp_f;
  float volts;

  // Read sensor data from memory and display it.
  read_sample(num_sample, &address, &temp_c, &temp_f, &volts);

  client->print("<br />\nNode Address: ");
  client->print(address, HEX);
  client->print("<br />\nTemperature: ");
  client->print(temp_c);
  client->print("C<br />\nTemperature: ");
  client->print(temp_f);
  client->print("F<br />\nVoltage: ");
  client->print(volts);
  client->println("V<br />");
}

void listener() {
  // listen for incoming clients
  WiFiClient client = server.available();
  if (client) {
```

```
Serial.println("Got a connection!");
// an http request ends with a blank line
boolean currentLineIsBlank = true;
while (client.connected()) {
  if (client.available()) {
    char c = client.read();
    // if you've gotten to the end of the line (received a
      newline
    // character) and the line is blank, the http request
      has ended,
    // so you can send a reply
    if (c == '\n' && currentLineIsBlank) {
      // send a standard http response header
      client.println("HTTP/1.1 200 OK");
      client.println("Content-Type: text/html");
      client.println();

      // Print header
      client.println("Welcome to the Arduino Data Aggregate
      Node!");
      client.println("<br />");

      // read sensor data
      byte num_samples = EEPROM.read(0);
      for (int i = 0; i < num_samples; i++) {
        send_sensor_data(&client, i);
      }
      // if no data, say so!
      if (num_samples == 0) {
        client.print("No samples to display.");
        client.println("<br />");
      }
      break;
```

```
      }
      if (c == '\n') {
        currentLineIsBlank = true;
      }
      else if (c != '\r') {
        currentLineIsBlank = false;
      }
    }
  }
  // give the web browser time to receive the data
  delay(100);
  // close the connection:
  client.stop();
  }
}

void setup() {
  Serial.begin(115200);
  while (!Serial); // wait for serial port to connect

  // WiFi section
  Serial.println("Starting WiFi.");
  int status = WiFi.begin(ssid, pass);
  // if you're not connected, stop here:
  if (status != WL_CONNECTED) {
    Serial.println("Couldn't get a WiFi connection!");
    while(true);
  }
  // if you are connected, print out info about the connection:
  else {
    Serial.println("Connected to network");
    IPAddress ip = WiFi.localIP();
```

```
    Serial.print("My IP address is: ");
    Serial.println(ip);
  }
  server.begin();

  soft_serial.begin(9600);
  xbee.setSerial(soft_serial);

  // Initialize the EEPROM
  EEPROM.write(0, 0);
}

void loop() {
  //attempt to read a packet
  xbee.readPacket();

  if (xbee.getResponse().isAvailable()) {
    // got something

    if (xbee.getResponse().getApiId() == ZB_IO_SAMPLE_RESPONSE) {

      // Get the packet
      xbee.getResponse().getZBRxIoSampleResponse(ioSample);

      // Get and store the data locally (in memory or on card?)
      record_sample(&ioSample);
    }
    else {
      Serial.print("Expected I/O Sample, but got ");
      Serial.print(xbee.getResponse().getApiId(), HEX);
    }
  } else if (xbee.getResponse().isError()) {
    Serial.print("Error reading packet.  Error code: ");
    Serial.println(xbee.getResponse().getErrorCode());
  } else {
```

```
    // Listen for client and respond.
    listener();
    delay(100);
  }
}
```

Take some time to go through the sketch until you are completely satisfied that you understand how everything works together. Once you are familiar and comfortable with the code, compile it and upload it to your Arduino.

Testing the Project

Once the code compiles and uploads successfully to your Arduino data-aggregate node and before any sensor nodes are powered on, connect to your Arduino via a web browser. Be sure to use the IP address you put in your sketch. Figure 10-5 shows the correct response. You can also open the serial monitor at this time.

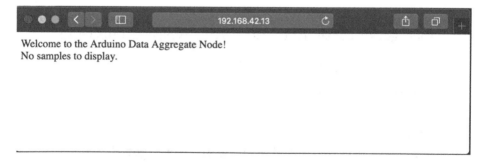

Figure 10-5. *Example response from a data-aggregate node with no sensors attached*

If you see this response, you have successfully written a very lightweight web server running on an Arduino! How cool is that? Now, power on one of your temperature sensor nodes and wait for 5–10 minutes.

If you haven't opened the serial monitor, do so now, and then wait for the sensor node data to arrive. You should see the message "`Received data from address: NNNNN`" in the serial monitor. When this happens, refresh your browser and notice the changes.

If you get some data back in the web browser, go ahead and power on all of your sensor nodes and wait for a while for several samples to arrive. The following shows what your serial monitor should be printing if you have three temperature sensor nodes running. Note that the addresses will be different and should match your XBee modules.

```
Starting WiFi.
Connected to network
My IP address is: 192.168.42.12
Got a connection!
Got a connection!
Got a connection!
```

Wait until you see several iterations of samples arrive, and then refresh your browser. You should see only one entry containing the latest sample for each sensor connected. The following shows an example result where there are three sensor nodes supplying data.

```
Welcome to the Arduino Data Aggregate Node!

Node Address: DB79
Temperature: 21.60C
Temperature: 70.88F
Voltage: 3.82V

Node Address: D45C
Temperature: 18.20C
Temperature: 64.77F
Voltage: 3.24V
```

```
Node Address: 29DB
Temperature: 11.52C
Temperature: 52.74F
Voltage: 3.15V
```

Wait for a few minutes, and then refresh your browser. You should see the sample values change. If they do not (or you just want to have some fun), carefully affect the values of the sensors by locating them nearer to heat or cool sources.

Note   If you do not see any data from your sensor nodes and there is nothing in the serial monitor indicating any data was received, use the troubleshooting section in Chapters 2 and 4 to diagnose possible issues with your XBee modules. Remember, they all must have the same version of the API firmware, and the sensor nodes must have the *ROUTER* role and the data-aggregate node the *COORDINATOR* role. Also, be sure to allow at least 10 minutes for the XBee modules to connect and form a network.

OK, that was a hoot, wasn't it? Yes indeed: you now have demonstrated mastery of the basic building blocks of a sensor network. Although you used only Arduino nodes to keep this easier to comprehend, the next project introduces the Raspberry Pi into the mix and further rounds out your cache of sensor networking tools.

Note   It is OK if your output varies from what is shown. In some cases, you may also notice a small discrepancy between what the sensor reports and measurements from more accurate devices. As long as you see values within tolerance for your particular sensor (check the vendor's datasheet for this), your sensor node is working properly.

For More Fun

There are a lot of really cool things you can do with this project. The
most obvious to me is replacing the XBee address with meaningful
labels. More specifically, label the sensor nodes by their location. For
example, XBee node CD0F is located on my porch, whereas node 29DB
is in my office. It would be more meaningful if the labels on the web
page stated Dr. Bell's Office and Mrs. Bell's Porch. Hint: Make a lookup
table for this data so that you can substitute the values when displayed
to the client.

Another area of exploration is to use the SD card rather than the
onboard EEPROM to store the data. Rather than store only the last value
for each sensor node, store a running list of values for each sensor in
a separate file. When the client requests the data, display only the last
values written to each file. This will demonstrate the minor changes
needed to make the local-storage data-aggregate node into a node that
permits storage of values over time. Be careful not to exceed the capacity
of the SD card!

There is one thing that this project does not have that would be
considered essential for cases where you want to know when a sample
was taken: the date and time of the sample! The project stores the latest
values for each sensor, but you don't know when the sample was taken.
For example, what if you receive data from one sensor only once and
something happens to cause the sensor to stop sending data? Without
a date and time reference, you have no way to know this. To resolve this
issue, you can modify the project to use a real-time clock module and store
the date and time of each sample as you saw in Chapter 7. Hint: You need
to extend the methods for storing the sample data by adding the real-time
clock value.

If you are looking for a significant challenge, modify the code to send
the data to the cloud, and use the cloud as your data-storage mechanism.

Remote-Storage Data Aggregator

A remote-storage data aggregator is a node designed to receive sensor data from one or more sensors or sensor nodes and store the data on a different node. Most often, it is the case that the other node is a system with a more robust storage device. For example, it may be a computer that can store large files or a database server that permits you to store the data in tables.

Remote-storage data-aggregate nodes can be less sophisticated than local-storage data-aggregate nodes because there is no need to process the data for display or storage in a local device. Rather, you merely pass the raw data to the remote node (system) for storage.

Remote storage is also the first choice for cases where you want to store the data for later processing. Although it may be the case that the loss of some values may be acceptable, it is more likely that you want to collect all the data produced so that your analysis can be more accurate.[5] You therefore want the connection from the data-aggregate node to the remote-storage node to be reliable.

It may also be the case that there are multiple nodes to which you send the data. Consider a situation in which you are working with different sensors or sensors that produce data in different formats. In this case, you may want to send data from some sensors to one remote node and other data to other node(s). The reasons for doing such are less paramount than those for using different local-storage data-aggregate nodes, but it is still a concern. I consider this and similar topics for planning sensor networks in the next chapter.

---

[5]Which reminds me of my advanced statistics professor, who opened the semester with the question, "How much data makes for a statistically relevant sample size?" He did not offer an answer, but he asked the question again at the end of the semester. To his delight, the answer presented by the students was "It depends on what you're doing with the data." When pressed for a numerical answer, his response was unwaveringly "42."

You see a working example of this form of data-aggregate node for both the Arduino and Raspberry Pi in the following sections.

Project: Arduino Data-Aggregate Node with Database Storage

This project uses the previous project as its basis. You can use similar hardware (board, shields) and software but with a slightly different sketch. If you have not built the components from the previous project or had problems getting it to work, you may want to go back and diagnose and correct the problem first.

Since we will be using the Connector/Arduino we saw in Chapter 9, we will need to use an Arduino board with more memory. For this project, I recommend using an Arduino Uno or, better, the Arduino Mega 2560 board. In fact, I will demonstrate the project using the Mega 2560.

Note   If you use a WiFi shield, be sure to refer to the vendor's datasheet or set up documentation to use the board correctly with the Arduino Mega 2560.

You also use the MySQL database server you created in Chapter 8 and the connection mechanism from Chapter 9. If you have not built the database server or have one installed on your PC, you need to go back to Chapter 8 and build it.

Note   If you have problems getting your Raspberry Pi configured with MySQL or want to simplify the project, you can use a MySQL server running on another computer. However, you should get your Raspberry Pi database server running if you plan to install or use this project as a basis for your own sensor network.

With that stated, it's time to build your sensor network storing the samples in a database. Savvy readers will realize you've already built examples of all the components in the previous chapters.

Hardware

This project uses the same sensor hardware as the previous project for the sensor nodes and the data-aggregate node. The difference is that you use a larger board for the data-aggregate node and we add a new node—the MySQL database server.

Recall from Chapter 8 that the MySQL database server is a Raspberry Pi with an external hard drive connected via a USB hub (the Raspberry Pi cannot power devices like hard drives via the USB bus). Please refer to the "Building a Raspberry Pi MySQL Server" section in Chapter 8 to build the MySQL database server if you have not done so already.

Go ahead and power on the database server and make sure it can accept connections. You can leave the server powered on and connected while working with the other nodes. It is best to leave the sensor nodes powered off until you get all the software changes completed for the data-aggregate node.

Software

As with the hardware, you use the same software as in the previous project, albeit with additional libraries for the MySQL connection and a few modifications to the sketch. Because you are using the same XBee configuration, all the code for reading data from the XBee modules is the same as in the previous project.

I omit the code for creating a web server and writing the data values to EEPROM. This removes a lot of the code, but the basic structure is the same. The new portions are the calls to the MySQL Connector Arduino library for connecting to the database server and issuing queries to save the data, as you saw in Chapter 9. You work through each of the new parts of the sketch in the following paragraphs. A later section looks at configuring the MySQL database.

Adding the MySQL Connector Code to the Sketch

If you haven't installed the MySQL Connector Arduino library yet, refer to Chapter 9 to install the library. Once you have the library installed, open a new sketch and name it Arduino_MySQL_Aggregate.ino. The following shows the libraries needed for reading data from the XBee module as well as the connector library:

```
#include <XBee.h>
#include <SoftwareSerial.h>
#include <WiFi.h>
#include <MySQL_Connection.h>
#include <MySQL_Cursor.h>
```

You reuse the variables for communicating with the XBee but add an instance of the MySQL_Connector class from the library, user, password, SQL INSERT, and default database strings as shown here:

```
char user[] = "arduino_user";      // MySQL user login username
char password[] = "secret";        // MySQL user login password
// Sample query
char INSERT_SQL[] = "INSERT INTO house.temperature (address,
raw_temp, voltage) VALUES('%s','$s','%s')";
char DEFAULT_DATABASE[] = "house";
...
WiFiClient client;
MySQL_Connection conn((Client *)&client);
```

You also need to store the IP address[6] of the MySQL database server. You do this via the following code. Be sure to use the correct IP address for your MySQL server—failure to use the correct address will result in connection errors when the sketch first starts (because you connect to the server in the setup() method):

```
IPAddress server_addr(192,168,42,8);  // IP of the MySQL
                                          *server* here
```

You keep the get_sample_data() method from the previous project but drop the listener(), send_sensor_data(), and EEPROM read and write methods. The record_sample() method requires rewriting, however. In this case, you still call get_sample_data(); but instead of calculating the temperature from the raw data and displaying it to the serial monitor, you build an INSERT SQL statement for saving the data in a table (I explain the database set up in the next section). This requires building the string to save the last four digits of the hexadecimal address, the raw temperature, and the voltage in the string. Once the string is built, you simply call the cmd_query() method of the MySQL Connector class instance (my_conn). The new method is shown next:

```
void record_sample(ZBRxIoSampleResponse *ioSample) {
  int saved_addr;
  char temp_buff[20];
  char voltage_buff[20];
  char query[128];

  // Get sample data from XBee
  get_sample_data(ioSample);
```

---

[6]It must be a valid IP address for the network segment to which your server is connected.

```
// Send data to MySQL
String addr(address, HEX);
dtostrf(temperature, 4, 4, temp_buff);
dtostrf(voltage, 4, 4, voltage_buff);
sprintf(query, addr.c_str(), temp_buff, voltage_buff);

Serial.println(&query[0]);
// Initiate the query class instance
MySQL_Cursor *cur_mem = new MySQL_Cursor(&conn);
// Execute the query
int res = cur_mem->execute(query);
if (!res) {
  Serial.println("Query failed.");
} else {
  Serial.println("Ok.");
}
delete cur_mem;
}
```

The changes to the setup() method require adding the code to
connect to the database server. You remove the calls to server.begin()
and EEPROM.write(0, 0) because you are neither initiating a web server
nor using the EEPROM to store the samples. Instead, add the following
code to the end of the setup() method:

```
// Now connect to MySQL
Serial.println("Connecting to MySQL...");
if (conn.connect(server_addr, 3306, user, password, DEFAULT_
DATABASE)) {
  delay(1000);
} else {
  Serial.println("Connection failed.");
}
```

Modifying the loop() method is much easier. All the calls are in place for reading from the XBee modules and calling the record_sample() method. The only thing left to do is to remove the last else statement that contains the call to the listener() method.

As you can see, the modifications to the sketch from the last project are very easy. In fact, if you want to save some time coding, you can copy the code from the previous project and remove the parts you do not need. Listing 10-5 shows the completed sketch, including all the parts reused from the last project.

Listing 10-5. Arduino Remote-Storage Data Aggregate

```
/**
   Beginning Sensor Networks Second Edition
   Sensor Networks Example Arduino Data Aggregate Node

   This project demonstrates how to receive sensor data from
   multiple XBee sensor nodes saving the samples in a MySQL
   database.

   It uses an Arduino with an XBee shield with an XBee
   coordinator installed.
*/

#include <XBee.h>
#include <SoftwareSerial.h>
#include <WiFi.h>
#include <MySQL_Connection.h>
#include <MySQL_Cursor.h>

// Setup pin definitions for XBee shield
uint8_t recv = 8;
uint8_t trans = 9;
SoftwareSerial soft_serial(recv, trans);
```

```
// assign a MAC address and IP address for the Arduino
byte mac_addr[] = { 0xDE, 0xAD, 0xBE, 0xEF, 0xFE, 0xED };

IPAddress server_addr(192,168,42,8);  // IP of the MySQL
                                          *server* here
char user[] = "arduino_user";       // MySQL user login username
char password[] = "secret";         // MySQL user login password
char ssid[] = "SSID";
char pass[] = "PASSWORD";
// Sample query
char INSERT_SQL[] = "INSERT INTO house.temperature (address,
raw_temp, voltage) VALUES('%s','$s','%s')";
char DEFAULT_DATABASE[] = "house";

WiFiClient client;
MySQL_Connection conn((Client *)&client);

// Start WiFi Server class with port 80
WiFiServer server(80);

// Instantiate an instance of the XBee library
XBee xbee = XBee();

// Instantiate an instance of the IO sample class
ZBRxIoSampleResponse ioSample = ZBRxIoSampleResponse();

// Sample data values
unsigned int address;   // Last 4 digits of XBee address
float temperature;      // Raw temperature value
float voltage;          // Reference voltage

// Get sample data
void get_sample_data(ZBRxIoSampleResponse *ioSample) {
  Serial.print("Received data from address: ");
  address = (ioSample->getRemoteAddress64().getMsb() << 8) +
            ioSample->getRemoteAddress64().getLsb();
```

```
  Serial.print(ioSample->getRemoteAddress64().getMsb(), HEX);
  Serial.println(ioSample->getRemoteAddress64().getLsb(), HEX);
  temperature = ioSample->getAnalog(3);
  int ref = xbee.getResponse().getFrameData()[17] << 8;
  ref += xbee.getResponse().getFrameData()[18];
  voltage = (float(ref) * float(1200.0 / 1024.0))/1000.0;
}

// Record a sample
void record_sample(ZBRxIoSampleResponse *ioSample) {
  int saved_addr;
  char temp_buff[20];
  char voltage_buff[20];
  char query[128];

  // Get sample data from XBee
  get_sample_data(ioSample);

  // Send data to MySQL
  String addr(address, HEX);
  dtostrf(temperature, 4, 4, temp_buff);
  dtostrf(voltage, 4, 4, voltage_buff);
  sprintf(query, addr.c_str(), temp_buff, voltage_buff);

  Serial.println(&query[0]);
  // Initiate the query class instance
  MySQL_Cursor *cur_mem = new MySQL_Cursor(&conn);
  // Execute the query
  int res = cur_mem->execute(query);
  if (!res) {
    Serial.println("Query failed.");
  } else {
```

```
    Serial.println("Ok.");
  }
  delete cur_mem;
}

void setup() {
  Serial.begin(115200);
  while (!Serial); // wait for serial port to connect

  // WiFi section
  Serial.println("Starting WiFi.");
  int status = WiFi.begin(ssid, pass);
  // if you're not connected, stop here:
  if (status != WL_CONNECTED) {
    Serial.println("Couldn't get a WiFi connection!");
    while(true);
  }
  // if you are connected, print out info about the connection:
  else {
    Serial.println("Connected to network");
    IPAddress ip = WiFi.localIP();
    Serial.print("My IP address is: ");
    Serial.println(ip);
  }
  soft_serial.begin(9600);
  xbee.setSerial(soft_serial);

  // Now connect to MySQL
  Serial.println("Connecting to MySQL...");
  if (conn.connect(server_addr, 3306, user, password,
  DEFAULT_DATABASE)) {
    delay(1000);
```

```
  } else {
    Serial.println("Connection failed.");
  }
}

void loop() {
  //attempt to read a packet
  xbee.readPacket();

  if (xbee.getResponse().isAvailable()) {
    // got something

    if (xbee.getResponse().getApiId() == ZB_IO_SAMPLE_RESPONSE) {
      // Get the packet
      xbee.getResponse().getZBRxIoSampleResponse(ioSample);

      // Get and store the data locally (in memory or on card?)
      record_sample(&ioSample);
    }
    else {
      Serial.print("Expected I/O Sample, but got ");
      Serial.print(xbee.getResponse().getApiId(), HEX);
    }
  } else if (xbee.getResponse().isError()) {
    Serial.print("Error reading packet.  Error code: ");
    Serial.println(xbee.getResponse().getErrorCode());
  }
}
```

You may be wondering why you remove the code for calculating the temperature in Fahrenheit and Celsius. You do this because you can move this functionality to the database server. Not only does this free up some processing power (a big help for smaller microcontrollers), but for platforms like the Arduino, it also frees up a small amount of memory. The savings for this project may be minimal, but consider the case for a very complex sketch or an Arduino that is doing other things. Any savings in memory could allow for more room to store data or work with more sensors.

For example, consider the need for building a node that not only serves as a data aggregate via an XBee network but also hosts a number of sensors on the Arduino connected via an I2C interface and displays data via some other hardware-specific interface such as an LCD panel or even a hard-copy printer.[7] All these components require the inclusion of libraries; and depending on the size of the Arduino, you may run low on memory. I have built sketches that have forced me to use an Arduino Mega not because of the size of my sketch but due to the sum of the memory needed for the libraries I needed to use.

Now that you have the sketch built, let's turn to the database server and see what needs to be done to support storing the samples in a table.

Setting Up the MySQL Database

This section discusses the work needed on the MySQL server to make a database for saving and reporting your sensor data. The first thing you need to do is create the database you want to use and populate it with the necessary objects. In this case, you need two tables and a trigger. I show you all the commands needed but omit most of the interaction with the server for brevity. Refer to Chapters 6 and 7 for a quick-start tutorial on MySQL if you have not read those chapters.

---

[7]Yes, these exist! See www.sparkfun.com/products/10438.

Connect to your MySQL database server. Recall that you can do this via the `mysql -uroot -p<password>` command if run on the Raspberry Pi or you can use the MySQL Shell via the `mysqlsh --uri root@ localhost:3306 --sql` command if run on your PC. Go ahead and create the database and name it house, as shown here:

```
CREATE DATABASE house;
USE house;
```

The data will be stored in a table. As mentioned previously, you want to store the address of the XBee sensor node (the last four hexadecimal digits of the 64-bit address), the raw temperature sample, and the voltage.

It is at this point you can consider adding some functionality to the database server that would otherwise require much more work on the data-aggregate node. For example, consider the fact that you want to know when the sample was taken. That is, you want to store the date and time of the sample. If you remember from earlier chapters, you must use a real-time clock module connected to the Arduino in order to display the date and time of the sample. Fortunately, you can avoid all that code and hardware by simply instructing the database server to store this data automatically by creating a column using the timestamp data type. This data type stores the current date and time when the row is inserted into the table. Very cool, eh?

But you may wonder how that works. The trick to making the server fill in the data for the field is to not pass a value in the `INSERT` statement. This is a special sentinel value that the server interprets to mean you want to calculate the timestamp and save it. Note that you can provide a specific timestamp for the column should you need to store a specific value.

You can also move the code to calculate the temperature in
Fahrenheit and Celsius to the database. This requires the use of
a trigger (a special block of code that can be executed at specific
moments when a row is inserted, updated, or deleted). You look at the
trigger in a moment; for now, you can simply add a column for each
temperature value.

Thus, you need a total of six columns: date and time of the
sample, address of the sensor node, raw temperature sample, voltage,
temperature in Fahrenheit, and temperature in Celsius. The CREATE
TABLE statement needed to realize this table is as follows. Name the table
temperature:

```
CREATE TABLE `temperature` (
  `sample_date` timestamp DEFAULT CURRENT_TIMESTAMP ON UPDATE
CURRENT_TIMESTAMP,
  `address` char(8) DEFAULT NULL,
  `raw_temp` float DEFAULT NULL,
  `voltage` float DEFAULT NULL,
  `fahrenheit` float DEFAULT '0',
  `celsius` float DEFAULT '0'
) ENGINE=InnoDB DEFAULT CHARSET=latin1[8];
```

Notice that you do not use a primary key. I leave it to you to consider
the implications, and I discuss considerations for database design in the
next chapter.

---

[8]What is missing here? Can you spot a potential problem with this table? I'll give
you a hint: can it accept duplicate rows? What about ordering of the rows? Are
these an issue?

WHAT ABOUT NODES WITHOUT XBEES? WHAT ADDRESS DO I USE?

The table you create here uses a short character string for the address of the
XBee sensor node. What do you use if you add a sensor node that doesn't use
XBees (it connects directly to the server for storing data) or if there are sensors
connected to the data-aggregate node? In either case, you can simply create
your own unique value for each sensor. You can use the convention of the last
four digits of the XBee 64-bit address and store the hexadecimal value. You
can just as easily number your sensor nodes and sensors with values starting
from 0000 to FFFF. This leaves you plenty of values to work with. But be sure
not to use the same value as one of your XBees.

Recall that one of the challenges from the last project is to use
meaningful names for each of the sensor nodes. You can move this to the
database server as well, in the form of a lookup table. In this case, you need
a column that matches the values stored in the temperature table and
another column for storing a more meaningful name. This allows you to
add more human-friendly data while preserving the original form of the
data. Later, you see how to retrieve this information when querying data on
the server. The following statements create the new table named sensor_
names and populate it with data. You conclude with a sample SELECT
statement to retrieve the data entered:

```
CREATE TABLE `sensor_names` (
  `address` char(8) DEFAULT NULL,
  `name` char(30) DEFAULT NULL
) ENGINE=InnoDB DEFAULT CHARSET=latin1;

INSERT INTO sensor_names VALUES ('DB79', 'New Porch');
INSERT INTO sensor_names VALUES ('D45C', 'Living Room');
INSERT INTO sensor_names VALUES ('29DB', 'Office');
```

```
SELECT * FROM house.sensor_names;
+---------+-------------+
| address | name        |
+---------+-------------+
| 29a2    | New Porch   |
| 29db    | Living Room |
| cd0f    | Office      |
+---------+-------------+
3 rows in set (0.00 sec)
```

Tip   Use the addresses for your own XBee nodes in the following
INSERT statements when you use them in your project.

Now let's consider the trigger. This is how you transplant the code
to calculate the temperature in the Fahrenheit and Celsius scales to the
database server. I encourage you to examine the syntax and use of triggers
in the online MySQL reference manual (https://dev.mysql.com/doc/
refman/8.0/en/create-trigger.html). In the meantime, I show you what
statements are needed to add the trigger you need.

You need to detect when a new row is added to the table. When that
happens, you want to perform the calculations and store the results in
the appropriate columns. Thus, you need to create a trigger that operates
before a new row is inserted. When that event occurs, you can perform the
calculations. The following code shows the trigger you need to create. The
calculations should look very familiar, albeit with a different syntax. Notice
the use of the new operator, which lets you reference the values from the
incoming (new) row to either read or write:

```
DELIMITER //
CREATE TRIGGER calc_temp BEFORE INSERT ON temperature
FOR EACH ROW
```

```
BEGIN
  declare c float;
  set c = ((new.raw_temp * 1200.0 / 1024.0) - 500.0) / 10.0;
  set new.celsius = c;
  set new.fahrenheit = ((c * 9.0)/5.0) + 32.0;
END;
//
DELIMITER ;
```

The first thing you may notice is the use of the DELIMITER command. This is a special command that can be used to replace the ; character that determines the end of a statement in the mysql client. In this case, you use // instead of ;.

The DELIMITER change is needed because the body of your trigger contains SQL statements that end with a semicolon. If you had not changed the delimiter, the mysql client would detect an end of statement and attempt to execute the partially coded trigger. If you run into syntax errors when creating this trigger, check to make sure you use the DELIMITER command as shown. Notice that the last thing you do is change the delimiter back to a semicolon.

Notice also that you set up the trigger to execute before an insert and you have a loop to process each new row. Although you're issuing single INSERT statements, this syntax is required because there may be cases where more than one new row is added at a time. For example, if there are transactions involved, the changes may not be committed (permanently stored) until several rows have been processed. In this case, the trigger will fire once, and the body will be processed once for each of the new rows.

You also need to grant access to the user if you haven't already done so in Chapter 9. You do this with the CREATE USER and GRANT statements:

```
CREATE USER 'arduino_user'@'%' IDENTIFIED WITH mysql_native_
password BY 'secret';
GRANT ALL ON *.* to 'arduino_user'@'%';
```

Now that you have your MySQL database server set up and the necessary database objects created, let's put it all together and see how it runs. It is at this time that you can upload the sketch to your Arduino data-aggregate node (making sure it is plugged in to your network) and power on the sensor nodes. Wait 3–5 minutes before powering on the sensor nodes.

Testing the Project

Once your sketch is loaded, open the serial monitor and observe the statements about connecting to the MySQL database server. If all is well, you should see a success message. If you do not, check the IP address you used, and be sure to check that your MySQL server is running and is accepting connections.

When you see the connection success message, you can power on your sensor nodes. You should start seeing a message printed in the serial monitor for each sensor node. Recall from Listing 10-5 that you print an announcement of data read from an XBee (and show the address). You also display the completed INSERT statement for the sample data.

If you let the sketch run for some time and have several sensor nodes powered on and communicating, you will start to see the sketch recording samples from those sensor nodes too. Listing 10-6 shows an example of the statements printed for samples from several sensor nodes.

Listing 10-6. Output from Arduino_MySQL_Aggregate Sketch

```
Connected to network
My IP address is: 192.168.42.12
Connecting...
...trying...
Connected to server version 8.0.19
Received data from address: 13A20040A0D45C
```

Query: INSERT INTO house.temperature (address, raw_temp,
voltage) VALUES ('d45c',573.0000,3.2062) ... Ok.
Received data from address: 13A200409029DB
Query: INSERT INTO house.temperature (address, raw_temp,
voltage) VALUES ('29db',546.0000,3.1688) ... Ok.
Received data from address: 13A2004192DB79
Query: INSERT INTO house.temperature (address, raw_temp,
voltage) VALUES ('db79',622.0000,3.8109) ... Ok.
Received data from address: 13A20040A0D45C
Query: INSERT INTO house.temperature (address, raw_temp,
voltage) VALUES ('d45c',572.0000,3.2109) ... Ok.
Received data from address: 13A200409029DB
Query: INSERT INTO house.temperature (address, raw_temp,
voltage) VALUES ('29db',547.0000,3.1734) ... Ok.
Received data from address: 13A2004192DB79
Query: INSERT INTO house.temperature (address, raw_temp,
voltage) VALUES ('db79',622.0000,3.8109) ... Ok.
Received data from address: 13A20040A0D45C
Query: INSERT INTO house.temperature (address, raw_temp,
voltage) VALUES ('d45c',572.0000,3.2109) ... Ok.
Received data from address: 13A200409029DB
Query: INSERT INTO house.temperature (address, raw_temp,
voltage) VALUES ('29db',546.0000,3.1688) ... Ok.
Received data from address: 13A2004192DB79
Query: INSERT INTO house.temperature (address, raw_temp,
voltage) VALUES ('db79',623.0000,3.8109) ... Ok.
Received data from address: 13A20040A0D45C
Query: INSERT INTO house.temperature (address, raw_temp,
voltage) VALUES ('d45c',572.0000,3.2109) ... Ok.
Received data from address: 13A200409029DB

```
Query: INSERT INTO house.temperature (address, raw_temp,
voltage) VALUES ('29db',546.0000,3.1734) ... Ok.
Received data from address: 13A2004192DB79
Query: INSERT INTO house.temperature (address, raw_temp,
voltage) VALUES ('db79',622.0000,3.8098) ... Ok.
```

If you see results similar to these examples, you've solved the project!
But what about the data in the database? How do you see it? Once the
sketch has run for some time, connect to your MySQL database server,
issue the following command, and observe the results:

```
> SELECT * FROM house.temperature;
```

sample_date	address	raw_temp	voltage	fahrenheit	celsius
2020-03-22 19:30:30	d45c	573	3.2062	62.8672	17.1484
2020-03-22 19:30:45	29db	546	3.1688	57.1719	13.9844
2020-03-22 19:31:00	db79	622	3.8109	73.2031	22.8906
2020-03-22 19:31:15	d45c	572	3.2109	62.6562	17.0312
2020-03-22 19:31:30	29db	547	3.1734	57.3828	14.1016
2020-03-22 19:31:45	db79	622	3.8109	73.2031	22.8906
2020-03-22 19:32:00	d45c	572	3.2109	62.6562	17.0312
2020-03-22 19:32:15	29db	546	3.1688	57.1719	13.9844
2020-03-22 19:32:30	db79	623	3.8109	73.4141	23.0078
2020-03-22 19:32:45	d45c	572	3.2109	62.6562	17.0312
2020-03-22 19:33:00	29db	546	3.1734	57.1719	13.9844
2020-03-22 19:33:15	db79	622	3.8098	73.2031	22.8906

```
12 rows in set (0.0007 sec)
```

Notice that I had many rows to see! This is because I set my XBee modules sleep time to a very low value. In practice, you would set the sleep time for more than a few seconds. It is fine to leave it sampling frequently for this project.

Notice also that you have data populated for the sample date, Fahrenheit, and Celsius columns! This shows that the timestamp data type worked and your trigger fired on INSERT, creating the calculated values. Isn't that slick and easier than making your poor overworked Arduino crank out the values?

Now let's consider another feature of the database server. Recall from the previous project that you could easily see the last known samples for each sensor node. How can you reproduce this feature if you never store those values any place? It is unlikely you will need to have this feature, but let's explore it in case you need similar features.

The answer is that you do store those values! You store every value in a sample. The problem is you don't know which row in the table is the latest for each sensor. But the answer is still there, isn't it?

This is where savvy SQL programmers earns their pay. You can indeed get to this data by using a bit of SQL magic called grouping and the MAX() function. In this case, you want the name of the sensor (not the address) and the temperature values in Fahrenheit and Celsius—just like what you had on the web server.

To get the name, you must join (combine the rows of two tables matching on a common set of columns) the temperature and sensor_ names tables, matching on address. Recall that the values in each table will match—that is, one row in the sensor_names table will match a specific number of rows in the temperature table.

But what about the last values? To get this data, you use the MAX() function on a subquery (a query executed from within another query) to return the latest timestamp for each group of addresses. Notice the GROUP BY clause in the subquery. You can use the results in the subquery to limit the output of your SELECT to only those rows that match the latest value for each address. The following code shows the complete SELECT statement and sample results:

```
SELECT name, fahrenheit, voltage
FROM temperature join sensor_names ON
temperature.address = sensor_names.address
WHERE sample_date IN (
SELECT MAX(sample_date)
FROM temperature
GROUP BY address
);
```

```
+-------------+------------+---------+
| name        | fahrenheit | voltage |
+-------------+------------+---------+
| Living Room |    62.6562 |  3.2109 |
| Office      |    57.1719 |  3.1734 |
| New Porch   |    73.2031 |  3.8098 |
+-------------+------------+---------+
3 rows in set (0.0034 sec)
```

If you are thinking that is a very complex query, don't feel bad. SQL can be quite a challenge when you start working with databases. If you find that you need to use such queries, it would be worth purchasing a book on learning SQL to become more familiar with the power and functionality available in SQL commands.

For More Fun

There are a number of things you can do with this project. In fact, all the challenges from the previous project apply. The only thing left to do is substitute a Raspberry Pi for one of the sensor nodes and substitute a Raspberry Pi for the data-aggregate node. You do the latter in the next project, but let's consider how to do the former.

Chapter 7 explores how to create a sensor node hosted by a Raspberry Pi. Consider taking this challenge one step further and combining it with what you learned in Chapter 7 regarding using the TMP36 sensor. Add such a node to your network.

For even more fun, you can add the web server components from the previous project to the sketch. Leaving these elements in place also introduces a form of the data-aggregate node discussed in Chapter 1—a hybrid data-aggregate node. Recall that the advantage here is that if the node loses connection to the server (or the server goes down), you can at least get the latest data from the data-aggregate node.

For those that need more power: if you find you need a more industrial-grade gateway, you can check out the Digi Industrial Gateway; an open source Python environment for developing complex applications that supports ZigBee and comes in a rugged case. See www.digi.com/products/networking/gateways/xbee-industrial-gateway for more details.

Now that you have mastered data-aggregate nodes with the Arduino, let's explore building data-aggregate nodes with the Raspberry Pi.

Project: Raspberry Pi Data-Aggregate Node with Database Storage

This project uses the sensor nodes from the previous project, but rather than use an Arduino as the host for the data-aggregate node, you use a Raspberry Pi. You also use the same MySQL database server from the previous project to store sensor data from the XBee sensor nodes via the Raspberry Pi data-aggregate node.

The goals of the project are to reproduce the functionality from the last project. That is, you want the Raspberry Pi to receive sensor samples from multiple sensor nodes via an XBee module (the coordinator) and save those results in your MySQL database. However, since we are using the XBee Python library, we will have to make a few minor changes to how we calculate the temperature based on the raw data. As you will see, the changes are subtle but not difficult.

The basis for this project is the Raspberry Pi XBee project from Chapter 5. It may be good to review that text to familiarize yourself with the task. I show the wiring diagram from Chapter 5 as a refresher.

Hardware

This project requires the XBee-hosted sensor nodes from the previous projects, a Raspberry Pi, a GPIO breakout board and cable, a breadboard, an XBee adapter, and some breadboard jumpers.

The wiring is the same as in the section "Project: Creating a Raspberry Pi Data Collector for XBee Sensor Nodes" in Chapter 5. Figure 10-6 shows the breadboard and wiring from Chapter 5. Wire the XBee adapter as shown, connect the GPIO cable to your Raspberry Pi, and then power up! You don't have to install the XBee yet, but it is a good idea to do so. Remember, you need your coordinator node.

617

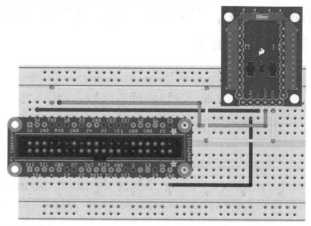

Figure 10-6. *Connecting an XBee to a Raspberry Pi*

Software

The software requirements for this project are the same as the project
from Chapter 5. That is, you're using the Connector/Python library.
Refer to Chapter 5 for information on how to download and install the
library. However, there is one other library you must install—the MySQL
Connector/Python library.

You can install the MySQL Connector/Python library on your
Raspberry Pi using the command shown in Listing 10-7, which will also
install any prerequisite libraries that may be needed.

Listing 10-7. Installing MySQL Connector/Python

```
$ pip3 install mysql-connector-python
Looking in indexes: https://pypi.org/simple, https://www.
piwheels.org/simple
Collecting mysql-connector-python
  Downloading https://files.pythonhosted.org/packages/5c/1e/3f
    372b31853b868153e453146d99ca787da3eb4bf0b654590b829b262afa/
    mysql_connector_python-8.0.19-py2.py3-none-any.whl (355kB)
```

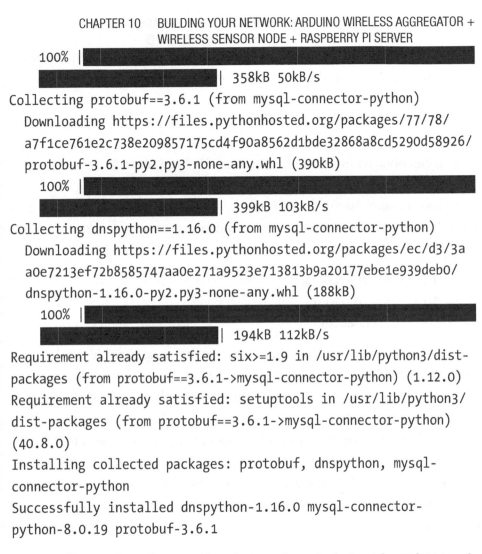

```
100% |████████████████████████████████████|
     |████████████████████|  358kB 50kB/s
Collecting protobuf==3.6.1 (from mysql-connector-python)
  Downloading https://files.pythonhosted.org/packages/77/78/
  a7f1ce761e2c738e209857175cd4f90a8562d1bde32868a8cd5290d58926/
  protobuf-3.6.1-py2.py3-none-any.whl (390kB)
    100% |████████████████████████████████████|
         |████████████████████|  399kB 103kB/s
Collecting dnspython==1.16.0 (from mysql-connector-python)
  Downloading https://files.pythonhosted.org/packages/ec/d3/3a
  a0e7213ef72b8585747aa0e271a9523e713813b9a20177ebe1e939deb0/
  dnspython-1.16.0-py2.py3-none-any.whl (188kB)
    100% |████████████████████████████████████|
         |████████████████████|  194kB 112kB/s
Requirement already satisfied: six>=1.9 in /usr/lib/python3/dist-
packages (from protobuf==3.6.1->mysql-connector-python) (1.12.0)
Requirement already satisfied: setuptools in /usr/lib/python3/
dist-packages (from protobuf==3.6.1->mysql-connector-python)
(40.8.0)
Installing collected packages: protobuf, dnspython, mysql-
connector-python
Successfully installed dnspython-1.16.0 mysql-connector-
python-8.0.19 protobuf-3.6.1
```

Recall I mentioned we need to change the calculations for Celsius and
Fahrenheit because we are using the XBee Python library to read the data.
If you recall from Chapter 5, we have to use a slightly different formula
for calculating the temperature. So, rather than using the existing trigger,
we will disable the trigger with the following command and place the
calculation in the code. This is fine since the Raspberry Pi has plenty of
power to do the calculation.

```
DROP TRIGGER house.calc_temp;
```

As you will see, we will also change the INSERT SQL command to pass the values for Celsius and Fahrenheit instead of allowing the trigger to populate those values.

Now let's start writing your Python script. If you want to copy the script from Chapter 5, you can. Simply copy it to a file named pi_xbee_mysql.py. Or you can open a new file and enter the code from scratch.

The first statements you need to enter are those for including the libraries you need. Recall from Chapter 5 that these include the serial and xbee libraries. You also add the mysql.connector library, as shown here:

```
import serial
from digi.xbee.devices import XBeeDevice
from digi.xbee.io import IOLine, IOMode
import mysql.connector
```

Next, you define some variables. You use the same variables and definitions from the project in Chapter 5 but add two new ones for your MySQL code. In this case, you need to add a variable to store the instance of a database connector class.

You also need to expand the constants to include those required to communicate with the MySQL server. You add the username, host (or IP), port, and password. These are the same values you would use to connect to the MySQL server via the mysql client. The following code shows all the constants and variables:

```
# MySQL constants
USER = 'arduino_user'         # MySQL user id
PASSWD = 'secret'             # MySQL password
HOST_OR_IP = '192.168.42.8'   # MySQL server IP address
PORT = 3306                   # MySQL port
# Query string
INSERT_SQL = ("INSERT INTO house.temperature (address,
raw_temp, voltage, celsius, fahrenheit) "
              "VALUES('{0}', {1}, {2}, {3}, {4})")
```

```python
# Serial port on Raspberry Pi
SERIAL_PORT = "/dev/ttyS0"
# BAUD rate for the XBee module connected to the Raspberry Pi
BAUD_RATE = 9600
# Analog pin we want to monitor/request data
ANALOG_LINE = IOLine.DIO3_AD3
# Sampling rate
SAMPLING_RATE = 15

# Get an instance of the XBee device class
device = XBeeDevice(SERIAL_PORT, BAUD_RATE)

# Variables for MySQL Connector/Python code
db_conn = None
```

Caution   Make sure all the constants match your XBee
configuration and specifics for accessing your MySQL database
server. If the script does not run correctly or you cannot connect to
MySQL, double-check these settings.

Rather than search the network for nodes by node id, we will search
the network once and get a list of all the nodes. While this example shows
how to do this at the start, you can use the XBee library to register a
callback to detect when new nodes are added. See the API documentation
at https://xbplib.readthedocs.io/en/latest/user_doc/discovering_
the_xbee_network.html for more details.

The following code shows how to use the XBee library to discover the
nodes on the network:

```python
def discover_nodes():
    """Get a list of the nodes (node ids) on the network
    Returns:
```

```
    """
    # Request the network class and search the network for the
      remote node
    xbee_network = device.get_network()
    xbee_network.start_discovery_process()
    print("Discovering network", end='')
    while xbee_network.is_discovery_running():
        print(".", end='')
        time.sleep(0.5)
    print("done.")
    devices = xbee_network.get_devices();
    node_ids= []
    for dev in devices:
        print("Found {0} at {1}.".format(dev.get_node_id(),
        dev.get_64bit_addr()))
        node_ids.append(dev.get_node_id())
    if not node_ids:
        print("WARNING: No nodes found.")
    return node_ids
```

Recall, we now need a method to get the XBee node in the network so we can capture the data it is reporting.

```
def get_remote_device():
    """Get the remote node from the network
    Returns:
    """
    # Request the network class and search the network for the
      remote node
    xbee_network = device.get_network()
    remote_device = xbee_network.discover_device(REMOTE_NODE_ID)
    if remote_device is None:
```

```
    print("ERROR: Remove node id {0} not found.".format
    (REMOVE_NODE_ID))
    exit(1)
remote_device.set_dest_address(device.get_64bit_addr())
remote_device.set_io_configuration(ANALOG_LINE, IOMode.ADC)
remote_device.set_io_sampling_rate(SAMPLING_RATE)
```

Next, we need a callback method to execute when the data is ready. In this case, we will form the INSERT query for the data in the same method and call the save_sample() method to execute it.

```
def io_sample_callback(sample, remote, time):
    address = str(remote.get_64bit_addr())
    # Get the raw temperature value
    raw_temp = sample.get_analog_value(ANALOG_LINE)
    # Calculate supply voltage
    volts = (sample.power_supply_value * (1200.0 / 1024.0)) /
    1000.0
    # Save results in the table
    short_addr = address[-4:]
    print("Reading from {0}: {1}, {2}.".format(short_addr,
    raw_temp, volts))
    # Get the temperature in Celsius
    temp_c = (sample.get_analog_value(ANALOG_LINE) / 1023.0 *
    1.25 - 0.5) * 100.0
    # Calculate temperature in Fahrenheit
    temp_f = ((temp_c * 9.0) / 5.0) + 32.0
    print("\tTemperature is {0:.2f}C. {1:.2f}F".format
    (temp_c, temp_f))
    query = (INSERT_SQL.format(short_addr, raw_temp, volts,
    temp_c, temp_f))
    save_sample(db_conn, query)
```

623

To use the save_sample() method, we pass it the database connection instance and a query string. The method creates a cursor, executes the query, and then checks for a result. If results are available, it returns them to the caller. The complete method is as follows:

```python
def save_sample(conn, query_str):
    results = None
    cur = conn.cursor(
        cursor_class=mysql.connector.cursor.
        MySQLCursorBufferedRaw)
    try:
        res = cur.execute(query_str)
    except mysql.connector.Error as e:
        cur.close()
        raise Exception("Query failed. " + e.__str__())
    try:
        results = cur.fetchall()
    except mysql.connector.errors.InterfaceError as e:
        if e.msg.lower() == "no result set to fetch from.":
            pass # This error means there were no results.
        else:    # otherwise, re-raise error
            raise e
    conn.commit()
    cur.close()
    return results
```

Now you get to the meat of the script using the same form as the project from Chapter 5 (one while infinity loop[9] with a break exception). But first, you connect to the database server (remember, function

---

[9]It is called an infinity loop because the test condition is always true. In this case, unless you kill the script or press *Ctrl+C*, it will continue to run as long as the hardware remains powered on and working.

declarations are not executed when encountered—only when called). You
create a dictionary of values, setting them to the constants shown earlier.
This is a technique you can use in any Python script to avoid passing a
large set of parameters. The following code attempts to connect to the
MySQL server and, if successful, returns an instance of the database
connector class:

```
# Connect to database server
try:
    parameters = {
        'user': USER,
        'host': HOST_OR_IP,
        'port': PORT,
        'passwd': PASSWD,
        }
    print("Connecting to MySQL...", end='')
    db_conn = mysql.connector.connect(**parameters)
    print("done.")
except mysql.connector.Error as e:
    raise Exception("ERROR: Cannot connect to MySQL Server!")
    exit(1)
```

If the connection fails, you throw an exception. If this happens, be sure
to check your constants for the correct values, and try connecting to the
MySQL server using the mysql client application using the same parameters.
Once you can connect successfully via the mysql client, try the script again.

The next portion is the while infinity loop, which is also taken from the
example in Chapter 5:

```
try:
    # Read and save temperature data
    print("Welcome to example of storing data from a set of
    remote TMP36 sensors in MySQL!")
```

```
    device.open()  # Open the device class
    # Get the nodes on the network
    remote_node_ids = discover_nodes()
    # Setup the remote device
    for remote_id in remote_node_ids:
        get_remote_device(remote_id)
    # Register a listener to handle the samples received by the
      local device
    device.add_io_sample_received_callback(io_sample_callback)
    while True:
        pass
except KeyboardInterrupt:
    if device is not None and device.is_open():
        device.close()
```

Once the while infinity loop is terminated, you must disconnect from
the server. The following code does that. In this case, you ignore any
errors—you are disconnecting, and you don't care if you fail because the
script will stop:

```
# Disconnect from the server
try:
    db_conn.disconnect()
except:
    pass
```

If you are thinking this isn't a lot of code, you are correct. The
Connector/Python library makes working with MySQL in Python very
easy. Listing 10-8 shows the complete code for this project. Take some
time to make sure everything is entered correctly before you attempt to
run the script.

Listing 10-8. Raspberry Pi Remote-Storage Data Aggregator

```
#
# Beginning Sensor Networks Second Edition
# RasPi XBee Remote Storage Data Aggregator
#
# For this script, we read data from an XBee coordinator
# node whenever data is received from an XBee sensor node.
# We also need a connection to a database server for saving
# the results in a table.
#
# The data read is from one sample (temperature from a
# XBee sensor node and the supply voltage at the source) for
# each device on the network by node id.
#
import serial
import time
from digi.xbee.devices import XBeeDevice
from digi.xbee.io import IOLine, IOMode
import mysql.connector

# MySQL constants
USER = 'arduino_user'       # MySQL user id
PASSWD = 'secret'           # MySQL password
HOST_OR_IP = '192.168.42.8' # MySQL server IP address
PORT = 3306                 # MySQL port
# Query string
INSERT_SQL = ("INSERT INTO house.temperature (address,
raw_temp, voltage, celsius, fahrenheit) "
              "VALUES('{0}', {1}, {2}, {3}, {4})")

# Serial port on Raspberry Pi
SERIAL_PORT = "/dev/ttyS0"
```

```python
# BAUD rate for the XBee module connected to the Raspberry Pi
  BAUD_RATE = 9600
# Analog pin we want to monitor/request data
ANALOG_LINE = IOLine.DIO3_AD3
# Sampling rate
SAMPLING_RATE = 15

# Get an instance of the XBee device class
device = XBeeDevice(SERIAL_PORT, BAUD_RATE)

# Variables for MySQL Connector/Python code
db_conn = None

# Save the sample in the database
def save_sample(conn, query_str):
    results = None
    cur = conn.cursor(
        cursor_class=mysql.connector.cursor.
        MySQLCursorBufferedRaw)
    try:
        res = cur.execute(query_str)
    except mysql.connector.Error as e:
        cur.close()
        raise Exception("Query failed. " + e.__str__())
    try:
        results = cur.fetchall()
    except mysql.connector.errors.InterfaceError as e:
        if e.msg.lower() == "no result set to fetch from.":
            pass # This error means there were no results.
        else:    # otherwise, re-raise error
            raise e
    conn.commit()
    cur.close()
    return results
```

```python
# Method to connect to the network and discover the nodes
def discover_nodes():
    """Get a list of the nodes (node ids) on the network
    Returns:
    """
    # Request the network class and search the network for the
      remote node
    xbee_network = device.get_network()
    xbee_network.start_discovery_process()
    print("Discovering network", end='')
    while xbee_network.is_discovery_running():
        print(".", end='')
        time.sleep(0.5)
    print("done.")
    devices = xbee_network.get_devices();
    node_ids= []
    for dev in devices:
        print("Found {0} at {1}.".format(dev.get_node_id(),
        dev.get_64bit_addr()))
        node_ids.append(dev.get_node_id())
    if not node_ids:
        print("WARNING: No nodes found.")
    return node_ids

# Method to connect to the network and get the remote node by id
def get_remote_device(remote_id):
    """Get the remote node from the network
    Returns:
    """
    # Request the network class and search the network for the
      remote node
    xbee_network = device.get_network()
```

```python
    remote_device = xbee_network.discover_device(remote_id)
    if remote_device is None:
        print("ERROR: Remote node id {0} not found."
        .format(remote_id))
        exit(1)
    remote_device.set_dest_address(device.get_64bit_addr())
    remote_device.set_io_configuration(ANALOG_LINE, IOMode.ADC)
    remote_device.set_io_sampling_rate(SAMPLING_RATE)

# Method to get the data when available from the remote node
def io_sample_callback(sample, remote, time):
    address = str(remote.get_64bit_addr())
    # Get the raw temperature value
    raw_temp = sample.get_analog_value(ANALOG_LINE)
    # Calculate supply voltage
    volts = (sample.power_supply_value * (1200.0 / 1024.0)) /
    1000.0
    # Save results in the table
    short_addr = address[-4:]
    print("Reading from {0}: {1}, {2}.".format(short_addr,
    raw_temp, volts))
    # Get the temperature in Celsius
    temp_c = (sample.get_analog_value(ANALOG_LINE) / 1023.0 *
    1.25 - 0.5) * 100.0
    # Calculate temperature in Fahrenheit
    temp_f = ((temp_c * 9.0) / 5.0) + 32.0
    print("\tTemperature is {0:.2f}C. {1:.2f}F".format
    (temp_c, temp_f))
    query = (INSERT_SQL.format(short_addr, raw_temp, volts,
    temp_c, temp_f))
    save_sample(db_conn, query)
```

```python
# Connect to database server
try:
    parameters = {
        'user': USER,
        'host': HOST_OR_IP,
        'port': PORT,
        'passwd': PASSWD,
        }
    print("Connecting to MySQL...", end='')
    db_conn = mysql.connector.connect(**parameters)
    print("done.")
except mysql.connector.Error as e:
    raise Exception("ERROR: Cannot connect to MySQL Server!")
    exit(1)

try:
    # Read and save temperature data
    print("Welcome to example of storing data from a set of
    remote TMP36 sensors in MySQL!")

    device.open()  # Open the device class
    # Get the nodes on the network
    remote_node_ids = discover_nodes()
    # Setup the remote device
    for remote_id in remote_node_ids:
        get_remote_device(remote_id)
    # Register a listener to handle the samples received by the
      local device
    device.add_io_sample_received_callback(io_sample_callback)
    while True:
        pass
```

```
except KeyboardInterrupt:
    if device is not None and device.is_open():
        device.close()

# Disconnect from the server
try:
    db_conn.disconnect()
except:
    pass
```

Testing the Project

To test the project, make sure your XBee coordinator node is installed
in the XBee adapter. Wait a few moments before you turn on your XBee
sensor nodes. Once all nodes are powered on, you're ready to go. Issue the
following command to launch the script:

```
$ python ./pi_xbee_mysql.py
```

If you see syntax errors or exceptions, be sure to fix them and rerun the
command. You know it is working (or at least doesn't have any errors) if
the script starts and nothing happens. Recall that the code is waiting for a
packet (sample) to be received from the XBee sensor nodes. When the nodes
start to send data, you see output similar to what is shown in Listing 10-9.
Remember, you can stop your script at any time by pressing *Ctrl+C*.

Listing 10-9. Example Output for pi_xbee_mysql.py

```
Connecting to MySQL...done.
Welcome to example of storing data from a set of remote TMP36
sensors in MySQL!
Discovering network............done.
Found TMP36_2 at 0013A20040A0D45C.
Found TMP36_1 at 0013A2004192DB79.
Found TMP36_3 at 0013A200409029DB.
```

```
Reading from D45C: 543, 3.15.
    Temperature is 16.35C. 61.43F
Reading from DB79: 539, 3.82734375.
    Temperature is 15.86C. 60.55F
Reading from 29DB: 523, 3.0796875.
    Temperature is 13.91C. 57.03F
Reading from D45C: 544, 3.15.
    Temperature is 16.47C. 61.65F
Reading from DB79: 539, 3.82734375.
    Temperature is 15.86C. 60.55F
Reading from 29DB: 523, 3.0796875.
    Temperature is 13.91C. 57.03F
Reading from D45C: 544, 3.15.
    Temperature is 16.47C. 61.65F
Reading from DB79: 540, 3.82734375.
    Temperature is 15.98C. 60.77F
Reading from 29DB: 523, 3.084375.
    Temperature is 13.91C. 57.03F
```

To check to see if your samples were saved in the database, connect to
the server and execute the following query:

```
> SELECT * FROM house.temperature;
+-------------+------+--------+--------+-----------+-----------+
| sample_date | address | raw_temp | voltage | fahrenheit | celsius |
+-------------+------+--------+--------+-----------+-----------+
| 2020-03-23 14:41:24 | D45C | 543 | 3.15    | 61.4282 | 16.349  |
| 2020-03-23 14:41:31 | DB79 |539 | 3.82734 | 60.5484 | 15.8602 |
| 2020-03-23 14:41:34 | 29DB | 523 | 3.07969 | 57.0293 | 13.9052 |
| 2020-03-23 14:41:39 | D45C | 544 | 3.15    | 61.6481 | 16.4712 |
| 2020-03-23 14:41:46 | DB79 | 539 | 3.82734 | 60.5484 | 15.8602 |
```

```
| 2020-03-23 14:41:49 | 29DB | 523 | 3.07969 | 57.0293 | 13.9052 |
| 2020-03-23 14:41:54 | D45C | 544 | 3.15    | 61.6481 | 16.4712 |
| 2020-03-23 14:42:02 | DB79 | 540 | 3.82734 | 60.7683 | 15.9824 |
| 2020-03-23 14:42:04 | 29DB | 523 | 3.08437 | 57.0293 | 13.9052 |
| 2020-03-23 14:42:09 | D45C | 544 | 3.15    | 61.6481 | 16.4712 |
| 2020-03-23 14:42:17 | DB79 | 539 | 3.825   | 60.5484 | 15.8602 |
| 2020-03-23 14:42:18 | 29DB | 523 | 3.07969 | 57.0293 | 13.9052 |
+---------------+-------+------+------+-------+------+
```

You should see a number of rows in the result set and be able to match the rows to the output from your script. Once you've verified it is working, congratulate yourself: you have now mastered building remote-storage data-aggregate nodes using both an Arduino and a Raspberry Pi!

Furthermore, you have demonstrated how versatile the XBee modules are by using the same XBee sensor nodes in each project. Take some time and experiment with the script and the data that is being stored in the database.

For More Fun

That was a lot of fun, wasn't it? You may be wondering what more you could do with such a solid bit of Python code. Well, there are some cool things you can do.

The biggest challenge I can suggest is taking this script and rewriting it slightly to get the data from a TMP36 sensor via an ADC module. In other words, change the Raspberry Pi data-aggregate node into a sensor node that stores its data directly into the database.

Aside from that, you may want to experiment with changing the script into a daemon so that you can run it in the background and still use your Raspberry Pi for other things.

Component Shopping List

There are no required components needed for the projects in this chapter.
Table 10-3 shows a list of the optional components that you may need to
complete the projects. The remaining components, such as XBee modules
and supporting hardware, are included in the shopping lists from other
chapters; these are shown in Table 10-4.

Table 10-3. *Components Needed*

Item	Vendors	Est. Cost USD	Qty Needed
Stackable header kit	www.sparkfun.com/ products/11417 www.adafruit.com/ products/85	$1.50–1.95	1*

*Optional and may not be needed.

Table 10-4. *Components Reused from Previous Chapters*

Item	Vendors	Est. Cost USD	Qty Needed
Arduino (any that support shields)	Various	$25.00 and up	1 for each node
XBee shield	www.sparkfun.com/ products/12847	$24.95	1
TMP36 sensor	www.sparkfun.com/ products/10988 www.adafruit.com/ products/165	$1.50	1 for each sensor node

(continued)

Table 10-4. (*continued*)

Item	Vendors	Est. Cost USD	Qty Needed
0.10uF capacitor	www.sparkfun.com/ products/8375	$0.25	1 for each sensor node
Breadboard (not mini)	www.sparkfun.com/ products/9567	$5.95	1 for each sensor node + 1 for Raspberry Pi
Breadboard jumper wires	www.sparkfun.com/ products/8431	$3.95	1
XBee-ZB (ZB) Series 2 or 2.5	www.sparkfun.com www.adafruit.com	$25.00	2–4 (1 for each node)
Raspberry Pi Model 3B+ or 4B 2GB or 4GB	Most online stores	$35.00 and up	2
HDMI or HDMI to DVI cable	Most online and retail stores	Varies	1
HDMI or DVI monitor	Most online and retail stores	Varies	1
USB keyboard	Most online and retail stores	Varies	1
USB power supply	Most online and retail stores	Varies	1
USB type A to micro-USB male	Most online and retail stores	Varies	1

(*continued*)

Table 10-4. (*continued*)

Item	Vendors	Est. Cost USD	Qty Needed
SD Card 2GB or more	Most online and retail stores	Varies	1
Surplus hard drive	Any USB hard drive (surplus or purchased)	Varies	1
Raspberry Pi Cobbler+	`www.adafruit.com/ product/2029`	$7.95	1
Wall adapter 9V (optional)	`www.sparkfun.com/ products/ 15314`	$5.95	1 for each node**
9V Battery Holder (optional)	`www.sparkfun.com/ products/10512` `www.adafruit.com/ products/67`	$2.95–3.95	1 for each node**
XBee Explorer Regulated with headers[10]	`www.sparkfun.com/ products/11373`	$10.95	1 for each sensor node + 1 for the Raspberry Pi

**You can mix and match these, provided you have enough to power all nodes.*

---

[10]You have used some in previous chapters, but you may need a few more
depending on how many sensor nodes you decide to add.

Summary

In this chapter, you explored how to build data-aggregate nodes and connect sensor nodes to them for building wireless sensor networks. You learned how to use local storage to store and display sensor data from sensors connected via a ZigBee (XBee) network, and you also discovered how to use the Raspberry Pi as a database server for storing and retrieving sensor data. You even explored how to build data-aggregate nodes with both an Arduino and a Raspberry Pi.

In the next chapter, I present considerations about planning sensor networks as well as more advanced sensor network topics. I discuss how to handle sensor data from multiple sensors, and you learn more about how to use the MySQL database to generate reports and views of the data for analysis.

CHAPTER 11

Putting It All Together

Now that you have learned the basic building blocks for constructing a wireless sensor network with the Arduino and Raspberry Pi, you can turn your attention to some of the more intricate details of designing and implementing sensor networks. This chapter explores considerations for planning sensor networks, discusses some advanced sensor network topics, and offers tips for designing databases.

Sensor Networks Best Practices

Let's begin with a discussion of some best practices[1] you can employ to make your sensor network projects more successful. In this section, I discuss practices for planning data-aggregate nodes, designing databases, and a number of tips and techniques for building sensor networks.

Considerations for Data-Aggregate Nodes

This section examines some important considerations for planning data-aggregate nodes. I discuss placement of the nodes in the network as well as design considerations for data storage.

---

[1] A cursory examination of professional and scholarly articles suggests there isn't a standard yet. However, I include some of the more commonly repeated practices as well as a few of my own.

© Charles Bell 2020
C. Bell, *Beginning Sensor Networks with XBee, Raspberry Pi, and Arduino*,
https://doi.org/10.1007/978-1-4842-5796-8_11

Network Type and Node Placement

An important consideration is the type of network connection available for the data-aggregate node. This may be dictated by the node's use or physical placement.

If you plan to have a data-aggregate node that you want to have access to via your computer, you must consider placing that node where you can connect it to your Ethernet network. This may be via a wireless Ethernet (WiFi) connection or via a cabled connection.

On the other hand, if your data-aggregate node communicates with sensor nodes via XBee modules, the range of the modules may dictate where you place your data-aggregate node. For example, if your sensor nodes are located in outbuildings or in or near ponds that are some distance from a building with a network connection or even too far away for WiFi, you may not be able to connect to the node with your computer and therefore will have to periodically physically visit the node to retrieve the data.

That doesn't mean you have to jump on your ATV or golf cart to run down to the old chicken house to get your data every night! In fact, there are alternatives you can and should consider. First, you can use intermediate XBee router nodes placed in series until you reach a location with a network connection where your data-aggregate node can be placed.

How does this work? It is one of the advantages of the ZigBee protocols—to create networks on the fly and relay information from one router to another to extend the maximum range. It comes as a consequence of using the API mode, but you can also control this easily with the AT mode and send your data to a specific router, which then sends the data to another (and another) until you reach your data-aggregate node.

Another possibility is to use a directional WiFi connection that focuses the WiFi signal using a line-of-sight, point-to-point connection. You don't have to spend a fortune to do it! In fact, if you or someone you know likes

Pringles, you can use a Pringles can to create a directional WiFi antenna (www.makeuseof.com/tag/how-to-make-a-wifi-antenna-out-of-a-pringles-can-nb/).

A more extreme solution involves using a cellular modem on the data-aggregate node to send data to another node via the Internet. Most cellular carriers frown on setting up web or database servers accessible from the Internet (some forbid it). Thus, you are limited to sending data from the data-aggregate node out of your home network to a web or database server. This option can incur recurring costs for the connection (you need a SIM card and a data plan from your carrier of choice).

Note   Although there is no pluggable cellular solution for the Raspberry Pi, you can use a cellular module with it. Doing so requires more work and perhaps building more complex software but should be possible.

For example, if you choose to use an Arduino for your data-aggregate node, you can use the LTE CAT M1/NB-IoT Shield—SARA-R4 shield from SparkFun (www.sparkfun.com/products/14997) along with a SIM card to connect your node to the Internet.[2] Figure 11-1 shows the shield. A sample sketch is on the SparkFun product page for using the modem. If you dial up modem AT commands,[3] you will recognize many of the commands shown in the online documentation.

---

[2]There is even an XBee3 cellular modem for that that wants to make a cellular gateway node. See www.digi.com/products/embedded-systems/digi-xbee/cellular-modems/xbee3-cellular-lte-m-nb-iot for more details.

[3]Ah, those were the days, eh? ATDT... screech, squawk, bleep, boop, brrrr, bleep, ding, ding, ding!

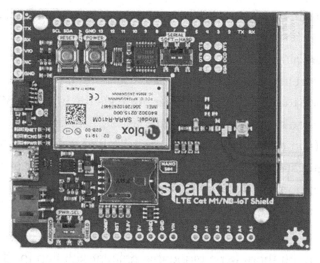

Figure 11-1. *LTE CAT M1/NB-IoT Shield (courtesy of SparkFun)*

If you find that none of these solutions will work because your sensor nodes and data-aggregate nodes are just too far away for any practical (and affordable) networking alternative, you may have to consider leaving those data-aggregate nodes as local storage nodes and collecting the data periodically to use in your analysis.

Storing Data

One major consideration for designing a data-aggregate node is the type of data it will store: that is, what sensors the node will support. It is typically better to use a data-aggregate node to store data for the same sensors or sensor nodes that generate the same type of data.

For example, if you are collecting temperature data from several locations as well as water levels from several ponds, the data produced by these two events differs. Temperature is normally a floating-point value; water level is most often a Boolean value (1 = water level ok, 0 = water level low), which corresponds to the most common form of measuring water level: a float and switch.[4]

Clearly, storing these two sets of sensor data together would require more work because you would be mixing different data types. This might require choices such as storing the data in different files or even in different databases. Furthermore, consuming the data and detecting what the data represents (the type of sensor) would require more logic, because you would need some way to detect what sensor node went with what data type.

Although the problem of storing water level and temperature may be easy to code around, consider storing samples from two sensors that produce the same data type but are interpreted differently. Recall the examples of reading barometric pressure. It too is represented as a floating-point number. For example, how would you know which sensor generated a value of 65.71929—the barometric or temperature sensor? It may be possible to write code specific to the sensor itself, but what if the sensor data is being relayed to another node? How then would you know how to interpret the data?

One solution to this problem is to use a different data-aggregate node for each group of like sensor nodes. In the example of using temperature and water-level sensor nodes, you would have one data aggregator for the temperature sensor nodes and another for the water-level sensors.

Another possibility for local storage on data-aggregate nodes is to store a special field that indicates from what sensor the data was read. You could include additional information as you saw in some of the example projects, such as date and time and a text string that represents a name you have given to the sensor. Listing 11-1 shows an example of a file format that employs a similar scheme. The first row is provided for documentation purposes and is not normally included in the file (but savvy programmers normally do include such things for documentation purposes).

---

[4]There are more sophisticated sensors that can sense water level over a range and provide a means to calculate water volume. These sensors typically produce either an integer or a float representing the water level.

Listing 11-1. Storing Additional Data with the Sample

```
# sensor_number, datetime, value, comment
3, 2020-02-09 14:25:21, 1, Water level Ok pond 1
1, 2020-02-09 14:30:01, 65.90013, Water temp pond 1
3, 2020-02-09 14:37:04, 1, Water level Ok pond 2
2, 2020-02-09 14:38:31, 65.81723, Water temp pond 2
1, 2020-02-09 14:45:23, 66.00123, Water temp pond 1
3, 2020-02-09 14:45:36, 0, Water level LOW! pond 2
3, 2020-02-09 14:54:17, 1, Water level Ok pond 1
2, 2020-02-09 14:59:54, 66.00011, Water temp pond 2
3, 2020-02-09 15:08:41, 1, Water level Ok pond 1
1, 2020-02-09 15:10:22, 65.99913, Water temp pond 1
```

Notice in the listing that the data is formatted as a comma-separated-value (CSV) file. This is an implementation choice (you could have chosen to use tabs, semicolons, and so on) that makes reading the file easier on a computer. If you use Python, you can read the file using only a few library calls.

If you examine the data, you see that you have to know something about the sensor number to be able to interpret the data. If the sensor number is 1 or 2, you know it is temperature; but if it is 3 or 4, it is water level. Again, this may not be that big of an issue, but if you have a data-aggregate node receiving samples from dozens of sensors (or worse, from sensors that have been added to the network after the code was written for the data-aggregate node), you could end up with unknown values in the sensor number—that is, values you don't know how to interpret because you don't know what kind of sensor generated them. You can solve this by having a separate data-aggregate node for each type of sample (sensor).

Notice also how the data is arranged. Do you see anything that suggests conformity? If you have knowledge and experience with databases, no doubt you have already realized this, but consider for a moment what a table in a database is made of: rows and columns, where the columns are the fields and the rows are data. In this case, you can define two tables, each with four columns. The water temperature data could be in one table, because its value is an integer (or Boolean, perhaps), and the water temperature data is a floating-point number.

Clearly, storing this data in a database makes sense. That's what databases are for—storing logically related groups of data for a single row (in this case, an event or a sample). With that in mind, let's look at considerations for using databases to store sensor data.

Considerations for Sensor Network Databases

In-depth, full coverage of the topic of database design is well beyond the scope of this book. Indeed, entire tomes and even several sets of volumes have been written about database design. Rather than go into all the theory and then relate that to practice, let's look at the subject from a slightly different angle: how you can best design your databases for easy storage and retrieval.

Note   I assume no prior knowledge of database design. If you have database design experience, you may want to skim this section.

As you saw in Chapter 8, you use the MySQL database system as the database server. Not only is it open source (it is free, as in free beer), but it is also the most popular choice for developers because it offers large database system features in a lightweight form that can run on just about any consumer computer hardware. MySQL is also very easy to use, and its popularity has given rise to many online and printed resources for learning and using the system. Despite this, the following examples and suggestions can be used with any relational database server (but may require slight changes to syntax for some).

How Data Is Organized

Let's begin by discussing how data is grouped in a database server. As you know, the server permits you to create any number of databases for storing data. Typically, you want to create a separate database for each of your sensor networks. This makes working with the data a logical whole so that data for one sensor network isn't intermixed with data from another.

The database itself is a container for a number of objects. You have seen examples of tables and even a trigger in Chapter 8. Here, you focus on the table. The table is a container that is designed specifically to hold instances of data described (or categorized) by its layout (the number of columns and their data types). For example, for the data shown in Listing 11-1, you can generate a table for the temperature sensors as follows:

```
CREATE TABLE `pond_monitor`.`pond_water_temp` (
  `sensor_number` int DEFAULT NULL,
  `sample_collected_on` timestamp DEFAULT CURRENT_TIMESTAMP,
  `temperature` float DEFAULT NULL
) ENGINE=InnoDB DEFAULT CHARSET=latin1;
```

Notice the `sample_collected_on` field. You define this as timestamp, which MySQL will fill in with the date and time when a row is inserted in the table. Unless you need absolute accuracy, setting this value shortly after the sample is collected will suffice to record the date and time at which the sample was taken.

As mentioned previously, the example in Listing 11-1 has data that is interleaved. You want to separate that data, and thus you generate a table to store the other samples as follows:

```
CREATE TABLE `pond_monitor`.`pond_water_level` (
  `sensor_number` int DEFAULT NULL,
  `sample_collected_on` timestamp DEFAULT CURRENT_TIMESTAMP,
  `water_level` tinyint DEFAULT '1'
) ENGINE=InnoDB DEFAULT CHARSET=latin1;
```

You may be wondering what happened to the comments. The comments field (column) is not really needed. Recall the discussion about storing a human-friendly name in Chapter 8. Here, you create a lookup table to store that data. For example, the lookup table allows you to equate a sensor number of 3 to a friendly name of Water Level Pond 1:

```
CREATE TABLE `pond_monitor`.`sensor_names` (
  `sensor_number` int(11) DEFAULT NULL,
  `sensor_name` char(64) DEFAULT NULL
) ENGINE=InnoDB DEFAULT CHARSET=latin1;
```

So, what have you done here? First, you designed two tables to store data from two different types of sensors (as defined by what data types are collected), and you added a lookup table to help eliminate duplicate data (storing Water Temp Pond 1 over and over again wastes space).

But what does this mean for the data-aggregate node? If you consider Listing 11-1 again, you see that the node has to write the sensor number, calculate and write the timestamp (perhaps from an onboard RTC or RTC module), write the value from the sensor, and (based on a lookup code) store a string for the comment (to make it easier for a human to read).

However, if you implement the previous tables, the data-aggregate node need only send the sensor number and the sample value to the database server. Sound familiar? That is exactly what you did in the project in Chapter 10.

Table Design Notes

Let's return to designing tables. When you design your tables, you should keep a few things in mind. First, consider what data types are needed for storing your samples. You should consider not only how many values each sample contains but also their format (data type). The basic data types available include integer, float, double, character, and Boolean. There are many others, including several for dates and times as well as binary large objects (blobs) for storing large blocks of data (like images), large texts (the same as blobs, but not interpreted as binary), and much more. See the online MySQL reference manual for a complete list and discussion of all data types (`https://dev.mysql.com/doc/refman/8.0/en/data-types.html`).

You can also consider adding additional columns such as a timestamp field, the address of the sensor node, perhaps a reference voltage, and so on. Write all of these down, and consider the data type for each.

Once you have decided on your table columns, the next thing you should consider is whether to allow duplicates in the table—that is, two or more rows that contain the same data. To avoid this, you can define a primary key (a special index) by specifying one or more columns as the key. You want to choose a column (or columns) that ensures that no two rows will have the same data for that column(s).

For example, if you choose `sensor_number` from the previous example as a primary key, you most certainly have a problem. Indeed, the database server will complain the instant you try to save a second value for each sensor. Why? Because to become the primary key, the `sensor_number` column must contain a unique value for every row in the table!

But the layout of the tables does not contain any column that is guaranteed to be unique. You may be thinking the timestamp field can be unique, but although that may be true, you typically do not use timestamp fields for the primary key. So, what do you do in this case?

You can use an automatically generated column as the primary key. It is called an auto-increment field property in MySQL. You can add this to any table, as shown here using the ALTER TABLE command:

```
ALTER TABLE `pond_monitor`.`pond_water_temp`
    ADD COLUMN id INT AUTO_INCREMENT PRIMARY KEY FIRST;
```

Here you add a new column named `id` that is an auto-incrementing field and is the primary key. You add the first modifier because primary key columns should be the first column in a table (not that order matters normally, but here it does).

You can do the same for both tables. Once this is done, when a new row is inserted, you specify NULL as you do for the timestamp field, and MySQL fills in the data for you. Listing 11-2 shows this principle at work.

Listing 11-2. Auto-Increment Fields

```
> INSERT INTO `pond_monitor`.`pond_water_temp` (sensor_number,
temperature) VALUES (3, 72.56);
Query OK, 1 row affected (0.00 sec)

> SELECT * FROM `pond_monitor`.`pond_water_temp`;
+----+---------------+---------------------+-------------+
| id | sensor_number | sample_collected_on | temperature |
+----+---------------+---------------------+-------------+
| 1  |             3 | 2020-02-10 11:39:51 |       72.56 |
+----+---------------+---------------------+-------------+
1 row in set (0.0004 sec)

> INSERT INTO `pond_monitor`.`pond_water_temp` (sensor_number,
temperature) VALUES (3, 82.01);
Query OK, 1 row affected (0.00 sec)

> SELECT * FROM `pond_monitor`.`pond_water_temp`;
+----+---------------+---------------------+-------------+
| id | sensor_number | sample_collected_on | temperature |
+----+---------------+---------------------+-------------+
| 1  |             3 | 2020-02-10 11:39:51 |       72.56 |
| 2  |             3 | 2020-02-10 11:40:53 |       82.01 |
+----+---------------+---------------------+-------------+
2 rows in set (0.0005 sec)
```

DOES THAT REALLY DO ANYTHING?

You may be thinking that this new field adds an artificial primary key to the table and doesn't really do anything. For the most part, you are correct.

This example is for illustration purposes and therefore teaches the concept of using a primary key as a practice you should consider whenever you design a table. The fact that the auto-increment key isn't used to reference another table or that it relates to the rows themselves is overlooked for the sake of practice.

Let's return to the lookup table. Although this table is unlikely to have many rows (it depends on the number of sensors), it is also true that one row in this table matches one and only one sensor. So, you can use the sensor_number column here as a primary key. I leave the ALTER TABLE statement for you to consider.

Note   Database designers sometimes forego the use of primary keys on tables with only a few rows, citing the additional overhead needed to maintain indexes and so on. The truth is it matters little either way because lookup tables are seldom modified (changed or data added) and if used frequently can result in the table being cached in its entirety. That being said, it does no harm to add a primary key.

Adding Indexes for Query Efficiency

A primary key is a special type of index. It is an index, but when used with auto-increment fields, it is a nice way of identifying a given row and allowing duplicate rows (among the other columns). However, there is another aspect of indexes that can make your data access much easier (and possibly faster).

Consider for the moment a table with many thousands of rows.[5] Suppose you want to see all the sensor samples for sensor number 2. How does the database server find all of these rows using the tables you defined earlier? You issue the following query, but what happens inside the server?

```
SELECT * FROM `pond_monitor`.`pond_water_temp` WHERE
sensor_number = 2;
```

Because the table has an index (the primary key on the column id that you added), it uses this to systematically read each and every row in order, choosing (returning) those rows that match the WHERE clause (in this case, sensor_number = 2). This is bad because the server does not know if these rows appear in the first N rows or even if sensor_number = 2 is in the last row in the table. Thus, it must read each and every row. This is called a table scan and is best avoided when working with tables with a lot of rows.

How do you do that? By adding another index called a secondary index! If you have an index on the sensor_number column, the server can use that index to examine each of the rows in a different order. It will look through the table starting with sensor_number 1 and then 2 and so on. It knows to stop after reading the last row whose sensor_number is 2. In fact, MySQL has some extra trickery included that permits the server (the part called the optimizer) to further expedite the query and skip to the first row with sensor_number = 2. Here is how you do it. You use the CREATE INDEX command:

```
CREATE INDEX s_num ON `pond_monitor`.`pond_water_temp`
(sensor_number);
```

The CREATE INDEX command allows you to name the index (s_num) and specify the table (ON pond_water_temp) and the column(s) you want to index in parentheses, (sensor_number). You can see a complete syntax explanation for this and all other commands supported by MySQL in the online MySQL reference manual.

---

[5]It may take several hundreds of thousands of rows for you to see this in action.

Now when you issue the earlier SELECT, the server uses the new index to read the rows in a different order. Note that the rows are not reordered on disk; rather, the index creates an alternate map or access method to find the rows in a specific order.

You may be thinking, "But wait: can't I do all of these table design steps in one go?" The answer is yes, you can! Let's look at the pond_water_temp table as a single CREATE statement:

```
CREATE TABLE `pond_monitor`.`pond_water_temp` (
  `id` int NOT NULL AUTO_INCREMENT,
  `sensor_number` int DEFAULT NULL,
  `sample_collected_on` timestamp NULL DEFAULT CURRENT_
  TIMESTAMP,
  `temperature` float DEFAULT NULL,
  PRIMARY KEY (`id`),
  KEY `s_num` (`sensor_number`)
) ENGINE=InnoDB AUTO_INCREMENT=3 DEFAULT CHARSET=latin1;
```

Notice that the auto-increment column is defined first, then your sensor number, the timestamp for when the sample was collected, the value (temperature), and the primary key and secondary index definitions. This statement replaces the three you just used—CREATE TABLE, ALTER TABLE, and CREATE INDEX. Cool, eh?

As you can see, creating tables in MySQL is easy once you understand the syntax (and know what you want to do). You can find all the syntax and many examples of each in the online MySQL reference manual (https://dev.mysql.com/doc/refman/8.0/en/sql-statements.html).

Once again, there is far more to consider for designing tables, but these at least are the things you need to know to make the most of your database system and to store and retrieve your data effectively.

Other Considerations

This section explores some additional best practices that can be helpful in making your work with sensor networks more enjoyable.

Stay Within Range of XBee Modules

XBee modules have an impressive range that belies their diminutive size. The specifications for the XBee series 2 modules you use in this book are

- *Indoor/urban*: Up to 133 feet

- *Outdoor line of sight*: Up to 400 feet

However, these maximums are very much influenced by interference from devices on similar frequencies and the composition of the building you are in.[6] For example, suppose your house is very old and has plaster walls and a tin roof. Wireless of any kind in your home operates well below the specified ranges. You need to test your XBee range in your own location to find your maximum range. If that is impractical, I recommend that you cut the specification values in half when planning your network to ensure that you don't place XBee-based sensor nodes out of range.

You can test the maximum range of your XBee modules before you develop your sensor network. One way is to create the XBee temperature sensor node project and use a USB XBee adapter on your laptop computer connected via the XCTU application. I include an unscientific method for determining a maximum reliable range next. For this to work, your sensor node should be set to deliver data every few seconds (say, every 10 seconds) and be running API firmware:

1. Connect the coordinator node to the laptop.

2. Connect to the coordinator via XCTU.

---

[6]You should avoid placing your XBee modules near large metal objects or at the bottom of concrete wells.

3. Place the sensor node in its intended location.

4. Hold your laptop near the sensor node (within a few feet), and power on the sensor node.

5. Wait until the XBee network is formed and you start receiving data.

6. Move slowly away, watching the data as the coordinator receives it.

7. When the coordinator starts presenting error packets or stops receiving data, you've gone too far.

This method is hardly scientific, but it can give you a rough gauge as to whether your sensor nodes are close enough (within range) to your data-aggregate node.

Keep an Engineering Logbook

Many developers, engineers, and scientists keep notes about their projects in paper notebooks or digital notebooks using apps like Evernote (http://evernote.com/). A voice recorder can also be handy in catching those impromptu ideas when you don't have time or it is too dangerous to use pen and paper.[7] Some people are more detailed than others, but most take notes during meetings and phone conversations, thereby providing a written record of verbal communications.

The best notetakers write down their ideas when they occur. Sometimes the mind works best when you are performing menial tasks and ideas come to you out of the blue. When this occurs, good engineers know to write down these ideas—even if they later turn to so much dirt—because the best ideas often start with a simple concept. Failure to write

---

[7]Like while driving. Sadly, I've seen drivers do this. Personal grooming seems to be the most popular form of activity people should never do while driving, after texting, email, tweeting, and so on.

down these tidbits can often lead to more experimentation and even wasted time working on alternatives.

If you aren't in the habit of keeping an engineering logbook, you should consider doing so. I have found a logbook to be a vital tool in my work. Yes, it does require more effort to write things down, and the log can get messy if you try to include all the various drawings and emails you find important (my notebooks are often bulging with clippings from important documents taped in place like some sort of engineer's scrapbook). The payoff is potentially huge, however.

This is especially true when designing sensor networks and the myriad of sensors and electronic circuits involved. You may be at a trade show (or a Maker Faire) and see something that really sparks an idea. Or maybe you see a circuit in a magazine or find a really cool sensor but need to design a circuit to host it. Writing down these ideas can enable you to achieve your goals.

It also helps you to remember concepts and critical information such as which way a sensor is wired, to avoid rework (or guesswork) that could lead to failed components and frustration. I am very thankful I keep a logbook of those times when I double-check my wiring, only to discover a misplaced jumper or wire routing. It has saved me time and money (not having to replace fried components).

Naturally, you can use any type of notebook you desire; but if you want to class up your notes a bit, you can purchase a notebook made especially for keeping engineering notes. These typically have subdued gridlines and sometimes text areas for recording key information like the project name and page number. One of my favorite notebooks is the Maker's Notebook from Maker Shed (www.makershed.com/products/makers-notebook-hard-bound).

This notebook features 150 numbered pages of graph paper, each with a special header for noting the project name, date, and page reference pointers. It also includes such nice additions as a space for a table of contents, a pocket for those small notes you write to yourself but later cannot read due to your own handwriting,[8] and stickers with electronic components for making circuits. This notebook is a bit more expensive than a run-of-the-mill lined or grid-filled notebook, but it is worth a look if you desire a good tool to help manage notes for multiple projects.

HOW TO MANAGE PAGES FOR MULTIPLE PROJECTS

One of the challenges of keeping a single notebook for multiple projects underway is how to manage pages. That is, if you are working on project X and write down some really cool ideas in the middle of working on project Y, how do you keep track of what pages belong to each project?

The Maker's Notebook solves this by allowing you room to note which page number is next at the bottom of each page. This can be really helpful when your project notes start to interleave (and they will). Think of it as a sort of manual linked list.

Another solution is to keep a living index at the front of your notebook that lists the page numbers for each project. This is not as nice as the Maker Shed solution, but it works.

Putting It All Together: Testing and Deploying Your Sensor Network

The projects in this book are designed to teach you how to build sensor networks by breaking the tasks into smaller components that you can combine. With the exception of the projects in Chapter 10 (they are complete sensor network examples), you can implement each in relative

---

[8]Unless your penmanship is far superior to most, this will happen to you eventually. Writing down an idea while riding a bucking train can often lead to illegible text. Sometimes reading such notes in the same environment where they were written helps.

isolation from the other projects. Some are alternative implementations, like the examples that show the same project first using an Arduino and then using a Raspberry Pi.

In some cases, especially in the "For More Fun" sections, I've suggested certain modifications and alternative solutions for you to experiment with. Experimentation is an excellent way to learn, but you should consider moving to a more formal evaluation of the solution when preparing your own sensor network.

In other words, test your network before deploying it. I cannot tell you how many times a well-planned hardware design has failed due to some unexpected consequence unrelated to the design. For example, you may find a physical obstruction that wasn't there or wasn't considered when you planned your network; or the cabling available or power in the area may be faulty; or you may find that the actual range of your radios in the target environment is shorter than anticipated. Whatever the case, usually bench-testing the solution prior to deploying it can help eliminate problems with the nodes themselves, allowing you to focus on what is different—the physical environment.

What I mean by bench-testing is to assemble the components in one location and power everything on as if it were deployed in the field. Not only does this allow you to ensure that the sensor network is working, but it also permits you to monitor the nodes themselves for anomalies. For example, incorrectly wiring a component may destroy it, but sometimes you can salvage the component by cutting power quickly.

Let's consider the last project in Chapter 10—a sensor network comprising a database node, a data-aggregate node, and several sensor nodes. There are several excellent methods to test a network like this, but the following approach can help you diagnose problems you may encounter when you deploy your own sensor networks. In this case,

I assume the software for each node is properly installed and working (i.e., the XBee nodes are configured correctly, and the sketches and scripts are working properly):

1. Starting with the database node, power it on and test connectivity from your network. Ensure that you can connect to MySQL as the user account you plan to use (and from the machines—IP addresses— that will need to access it) and that the user has privileges to update the databases you've designed. For more information about granting privileges to users, see the online MySQL reference manual.

2. Move to the data-aggregate node, and modify the sketch to insert dummy data into the database. Go back to the database, and ensure that the data has been inserted.

3. Power down your data-aggregate node, and move the coordinator XBee module to a USB XBee adapter. Connect it to your laptop, open a terminal application, and connect to the USB port with the XBee module.

4. Power on each of your sensor nodes, one at a time, and observe the terminal window. Ensure that each of the sensor nodes sends data and that the data is received (echoed in the terminal). Power down all XBee nodes, and remove the coordinator node from your laptop.

5. Return the data-aggregate node to its operational state (including running the final sketch or script), and power it up. Wait about 5 minutes, and then power on your sensor nodes. Connect to your database server, and ensure that data is being inserted into the table.

Once you have your sensor network assembled and running correctly, you can begin considering deployment. I prefer to deploy the sensor nodes first and (if possible) move my data-aggregate node and database server closer to the sensor nodes. I then power everything on, starting with the database server and then the data-aggregate node; then I wait 5 minutes and power on the sensor nodes.

Moving the data-aggregate node close to the actual location of the sensor nodes helps minimize any issues with ranges or obstructions. When I see that the network is operating correctly, I power everything off and deploy my data-aggregate node to its proper location and start the process again. Once that stage works, I deploy the database server and test the network one more time. When everything is working correctly, I power it all down again, erase the data (use DELETE SQL statement) the sample data, and power everything up. At this point, my deployment is complete, and I can work on the next stage: consuming the accumulated data for analysis.

With these best practices and considerations in mind, let's look at a topic that can sometimes lead to impromptu tinkering.[9]

Note   The projects in this chapter are intended for demonstration purposes and therefore do not include all the steps for building each project. However, given your knowledge level at this point, you can easily fill in the missing parts.

Choosing Sensor Nodes

When you consider how to host a sensor, you have some choices to make. Sometimes this decision is based on the type of sensor and the data it

---

[9]In other words, an emergency redesign of a failed implementation—fancy words for a poor design choice.

produces. For example, you can host almost any sensor with an Arduino. With some additional hardware, you can do so with the Raspberry Pi; and you can also host certain sensors with XBee modules (see Chapter 2).

But other things can determine the configuration of your sensor nodes and your data-aggregate nodes. These include the type of networking to use and whether the sensor node will use Ethernet or XBee (ZigBee) to communicate. There are also a number of alternative configurations for your sensor nodes that you have not explored thus far. I discuss each of these aspects in more detail in this section.

Wired or Wireless?

I mentioned in Chapter 10 that I consider a wired Ethernet connection a requirement for a data-aggregate node. But that is just the most typical case. It may be that you have WiFi Ethernet instead.

The main reason is that the data-aggregate node is typically accessed much more frequently than the sensor nodes. You may include data-aggregate nodes that have web servers, as you saw in Chapter 10, or you may decide to have the data-aggregate nodes send the data to another node (such as a database) for storage. In these cases, having a fast and reliable network is a must.

Typically, you use XBee modules and the ZigBee protocols to connect a data-aggregate node to sensor nodes. However, you can use the API protocols in ZigBee to communicate with your data-aggregate nodes. The challenge is to build a set of routines to match how you intend to interact with the data-aggregate nodes. It is not impossible (and I have seen proof of people who have designed such networks), but it takes a lot more work and eliminates a number of possibilities for data access.

The main consideration is to place your data-aggregate nodes on the most reliable network medium. Wired Ethernet is the most robust, followed by WiFi and then ZigBee. If the data will be stored locally and retrieved manually, then the choice of network medium may not matter. However, if you need to access the data remotely or store it on a remote node (such as a database server), then wired Ethernet is definitely the right choice.

Arduino or Raspberry Pi?

Choosing an Arduino or a Raspberry Pi should be based on a number of factors. These include cost, security, functionality, expandability, and connectivity. Your choice will likely be based on one or more of these and may dictate (or limit) your implementation of your sensor or data-aggregate node.

Cost

If you are planning a large network or have a limited budget, cost may be a primary concern. This is likely to be seen in the per-node cost. Sensors are typically commodities, and the prices normally don't vary much from one vendor to another. But the price of the host itself may make a difference. Let's look at each board with cost in mind.

The current average cost of the Raspberry Pi 3B (in the United States) is about $40. This is about $5.00 more than the MSRP should be for these boards, but given the high demand and somewhat limited supply, it is no surprise vendors are charging more.

The cost for an Arduino is a bit harder to pin down. Because the Raspberry Pi is closed source whereas the Arduino is open source, you can find a lot of different vendors selling a variety of Arduino-compatible boards. Although you can buy a Raspberry Pi from different vendors, there are no Raspberry Pi clones. As a consequence, you can find any number of varieties of Arduino-compatible boards starting from as low as $15.00. Currently, the average price (on eBay and Amazon) for an Uno or Leonardo clone is about $20.00.

If you are planning 20 sensor nodes (and none are XBee-based), your cost savings through choosing an Arduino over a Raspberry Pi could be significant. For example, if you find Raspberry Pi boards for $40.00 each and Arduino-compatible boards for $20.00 each, it will cost you $400.00 more to use Raspberry Pi boards than Arduino boards.

However, if you must augment your Arduino boards with shields, the cost of the shield could bring your total outlay much closer to the cost of the Raspberry Pi (unless you buy the Uno WiFi version). In some cases, it could even cost more to buy an Arduino and a shield than a Raspberry Pi. On the whole, the takeaway is that if cost is an issue, the Arduino is often the less expensive choice.

Security

I have not said much about security or securing your sensor and data-aggregate nodes in this book. Let's take a moment to briefly consider this topic.

We generally can agree that a database node should be secure with a modicum of password security and access restrictions,[10] what about the sensor nodes themselves? Theft may be less of a concern, but you should at least consider securing your sensor nodes against theft. The average thief looking for a target of opportunity is not likely to steal your sensor node.[11]

However, physical access to the nodes is a concern. Although it is possible for someone to exploit an Arduino node if they have direct access, it is much harder to do so with an Arduino than a Raspberry Pi. The primary reason is that the Arduino is loaded electronically; someone could reprogram the microcontroller, but there is little they can do without

---

[10]Don't mount it to the outside of your house and put a huge sticker on that says "database server."

[11]Let's hope not, anyway.

knowing how the sketch was written. But all that is needed to exploit a Raspberry Pi node is an SD card with a fresh OS loaded.[12] Thus, you should consider making it as difficult as possible for someone to get physical access to your Raspberry Pi nodes—especially if they are connected to your local network or the Internet.

Sadly, there is another concern—electronic intrusion. Because the Arduino is a microcontroller, it is not likely that someone will attempt to connect to it for nefarious activities. There is a much greater likelihood that someone will attempt to exploit a Raspberry Pi node. This means you have to be more careful when deploying Raspberry Pi-based nodes. Basic security practices go a long way, but if you don't take care and plan against intrusion, your Raspberry Pi nodes could be vulnerable.

If you are concerned about the security of your nodes, you should consider reading more about sensor network security. However, the bottom line here is that Raspberry Pi nodes tend to be easier to exploit than Arduino nodes.

Functionality

The functionality provided by the host is another area where you may want to focus. If you are looking to add functionality, such as a web server, a local database server, or remote access via SSH, or connectivity to peripherals such as hard disks, keyboard, display, and so on, there is really no choice. The Raspberry Pi is a fully functional personal computer (and mini server).

On the other hand, the Arduino is very easy to program and has a much wider hardware support base, making it possible to host a much wider array of sensor options and even electronic circuits. This is because the Arduino has a more robust hardware interface than the GPIO of the Raspberry Pi.

---

[12]Most disconcerting, isn't it?

663

For example, consider that the Raspberry Pi requires an ADC to interface with analog sensors. Thus, if you plan to use only analog sensors but still need the features of the Raspberry Pi, the cost of your sensor will be a bit higher (for the price of the ADC module).

The decision rests on whether you need computer-like features or better hardware support options. If you require personal computer or server features for your node, you should choose a Raspberry Pi. If you need to support a more diverse set of sensors and related hardware, you should choose the Arduino.

Expandability

Expandability (can also be called scalability) is closely related to functionality. I focus on this as a separate consideration because it has a bearing on sensor networks. There are two aspects of expandability that you should consider: the availability of pluggable modules and the ability to add more features to the node.

The clear winner in the availability of pluggable modules is the Arduino. There are dozens of shields that support all manner of hardware features. From simple sensor boards to XBee hosting to advanced motor control and robotics, there is a shield for just about anything you want to do for a sensor network.

That doesn't mean you should count the Raspberry Pi out. If you need to store a lot of data on a node, you are less likely to choose the Arduino because it is very easy to add a local hard disk to the Raspberry Pi. Similarly, if you need complex display capabilities, the Raspberry Pi requires no additional hardware (just use a monitor).

Note   You can indeed use small to medium-sized LCD panels on the Arduino. There are many examples, including example sketches, in the Arduino IDE. However, it is a lot easier to write a Python script to produce screen output than it is to try to cram a lot of information on a small LCD.

Thus, if you need expandability from an electronics perspective, you should choose the Arduino. If you need more expandability for attaching storage devices or displaying a lot of data, you should choose the Raspberry Pi.

Connectivity

The last area to consider is connectivity. Once again, this depends on your perspective. If you want to connect your node to other nodes via XBee modules, the platforms are equally capable.

If you plan to connect your node to an Ethernet network, you must consider the fact that the Raspberry Pi 3B, 3B+, and 4B comes Internet-ready with a LAN port (Ethernet) as well as WiFi, whereas the Arduino (excluding the Yun and Arduino Uno Ethernet variant) requires an Ethernet or WiFi shield; therefore, the cost may be much closer. For example, you can purchase a basic Arduino Ethernet clone shield for about $30.00. Given that the Arduino costs about $20.00 for an older clone board, your cost has exceeded that of the Raspberry Pi.

However, the Arduino currently has one advantage over the Raspberry Pi for when it comes to connectivity: it is much easier to interface specialized hardware. Recall the discussion earlier on the use of cellular modems to connect your nodes to the Internet for collecting data. Because there is no pluggable solution for the Raspberry Pi, the Arduino is the better choice in this case. This may also apply to other forms of connectivity provided by the use of specialized shields.

Thus, the consideration of connectivity for Ethernet and Bluetooth gives the advantage to the Raspberry Pi, whereas specialized communication such as a cellular modem gives the advantage to the Arduino.

Tip   There may be cases where you want to have the power of a Raspberry Pi but the flexibility and expandability of an Arduino. I'll reveal one such solution in the next section.

Now that you have seen some considerations for choosing what host to use, let's look at a couple of alternative solutions that you may want to consider—starting with a purpose-built sensor node.

Alternative Hosts

This section considers two alternatives for basing your sensor and data-aggregate nodes. You see an Arduino-compatible board designed expressly for sensor networks and outdoor operation as well as a daughter board designed to create a hybrid node combining a Raspberry Pi with an Arduino.

Seeed Studio Wireless Sensor Kit

One of the best Arduino-compatible kits is the Seeed Studio Wireless Sensor Kit—also called the Stalker Waterproof Solar Kit (http://wiki. seeedstudio.com/Seeeduino_Stalker_V3-Waterproof_Solar_Kit/). The kit consists of a Seeed Studio Stalker board, a solar panel, battery pack, case (a glass jar!), XBee adapter, hardware, and accessories. Figure 11-2 shows what is included in the kit.

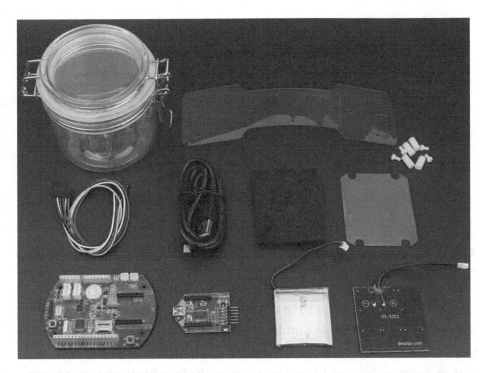

Figure 11-2. *Seeed Studio Stalker wireless sensor node (courtesy of Seeed Studio)*

The Seeed Studio Stalker board is a Seeeduino (Arduino-compatible) board and is the true gem in this kit. Not only is it fully compatible with Arduino (because it has the same processor), but it also has an onboard RTC, XBee headers, microSD card drive, real-time clock (for recording sample datetime), Grove connectors, and more. The full specifications can be found at http://wiki.seeedstudio.com/Seeeduino-Stalker_v3/. Figure 11-3 shows a photo of the Stalker board in more detail.

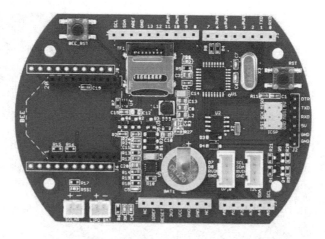

Figure 11-3. *Seeeduino Stalker Arduino-compatible board (courtesy of Seeed Studio)*

The Stalker is marketed as a wireless sensor node based on its onboard XBee support. You may be wondering why I have left the discussion of this board to the end of the book. Simply put, the Stalker is a specialized board that requires building your sensor nodes with very specific hardware and software. Although it can indeed make building sensor networks easier by taking away a lot of the harder work of connecting modules and interfacing with them, this very nature makes it less valuable for learning how sensor nodes are built.

It is better to learn the basic building blocks of putting together sensor nodes so that when you begin working with more advanced sensor networks or incorporating advanced sensors into your sensor nodes, you have the proper experience and knowledge to use them. Besides, it is a lot more fun to build something from scratch.[13]

---

[13]You can learn quite a lot about hardware by this approach. You haven't truly pushed yourself to learn until you've made a few mistakes. If you take the proper care and precautions, the end result of minor mistakes is nothing more than a fried component or two.

However, if the features of the board are what you need, then you should consider using as many of these as you require. The cost is a bit higher, as you can imagine. The cost of the kit is about $59.50, and the board itself is $39.00. If you consider that the board has an RTC as well as XBee headers, the $39.00 cost is less than buying an Arduino, separate XBee shield, and RTC module combined.

All the onboard features can be used in your sketches. For example, you can read temperature from the onboard RTC (the DS3231 chip has a temperature sensor) using only a single method call. To get this functionality, you must download and install the DS3231 library from `https://jeelabs.org/pub/docs/rtclib/`.

The DS3231 library and the Stalker make building and deploying a temperature sensor node very easy. All you need to do is add the XBee code you've explored in previous projects, and you can quickly build a solar-powered wireless temperature sensor node. Cool.

Tip   You can find a lot more information about programming the Seeed Studio Stalker on the company wiki for this board (`http://wiki.seeedstudio.com/Seeeduino_Stalker_V3.1/`).

Getting back to the solar part of the kit, the Stalker has a lithium polymer (LiPo) battery-charging circuit designed specifically for attaching a solar panel and a LiPo battery. The solar panel charges the battery during the day, providing adequate power for the node to run overnight (assuming your XBee is utilizing sleep mode and you don't have a lot of circuitry drawing power). This means you can build this kit and use it outdoors to communicate sensor data to your sensor network without worry of providing power or network connections. If you have a property with outbuildings without power (or ponds), this kit has the features you need to install a remote sensor.

The thing I like most about the Seeed Studio Stalker is that it is a fully compatible Arduino clone. If you do not use the Stalker in its waterproof case, you can use it in place of one of your Arduino nodes (because it is an Arduino). With the onboard RTC, XBee headers, and microSD card drive, you may even be able to use this board for all of your sensor nodes—data aggregators included.

If you are planning a home temperature-monitoring sensor network, you should consider using this board for your remote sensors at the least. However, considering all the goodies you get in the wireless sensor kit, it is an excellent value.

Raspberry Pi Alamode

Another variant you may want to consider is the Raspberry Pi Alamode. This board is a very special piece of hardware designed to bridge the gap between the Arduino and the Raspberry Pi. While originally developed for earlier versions of the Raspberry Pi, the Alamode is a daughter board for the Raspberry Pi that plugs into the GPIO header and features a fully compatible Arduino clone.

This board is also available from Seeed Studio and has a lot of the same features. See www.seeedstudio.com/Alamode-Arduino-Compatible-Raspberry-Pi-Plate-p-1285.html for more details. Figure 11-4 shows a photo of the board.

Figure 11-4. Raspberry Pi Alamode (courtesy of Seeed Studio)

More specifically, the Alamode is an Arduino-compatible board that
you can connect to your Raspberry Pi; and you can write sketches that you
can interact with via another program on the Raspberry Pi. Like the Seeed
Studio Stalker, it also supports Arduino shields so you can write sketches
that take advantage of the shields and pass the functionality on to the
Raspberry Pi via a sketch on the Alamode. You can also run the Arduino
IDE on the Raspberry Pi to load sketches on the Alamode. Some of the best
features of the Alamode include the following:

- Arduino compatible

- Connects to the Raspberry Pi via the GPIO header

- Automatically controls voltage on the GPIO header,
  providing 3.3V safe voltage on the GPIO but powering
  the Alamode with 5V

- Has a separate micro-USB port for powering the Alamode

- Supports headers for controlling servos

- MicroSD drive

- Onboard RTC that can be used by the Raspberry Pi

- Supports additional headers for FTDI, ICSP, and a GPS module

The Alamode represents a unique hardware solution for sensor nodes. It permits you to use the best of both platforms on a single node. Let's say you need to use a special component or feature that is only available for the Arduino, but you also need computer resources such as a full-featured web server and lots of storage for your data-aggregate node. To solve this problem, you must find a way to connect the Arduino to your Raspberry Pi. The Alamode is that bridge. You can write sketches for the Alamode (even directly from the Raspberry Pi!) that provide the data from whatever shield, sensor, or other hardware you connect to the Alamode Arduino headers.

For example, you can access the RTC on the Alamode from the Raspberry Pi. To do this, you must have the I2C drivers on the Raspberry Pi. Fortunately, you achieved this earlier in the book. The setup is not overly complicated and involves adding a new module to the Raspberry Pi so that it can get its date and time from the RTC on the Alamode via the I2C interface. In fact, you access it as you would any I2C RTC module. A complete walk-through of accessing an RTC via I2C is available from Adafruit (`http://learn.adafruit.com/adding-a-real-time-clock-to-raspberry-pi`).

As a consequence of its uniqueness and implementation, there are some limitations. First, although it is true that you can use the Arduino IDE from the Raspberry Pi, doing so requires installing a special patch for the IDE that changes the IDE slightly to recognize the Alamode. You can download the patch and apply it using the following commands on the Raspberry Pi:

```
$ wget www.wyolum.com/downloads/alamode-setup.tar.gz
$ tar -xvzf alamode-setup.tar.gz
$ cd alamode-setup
$ sudo ./setup
```

Once you complete these steps and restart the IDE, you see the Alamode listed under the Board submenu. To set up the Alamode, select it from this menu and then select the /dev/ttyS0 serial port.

Tip   A complete walk-through of getting started with the Alamode can be found at `http://wyolum.com/projects/alamode/alamode-getting-started/`.

Communication between the Alamode and the Raspberry Pi can be accomplished using the Firmata library, which is built into the Arduino IDE. Fortunately, there are a number of examples you can explore in the Arduino IDE. There are also walk-throughs on the Alamode wiki (`http://wyolum.com/projects/alamode/`).

The Raspberry Pi Alamode is still a very new product and as yet has not been used (or at least reported or documented) enough to realize its full potential. However, I believe that if you need a special piece of hardware that is available for the Arduino, but you need to use it directly on a Raspberry Pi (like that cellular shield), this product may provide an excellent solution.

Project: Home Temperature-Monitoring Network

This chapter would not seem complete if I didn't have a project to discuss. By this point, though, you have all the knowledge you need to build sensor networks using Arduino boards, Raspberry Pi computers, and even dedicated XBee sensor nodes. Thus, rather than provide yet another step-by-step example, this section presents a walk-through of the planning stages of creating a home temperature-monitoring network.

This project will seem a lot like the projects from Chapter 10. That is intentional. Everything you need to build this network was demonstrated in that project. What I am discussing here are the considerations for actually designing and deploying such a sensor network. The intent of the project is to provide one possible practical example for how to get started planning and implementing a sensor network.

Planning Considerations

The first question you need to ask when planning a sensor network is "Why?" The second question is "What do I expect to get from the data?" The reasons for creating a home temperature network are many and varied, but generally you expect to be able to track the ambient temperature of the home so that you can either plan changes to the heating and cooling systems or verify that they are working correctly (the thermostat settings match the actual temperatures measured).

As for why you would create the network, consider cases where the house is large, has several heating and air conditioning systems (HVAC), or was expanded over time to include rooms that are isolated or poorly supported by different HVAC systems. Or perhaps you have more personal reasons like differing opinions of hot/cold among family members or the need to protect sensitive medical equipment. Whatever the reasons, they should be considered a design element.

For this example, suppose the reason is that your home has multiple HVAC systems and has been expanded over the years in such a way that some rooms are noticeably warmer or cooler during different seasons of the year. In this case, you want to be able to predict the effects of outside climate (temperature) on the inside of the home.

Planning the Nodes

The next thing you should do is evaluate the resources available for a sensor network. Let's assume the home has two floors and only the first floor and one room on the second floor are wired for Ethernet, but there is a wireless Ethernet router (wireless access port) that can be accessed from anywhere in the home. There are four bedrooms, a den, a kitchen, a formal dining room, three bathrooms, and a sunroom (enclosed porch). The construction of the home limits radio signals to no more than 30–40 feet.

These criteria mean you must design the sensor network following a specific model. Namely, you need to collect data over time from multiple sensors. You could use as many as 12 (11 inside and 1 outside), but let's say you identify 5 zones in the home representing key areas where the temperature can differ from the rest of the home.

If you take sensor samples six times every 24 hours, you will be storing 36 samples per day (6 per sensor), more than 256 per week, and more than 91,000 per year. If you are measuring temperature, this could result in as much as a few megabytes of data per year. Although this isn't too much data to store on an SD card, if you want to compute averages over time compared to an outside variable (the outside climate), you must read the data and calculate the comparisons at some point (perhaps several times a month). Thus, you would be better suited to use a database server to store the data. Also, because you want to know when each sample was taken, you need to design the database table to store a timestamp for each sample.

If you consider the radio limitations of the home and the fact that it has multiple floors and a number of rooms, you can expect to require at least one data-aggregate node that is centrally located in the home. However, it is possible you could need more, depending on the placement of the sensors and the effects of the limited range.

For this project, assume that a centrally located data-aggregate node will suffice. In addition, you decide the data-aggregate nodes will connect to the database node via Ethernet, but the sensor nodes will communicate with the data-aggregate node using XBee modules.

You will implement the five internal sensor nodes using XBee modules (to which you can connect the TMP36 directly), but for the outside node, you will use the Seeed Studio Wireless Sensor Kit discussed earlier.

As for powering the nodes, you can use common 5V–9V wall wart power supplies for all sensor nodes. Also assume that the peripherals for the Raspberry Pi database node are gathered from on-hand surplus components.

Cost Considerations

Finally, you want to limit the cost of the network as much as possible. You also want to keep the samples relative in scale. The best way to do this is to use the same temperature sensor for each node. The most cost-effective solution is to use a sensor like the TMP36.

To sum up your node requirements, you need six sensor nodes (including one that can be installed outside), a database node, and a data-aggregate node. Taking all this into consideration, one possible hardware shopping list is shown in Table 11-1.

Table 11-1. *Sample Shopping List for the Home Temperature Sensor Network*

Description	Qty	Cost USD	Ext. Cost USD
Raspberry Pi (database server)	1	$35.00	$35.00
TMP36 sensors with resistor	6	$1.50	$9.00
Seeed Studio Wireless Sensor Kit	1	$59.50	$59.50
XBee-ZB (ZB) Series 2 or 2.5	7	$25.00	$175.00
Arduino-compatible boards	1	$21.00	$21.00
Power adapters (1 for each node)	8	$6.95	$55.60
Ethernet shields	1	$45.00	$45.00
Arduino XBee shield	1	$24.95	$24.95
		Total	**$425.10**

I leave out some of the finer details for brevity, but the more costly items are listed. That is, I omit the cost of breadboards, cases, and so on for the sensor nodes because these are only one way to implement the circuitry. You could just as easily build a circuit on a preprinted circuit prototyping board and place each in a small enclosure (bits like this are called vitamins in the 3D printing world—an appropriate description I think).

One of the newest prototyping boards are the Perma-Proto Breadboard PCBs from Adafruit (www.adafruit.com/category/466). They come in a variety of sizes as well as multi-packs for a bit of savings and can be used just like a breadboard, but in this case, you solder the components rather than plug them in. Thus, Perma-Proto Breadboard PCB makes it much easier to transfer a project from a breadboard onto a permanent circuit board that you can mount. Figure 11-5 shows a half-sized Perma-Proto Breadboard PCB from Adafruit (www.adafruit.com/product/1609).

677

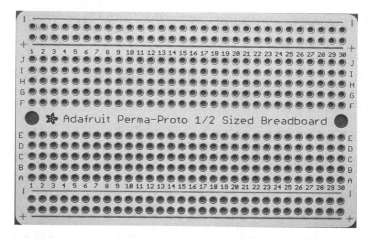

Figure 11-5. *Prototyping circuit board (courtesy of SparkFun)*

As for enclosures, there are many examples out there that you can use. Some are waterproof (most are not), some are made of plastic, and others are metal. I even found some that are made from laser-cut plywood and acrylic sheets. If you want a simple enclosure large enough for an Arduino board and even a small PCB, take a look at the Big Red Box enclosure from SparkFun (www.sparkfun.com/products/11366) as shown in Figure 11-6.

Figure 11-6. *Big Red Box enclosure (courtesy of SparkFun)*

What About Implementation?

Recall that at the start of this project, I said you have all the knowledge you need to implement this project. If you consider the nodes you need, you can find examples of how to build each one in previous chapters. The database node is found in Chapter 8, the Arduino data-aggregate node is also in Chapter 10, the XBee sensor nodes are in Chapters 3 and 4, and an example of the outdoor sensor node is included in this chapter (the Seeed Studio Wireless Sensor Kit).

I therefore leave the implementation to you; you can study those examples and implement them. Fortunately, little or no modification should be necessary. Other than perhaps substituting prototype circuit boards for the breadboards and sturdy enclosures for all the nodes, your implementation should be the same as the examples.

Conclusion

Once you have purchased all the components and assembled the sensor nodes in their final form, you can bench-test the entire network and then deploy the sensor nodes, testing for reliable connections between the sensor nodes and the data-aggregate node. Once all this checks out, you secure the sensor nodes in their locations, the data-aggregate node is installed in the central location, and the database node is installed in a secure area.

Returning to what you expect to get from the network, after it has run for some time—a week perhaps—without errors or problems, you can start issuing queries on the database to check for differences observed between the outside sensor values and the indoor sensor values. Once you have several months' worth of data, you can start to consider grouping the data by season (through a selection on the timestamp column).

I hope this example has reinforced the material in the book as way to validate your efforts in constructing all the projects and experimenting with them. I am fully confident that doing so will mean, should you follow this example to form a similar network, you succeed handily.

For More Fun

The total cost of these components is approximately $425.00, not including miscellaneous vitamins and shipping costs. This may sound like a lot, but consider substituting other components such as using fewer XBee sensor nodes and more Arduino sensor nodes with WiFi shields or the use of a Raspberry Pi for the data-aggregate node.

Optional Component Shopping List

No required components are needed for the examples in this chapter. Rather, the components and accessories listed in this chapter are optional—things you may want to consider purchasing if needed. Table 11-2 shows a list of the components mentioned in this chapter.

Table 11-2. *Optional Components*

Item	Vendors	Est. Cost USD
Seeed Studio Stalker Wireless Sensor Kit	`http://wiki.seeedstudio.com/ Seeeduino_Stalker_V3-Waterproof_ Solar_Kit/`	$59.50
Seeed Studio Stalker Board	`http://wiki.seeedstudio.com/ Seeeduino_Stalker_V3.1/`	$39.00
Raspberry Pi Alamode	`www.seeedstudio.com/Alamode- Arduino-Compatible-Raspberry- Pi-Plate-p-1285.html`	$35.00
LTE CAT M1/NB-IoT Shield	`www.sparkfun.com/products/14997`	$79.95
Perma-Proto Boards	`www.adafruit.com/category/466`	$2.50 and up
Enclosure	`www.sparkfun.com/products/11366`	$8.95

Summary

This chapter explored some of the nuances of designing and implementing wireless sensor networks. I discussed some of the more popular best practices for sensor networks, considerations for planning databases to store the sensor data, how best to retrieve and use the data from a database, and how to choose what type of host to use for each sensor node. You also explored the design of a whole home temperature-monitoring system with special considerations for selecting hardware for the sensors.

Now that you have a basic (and some more advanced) understanding of wireless sensor networks, you can put down this book in triumph and start thinking of some really cool ways you can implement what you have learned. Perhaps you want to monitor the temperature in your house, workshop, or garage. Or perhaps you want to design a more complex network that monitors sound, movement, and ambient temperature changes (like a home security system).

An even more ambitious project would be to build your own weather station from discrete components, with a sensor node for each data sample (wind speed, temperature, gas readings, rain gauge, and so on). All that and more is possible with what you have learned in this book. Good luck, and happy sensor networks!

APPENDIX

This appendix contains the consolidated shopping list for all components required for building all the projects in this book. We will also cover three optional component connector systems that you may find helpful in developing your own sensor networks.

Consolidated Shopping Lists

The tables in this section cover the projects from Chapters 2 and 4–10 (Table A-1). Also contained is the optional shopping list for the projects in Chapter 10 (Table A-2). The lists have been sorted by item name for easier reference.

Table A-1. *Consolidated Component Shopping List*

Item	Vendors	Est. Cost USD	Qty Needed
0.10mF capacitor	Most online and retail stores	Varies	3
10K Ohm resistor	Most online and retail stores	Varies	1
12-bit ADC module	www.adafruit.com/products/1083	$9.95	1
150 Ohm Resistor	Most online and retail stores	Varies	1
4.7K Ohm resistor	Most online and retail stores	Varies	2
5V Power Supply (3A, 3B, 3B+)	www.pishop.us/product/wall-adapter-power-supply-micro-usb-2-4a-5-25v/	$9.95	1

(continued)

© Charles Bell 2020
C. Bell, *Beginning Sensor Networks with XBee, Raspberry Pi, and Arduino,*
https://doi.org/10.1007/978-1-4842-5796-8

Table A-1. (*continued*)

Item	Vendors	Est. Cost USD	Qty Needed
5V Power Supply (4B)	www.raspberrypi.org/ products/type-c-power- supply/	$8.00	1
9V Battery Holder (optional)	www.adafruit.com/ products/67 www.sparkfun.com/ products/10512	$2.95–3.95	1 for each node
Arduino Ethernet Shield	www.sparkfun.com/ products/9026	$24.95	1
Arduino Ethernet Shield 2	www.sparkfun.com/ products/11166	$24.95 and up	1
Arduino Uno (any that supports shields)	Various	$25.00 and up	1
Arduino Uno or Mega 2560	Various	$25.00 and up	1 for each node
Arduino Uno, Leonardo (any that supports shields)	Various	$25.00 and up	1
Arduino WiFi Shield	www.sparkfun.com/ products/13287	$16.95	1
Arduino XBee shield	www.sparkfun.com/ products/10854	$24.95	1

(*continued*)

Table A-1. (*continued*)

Item	Vendors	Est. Cost USD	Qty Needed
BMP280 breakout board	www.adafruit.com/product/2651	$9.95–14.95	1
	www.sparkfun.com/products/15440		
BMP280 Grove Sensor (optional)	www.seeedstudio.com/catalogsearch/result/?q=bmp280	$8.95	1
BMP280 Sensor	www.adafruit.com/products/2651	$9.95	1
Breadboard (not mini)	www.adafruit.com/product/64	$5.95	1 for each node
Breadboard (not mini)	www.sparkfun.com/products/9567		
Breadboard jumper wires	www.adafruit.com/product/758	$3.95	1
	www.sparkfun.com/products/8431		
Breadboard power supply	www.sparkfun.com/products/10804	$14.95	1
Breakaway male headers (optional)	www.adafruit.com/products/392	$4.95	1
Cobbler+	www.adafruit.com/products/914	$7.95	1

(*continued*)

Table A-1. (*continued*)

Item	Vendors	Est. Cost USD	Qty Needed
Data Logging shield for Arduino	www.adafruit.com/ products/1141	$19.95	1
DHT22	www.adafruit.com/ products/385 www.sparkfun.com/ products/10167	$9.95	1
DS1307 Real-Time Clock breakout board	www.adafruit.com/ product/3296	$7.50	1 for each node
DS18B20 Digital Temperature Sensor	www.adafruit.com/ product/374	$3.95	1
Grove to Female Jumper (optional)	www.seeedstudio.com/ Grove-4-pin-Female- Jumper-to-Grove-4-pin- Conversion-Cable-5- PCs-per-PAck.html	$3.90	1
HDMI or DVI monitor	Most online and retail stores	Varies	1
HDMI or HDMI to DVI cable	Most online and retail stores	Varies	1
I2C EEPROM	www.sparkfun.com/ products/525	$1.95	1
LED	Most online and retail stores	Varies	1
microSD Shield	www.sparkfun.com/ products/9802	$14.95	1

(*continued*)

Table A-1. (*continued*)

Item	Vendors	Est. Cost USD	Qty Needed
Mini-HDMI cable	Most online and retail stores	Varies	1
Pushbutton (breadboard mount)	`www.sparkfun.com/products/97`	$0.35	1
Raspberry Pi 3B, 3B+, or 4B	Most online and retail stores	$35.00 and up	1

Raspberry Pi Cobbler+ (you can also use the T-Cobbler+)	`www.adafruit.com/products/2028`
	
	`www.adafruit.com/products/2029`
		$7.95	1

Raspberry Pi Model 3B+ or 4B 2GB or 4GB	Most online stores	$35.00 and up	2

Raspberry Pi Model 4B 2GB or 4GB RAM	`sparkfun.com,`
	`adafruit.com,`
	`thepithut.com`
		$50.00 and up	1

Real-Time Clock module	`www.sparkfun.com/products/99`	$14.95	1 for each node
SD Card, 2GB or more	Most online and retail stores	Varies	1
SD card, 16GB or more	Most online and retail stores	Varies	1
Soldering iron and solder (optional)	Most online and retail stores	Varies	1
SparkFun XBee shield	`www.sparkfun.com/products/10854`	$24.95	1

(*continued*)

Table A-1. (*continued*)

Item	Vendors	Est. Cost USD	Qty Needed
Stackable header kit	www.sparkfun.com/products/11417	$1.50–1.95	1
Surplus hard drive	Any USB hard drive (surplus or purchased)	Varies	1
TMP36 sensor	www.adafruit.com/products/165 www.sparkfun.com/products/10988	$1.50	1 for each sensor node
USB keyboard	Most online and retail stores	Varies	1
USB power supply	Most online and retail stores	Varies	1
USB power supply	Most online and retail stores	Varies	1
USB Type A to micro-USB male	Most online and retail stores	Varies	1
USB XBee Adapter	www.adafruit.com/product/247	$29.95	1 for each node
USB-C power supply	Most online and retail stores	Varies	1
USB-to-mini USB cable for use with the XBee Explorer USB	www.sparkfun.com/products/11301	$3.95	1
Wall adapter 9V (optional)	www.sparkfun.com/products/ 15314	$5.95	1 for each node**

(*continued*)

Table A-1. (*continued*)

Item	Vendors	Est. Cost USD	Qty Needed
Wall power supply (6V–12V)	www.sparkfun.com/products/15314	$5.95	1
XBee Explorer Dongle	www.sparkfun.com/products/ 11697	$24.95	1 for each node
XBee Explorer Regulated	www.sparkfun.com/products/11373	$9.95	2
XBee Explorer USB	www.sparkfun.com/products/ 11812	$29.95	1 for each node
XBee Explorer Regulated with headers	www.sparkfun.com/products/11373	$10.95	1 for each sensor node + 1 for the Raspberry Pi
XBee shield	www.sparkfun.com/products/12847	$24.95	1
XBee-ZB (ZB) series 2, 2.5, or 3	www.adafruit.com www.sparkfun.com	$25.00–48.00	2–4 (1 for each node)

Table A-2. *Optional Component Shopping List*

Item	Vendors	Est. Cost USD
Enclosure	www.sparkfun.com/products/11366	$8.95
LTE CAT M1/NB-IoT Shield	www.sparkfun.com/products/14997	$79.95
Perma-Proto Boards	www.adafruit.com/category/466	$2.50 and up
Raspberry Pi Alamode	www.seeedstudio.com/Alamode-Arduino-Compatible-Raspberry-Pi-Plate-p-1285.html	$35.00
Seeed Studio Stalker Board	http://wiki.seeedstudio.com/Seeeduino_Stalker_V3.1/	$39.00
Seeed Studio Stalker Wireless Sensor Kit	http://wiki.seeedstudio.com/Seeeduino_Stalker_V3-Waterproof_Solar_Kit/	$59.50
XBee Grove Development Board	www.digikey.com/products/en?mpart=76000956&v=602	$25.00

Alternative Connection Systems

If you've been working with microcontrollers and discrete components for some time, chances are you're an expert at wiring components to a breadboard and connecting them together. However, if working with electronics is new to you or you find wiring things together tedious, you've probably wondered if there is a better way. It turns out there are better ways!

As we saw in Chapter 5, there are connection systems designed to allow you to connect sensors and other components together using one set of wiring and connectors that connect to a platform-specific host board (shield, hat). These systems typically support a specific communication protocol such as I2C, SPI, and so on. Even so, manufacturers offer the components as modules that "speak" the same protocol. For example, you can get sensors and displays that can be connected together. These connection systems cost a little more, but the cost is easily offset by ease of use and keyed connectors that prevent cross or simply incorrect hookups.

In the following sections, we will see a short overview of three of the most popular connection systems you may want to consider using in your own projects. The examples are presented without detailed explanations for the reader to explore. That is, they represent a small glimpse into what is possible.

Grove

We first introduce the Grove system from Seeed Studio in Chapter 5. Grove is open source that utilizes a four-wire keyed connector that makes assembling electronic components easy and fast while also simplifying the learning process. The Grove system consists of a host board (shield/hat) with each module having a single, dedicated connector using one of several protocols. Connections are made in a star pattern where each component requiring a connection on the host or multiplex boards. Each Grove module addresses a single function such as a sensor, button, or display. With over 200 modules available, you are sure to find the modules you need for your project.

Since we have already discussed a sample Raspberry Pi Grove project in Chapter 5, Listing A-1 shows another example of a Grove project using the Arduino. In this case, we use a Grove Arduino base shield, DHT11 sensor, and a 16x2 LCD to display the data. All of the code is taken from the excellent example sketches.

Listing A-1. Grove Arduino Example Sketch

```
/**
  Beginning Sensor Networks Second Edition
  Sensor Networks Example Grove Temperature Node

  This project demonstrates how to use a Grove DHT11 sensor and
  LCD display. It shows how easy it is to use the Grove family
  of sensors as an alternative to hard wiring.
*/
#include "DHT.h"
#include "rgb_lcd.h"

const int colorR = 255;
const int colorG = 0;
const int colorB = 0;

#define DHTPIN A2
#define DHTTYPE DHT11

DHT dht(DHTPIN, DHTTYPE);
rgb_lcd lcd;
```

```
void setup()
{
  Serial.begin(115200);
  while(!Serial);
  Serial.println("Welcome to the Grove DHT11 example!");
  Wire.begin();
  dht.begin();
  // set up the LCD's number of columns and rows:
  lcd.begin(16, 2);
  lcd.setRGB(colorR, colorG, colorB);
}

void loop()
{
  float temp_hum_val[2] = {0};

  if(!dht.readTempAndHumidity(temp_hum_val)){
    lcd.clear();
    lcd.setCursor(0, 0);
    lcd.print("Humidity: ");
    lcd.print(temp_hum_val[0]);
    lcd.print("%");
    lcd.setCursor(0, 1);
    lcd.print("Temp: ");
    lcd.print(temp_hum_val[1]);
    lcd.print("C");
  }
  else{
    Serial.println("Failed to get temperature and humidity
    value.");
  }

  delay(1000);
}
```

To run this sketch, you must install the following libraries using the library manager:

- *Grove Temperature and Humidity Sensor*—DHT11

- *Grove LCD RGB Backlight*—16x2 LCD

Figure A-1 shows the hardware for the project including an Arduino Uno, Grove Arduino Base Shield, DHT11 humidity/temperature sensor, and a 2x16 LCD module.

Figure A-1. *Grove Arduino example hardware*

See www.seeedstudio.com/category/Grove-c-1003.html for more information about the Grove family of products.

Qwiic

SparkFun's Qwiic connect system uses a smaller four-pin cable with JST connectors to quickly interface host and development boards with sensors, LCDs, and more. In fact, SparkFun has introduced many of its development boards with Qwiic connectors to make experiments and projects easier.

With the Qwiic system, there is no soldering and modules just plug together. No searching for the "right" connector; just plug it in and go. You can't cross-connect since the connectors are polarized and keyed to plug in only on way. Better still, unlike the Grove system, Qwiic modules have two connectors permitting you to daisy-chain modules together, thereby saving space on the host board.

Qwiic host boards connect the I2C bus (GND, 3.3V, SDA, and SCL) on your Arduino, Raspberry Pi, Photon, and so on to a series of SparkFun Qwiic connectors. Some host boards have circuitry to convert the 5V given to the 3.3V required by I2C boards in the Qwiic system.

One nice feature of the Arduino host shield also is the ability to mount Qwiic boards on top using two through holes that line up with the modules. This permits you to securely stack the modules on top. Nice.

The list of sensors along with supported host platforms and accessories for the Qwiic system from SparkFun is quite impressive. You are sure to find all manner of ideas just by browsing the catalog. In fact, if you own multiple microcontroller boards like I do, you'll be extra pleased to know you need only change the host board and you can reuse your Qwiic modules across your fleet of microcontroller boards.

To show how easy the Qwiic system is to use, Listing A-2 shows an example of a Qwiic project using the Arduino. In this case, we use a Qwiic Arduino shield, environmental sensor, and a tiny OLED to display the data. All of the code is taken from the excellent example sketches.

Listing A-2. Qwiic Arduino Example Sketch

```
/**
  Beginning Sensor Networks Second Edition
  Sensor Networks Example Qwiic Temperature Node

  This project demonstrates how to use a Qwiic BME280 sensor and
  OLED display. It shows how easy it is to use the Qwiic family
  of sensors as an alternative to hard wiring.
*/
#include <Wire.h>
#include <SFE_MicroOLED.h>
#include "SparkFunBME280.h"

// MicroOLED Definition
#define PIN_RESET 9
#define DC_JUMPER 1
// MicroOLED Object Declaration
MicroOLED oled(PIN_RESET, DC_JUMPER);
// BME280 Sensor
BME280 mySensor;

void setup() {
  Serial.begin(115200);
  while(!Serial);
  Serial.println("Reading basic values from BME280 and display
  on OLED.");
  Wire.begin();
  if (mySensor.beginI2C() == false) {
    Serial.println("The sensor did not respond. Please check
    wiring.");
    while(1); //Freeze
  }
```

```
  oled.begin();    // Initialize the OLED
  oled.clear(ALL); // Clear the display's internal memory
  oled.display();  // Display what's in the buffer
                        (splashscreen)
  delay(1000);     // Delay 1000 ms
  oled.clear(PAGE); // Clear the buffer.
}

void loop() {
  float temp_c = 0.0;
  float temp_f = 0.0;

  delay(1000);
  temp_c = mySensor.readTempC();
  temp_f = mySensor.readTempF();

  oled.clear(PAGE);
  oled.setCursor(0, 0);
  oled.setFontType(1);
  oled.print(temp_c);
  oled.print("C");
  oled.setCursor(0, 16);
  oled.print(temp_f);
  oled.print("F");
  oled.display();
}
```

To run this sketch, you must install the following libraries using the library manager:

- *SparkFun Micro OLED Breakout*—OLED

- *SparkFun BME280*—BME280

- *SparkFun CCS811 Arduino Library*—CCS811 (optional)

Figure A-2 shows the hardware for the project including an Arduino Uno, Qwiic Arduino shield, BME280 environment sensor, and an OLED module.

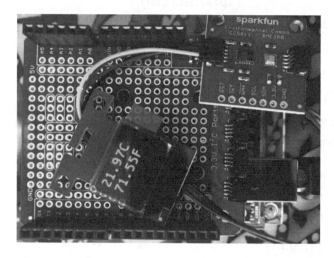

Figure A-2. *Qwiic Arduino example hardware*

There are two things I like about the Qwiic system: (1) the wide variety of platforms supported and (2) the ability to incorporate I2C devices that aren't in the SparkFun catalog. Figure A-3 shows an excerpt of the Qwiic host boards available including a nifty, tiny Raspberry Pi board.

HATs, Shields, and Carrier Boards

SparkFun Qwiic Shield for Arduino $6.95	SparkFun Qwiic HAT for Raspberry Pi $5.95 ★★★★☆ 3	SparkFun Qwiic Shield for Photon $5.95	SparkFun LTE CAT M1/NB-IoT Shield - SARA-R4 $79.95 ★★★★☆ 2
Qwiic Expansion Board for Onion Omega $15.00	SparkFun Qwiic pHAT v2.0 for Raspberry Pi $5.95	SparkFun Servo pHAT for Raspberry Pi $10.95 ★★★★★ 1	SparkFun Qwiic SHIM for Raspberry Pi $0.95
SparkFun Qwiic Shield for Arduino Nano $3.50	SparkFun Qwiic Shield for Thing Plus $3.50	SparkFun weather:bit - micro:bit Carrier Board (Qwiic) $15.95	SparkFun moto:bit - micro:bit Carrier Board (Qwiic) $15.95

Figure A-3. Qwiic host boards (courtesy of SparkFun)

While you can add devices to the Grove system, SparkFun makes it easier with the SparkFun Qwiic Adapter, a tiny board that has the I2C pins broken out in breadboard-friendly pins along with the customary two connectors. This permits you to create your own Qwiic modules from older I2C devices. Very cool. Figure A-4 shows the SparkFun Qwiic Adapter from SparkFun.

Figure A-4. SparkFun Qwiic Adapter (courtesy of SparkFun)

Finally, SparkFun offers a number of Qwiic starter kits for most platforms. These kits are often cheaper than buying the components separately and come ready to use in example projects.

See `www.sparkfun.com/qwiic?_ga=2.26742462.2046856991.1585058029-656283068.1580489631` for more information about the Qwiic family of products.

STEMMA QT

The STEMMA/QT system is another modular connection system from Adafruit. It supports both three- and four-pin JST connectors. Like Grove and Qwiic, it is Adafruit's way of making it easy to plug and play various sensors and devices without a lot of wiring.

While it isn't an original idea, Adafruit wanted to create something that could work within an ecosystem of other plug-and-play systems originally intended to be compatible with Grove, but when Qwiic was introduced, Adafruit added a smaller connector so it could work with both systems. However, there are a few exceptions.

STEMMA four-pin cables are cross-compatible with Grove modules, and Adafruit provides an optional cable for connecting Grove modules. STEMMA uses the same voltage as Grove—power is 3–5VDC and data is 3–5VDC with level shifting/regulators on devices. However, Qwiic only has level shifting and voltage regulation on the controller, not on the modules. Thus, while you can use STEMMA modules with any Qwiic controller, you can use Qwiic devices on a STEMMA controller only if you set the voltage jumper from 5V to 3V.

While these differences are subtle, you can acquire any of the STEMMA devices and modules and mix them with your Grove and Qwiic systems. Just be careful about how you connect them and how the devices are powered.

For more information about STEMMA and especially compatibility with other systems, see `https://learn.adafruit.com/introducing-adafruit-stemma-qt/what-is-stemma`.

Summary

There is a great sense of accomplishment when wiring up your projects and seeing them record sensor data. However, for some the task of wiring various components together can be tedious and sometimes error prone. Fortunately, the nice folks at Seeed Studio, SparkFun, and Adafruit feel your pain and have delivered excellent easy connect solutions.

While either system will work well, choosing one over another may come down to which system has the modules you need most. For example, the Qwiic system from SparkFun has an impressive and growing list of modules to choose from. However, it only supports the I2C protocol. If you need to use modules requiring other protocols, the Grove system may be a slightly better choice. Regardless of which you choose, these optional connector systems will make your projects assemble faster with fewer errors, and that's always a good thing.

Index

A

© Charles Bell 2020
C. Bell, *Beginning Sensor Networks with XBee, Raspberry Pi, and Arduino*,
https://doi.org/10.1007/978-1-4842-5796-8

I, J, K

L

N

O

P

Z

Printed in the United States
By Bookmasters